ERNESTO LACLAU

Ernesto Laclau blazed a unique trail in political theory and philosophy since the early 1970s. In so doing, he has articulated a range of philosophical and theoretical currents into a coherent alternative to mainstream models and practices of conducting social and political science. The editors have focused on work in three key areas:

Post-Marxist political theory: discourse, hegemony, signification

Laclau has developed an original conception of post-Marxist political theory that is grounded on a materialist theory of discourse. The latter is constructed from a range of theoretical and philosophical sources, including poststructuralism, psychoanalysis, linguistic theory and post-analytical philosophy. The centrepiece of this approach is the category of hegemony, which develops Antonio Gramsci's seminal contribution to Marxist theory, and is in turn connected to a web of related concepts, including articulation, dislocation, the logics of equivalence and difference, political identification, myth and social imaginary. These ideas have informed a number of empirical and theoretical studies associated with the Essex School of Discourse Theory.

Analysing populism

A central concern of Laclau's writings has been the question of populism, both in Latin America where he began his interrogation of the phenomenon (especially the experience of Peronism), and then in his engagement with the "new social movements" and socialist strategy more generally. The concept of populism becomes a general way of exploring the "primacy of politics" in society.

Critical engagements

Laclau is first and foremost an engaged intellectual who has consistently sought to theorize contemporary events and reality, and to debate with the leading intellectual figures of the day, with respect to questions of political principle and strategy. His recent debates with Judith Butler and Slavoj Žižek in *Contingency, Hegemony, Universality: Contemporary Dialogues on the Left*, published in 2000 (London: Verso), exemplify this critical ethos. He continues to elaborate his approach by challenging and articulating related approaches, and by situating his work in connection to the democratic Left.

David Howarth is a Reader in the Department of Government and Co-Director of the Centre for Theoretical Studies at the University of Essex, UK.

Routledge Innovators in Political Theory
Edited by Terrell Carver, University of Bristol and Samuel A. Chambers, The Johns Hopkins University

Routledge Innovators in Political Theory focuses on leading contemporary thinkers in political theory, highlighting the major innovations in their thought that have reshaped the field. Each volume collects both published and unpublished texts, and combines them with an interview with the thinker. The editorial introduction articulates the innovator's key contributions in relation to political theory, and contextualises the writer's work. Volumes in the series will be required reading for both students and scholars of twenty-first century politics.

1 **William E. Connolly**
   Democracy, pluralism and political theory
   Edited by Samuel A. Chambers and Terrell Carver

2 **Carole Pateman**
   Democracy, feminism, welfare
   Edited by Terrell Carver and Samuel A. Chambers

3 **Michael J. Shapiro**
   Discourse, culture & violence
   Edited by Terrell Carver and Samuel A. Chambers

4 **Chantal Mouffe**
   Hegemony, radical democracy, and the political
   Edited by James Martin

5 **Ernesto Laclau**
   Post-Marxism, populism, and critique
   Edited by David Howarth

ERNESTO LACLAU

Post-Marxism, populism and critique

Edited by
David Howarth

Routledge
Taylor & Francis Group
LONDON AND NEW YORK

First published 2015
by Routledge
2 Park Square, Milton Park, Abingdon, Oxon OX14 4RN

and by Routledge
711 Third Avenue, New York, NY 10017

Routledge is an imprint of the Taylor & Francis Group, an informa business

© 2015 selection and editorial matter David Howarth; contributors their contributions.

The right of David Howarth to be identified as editor of this work has been asserted by him in accordance with the Copyright, Designs and Patent Act 1988.

All rights reserved. No part of this book may be reprinted or reproduced or utilised in any form or by any electronic, mechanical, or other means, now known or hereafter invented, including photocopying and recording, or in any information storage or retrieval system, without permission in writing from the publishers.

Trademark notice: Product or corporate names may be trademarks or registered trademarks, and are used only for identification and explanation without intent to infringe.

British Library Cataloguing in Publication Data
A catalogue record for this book is available from the British Library

Library of Congress Cataloging in Publication Data
Laclau, Ernesto
[Essays. Selections]
Ernesto Laclau : post-marxism, populism, and critique / edited by David Howarth.
pages cm -- (Routledge innovators in political theory ; 5)
Includes bibliographical references and index.
1. Populism--Philosophy. 2. Socialism--Philosophy. I. Howarth, David R., editor of compilation. II. Title.
JC423.L25 2014
320.01--dc23
2013049230

ISBN: 978-0-415-87086-3 (hbk)
ISBN: 978-0-415-87087-0 (pbk)
ISBN: 978-0-203-76228-8 (ebk)

Typeset in Bembo
by Integra Software Services Pvt. Ltd.

Printed and bound in Great Britain by
TJ International Ltd, Padstow, Cornwall

CONTENTS

Acknowledgements   vii

Introduction: discourse, hegemony and populism:
Ernesto Laclau's political theory   1
David Howarth

PART I
Post-Marxist political theory: discourse, hegemony, signification   21

1. Discourse (1993)   23

2. Dislocation and capitalism, social imaginary and democratic revolution (1990)   30

3. Why do empty signifiers matter to politics? (1994)   66

4. The death and resurrection of the theory of ideology (1996)   75

5. Ideology and post-Marxism (2007)   96

PART II
Analysing populism   109

6. Towards a theory of populism (1977)   111

7. Populism: what's in a name? (2005)   152

8 Why constructing a people is the main task of
radical politics (2006) 165

PART III
Critical engagements 197

9 'The time is out of joint' (1995) 199

10 Can immanence explain social struggles? (2003) 213

11 On 'real' and 'absolute' enemies (2005) 223

12 Bare life or social indeterminacy? (2005) 231

13 Community and its paradoxes: Richard Rorty's
"Liberal Utopia" (1991) 242

An interview with Ernesto Laclau: questions from David Howarth 257

Index 272

ACKNOWLEDGEMENTS

In the final stages of editing this volume, we learned that Ernesto Laclau died suddenly while attending a conference in Valencia, Spain. This book is dedicated to the memory of Ernesto—an inspirational thinker and generous teacher and mentor. I would also like to thank Terrell Carver, Sam Chambers and the editorial team at Routledge for their patience and good cheer in ensuring the completion of this book.

David Howarth
University of Essex

INTRODUCTION

Discourse, hegemony and populism: Ernesto Laclau's political theory

David Howarth

Ernesto Laclau, an Argentinian political theorist and philosopher, has taught and conducted research at a number of leading universities in the UK, North America and in his native Latin America. He is the foremost exponent of a distinctively post-Marxist approach to social analysis, which has developed over the past thirty or forty years. In elaborating this approach, he has articulated currents within poststructuralist theory (e.g. Derrida and Foucault) and post-analytical philosophy (e.g. Wittgenstein and Rorty), together with psychoanalysis (e.g. Freud and Lacan), so as to elaborate a novel method of discourse analysis. This approach is underpinned by a materialist conception of discourse, which deconstructs the realism/idealism opposition, as well as the traditional dichotomies between thought and reality, linguistic and non-linguistic practices and mind and matter. His work has inspired a number of scholars in the social sciences and humanities, who have endeavoured to apply and develop his theoretical and methodological approach in various ways.[1]

In general, his work can be divided into three basic phases: an initial attempt to develop a Marxist theory of ideology and politics, which draws upon and extends the work of Antonio Gramsci and Louis Althusser; the development of a post-Marxist theory of hegemony that incorporates poststructuralist philosophy, thus breaking decisively with the residual determinism and essentialism of the Marxist paradigm; and the further development of this post-Marxist approach through a deeper engagement with Jacques Derrida's deconstructionist philosophy and Jacques Lacan's interpretation of Freudian psychoanalysis. His work is indispensable for characterizing and explaining the emergence and dissolution of political ideologies and the social formations within which they are constructed, as well as the constitution of social subjects. On a more normative register, together with Chantal Mouffe, he has constructed and advocated a project for a radical and plural democracy (Laclau, 2005b; Laclau and Mouffe, 1985; Mouffe, 1993; 2000; 2005).

Much of this work focuses on a radical rethinking of populist politics and its implications for the extension and deepening of democratic forms and practices.

There are multiple ways to classify and present a thinker's work. In a genealogical mode, one might explore the contingent emergence and transfiguration of an author's concepts and preoccupations, or following in the footsteps of Quentin Skinner one might carefully connect their central ideas to the particular contexts in which he or she wrote. Another method is to abstract the key concepts and logics that have been developed, with a view to capturing and evaluating the essence of a thinker's contribution. In this introductory chapter, I have chosen to pursue the latter, though this should not come at the expense of the other logics of presentation, as each strategy offers important theoretical and methodological resources. In this spirit, I shall focus on Laclau's conceptions of discourse, hegemony and populism, which in my view constitute the nodal points of his theoretical contribution. But I shall begin by locating his approach in the wider debate about poststructuralism and its connection to contemporary critical theory.

Philosophical background: the debate about poststructuralism

In recent years, poststructuralist thought has attracted widespread interest and not a little opprobrium. Critics have alleged that this tradition of theory reduces reality to linguistic and textual structures; subscribes to a self-defeating relativism, which abandons truth and knowledge in the name of 'anything goes'; dissolves the impact of social structures on political life, on the one hand, or reduces social agents to the abstract logics of discourse, on the other; and exhibits a crippling 'normative deficit', which is complicit with the most powerful relations of domination and oppression in existing capitalist systems. Rationalists like Jürgen Habermas and Charles Taylor argue that poststructuralists abandon the role of reason, autonomous subjectivity and human emancipation, whereas Marxists and critical realists discern a failure to emphasize the importance of economic structures and social institutions in the structuring of social relations. Positivists accuse poststructuralists of reducing scientific investigation to the description of particularities, or the free play of competing narratives.

In his various writings, Laclau elaborates a more nuanced account of the poststructuralist project. His alternative reading of poststructuralism hinges on the positing of an undecidable play between the logics of necessity and impossibility in social life, as well as a deconstructive reading of the binary opposition between the categories of essence and contingency (Laclau and Mouffe, 1985; Laclau, 2000a, p. 75). He posits a progressive anti-essentialist movement in twentieth-century philosophy and social theory, which emerges in structuralism, phenomenology, Marxism, psychoanalysis and analytical philosophy. Laclau alleges that in each of these traditions an unmediated given or objectivity – the facts of the matter, the phenomenon or a grounded reason, for example – is shown to be constructed and contingent. Situating poststructuralism within the so-called 'linguistic turn' in Western philosophy and theory (Rorty, 1967), Laclau thus charts a shift from an 'illusion of immediacy', in which thought is predicated on the existence of a presence or reality that is simply given to consciousness, to the constructed, mediated and ultimately contingent character of all objectivity.

Laclau argues that the internal development of the aforementioned intellectual traditions has brought a weakening of their underlying presuppositions. First, post-analytical philosophers such as the later Wittgenstein, Donald Davidson and Richard Rorty questioned the commitment to any foundational connection between a name and a thing by introducing notions like 'language games', 'forms of life' and the totality of actual linguistic behaviour, which necessarily precedes any logic of reference. In a parallel way, Heidegger's existential phenomenology challenges the concept of a transcendental subjectivity that confronts a phenomenon, and which appears in its consciousness by situating all such 'subjects' and phenomena within the context of meaningful practices. And, finally, post-structuralists such as Barthes, Derrida, Foucault and Kristeva sought to deconstruct the metaphysical connotations of the linguistic sign, especially the sharp distinction between the signifier and the signified, by proposing the idea of incomplete structures of signification that are marked by an irreducible play of meaning. Laclau combines these poststructuralist themes with Gramsci's 'philosophy of praxis' to elaborate a distinctive post-Marxist social and political theory (Howarth, 2013). I shall return to this synthesis at various points later in this chapter.

Marxism, discourse and the post-Marxist turn

The elaboration of a novel theoretical approach, such as poststructuralist discourse theory, is best explicated by exploring the problems to which it has responded, as well as the range of philosophical and analytical resources its protagonists draw upon in its development. Put somewhat bluntly, the anomalies that stimulated the emergence of Laclau's approach presented themselves in the form of a debilitating class reductionism and economic determinism, which permeated Western Marxist theory from the 1950s until the 1970s, despite the efforts of various schools to rework the Marxist problematic in a non-reductionist and non-deterministic direction. The latter included the different generations of the Frankfurt school and the structuralist Marxism of Althusser, Balibar, Poulantzas and others. But it also encompassed various neo-Gramscian accounts of the State and civil society, critical realist theories of structure and society, and various endeavours to articulate a more democratic and humanist Marxism in multiple contexts.

The key theoretical anomalies that are tarried with in Laclau's writings are best captured by the problem of a rationalist essentialism, whereby successive Marxist approaches presumed the existence of objects, whether they be the 'laws of history', determinate social formations, or social subjects and political agents, which could be rationally grasped through systematic theoretical and empirical investigation. Indeed, as Foucault noted in *The Order of Things*, the problem of essentialism signifies a more general problem in the human and social sciences – predicated on the rigid separation of a given subject and object – in which the latter can be rationally grasped by a reasoning subject that stands outside the locus of its theoretical and scientific gaze (Foucault, 1970). In equal fashion, drawing on Nietzsche's critique of metaphysical thinking, essentialism can take the form of a prioritization of 'being' over 'becoming', which Foucault (amongst others) dismantled in the name of an anti-essentialist approach to the study of history and society. As Foucault neatly puts it, 'nothing in man – not even his body – is sufficiently stable to serve as the basis for self-recognition or for understanding other men' (Foucault, 1984, p. 88).

Laclau's radical solution to the problem of essentialism is to draw upon the resources of poststructuralist theory in order to deconstruct the opposition between subject and object, and thus to rework the metaphysical dualisms between, for example, essence and contingency, necessity and impossibility, structure and agency, ideology and science, language and reality, which have dominated Marxist (and other) research programmes over the past fifty or so years. Critical to this task has been the elaboration of a complex and multidimensional category of discourse, which is designed to problematize the dominant oppositions in Western philosophy, and lay the basis for an alternative model of social and political analysis.

A great deal of excitement has been generated in recent years about the concept of discourse and the role of discourse analysis in reworking the human and social sciences. Perhaps understandably this has led to a growing set of contested definitions and competing theoretical assumptions, as well as rival methods and research strategies. Alongside traditional concerns with the importance of 'talk and text in context', which includes conversation analysis, speech act theory and various forms of hermeneutical research, others have taken their lead from Michel Foucault's innovative conceptions of discourse, though the latter also vary considerably with respect to *what* is included in the concept and *how* the concept is used to problematize and explore issues in the social and political world. Amongst the latter, Norman Fairclough, Lillie Chouliaraki and others have elaborated 'critical discourse analysis', while Ruth Wodak and Martin Reisigl have articulated a distinctive form of 'historical discourse analysis' (e.g. Fairclough, 1995; Fairclough and Wodak, 1997; Reisigl and Wodak, 2001; Wodak and Meyer, 2001). Maarten Hajer has developed a novel form of argumentative discourse analysis in his exploration of environmental policy and new types of governance (Hajer, 1995).

One pressing bone of contention concerns the scope, content and complexity of discourse, especially with respect to the distinction between the discursive, non-discursive or extra-discursive aspects of (social) reality. Even within the limits of Foucault's texts, for example, the concept of discourse varies between a narrow version of the term, where it refers to the historically specific 'rules of formation' that inform the discursive practices which constitute statements, and a much broader conception, in which discourse is equated with historically specific regimes of power/knowledge, as well as a strategic orientation in which discourses are understood to be 'tactical elements' or 'blocks' operating in a field of force relations (Foucault, 1979, pp. 101–2; see also 1972; 1981). Yet, despite this variation, it is clear that in Foucault's writings – and in most other approaches – discourses are generally understood to be a particular *subset* of linguistic or symbolic practices, such as speaking, writing, representing or communicating, which can and ought to be distinguished from other activities, such as striking or hitting an object on a court, as well as the 'real' objects and entities that compose such actions and practices.

According to Laclau and Mouffe, however, this is a problematical conclusion, for they insist that activities like hitting a ball are not without meaning, nor are the objects that are integral to such a practice external to particular systems of sense and signification. Striking an object in a particular context is an action, but it acquires its meaning and significance only within the context of playing a tennis match, for example. Its meaning thus differs from the angry response of a player, who propels the ball into a nearby street, or throws his racket to the ground in disgust, after he has plopped a forehand into the net. At the same time, different social practices are themselves meaningful entities: they are thus instances of playing tennis or explosions of anger and frustration.

In this way, Laclau and Mouffe's poststructuralist account of discourse theory offers a fruitful way to conceptualize and integrate these various distinctions. More precisely, they reject a purely linguistic or cognitive approach to discourse analysis by defining discourse as an *articulatory practice* that constitutes social relations and formations, and thus constructs their meaning. Discourse is articulatory in that it links together contingent elements – linguistic and non-linguistic, natural and social – into relational *systems*, in which the identity of the elements is modified as a result of the articulatory practice. A key *condition* of this approach is that all such elements are contingent and unfixed, so that their meaning and identity is only partially fixed by articulatory practices. The outcomes of such practices are incomplete *systems* of meaning and practice (Laclau, 2005a; Laclau and Mouffe, 1985; 1988).

Rooted in the structural linguistics inspired by Saussure, and then developed by Benveniste, Hjelmslev and Jacobson, Laclau and Mouffe conceptualize discourses in terms of systems of difference, in which the identity of an individuated element is defined and positioned by reference to the other components of the structure. But, notwithstanding an initial decentring of language, which moves linguistics away from a purely referential model of meaning and identity – because such systems are closed and complete structures, which fix the relations between signifier ('sound-image') and signified ('concept') in a necessary fashion – structuralism can easily function as a new form of essentialism. Instead, if the radical consequences of the structuralist problematic are to be properly harvested, then the elements of linguistics structures, as well as the systems within which the elements acquire their identity, require further deconstruction.

So, following thinkers like Heidegger, Lacan and Derrida, in which no structure or system can fully exhaust the horizon or space within which it is constructed, Laclau and Mouffe posit the radical contingency and historicity of the different elements that are encountered in a particular 'field of discursivity', as well as the finitude of the structures that are constituted therein. As they put it, 'the transition to the relational totality that we have called "discourse", would hardly be able to solve our initial problems if the relational and differential logic of the discursive totality prevailed without any limitation'. This is because the result would be 'pure relations of necessity', in which the potential elements of a system would fully coincide with the actually articulated moments of a discourse, so the latter would be no more than the components 'of a closed and fully constituted totality where every moment is subsumed from the beginning under the principle of repetition' (Laclau and Mouffe, 1985, pp. 110, 106).

Yet, as they continue, this conclusion only arises 'if we allow that the relational logic of discourse be carried through to its ultimate consequences, without limitation by any exterior', where the latter is composed of other discourses (Laclau and Mouffe, 1985, p. 110). Hence they argue that 'a discursive totality never exists in the form of a simply *given and delimited* positivity', because 'the relational logic will be incomplete and pierced by contingency', which means that 'the transition from the "elements" to the "moments" is never entirely fulfilled' (Laclau and Mouffe, 1985, p. 110). In short, 'if contingency and articulation are possible', it is only 'because no discursive formation is a sutured totality and the transformation of the elements into moments is never complete' (Laclau and Mouffe, 1985, pp. 106–7).

In accounting for the emergence and formation of discourses, Laclau stresses the primacy of politics and power (Laclau, 1990; Laclau and Mouffe, 1985). Discourses are constructed by the drawing of political frontiers between differently positioned social subjects via the exercise of power, in which certain elements are included in a discourse or political project and others are not. In this model, one force endeavours to universalize its values and norms by winning the consent of its allies and by securing the compliance of its others, though coercion and violence may be required to subject its opponents. The logic of hegemony, which I shall elaborate upon in more detail below, captures this complex set of processes. An important condition for any articulatory practice (including hegemonic practices) is the radical contingency of all social and natural elements, which can always be constructed in different ways.

Such ontological postulates enable Laclau to re-engineer the basic contours of the Marxist problematic, thus deepening the work of theorists like Luxemburg, Gramsci, Althusser and Poulantzas. A first manoeuvre focuses on the Marxist concept of totality. During the 1960s and 1970s, structural Marxists such as Althusser, Badiou, Poulantzas and others had gone some way in problematizing the reduction of concrete social formations to abstract modes of production by arguing that an actual social totality is a complex articulation of multiple modes of production in which there is no coincidence between the dominant and determinant contradictions of a particular historical formation, even though the economy was ultimately primary in shaping the overall contours and logic of any given social order. Laclau and Mouffe deepen this initial complexifying and decentring operation by abandoning the concept of society as 'a sutured and self-defined totality', and thus as a 'valid object of discourse' (Laclau and Mouffe, 1985, p. 111). 'Society' is distinguished from the 'surplus of the social', where the latter always exeeds the former, and any particular 'society' is understood to be the *outcome* of a series of political and ideological struggles, which involve the drawing of political frontiers and the exercise of power.

Secondly, they problematize the notion of a topographical division of society into distinct spheres, which is most famously captured by Marx's base–superstructure model of social relations, but is also evident in the Althusserian division of the social formation into three relatively autonomous regions of social practice: the economic, the political and the ideological. Instead, building on the work of Gramsci, Laclau and Mouffe argue that societies are composed of relational blocs, which are forged out of a heterogeneous series of elements through the exclusion of certain possibilities. What is more, in keeping with this logic, they also affirm, thirdly, the 'primacy of politics', rather than the economy, in accounting for the emergence and ultimate character of any configuration of elements and relations. Politics is not a particular region of society, or a specific set of institutions like government or the State, which can be distinguished from civil society, but an ontological dimension of social relations, which can be captured by the operation of political logics and their novel concept of hegemony.

Fourthly, they contest a purely negative, and ultimately epistemological, conception of ideology, where the latter is understood to distort or conceal the ultimate structure of reality, which only Marxist science can demystify and render intelligible. In part, their deconstruction of the distinction between science and ideology is predicated on a questioning of a sharp split between thought (in its various representational guises) and reality, and by the elaboration of their concept of discourse, which embraces ideational, linguistic and non-linguistic forms. But it is also based on a rejection of both a topographical conception of the social and the privileging of a foundational conception of (Marxist) science. In his later writings, Laclau reworks the concept of ideology in order to identify and account for the way in which certain discursive forms cover over the ultimate contingency of social relations (Laclau, 1997).

Finally, on a normative register, Laclau and Mouffe propose a project of radical and plural democracy that is designed to replace the orthodox Marxist account of social change and political agency – a revolutionary break with a previously existing mode of production led by a fundamental social class such as the proletariat – as well as its preferred alternative to capitalist liberal democracies, namely a fully emancipated and transparent system of communism. Rather than rejecting the gains of the democratic revolution, radical democracy involves a deepening and extension of the values and ideals of democracy – the ideas of equality, freedom and solidarity – into ever-widening sites and sets of social relations, and involves the linking together of various demands, claims, identities and interests, none of which has a necessary or determining class orientation. Hegemony is the name that Laclau and Mouffe give to this political practice of linking disparate elements together, as well as the processes through which a putative hegemonic project 'becomes state' (to use Gramsci's term), and it is to this key concept that I now turn.

Three models of hegemony

As I have suggested, the concept of hegemony constitutes a nodal point in Laclau's political theory. However, this conceptualization of hegemony has mutated in subtle ways as his theory has developed. Indeed, it is possible to discern at least three models of hegemony at work in his writings, beginning with his initial efforts to harness the resources of Gramsci and Althusser to rethink the emergence and character of ideologies like fascism, populism, authoritarianism and nationalism in Marxist theory, as well as the role of institutions such as the capitalist State. Hegemony is then linked to Laclau and Mouffe's post-Marxist conception of politics and society, in which it is conceptualized as a special type of articulatory practice that constitutes social formations. Finally, it is fleshed out in more explicitly Derridean and Lacanian terms, so that it refers to the process in which 'one difference, without ceasing to be a *particular* difference, assumes the representation of an incommensurable totality' (Laclau, 2005a, p. 70).

As its title suggests, *Politics and Ideology in Marxist Theory* seeks to furnish a theory of the political and ideological superstructures, as against an underlying economic base or foundation, by tackling the problems of economic determinism and class reductionism in Marxist theory. By positing a paradigmatic and unchanging connection between certain ideological elements and pre-existing social classes, where ideological elements take the form of various appeals, demands, identities and representations, Laclau argues that in orthodox Marxist theory 'contradictions are seen in a hierarchical system that can be directly or indirectly reduced to a class contradiction. Any element or contradiction at the political and ideological level is, therefore, a class appurtenance. The paradoxical result is that theoretical practice has no need to correct the connotative articulations of political discourse' (Laclau, 1977, p. 11).

Opposing the reduction of the *content* of political ideologies, as well as the *forms* of the State and other institutional complexes, to the interests of the dominant social classes in a society (class reductionism), or the restriction of these forms to the role of mirroring or reflecting underlying material processes (economic determinism), Laclau argues that not all ideological elements have 'a necessary class connotation' (Laclau, 1977, p. 99). In even the most sophisticated renditions of Western Marxism, such as the one proposed by Nicos Poulantzas in his analysis of fascism and dictatorship, 'pronouncing the class belonging of elements of concrete ideologies is a purely arbitrary one', whose 'method, inspired by the metaphysical assignment to classes of certain ideological elements, can only lead to a multiplication ad infinitum of increasingly formal distinctions'. By contrast, Laclau proposes to reverse the dominant method by accepting

> that ideological "elements" taken in isolation have no necessary class connotation, and that this connotation is only the result of the articulation of those elements in a concrete ideological discourse. This means that the precondition for analyzing the class nature of an ideology is to conduct the inquiry through that which constitutes the distinctive unity of an ideological discourse.
> (Laclau, 1977, p. 99; emphasis in original)

Using this conceptual schema, Laclau is also able to explore what he terms the 'distinctive unity' of an 'ideological discourse', as well as the way in which ideologies are transformed. Drawing on the work of Althusser, his response to the first issue – the 'unifying principle of an ideological discourse' – focuses on the particular *subject* that is interpellated and thus constituted through the discourse. This means that the isolated and dispersed elements of a discourse do not express any determinate meaning. Instead, it is only by reconstructing the interpellative structures of such discourses via an empirical investigation of the different types and logics of interpellation, together with a conjunctural analysis of particular social formations, that the character and durability of discursive unity is explicable. Secondly, with respect to the question of ideological change, Laclau advances the thesis that it is '*through class struggle, which is carried out through the production of subjects and the articulation/disarticulation of discourses*' that a particular ideology is transformed (Laclau, 1977, p. 109; emphasis in original). In short, it is via the logic of class struggle, in which the identities of classes are forged in conflict with other classes, that the components of ideological discourses are broken down and then recomposed.

In this first model, then, the logic of hegemony involves the multifarious practices through which a fundamental social class endeavours to colonize the meaning of those ideological elements that do not have a necessary class belonging (appeals to 'the nation', for example, or a range of popular democratic demands) into a project that can transform – or indeed sustain – a social formation, where the latter is organized around a dominant and determinant mode of production. Such projects involve the production of new subjects, which turn individuals into social actors with an identity. Laclau's early writings thus pluralize the contradictions in a social formation, so that not all contradictions are class contradictions, and they disclose a contingent domain of interpellations (especially those he labels 'popular-democratic') that are made available for political articulation under certain circumstances.

But Laclau's initial model still presupposes that each social formation, albeit at the abstract level, is organized around a class contradiction, and that the ultimate meaning of ideological discourses (at the more concrete level of the social formation) is always 'overdetermined' by the class struggle. In contrast, *Hegemony and Socialist Strategy* (1985), which was co-authored with Chantal Mouffe, breaks with Laclau's erstwhile commitment to the idea that a 'fundamental social class' – either the bourgeoisie or the proletariat in capitalist society – shapes the meaning of ideological elements such as 'the people' or 'the nation' in the struggle to construct hegemony. Instead, he argues that there is no privileged agent of hegemonic struggle, and he extends his theory of ideological elements with 'no necessary class belonging' to *all* elements situated in the field of discursivity. Ideology is no longer viewed as a distinct region of the social, but a fundamental dimension of social relations, and all elements are viewed as contingent signifiers, which in precise social circumstances, such as an 'organic crisis', are subject to ongoing practices of disarticulation and rearticulation. He thus considerably widens the sphere of political intervention, while inaugurating the move to a post-Marxist stance.

Hegemony is thus a special type of a political practice that involves the construction and deconstruction of hegemonic projects. Such projects either challenge the dominant terms of political discourse, or seek to expand the existing order of things by negating or incorporating demands and grievances, which are articulated by oppositional projects and subjectivities. As I have noted, this second conception of hegemony is predicated on a poststructuralist theory of discourse, in which discourse is first and foremost a kind of social practice that links together and modifies heterogeneous elements in changing historical formations (Laclau and Mouffe, 1985, p. 96). The outcomes of such practices are discursive formations, in which the linkages between the elements of these systems are relational and differential. Discursive formations are finite, uneven and incomplete. Both as a practice and as an incomplete system of related moments, discourse thus presupposes a world of contingent elements – linguistic and non-linguistic, social and natural – which can be linked together in various ways.

In this second model of hegemony, such elements are conceived of as 'floating signifiers', which, in certain circumstances, can be articulated by rival political projects seeking to fix their meaning and import, whereas moments are those elements that are firmly positioned in a particular discourse. Nodal points are those privileged points of signification within a discourse that partially fix the meaning of practices and institutional configurations. For example, in the discourse of Thatcherism in the UK during the 1970s and 1980s, signifiers such as 'the free economy', 'the strong State', 'individual freedom', 'law and order' and a return to 'traditional morality' were welded together into a new political ideology that was able to recruit or 'interpellate' social subjects, who were dislocated by the intensified political, economic and ideological crisis of the 1970s (crystallized in the so-called 'Winter of Discontent') by making available new subject positions, while promising and conferring a new identity. The linking together and partial fixing of the meaning of signifiers is thus a social and political practice, but one which presupposes the ultimate contingency of all identity and meaning.

Crucial to the fixing of the meaning of floating signifiers in fields of discursivity are the actions of social forces, which draw political frontiers between differently positioned agents, thus establishing boundaries between the 'insiders' and 'outsiders' of a discourse. In the case of Thatcherism, for example, the outsiders – the so-called 'welfare scroungers', the trade unions (the infamous 'enemy within'), socialists, deviant social groups such as gays, immigrants and single parents, overweening bureaucrats, and so forth – were central for constructing the identities of the insiders, precisely because they were seen to threaten the dominant social values and traditions. In accounting for the creation of political boundaries, which temporarily stabilize and fix the meaning of identities, Laclau's concept of antagonism emphasizes the constitutive role of negativity in political life. Social antagonisms occur when the presence of 'an Other' is discursively constructed as blocking or impeding the attainment of identity by a subject (Laclau and Mouffe, 1985). For instance, gays and lesbians in Britain during the 1980s came under assault because their alternative ways of life were deemed to threaten the 'normal', heterosexual majority. Vociferous debates about the introduction of Section 28 of the Local Government Act of 1988 exemplify such struggles in the Thatcher period. The amendment declared that a local authority 'shall not intentionally promote homosexuality or publish material with the intention of promoting homosexuality', or 'promote the teaching in any maintained school of the acceptability of homosexuality as a pretended family relationship' (Local Government Act, 1988), and was deemed by many gays and lesbians to be an explicit attack on their alternative sexual identities and lifestyles, which provoked intense conflict and antagonism (Smith, 1994). At the same time, coal-miners faced by the closure of their pits, and thus an end to their particular way of life, constructed the Thatcher government and the British Coal Board as a threatening 'Other' that blocked their identities and interests, thus provoking sustained resistance and conflict via their trade union led by Arthur Scargill.

One of the main objectives of post-Marxist discourse theory is to explore the way in which social antagonisms are constructed; what precise forms they take; and how they may be accommodated within democratic forms of social life. In so doing, Laclau develops the logics of equivalence and difference, which are derived in part from Saussure's paradigmatic and syntagmatic poles of language, where the former refers to the construction of equivalences between different demands and identities, thus dividing social relations into opposed camps, and the latter to the process of disarticulating the elements of an equivalential chain and reconfiguring them as mere differences, thus relegating social antagonisms and the division of the social to the margins of society. Finally, Laclau distinguishes between popular democratic projects, which challenge tendentially authoritarian and exclusionary political regimes, and struggles for radical democracy, which endeavour to radicalize the terms of liberal democracies by widening and intensifying the dominant principles, ideals and values of established democratic orders.

In what I shall call his third model of hegemony, which is developed in books such as *New Reflections on the Revolution of Our Time* (1990), *Emancipation(s)* (1996), *Contingency, Hegemony, Universality* (2000b) and *On Populist Reason* (2005a), Laclau has responded to important commentaries and criticisms of his approach, especially those made by Žižek (1989; 1990; 1999), by developing the deconstructionist and psychoanalytic themes more prominently. In this view, all social relations are built upon a fundamental 'structural undecidability' or 'lack' that can never be fully sutured. At best, these gaps in a symbolic order are rendered visible by dislocatory events that can be symbolized in different ways. One such symbolization is achieved by the construction of social antagonisms that divide the social into opposed camps; other symbolizations may pre-empt or contain such antagonistic constructions. The struggle for hegemony is now conceived in terms of the production of 'empty signifiers', which function to represent the 'absent fullness' of an ontologically lacking social order.

Three further elements are added to this picture. In the first place, Laclau develops a theory of political subjectivity or agency that emerges in the space opened up by a dislocated structure. If 'subject positions' are available places for identification in a sedimented social structure, then the failure of such structures to stabilize meaning and identity gives rise to new political subjects that seek to reorder social relations in new ways by proposing alternative myths and instituting a different collective social imaginary. Allied to this reworking of subjectivity and agency is a fleshing out of the processes through which a hegemonic project becomes universalized and sedimented. Here Laclau introduces the concepts of 'myth' and 'social imaginary' to account for the way in which particular attempts to cover over a dislocated structure by the production of social myths, which are created in the endeavour to repair a dislocated structure by positing a pure form of order, are transformed into broad horizons within which many demands and identities can be accommodated (Laclau, 1990).

Finally, Laclau introduces the notion of an empty signifier to supplement the role of nodal points in the partial fixation of meaning (Laclau, 1995). Whereas nodal points are those privileged points of signification within a discourse that partially fix the meaning of practices and institutional configurations, empty signifiers provide the symbolic means to represent these essentially incomplete orders. The function of the latter is to incarnate the 'absent fullness' of an essentially incomplete discursive system. At the same time, if floating signifiers are ideological elements that are not securely fixed in a particular discourse and can thus be constructed in diverse ways, then empty signifiers are points of fixation that can hold together multiple and even contradictory demands in a precarious unity (Laclau, 1995; 1996; 2004).

The logic of populism

In his most recent writings, Laclau's third model of hegemony leads to a further set of reflections on the phenomenon of populism, which in many respects remains his key object of investigation. As I have noted, in *Politics and Ideology in Marxist Theory* (1977), populist interpellations are crucial to the understanding of concrete social formations in capitalist society, because they are often the objects of hegemonic struggle, thus defining the principal relations of political domination in a particular social order. And even though popular struggles are distinguished from democratic struggles in *Hegemony and Socialist Strategy* (1985), they still assume an important role in explaining the politics of many societies. In his final model of hegemony, and especially in *On Populist Reason* (2005a), populist politics once again occupies centre stage, where it is made virtually synonymous with the concept of politics itself.

Central to this last perspective is a reconsideration of populism itself. We often speak of a populist stance, gesture, action, policy or movement, when it seemingly appeals to the interests of the ordinary people, or is perceived to be popular by a large majority of a country's population. A politician's populist gesture – a call to 'crack down on welfare scroungers', for example, or a policy designed to 'tax the rich until the pips squeak' – is frequently taken as a pejorative description of a politician's speech or decision, which allegedly appeals to the baser instincts of the mass of a country's *populus*. Yet, even a cursory acquaintance with everyday discourses makes it clear that the term 'populism' can be used to describe a wide and diffuse range of locutions, actions and groups. In equal measure, the academic discourse on populism displays a similarly chaotic and confusing mixture of theories and usages. There is much theoretical confusion about the concept of populism and its application, and there is a good deal of slippage between the ethnographic and theoretical usages of the term. Indeed, as Laclau suggests, it is important not to confuse our commonsensical views and prejudices about certain political practices and forms with a properly worked out theory of populism (Laclau, 2005a; 2005c).

Set against this backdrop, Laclau seeks to construct a theory of populism that focuses on the construction of equivalential linkages between dispersed social and political demands, in which the latter requires the production of specific means of representation – 'floating' and 'empty' signifiers – that can serve as points of subjective identification (Laclau, 2005a; 2005c). In this conception, populism is not a specific ideological *content*, which is embodied in a series of rhetorical appeals or demands, though this does not mean that rhetoric is an insignificant element of populist discourse – on the contrary, as Laclau insists, rhetoric is constitutive of *all* political practice. Nor is populism confined to a certain *type* of movement, political party or leader, who is against the system, for example. Populist discourse and practice speaks, instead, directly to the political *dimension* of social relations. That is to say, if the political refers to the contestation and institution of various social relations, then the logic of populism captures the practices through which society is divided into opposed camps in the endless struggle for hegemony (Laclau and Mouffe, 1985; Glynos and Howarth, 2007). A populist politics thus involves the construction of a collective agency or project – 'the people', for instance – through the drawing of a political frontier between a 'we' and a 'they' within a social formation; and the latter presupposes a set of antagonisms and the availability of indeterminate ideological elements (or floating signifiers) that can be woven together into a particular ideological formation.

Simplifying, then, Laclau's more formal and structural logic of populism consists of five basic features (Griggs and Howarth, 2008). First, the articulators of a populist discourse appeal to a collective subject such as 'the people' or 'the community' as the privileged subject of interpellation. Such discourses seek to construct and naturalize a certain meaning of 'the people' or its functional equivalent, using such appeals to forge political identities and thus recruit differently positioned subjects. Secondly, the articulation of populist discourse involves the drawing of political frontiers, which, if successful, pits 'the people' against a defined enemy or adversary, whether the latter takes the form of a 'power elite', the government or vested interests. Thirdly, the establishment of this political boundary, which divides the people from its 'other', is grounded on the creation of equivalential relations between particular social *demands*, which are linked together in a more universalistic, populist discourse. This presupposes that demands are internally split between their particular content – the particular thing that is demanded (such as 'higher wages' or 'better hospitals') – and the fact that a particular demand also expresses a more universal opposition to the system as a whole. Thus populist discourses invariably speak in the name of 'the people', 'the nation' or 'the community', and their rhetoric seeks to galvanize a common set of values, beliefs and symbols which can advance the interests of such collective subjects. The identity of the demands that constitute a populist movement thus depends upon the hegemonic practices that confer meaning in a particular historical context (Howarth, 2005; 2008). Fourthly, the construction of a people requires the production of empty signifiers – symbols that can unite heterogeneous elements into a singular identity by standing in for a community's 'absent fullness' – which in populist discourses tends to be invested in the name and body of particular political leaders (Laclau, 2005a, pp. 99–100).

The first four elements of Laclau's approach go some way in accounting for the *form* and *structuring* of popular identities. But, in adding a final element to his approach, Laclau goes on to stress the *force* of a subject's attachments to particular signifiers by reference to the role of what he calls 'radical investment' (or *affect*) in social life (Laclau, 2005a, p. 110). Drawing parallels between his neo-Gramscian theory of hegemony and psychoanalysis, especially the logic of the *object petit a*, which has been developed by Lacan, Žižek and Copjec, Laclau stresses the way in which 'a certain particularity ... assumes the role of an impossible universality' (Laclau, 2005a, p. 115). In other words, a certain partial object assumes the dignity of 'a Thing' – thereby embodying the whole – which serves as an (impossible) point of 'passionate attachment'. Moreover, whilst this radical investment in a cathected object is radically contingent – nothing predetermines the fact that one signifier performs this role – 'once a certain part has assumed such a function', it retains a grip that 'cannot be changed at will'; indeed, 'it is its very materiality as a part which becomes a source of enjoyment', thus 'making an object the embodiment of a mythical fullness' (Laclau, 2005a, p. 115). This means, in short, that the logic of populist hegemony is 'nothing more than the investment, in a partial object, of a fullness which will always evade us because it is purely mythical' (Laclau, 2005a, p. 116).

Laclau complexifies this basic model by admitting the prospect of multiple equivalences and lines of flight in the structuring of social relations, so that there is always the possibility of new political frontiers that can destabilize and reorientate blocs and systems of power. Hence partially fixed moments of a discourse can become destabilized and then tethered to rival projects and assemblages; such moments become floating signifiers which are available for alternative resignifications. All demands and identities are thus vulnerable to disarticulations and rearticulations. Even more importantly, he notes the importance of grievances and demands that stand outside the settled horizon of agreements and disagreements, and which are crystallized, for example, in the division of the social into opposed chains of equivalence within a particular site of the social. Such demands are marginalized and excluded demands are essential for the creation of a 'people', but they are also partly constitutive of the existing spaces of representation and the narratives which are elaborated in such spaces (Laclau, 2006, p. 672). In short, then, in addition to the 'displacement of political frontiers', Laclau's most fully-fledged model of populism makes room for those demands which are put forward by 'outsiders' or 'underdogs' – a process that foregrounds what he calls the element of 'heterogeneity' in his approach – which are integral in shaping the formation of collective popular identities (Laclau, 2005a, pp. 107–8). Not only does this model of populism push us to rethink the role and impact of collective subjects, but it also raises questions about democratic politics, especially the conceptualization of radical democracy, to which I shall now turn.

Populism, politics and radical democracy

An important implication of this approach is the distinction between populist and non-populist forms of politics. In Laclau's terms, populism refers to the *degree* of division and contestation brought about by a particular project or practice (Laclau, 2005b, p. 45). To put it in quantitative terms, the greater the number of *demands* articulated into an equivalential chain across a greater number of *social spaces*, the greater the degree of populism. On the other hand, the failure to articulate different demands across a multiple range of contested sites – or indeed the struggle to disarticulate equivalential demands – is a feature of a more non-populist, or what might be termed an *institutional* form of politics. Instead of an equivalentially based politics, the latter is characterized by the primacy of a differential logic, in which demands are intercepted and negotiated in a piecemeal fashion, rather than part and parcel of a wider set of struggles. And, while populist politics serves to split different social spaces into opposed camps, a more institutionally bound politics tends to operate within the existing rules of the political game. More formally, populist and non-populist politics are best viewed as two endpoints of a spectrum – both of which are no more than regulative ideals – where non-populism involves no equivalence or the disarticulation of equivalence, and populism the precise inverse (see Griggs and Howarth, 2008; 2013).

Three further aspects are worth noting in this regard. First, it is important to stress that the logic of populism is not conceded a normative or explanatory priority in this theoretical approach; populism is not *necessarily* more radical or progressive than a more institutional form of politics. Nor does the logic of populism partake of an either/or logic, in which populism and a more institutional politics are separated by an unbridgeable chasm. Instead, the construction and deconstruction of social relations always involves the continuous interplay between the two logics. In this regard, Margaret Canovan's idea of two styles of democratic politics – the *pragmatic* and the *redemptive* – where the former refers to a form of managing antagonisms, while the latter is a 'politics of faith' in which 'the people' believe they can build a better world by taking control of their lives, displays some resonances with Laclau's model (Canovan, 1999; see also Canovan, 2005). In Laclau's terms, the pragmatic style is akin to the institutional, while the redemptive shares a strong resemblance with the logic of populism. For Laclau, then, the logic of populism does not exhaust democratic politics: while it is an important aspect of political life, and democratic politics must be attentive to it, new projects are always institutionalized and sedimented in various contingent and precarious ways; and they are always vulnerable to new (populist) challenges.

Secondly, in developing his model, Laclau elaborates a more complicated notion of political representation. Representation in this view is not just confined to the practices of liberal democracies, such as voting in elections and assemblies, or participating in various forms of democratic consultation or deliberation, but involves a complex process of constructing identities and interests. In this conception, the building of a hegemonic project requires a constant mediation between leaders/representatives, on the one hand, and those they seek to represent, on the other. Rather than transparently transmitting pre-existing interests and identities, or simply constituting such interests or identities in a top-down fashion, the practices of representation comprise a to-and-fro movement between leader and led – those that represent and those that are represented – during which interests and identities are constantly modified and adapted as they are iterated in different institutional contexts (Laclau, 2005a, pp. 167–74).

A final implication concerns the relationship between Laclau's conception of populism and democracy. As against aggregative, deliberative and agonistic models of democratic politics, Laclau fleshes out his commitment to radical democracy in terms of hegemony and populism, rather than bargaining, human reasoning or a distinctive sensibility or ethos. In *Hegemony and Socialist Strategy*, Laclau and Mouffe aver that universalism is incompatible with the project of radical and plural democracy (Laclau and Mouffe, 1985, p. 191). But, in his later writings, the notion of universality is not rejected in the name of a commitment to pluralism and diversity. Instead, he stresses 'the constitutive asymmetry between universality and particularity', which he argues is the condition for democracy and hegemonic politics. In this picture, every hegemonic project – every set of equivalential linkages between a disparate series of demands – seeks (necessarily) to universalize its discourse by constructing an empty signifier in the struggle to 'occupy the empty place of power', if not necessarily to 'identify with it' (Laclau, 2001, p. 7).

In *On Populist Reason*, Laclau draws a strong link between populism and democracy, in that 'democracy is grounded only on the existence of a democratic subject, whose emergence depends on the horizontal articulation between equivalential demands' (Laclau, 2005a, p. 171). One implication is that the articulation between democracy and liberalism is contingent. This is because, first,

> other contingent articulations are also possible, so that there are forms of democracy outside the liberal symbolic framework (the problem of democracy, seen in its true universality, becomes that of the plurality of frameworks which make the emergence of a "people" possible)

and, secondly, 'since the emergence of a "people" is no longer the direct effect of any particular framework, the question of the constitution of a popular subjectivity becomes an integral part of the question of democracy' (Laclau 2005a, p. 167). A more general implication is the distancing of democracy from any particular institutional or organizational form, even 'an empty place of power', which is characteristic of Claude Lefort's analysis of democracy (Lefort, 1986). Whereas Lefort focuses on the form and logic of liberal-democratic regimes in modernity, which are in turn located within the symbolic framework of modern society, Laclau is more concerned with the production and actions of popular-democratic subjects, and the way in which 'emptiness' emerges from the creation of collective identities in particular configurations (Laclau, 2005a, p. 166).

Such ideas are developed in a short essay entitled 'The Future of Radical Democracy', where Laclau argues that radical democracy denotes a 'cluster of dimensions', each of which is lacking in itself, and when taken together do not 'easily cohere' (Laclau, 2005b, p. 258). The three conceptions are: (1) democracy as a political regime, that is, a universal system of institutional rules (e.g. freedom and equality for all); (2) democracy as a particular form of democratic subjectivity – the constitution of 'the people' for example, which Laclau identifies as 'populist'; and (3) the connection between radical democracy and pluralism, in which the notion of universality is questioned in the name of difference and particularity (Laclau, 2005b, pp. 259–61).

Laclau goes on to discern serious deficiencies in each conception. In the formal conception of democracy, the principles and rules of liberal democracy, taken on their own terms, are deemed to be too narrow and thin. They are thus compatible with various inequalities in civil society, while also concealing relations of domination and hierarchy in the name of universalism. A purely populist democracy, on the other hand, runs the risk of identifying the community with a particular section of it, thus ruling out pluralism and 'democratic interaction' (Laclau, 2005b, p. 261). Finally, if radical democracy were to be equated with the simple affirmation of pluralism and difference, it would deprive the concept of a common symbolic order within which such claims and grievances could be affirmed. By contrast, Laclau argues that a properly constituted model of radical democracy needs a *political articulation* between these three dimensions, rather than a *logical mediation* between them, or the logic of *subsuming* two of them under one particular conception. In his words, the 'undecidable character of this interaction, the impossibility of conceptually mastering the contingent forms in which it crystallises, is exactly what we call radical democracy' (Laclau, 2005b, p. 261).

Conclusion

This introductory chapter has focused on the concepts of discourse, hegemony and populism, which in my view constitute the three key theoretical concepts of Laclau's political philosophy, because he uses them to analyse and explain a range of problematized social phenomena and processes. Such concepts also inform his commitment to radical democracy, though this normative affirmation is not derived or deduced from his theoretical grammar of concepts and logics. But in this context they have also provided the key organizational matrix for selecting and presenting this collection of Laclau's writings. The first part of the book presents the key ontological assumptions and postulates of Laclau's mature theory, focusing especially on his concept of discourse and its implications for social and political analysis. The second part concentrates on his various theorizations of populism, beginning with his earlier Gramscian-Althusserian account, as well as his more recent account of populism, which is best expressed in his *On Populist Reason*.

The first two parts of the book thus cover the basic theoretical approach put forward by Laclau and applied to the experience of populist politics in different historical contexts. Yet, in elaborating his approach, Laclau has attracted various criticisms, while consistently pitting his assumptions, concepts and political arguments against neighbouring and competing perspectives, many of which are articulated by the leading thinkers of the progressive Left. Such voices include critical realists like Roy Bhaskar (Laclau and Bhaskar, 1998), Norman Geras (1987; 1988) and Bob Jessop (1982; 1990). But it also encompasses Lacanian Marxists, such as Slavoj Žižek, and other postmodernists and poststructuralists, including Judith Butler, William Connolly and Richard Rorty. Coming to terms with the range and complexity of such criticisms and commentaries is beyond the scope of this introductory chapter. Nonetheless, the last part of the book endeavours to capture some of the flavour of Laclau's critical engagements by publishing a series of essays in which Laclau engages with the work of Giorgio Agamben, Alain Badiou, Jacques Derrida, Michael Hardt and Antonio Negri and Richard Rorty. Laclau also addresses such engagements in an especially commissioned interview, which concludes this volume.

Note

1 See, for example, Critchley and Marchart, 2004; Daly, 1991; Davila, 2000; Dyrberg, 1997; Glynos, 2001; 2003; Glynos and Howarth, 2007; Griggs and Howarth, 2013; Howarth, 2000; 2005; 2006; Howarth, Norval, and Stavrakakis, 2000; Marchart, 2007; Norval, 1994; 1999; 2004; Panizza, 2005; Smith, 1994; Stäheli, 2012; Stavrakakis, 1999; 2005; 2007; Torfing, 1998; 1999.

Bibliography

Althusser, L. (1969) *For Marx*. London: Verso.
—— (1971) *Lenin and Philosophy, and Other Essays*. New York: Monthly Review Press.
Althusser, L. and Balibar, E. (1997) *Reading 'Capital'*. London: Verso.
Butler, J., Laclau, E. and Žižek, S. (2000) *Contingency, Hegemony, Universality*. London: Verso.
Canovan, M. (1999) Trust the People! Populism and the Two Faces of Democracy, *Political Studies* 47(1): 2–16.
—— (2005) *The People*. Cambridge: Polity Press.
Critchley, S. and Marchart, O. (eds) (2004) *Laclau: A Critical Reader*. London: Palgrave.
Daly, G. (1991) The Discursive Construction of Economic Space, *Economy and Society* 20(1): 79–102.
Davila, L. R. (2000) The Rise and Fall and Rise of Populism in Venezuela, *Bulletin of Latin American Research* 19(2): 223–38.
Dyrberg, T. (1997) *The Circular Structure of Power*. London: Verso.
Fairclough, N. (1995) *Critical Discourse Analysis: The Critical Study of Language*. London: Longman.

Fairclough, N. and Wodak, R. (1997) Critical Discourse Analysis, in T. van Dijk (ed.), *Discourse as Social Interaction*. London: Sage.
Foucault, M. (1970) *The Order of Things*. London: Tavistock.
—— (1972) *The Archaeology of Knowledge*. London: Tavistock.
—— (1977) *Discipline and Punish*. Harmondsworth: Penguin Books.
—— (1979) *The History of Sexuality*. London: Allen Lane.
—— (1981) The Order of Discourse, in R. Young (ed.), *Untying the Text*. London: Routledge.
—— (1984) Nietzsche, Genealogy, History, in P. Rabinow (ed.), *The Foucault Reader*. Harmondsworth: Penguin Books.
Geras, N. (1987) Post-Marxism? *New Left Review* 163: 40–82.
—— (1988) Ex-Marxism without Substance, *New Left Review* 169: 34–61.
Glynos, J. (2001) The Grip of Ideology, *Journal of Political Ideologies* 6(2): 191–214.
—— (2003) Self-Transgression and Freedom, *Critical Review of International Social and Political Philosophy* 6(2): 1–20.
Glynos, J. and Howarth, D. (2007) *Logics of Critical Explanation in Social and Political Theory*. London: Routledge.
Griggs, S. and Howarth, D. (2008) Populism, Localism and Environmental Politics: The Logic and Rhetoric of the Stop Stansted Expansion Campaign in the United Kingdom, *Planning Theory* 7(2): 123–44.
—— (2013) *The Politics of Airport Expansion in the United Kingdom: Hegemony, Policy and the Rhetoric of 'Sustainable Aviation'*. Manchester: Manchester University Press.
Hajer, M. (1995) *The Politics of Environmental Discourse*. Oxford: Oxford University Press.
Howarth, D. (2000) *Discourse*. Buckingham: Open University Press.
—— (2005) Populism or Popular Democracy?, in F. Panizza (ed.), *Populism and the Mirror of Nature*. London: Verso.
—— (2006) Space, Subjectivity and Politics, *Alternatives* 31(2): 105–34.
—— (2008) Ethos, Agonism and Populism: William Connolly and the Case for Radical Democracy, *British Journal of Politics and International Relations* 3(3–4): 309–35.
—— (2013) *Poststructuralism and After: Structure, Agency and Power*. London: Palgrave.
Howarth, D., Norval, A. J. and Stavrakakis, Y. (eds) (2000) *Discourse Theory and Political Analysis*. Manchester: Manchester University Press.
Jessop, B. (1982) *The Capitalist State: Marxist Theories and Methods*. Oxford: Martin Robertson.
—— (1990) *State Theory*. Cambridge: Polity.
Laclau, E. (1977) *Politics and Ideology in Marxist Theory*. London: Verso.
—— (1988) Building a New Left: An Interview with E. Laclau, *Strategies: Journal of Theory, Culture, and Politics* 1: 10–28.
—— (1990) *New Reflections on the Revolution of Our Time*. London: Verso.
—— (1993) Discourse, in R. E. Goodin and P. Pettit (eds), *A Companion to Contemporary Political Philosophy*. Oxford: Blackwell.
—— (1995) Why Do Empty Signifiers Matter to Politics? in J. Weeks (ed.), *The Greater Evil and the Lesser Good*. London: Rivers Oram.
—— (1996) *Emancipation(s)*. London: Verso.
—— (1997) The Death and Resurrection of the Theory of Ideology, *Journal of Political Ideologies* 112: 297–321.
—— (2000a) Identity and Hegemony, in J. Butler, E. Laclau and S. Žižek, *Contingency, Hegemony, Universality*. London: Verso.
—— (2000b) Constructing Universality, in J. Butler, E. Laclau and S. Žižek, *Contingency, Hegemony, Universality*. London: Verso.
—— (2001) Democracy and the Question of Power, *Constellations* 8(1): 3–14.
—— (2004) Reply, in S. Critchley and O. Marchart (eds), *Laclau: A Critical Reader*. London: Routledge.
—— (2005a) *On Populist Reason*. London: Verso.
—— (2005b) The Future of Radical Democracy, in L. Tønder, and L. Thomassen (eds), *Radical Democracy: Politics between Abundance and Lack*. Manchester: Manchester University Press.

——(2005c) Populism: What's in a Name?, in F. Panizza (ed.), *Populism and the Mirror of Nature*. London: Verso.
——(2006) Why Constructing a People is the Main Task of Radical Politics, *Critical Inquiry* 32: 646–80.
Laclau, E. and Bhaskar, R. (1998) Discourse Theory vs. Critical Realism, *Alethia* 1(2): 9–14.
Laclau, E. and Mouffe, C. (1985) *Hegemony and Socialist Strategy*. London: Verso.
——(1988) Post-Marxism without Apologies, *New Left Review* 166: 79–106.
Lefort, C. (1986) The Political Forms of Modern Society: Bureaucracy, Democracy, Totalitarianism. Cambridge, MA: MIT Press.
Local Government Act. (1988) (c. 9), *Section 28*. http://www.legislation.gov.uk/ukpga/1988/9/introduction. Accessed 18 August 2013.
Marchart, O. (2007) *Post-foundational Political Thought*. Edinburgh: Edinburgh University Press.
Mouffe, C. (1993) *The Return of the Political*. London: Verso.
——(2000) *The Democratic Paradox*. London: Verso.
——(2002) Politics and Passions: Introduction, *Philosophy and Social Criticism* 28(6): 615–16.
——(2005) *On the Political*. London: Routledge.
Norval, A. J. (1994) 'Social Ambiguity and the Crisis of Apartheid', in E. Laclau (ed.), *The Making of Political Identities*, London: Verso.
——(1999) *Deconstructing Apartheid Discourse*, London: Verso.
——(2004) Hegemony after Deconstruction: The Consequences of Undecidability, *Journal of Political Ideologies* 9(2): 139–57.
Osborne, P. (1991) Radicalism without Limit, in P. Osborne (ed.), *Socialism and the Limits of Liberalism*. London: Verso.
Panizza, F. (ed.) (2005) *Populism and the Mirror of Nature*. London: Verso.
Reisigl, M. and Wodak, R. (2001) *Discourse and Discrimination: Rhetorics of Race and Immigration*. London: Routledge.
Rorty, R. (1967) *The Linguistic Turn: Recent Essays in Philosophical Method*. Chicago: University of Chicago Press.
Smith, A. M. (1994) *New Right Discourse on Race and Sexuality: Britain 1968–1990*. Cambridge: Cambridge University Press.
Stäheli, U. (2012) Decentering the Economy: Governmentality Studies and Beyond, in U. Bröckling, S. Krasmann and T. Lemke (eds), *Governmentality: Current Issues and Future Challenges*. London: Routledge.
Stavrakakis, Y. (1999) *Lacan and the Political*. London: Routledge.
——(2005) Passions of Identification, in D. Howarth and J. Torfing (eds), *Discourse Theory in European Politics*. Basingstoke: Palgrave Macmillan.
——(2007) *The Lacanian Left*. Edinburgh: Edinburgh University Press.
Torfing, J. 1998. *Politics, Regulation and the Modern Welfare State*. London: Macmillan.
——(1999) *New Theories of Discourse: Laclau, Mouffe and Žižek*. Oxford: Blackwell.
Wodak, R. and Meyer, M. (2001) *Methods of Critical Discourse Analysis*. London: Sage.
Žižek, S. (1989) *The Sublime Object of Ideology*. London: Verso.
——(1990) Beyond Discourse-analysis, in E. Laclau, *New Reflections on the Revolution of Our Time*. London: Verso.
——(1999) *The Ticklish Subject*. London: Verso.

PART I
Post-Marxist political theory
Discourse, hegemony, signification

1

DISCOURSE (1993)

The notion of 'discourse', as developed in some contemporary approaches to political analysis, has its distant roots in what can be called the transcendental turn in modern philosophy – i.e. a type of analysis primarily addressed not to *facts* but to their *conditions of possibility*. The basic hypothesis of a discursive approach is that the very possibility of perception, thought and action depends on the structuration of a certain meaningful field which pre-exists any factual immediacy. A transcendental enquiry as an investigation of the conditions of possibility of experience started with Kant, for whom space, time and the categories of understanding constitute the *a priori* dimension in the constitution of phenomena. And in the early twentieth century Husserl's phenomenology strictly differentiated an intuition of facts from an intuition of essences, and asserted that the latter is constitutive of all 'givenness'. These classical transcendental approaches differ, however, in two crucial respects from contemporary theories of discourse. The first is that, while in a philosophy like Kant's the *a priori* constitutes a basic structure of the mind which transcends all historical variations, contemporary discourse theories are eminently historical and try to study discursive fields which experience temporal variations in spite of their transcendental role – i.e. that the line separating the 'empirical' and the 'transcendental' is an impure one, submitted to continuous displacements. A second differentiating feature is that the concept of 'discursive fields' in contemporary approaches depends on a notion of structure which has received the full impact of Saussurean and post-Saussurean linguistics.

Even within this very general characterization we must differentiate between those theories of discourse that are strongly related to transformations in the field of structural linguistics and those whose links to structural analysis are more distant and do not pass through an internal critique of the Saussurean notion of the sign. The first approach is represented by poststructuralism conceived in a broad sense, the second by the work of Michel Foucault and his school. We will treat these two trends successively and will later deal with the consequences of such developments for the conceptualization of politics.

Theories of discourse

The linguistic theory of Ferdinand de Saussure (1959), originally presented in three courses given in Geneva between 1906 and 1911, turn around the notion of the sign conceived as the relation between an acoustic image (the *signifier*) and a concept (the *signified*). According to Saussure there are two basic principles around which structural linguistics is organized. The first is that in language there are no positive terms, only differences. To understand the meaning of the term 'father' I have to understand the meaning of the terms 'mother', 'son', etc. This purely relational and differential character of linguistic identities means that language constitutes a *system* in which no element can be defined independently of the others. The second principle is that language is *form* and not *substance* – that is, that each element of the system is exclusively defined by the rules of its combinations and substitutions with the other elements. To use Saussure's analogy, if I substitute the wooden pieces in a chessboard with marbles or even pieces of paper, I can still play chess in so far as the rules governing the movements of the pieces remain the same. In this entirely differential universe, dominated by purely formal rules, there is strict isomorphism: to each stream of sounds constituting a word corresponds one and only one concept. The order of the signifier and the order of the signified strictly overlap.

There were, however, for Saussure, strict limits to the possibility of developing a linguistic theory of discourse. From a Saussurean point of view discourse is any linguistic sequence more extended than the sentence. Now, in a Saussurean perspective a linguistics of discourse is impossible because a succession of sentences is only governed by the whims of the speaker and does not present any structural regularity graspable by a general theory. With this Cartesian assertion of the omnipotence of the subject, the very possibility of a linguistic theory of discourse was ruled out. On top of that, the Saussurean theory of the sign was ultimately inconsistent, for if language is form and not substance, and if there is a strict isomorphism between the order of the signifier and the order of the signified, the two orders become – from a formal point of view – indistinguishable from each other, and the duality of the linguistic sign cannot be maintained. At this point Saussure had to reintroduce surreptitiously the distinction between phonic and conceptual *substances,* with the result that structural analysis became even more closely tied to the linguistic sign. Although he had vaguely announced the possibility of a semiology as a general science of signs in society, his dependence on linguistic *substances* made difficult this enlargement of the fields of application of structural principles.

It was only with the *glossematic school* of Copenhagen that these internal inconsistencies of Saussureanism were properly addressed. The result was the formulation of a second model of structural linguistics, which clearly advanced in the direction of an increasing formalism. Hjelmslev (1961; 1970) broke with Saussure's isomorphic conception of the relation between signifier and signified by subdividing both orders into units smaller than the sign:

> phonologists ... have brought to light linguistic units smaller than signs: the phonemes ... (the sign *calf is* made up of the three phonemes /k/, /ae/ and /f/). The same method applied to content allows the distinction, in the same sign, of at least three elements ... or semes ... bovine/male/young. Now it is clear that the semantic and the phonic units thus located can be distinguished from the formal point of view: the combinatorial laws concerning the phonemes of a language and those applied to the semes cannot be shown to correspond to each other ...
>
> *(Ducrot and Todorov 1980, p. 22)*

The consequences of this trend towards formalism were far-reaching as far as a theory of discourse is concerned. The main ones are listed below:

(1) If the abstract system of formal rules governing the combination and substitution between elements is no longer necessarily attached to any particular substance, *any* signifying system in society – the alimentary code, furniture, fashion, etc. – can be described in terms of that system. This was the direction that semiology took from the 1960s, starting with the pioneering works of Roland Barthes (1967; 1972; 1983; see also Kristeva 1969). In fact, there was an increasing realization that 'discourse' did not refer to a particular set of objects, but to a viewpoint from which it was possible to redescribe the totality of social life.

(2) If formalism strictly applies, this means that the *substantial* differences between the linguistic and the non-linguistic also have to be dropped – in other terms, that the distinction between action and structure becomes a secondary distinction within the wider category of meaningful totalities. This point has been particularly stressed in Laclau and Mouffe (1985), and it brings discourse theory close to the conclusions reached by the work of the later Wittgenstein, i.e. the notion that 'language games' embrace both language and the actions in which it is woven (Wittgenstein 1983, p. 5).

(3) Finally, strict formalism also made it possible to overcome the other obstacle to the formulation of a linguistic theory of discourse: as all distinctions had to be considered as merely differential – i.e. as internal to the structure – and the subject could no longer be conceived as *the source* of meaning but, instead, as just one more particular location within a meaningful totality. The 'death of the subject' was one of the battle cries of classical structuralism. The way in which the speaker put sentences together could no longer be conceived as the expression of the whims of an entirely autonomous subject but, rather, as largely determined by the way in which institutions are structured, by what is 'sayable' in some contexts, etc. The task of discourse analysis for classical structuralism was to uncover these basic regularities which govern the production of meaning in social life. This programme was carried out, from a technical point

of view, by putting together the contributions of various disciplines such as the theory of argumentation, the theory of enunciation, speech-act theory, semantic and syntactic analysis, etc.

In recent years the structuralist tradition has experienced, from various quarters, a series of reformulations which have led to what can properly be called a post-structuralist moment. The common denominator of these revisions has been to put into question the notion of closed totality, which was the cornerstone of classical structuralism. (If identities are only differences within a discursive system, no identity can be fully constituted unless the system is a closed one.) The post-structuralist trend has been to experiment with the logic of subversion of discursive identities which follows from the logical impossibility of constituting a closed system. The main currents within this trend are the following:

(1) The reformulation of the logic of meaning in the later work of Roland Barthes (1974). While in his early semiological works Barthes believed in a strict differentiation between denotative and connotative meanings, he realized later that no strict differentiation between both can be established. This led to the notion of a *plural text,* whose signifiers cannot be permanently attached to particular signifieds.
(2) A similar loosening of the relation between signifier and signified takes place in the psychoanalytic current inspired by Jacques Lacan (1977). Freudian theory, through its emphasis on the process of overdetermination (condensation and displacement), which intervenes in the constitution of all psychical formations, had already insisted on the impossibility of fixing meaning through a strict correlation between signifier and signified. This tendency is radicalized by Lacanian theory in what is called the *logic of the signifier,* i.e. the permanent slide of the signified under the signifier (the latter becoming the stable element).
(3) Finally, the *deconstructionist* movement, initiated by Jacques Derrida (1976; also Gasché 1986), attempts to show the elements of radical undecidability to be found in all structural arrangements (in a way not dissimilar to Gödel's theorem) and how no structure of signification can find in itself the principle of its own closure. The latter requires, consequently, a dimension of force which has to operate from outside the structure.

An entirely different approach to a theory of what he calls 'discursive formations' is to be found in the work of Michel Foucault. While both structuralism and post-structuralism start from the logic of the sign and its subversion once the conditions of total closure do not obtain, Foucault's starting point is a second-level phenomenology trying to isolate the totalities within which any production of meaning takes place. Classical phenomenology had focused on the meaning of statements by bracketing their reference to any external reality. Foucault proceeds to a second bracketing by showing that meaning itself presupposes conditions of production which are not themselves reducible to meaning. This 'quasi-transcendental' move leads to the isolation of a stratum of phenomena which Foucault calls discourse. The central problem in his analysis is to determine what constitutes the unity and principle of coherence of a discursive formation. The minimal unit of any discourse is, for Foucault, the *statement (énoncé)*. A statement cannot be considered as a proposition because the same proposition can involve two different statements (both I and a doctor can say that somebody has a cancer, but only the latter's proposition can be considered as a medical statement). It cannot be considered as an utterance either, because different utterances can involve the same statement. Finally, statements cannot be identified with speech-acts, given that the former are restricted by Foucault to what he calls 'serious speech-acts' – those that are not ordinary, everyday speech-acts, but are constituted through an authoritative or autonomous activity (like the medical discourse). But this is just to put the same problem in a different way: what constitutes the principle of unity of a particular discursive field or formation? For a while Foucault played with the idea of finding this principle of unity in what he called an *episteme:* a basic outlook which unifies the intellectual production during a certain age. 'By *episteme* we mean ... the total set of relations that unite, at a given period, the discursive practices that give rise to epistemological figures, sciences, and possibly formalized systems' (Foucault 1972, p. 191). In this sense he tried to isolate the basic *epistemes* of the ages that he conventionally called the Renaissance, the Classical Age and Modernity (Foucault 1973). The intellectual operation of uncovering these basic discursive strategies is what he called *archaeology*. But the main trend of his thought led him to the increasing realization that the heterogeneity of a discursive formation cannot be reduced to such a simple principle of unity. So, he concluded that the principle of unity of a discursive formation cannot be found in the reference to the same object, or in a common style in the production of statements, or in the constancy of the concepts, or in the reference to a common theme, but in what he called 'regularity in dispersion' – the constancy in the external relations between elements which do not obey any underlying or essential principle of structuration. However, if regularity in dispersion is the only principle of unity of a discursive formation, what remains open is the question of the frontiers between discursive formations, a question to which Foucault, at this stage, was unable to give any precise answer.

Discourse theory and politics

The main contributions of discourse theory to the field of politics have been linked so far to the conceptualization of power. The same broad division pointed out earlier applies here: we have, on the one hand, analysts whose theoretical roots are to be found in the post-structuralist theory of the sign and, on the other, those whose roots are mainly linked to the reformulation of Foucault's intellectual project in his later work.

The first tendency can be found especially in the work of Laclau and Mouffe (Laclau and Mouffe 1985; Laclau 1990). Two aspects of the post-structuralist tradition have been important in their formulation of an approach to political power centred in the category of *hegemony*. The first is the notion of 'discourse' as a meaningful totality which transcends the distinction between the linguistic and the extra-linguistic. As we have seen, the impossibility of a closed totality unties the connection between signifier and signified. In that sense there is a proliferation of 'floating signifiers' in society, and political competition can be seen as attempts by rival political forces to partially fix those signifiers to particular signifying configurations. Discursive struggles about the ways of fixing the meaning of a signifier like 'democracy', for instance, are central to explaining the political semantics of our contemporary political world. This partial fixing of the relation between signifier and signified is what in these works is called 'hegemony'. The second aspect in which post-structuralism contributes to a theory of hegemony is closely connected with the first. As we have seen, deconstruction shows that the various possible connections between elements of the structure are, in their own terms, undecidable. As, however, one configuration rather than the other possible ones has been actualized, it follows: (1) that the actually existing configuration is essentially contingent: (2) that it cannot be explained by the structure itself but by a force which has to be partially external to the structure. This is the role of a hegemonic force. 'Hegemony' is a theory of the decisions taken in an undecidable terrain. The conclusion is, as deconstruction shows, that as undecidability operates at the very ground of the social, objectivity and power become indistinguishable. It is in these terms that it has been asserted that power is the trace of contingency within the structure (Laclau 1990). Laclau and Mouffe present a history of Marxism, from the Second International to Gramsci, as a progressive recognition of the contingent character of social links which had previously been considered as grounded in the necessary laws of History. This is what has continually extended the area of operativity of hegemonic links.

There has also been an important attempt by Slavoj Žižek (1989) to extend discourse theory to the field of political analysis through an approach which brings together Lacanian psychoanalysis, Hegelian philosophy and some trends in analytical philosophy, especially Saul Kripke's anti-descriptivism. The central aspect of Žižek's approach is his attempt to reintroduce the category of the subject without any kind of essentialist connotation. His 'subject' is not the substantial *cogito* of the philosophical tradition of modernity, but nor is it the dispersion of *subject positions* that structuralism had postulated. The subject is rather – following Lacan – the place of the *lack,* an empty place that various attempts at identification try to fill. Žižek shows the complexity involved in any process of *identification* (in the psychoanalytic sense) and attempts to explain on that basis the constitution of political identities.

The later work of Foucault (1979; 1980) was an attempt to deal with the difficulties to which his analysis of discursive formations had led. Foucault had defined the realm of discourse as just one object among others. Discourse related to the statement as one object of analysis sharply separated from the others: discursive regularities did not cut across the frontier between the linguistic and the non-linguistic. As a result, the presence of certain discursive configurations had to be explained in terms which for him were extra-discursive. This led to a new kind of approach, which he called *genealogy*. While archaeology *presupposed* the unity of a discursive field which could not appeal to any deeper principle of unification, genealogy tried to locate the elements entering a discursive configuration within the framework of a discontinuous history whose elements did not have any principle of teleological unity. The external character of the unifying forces behind the genealogical dispersion of elements is at the basis of the Foucauldian conception of power: power is ubiquitous because elements are discontinuous, and their being linked is nothing that we can explain through the elements themselves. So, while post-structuralism and genealogy both deal with the question of discontinuity and its production out of unsutured identities, they approach discontinuity from two different angles: in the first case it is a question of extending the category of discourse to the point at which it embraces its radical other – i.e. it is a question of showing the working of a logic of *difference* which cuts across any distinction between the linguistic and the non-linguistic; in the second case it is a question of showing how linguistic regularities depend on putting together elements which can only be conceived in non-discursive terms.

Bibliography

Barthes, R. 1967. *Elements of Semiology*. Trans. A. Lavers and C. Smith. New York: Hill and Wang.
——1972. *Mythologies*. Trans. A. Lavers. London: Jonathan Cape.
——1974. *S/Z*. London: Jonathan Cape.
——1983. *The Fashion System*. Trans. M. Ward and R. Howard. New York: Hill and Wang.
Derrida, J. 1976. *Of Grammatology*. Trans. G. C. Spivak. Baltimore, MD: Johns Hopkins University Press.
Ducrot, O. and Todorov, T. 1979. *Encyclopedic Dictionary of the Sciences of Languages*. Baltimore, MD: Johns Hopkins University Press.
Foucault, M. 1972. *The Archaeology of Knowledge*. Trans. A. M. Sheridan Smith. London: Tavistock.
——1973. *The Order of Things: An Archaeology of the Human Sciences*. New York: Pantheon.
——1977. Nietzsche, genealogy and history. In *Michel Foucault: Language, Counter-Memory, Practice: Selected Essays and Interviews*, ed. D. F. Bouchard. New York: Vintage Books.
——1979. *Discipline and Punish: The Birth of the Prison*. Trans. A. Sheridan. New York: Vintage.
——1980. *The History of Sexuality*, vol. I: *An Introduction*. Trans. R. Hurley. New York: Pantheon.
Gasché, R. 1986. *The Tain of the Mirror*. Cambridge, MA: Harvard University Press.
Hjelmslev, L. 1961. *Prolegomena to a Theory of Language*. Trans. F. A. Whitfield. Madison, WI: University of Wisconsin Press.
——1970. *Language: An Introduction*. Trans. F. A. Whitfield. Madison, WI: University of Wisconsin Press.
Kristeva, J. 1969. *Semeiotike*. Paris: Editions du Seuil.
Lacan, J. 1977. *Écrits. A Selection*. Trans. A. Sheridan. New York: Norton.
Laclau, E. 1990. *New Reflections on the Revolution of Our Time*. London: Verso.
Laclau, E. and Mouffe, C. 1985. *Hegemony and Socialist Strategy: Towards a Radical Democratic Politics*. London: Verso.
Saussure, F. de 1959. *Course in General Linguistics*. Trans. C. Bailey and A. Sechehaye. New York: McGraw-Hill.
Wittgenstein, L. 1983. *Philosophical Investigations*. Oxford: Blackwell.
Žižek, S. 1989. *The Sublime Object of Ideology*. London: Verso.

2

DISLOCATION AND CAPITALISM, SOCIAL IMAGINARY AND DEMOCRATIC REVOLUTION (1990)

Let us begin by identifying three dimensions of the relationship of dislocation that are crucial to our analysis. *The first is that dislocation is the very form of temporality.* And temporality must be conceived as the exact opposite of space. The 'spatialization' of an event consists of eliminating its temporality. Let us consider the case of Freud's *Fort/Da* game. Through the game the child symbolizes the absence of the mother, which is a traumatic event. If the child comes to terms with that absence in this way, it is because absence is no longer *just* absence but becomes a moment of the presence—absence succession. Symbolization means that the total succession is present in each of its moments. This synchronicity of the successive means that the succession is in fact a total *structure,* a space for symbolic representation and constitution. The spatialization of the event's temporality takes place through repetition, through the reduction of its variation to an invariable nucleus which is an internal moment of the pre-given structure. And note that when we refer to space, we do not do so in a metaphorical sense, out of analogy with physical space. There is no metaphor here. Any repetition that is governed by a structural law of successions is space. If physical space is also space, it is because it participates in this general form of spatiality. The representation of time as a cyclical succession, common in peasant communities, is in this sense a reduction of time to space. Any teleological conception of change is therefore also essentially spatialist. It is important to note that we are not dealing with the synchrony/diachrony opposition here. Diachrony, insofar as it is subject to rules and attempts to capture the *sense* of a succession, is also synchronic in our terms. But this means that only the dislocation of the structure, only a maladjustment which is spatially unrepresentable, is an event. Through dislocation time is overcome by space. But while we can speak of the hegemonization of time by space (through repetition), it must be emphasized that the opposite is not possible: time cannot hegemonize anything, since it is a pure effect of dislocation. The ultimate failure of all hegemonization, then, means that the real – including physical space – is in the ultimate instance temporal.

The second dimension is that *dislocation is the very form of possibility*. To understand this, let us again return to Aristotle. Movement (in the broad sense of change in general) is defined in the *Metaphysics* as the actuality of the possible as possible. Let us imagine the case of a white object which becomes black. At moment 'A' the object is white as actuality and black as potentiality, at moment 'B' it is actually black. But what about the specific moment of change, or the ontological status of 'blackening'? At that point the object is no longer white, but nor is it yet black. The Aristotelian formula of 'actuality of the possible as possible' tries to grasp this situation conceptually: what the change reveals is the *possibility* of the object becoming black. The Aristotelian possibility, however, is a single possibility because the process of change is conceived as *development* and thus appears dominated by the *telos* of the transition from potentiality to actuality. In this sense, it is a spurious possibility, one for our eyes alone. It is not the possibility we are referring to when we assert that a situation 'opens possibilities', for example. Possibility appears completely 'spatialized' in the sense we mentioned earlier. But *with dislocation there is no telos which governs change; possibility therefore becomes an authentic possibility, a possibility in the radical sense of the term.* This means that *there must be other possibilities, since the idea of a single possibility denies what is involved in the very concept of possibility.* As we have seen, because *structural dislocation is constitutive*, the dislocated structure cannot provide the principle of its transformations. The dislocated structure thus opens possibilities of multiple and indeterminate rearticulations for those freed from its coercive force and who are consequently outside it. And the very possibility of this dislocation reveals the character of *mere possibility* of the articulatory ensemble forming the structure before dislocation. The pure form of temporality and the pure form of possibility thus coincide. Just as, in the final instance, time always overcomes space, we can also say that the character of mere possibility of any kind of arrangement imposes itself, in the long term, on all structural necessity. To avoid any misunderstanding, we must once again emphasize that the dislocation of a structure does not mean that *everything* becomes possible or that *all* symbolic frameworks disappear, since no dislocation could take place in that psychotic universe: a structure must be there for it to be dislocated. The situation of dislocation is that of a lack which involves a structural reference. There is a *temporalization of spaces or a widening of the field of the possible, but this takes place in a determinate situation: that is, one in which there is always a relative structuration.*

The third dimension is that dislocation is *the very form of freedom*. Freedom is the absence of determination. Whoever is *causa sui* is free. Let us consider various possibilities on this basis. One is the Spinozan formula: any individual entity is merely a link in a chain of determinations surpassing it. As a result, freedom can only be attributed to the totality of the existent *(Deus sive Natura);* or in its structuralist version: it is not me who is speaking, but the structures which are speaking through me. Total freedom and total determination coincide and freedom comes from the 'self' of self-determination. This identity between freedom and self-determination persists when we move to a second possibility: that each individual identity in the universe ideologically tends towards the purpose fixed in advance by its nature. The alternative, then, is either a total liberty – if that purpose is guaranteed by a pre-established harmony assuring the absence of interaction with other entities – or that that interaction is inevitable, in which case freedom can only be relative. In contrast with these two variants of the notion of freedom conceived as self-determination, we have a third possibility, which is the existentialist conception of freedom. Man is condemned to be free; he is transformed into an absolute chooser by the absence of any predetermined nature; but he is a chooser who no longer has any reason to choose.

At this point, however, a different possibility opens up. Let us assume we fully accept the structuralist vision: I am a product of structures; there is nothing in me with a separate substantiality from the discourses making me up; a total determinism governs my actions. Very well, let us concede the whole argument. But the question immediately arises: what happens if the structure I am determined by does not manage to constitute itself, if a *radical* outside – which does not share a common measure or foundation with the inside of the structure – dislocates it? The structure will obviously not be able to determine me, not because I have an essence independent from the structure, but because the structure has failed to constitute itself fully and thus to constitute me as a subject as well. There is nothing in me which was oppressed by the structure or is freed by its dislocation; I am simply *thrown up* in my condition as a subject because I have not achieved constitution as an object. The freedom thus won in relation to the structure is therefore a traumatic fact initially: I am *condemned* to be free, not because I have no structural identity as the existentialists assert, but because I have a *failed* structural identity. This means that the subject is partially self-determined. However, as this self-determination is not the expression of what the subject *already* is but the result of its lack of being instead, self-determination can only proceed through processes of *identification*. As can be gathered, the greater the structural indetermination, the freer a society will be. We shall come back to this point.

These three dimensions of the relationship of dislocation – temporality, possibility and freedom – are mutually involved. If temporality was not radical, in other words if the event was not essentially exterior to the structure, it could be inscribed as an internal moment of the latter. This would mean that the possibilities would be those *of* the structure and not those emerging from structural dislocation. In that case there would be no self-determination, and thus no freedom either. Once again we find the paradox dominating the whole of social action: freedom exists because society does not achieve constitution as a structural objective order, but any social action tends towards the constitution of that impossible object, and thus towards the elimination of the conditions of liberty itself. This paradox has no solution; if it did, we would have simply returned to the sociological objectivism we are taking issue with in this chapter. It is because it is insoluble that dislocation is the primary ontological level of constitution of the social. *To understand social reality, then, is not to understand what society* is, *but what prevents it from being*. However, if what we have argued previously is true, in that case there is *no common measure between the paradox as such and the possibilities of historic action – the language games – that it opens up*. Such possibilities are therefore not a necessary structural development of the paradox, but can be taken advantage of by someone outside it. It is to this set of possibilities that we must now turn our attention. As a result of our previous argument, we will divide the discussion in two parts. In the first, to which the rest of this section will be dedicated, we will analyse the dislocatory tendencies operating in contemporary capitalism and the new possibilities of political intervention it opens up. In the section that follows, we will discuss the question of agency – that is the new forms of political subjectivity that are constructed on the basis of those possibilities (and which, as we said, are not *determined* by the dislocated structures). Our basic thesis is that the *possibility* of a radical democracy is directly linked to the level and extension of structural dislocations operating in contemporary capitalism.

It is important to remember that reflection on dislocation and its possible political fruitfulness does have a tradition within Marxism: it is a feature of the group of phenomena linked to 'permanent revolution' and 'uneven and combined development'. As has been pointed out, the concept of 'bourgeois—democratic revolution' which was to become the cornerstone of the stagist Marxism of the Second International, was never explicitly formalized in the works of Marx and Engels, and both had growing doubts about its possible generalization as a historical category. The concept was clearly linked to the historic experience of the French Revolution and combined the bourgeois objectives of the Revolution with its character of mobilization 'from below'. But it was precisely this combination that later developments in Europe placed in question. The bourgeoisie was increasingly able to achieve its objectives through non-revolutionary means. In his introduction to Marx's *Class Struggles in France* in 1895, Engels concluded that the cycle of bourgeois revolutions from below had closed after the experiences under Napoleon III and Bismarck and that a period of revolutions from above was beginning. But the other side of the situation was that if bourgeois revolution appeared less and less linked to democracy, democratic revolution was assuming an increasingly less bourgeois character. Hence Marx's texts on permanent revolution which go back to the very beginning of his work and coexist with those upholding economistic stagism. Take the following well-known passage, for example:

> The Communists turn their attention chiefly to Germany, because that country is on the eve of a bourgeois revolution that is bound to be carried out under more advanced conditions of European civilization, and with a much more developed proletariat than that of England was in the seventeenth, and of France in the eighteenth century, and because the bourgeois revolution in Germany will be the prelude to an immediately following proletarian revolution.
> (Marx 1973, p. 98).[1]

It is easy to note that, in this text, it is structural dislocation which creates the revolutionary juncture. The internal laws of the structure, which would have required a full introduction of capitalist relations of production until they became incompatible with any further development of the productive forces, are interrupted here by a dislocation that creates a new political possibility. The late development of capitalism in Germany (which would fall under what Trotsky called 'the privilege of backwardness') gives a political strength to the proletariat that bears no relation to the level of development of German capitalism. It should be noted that it is not a case of replacing one conception of structural laws with another here. On the contrary, it is the *dislocation* of structural laws which creates the *possibility* of a revolutionary politics. Here we find the seed of a vision of history that is different from economistic stagism: a succession of dislocatory junctures that may or may not be taken advantage of.

This different vision of history is insinuated in several of Marx's texts. Take the famous letter to Vera Zasulich in 1881, for example.

> Russia finds itself in a modern historical environment. It is contemporaneous with a superior civilization, it is tied to a world market in which capitalist production predominates. By appropriating the positive results of this mode of production, it is in a position to develop and transform the yet archaic form of its village community, instead of destroying it.
> *(Marx and Engels 1953, pp. 222–23)*

The key issue lies in determining whether this 'appropriation' is a contingent historical *possibility* arising from the unevenness – and thus dislocation – of the development of capitalism in Russia, or whether it is the result of a necessary structural law. Marx's whole argument on the issue moves in the first direction. In his prologue with Engels for the Russian edition of the *Manifesto* (1882), for example, the interrelationship between a revolution in Russia and a proletarian revolution in the West is affirmed and the possible maintenance of the Russian peasant community is made a condition for that revolution. We are not dealing at all with a process that is dominated by necessary infrastructural laws, but with a body of contingent articulations that have been made possible by junctures depending on the uneven development of world capitalism.

It is important to note that by dislocation and unevenness we do not mean 'contradiction' in the classical Hegelian—Marxist sense of the term. Contradiction is a necessary moment of the structure and is therefore internal to it. Contradiction has a theoretical *space* of representation. As we saw, however, dislocation is not a necessary moment in the self-transformation of the structure but is its failure to achieve constitution and is mere temporality in this sense. For that reason it opens different *possibilities* and expands the area of *freedom* of the historical subjects.

This tendency to make structural dislocation the very crux of political strategy is later accentuated in the work of Trotsky where it develops much of its potential richness. For Trotsky, the very possibility of revolutionary action depends on structural unevenness. Let us consider, first of all, the formulation of the permanent revolution perspective in his writings on the revolution of 1905. Trotsky borrowed from Parvus the idea that the capitalist system should be seen as a global totality and that the prospects for revolution should be viewed in terms of the dislocations experienced by that total structure. Hence his well-known description of the peculiarities of Russian history, the hypertrophied development of the state as a military centre to contain Asian invasions; the consequent preponderance of the state with respect to civil society, the bureaucratic nature of cities which, unlike those of Western Europe, did not develop primarily as centres of craft and trade. To this must be added the late development of capitalism in Russia and its main feature: that its predominant sources of finance were investments by foreign capital. As a result, the local bourgeoisie was weak, and, given the high concentration of capital invested in Russia, the working class gained increasingly in social and political influence. This structural imbalance between bourgeoisie and proletariat was at the heart of the bourgeoisie's inability to lead the democratic revolution. The democratic revolution was hegemonized by the proletariat and, according to Trotsky's conception of the revolution, this involved the need to go beyond democratic tasks and to move in a socialist direction.

As can be seen, in this schema the *totality* of the revolutionary strategy appears based on a succession of dislocations. In the first place, the dislocation of the relation between base and superstructure: the military-bureaucratized state of tsarism inverts the 'normal' relations between state and civil society. In the second place, the dislocation of the relation between democratic revolution and the bourgeoisie as the agent to carry it through: the break in the relation between the two, which had already been predicated incipiently by Marx in connection with the countries of Central and Western Europe, is even more the case in Russia. And finally, the dislocation of the relation between democracy and socialism, which should have been a relation of succession but which now becomes a relation of articulation. The possibility of revolution does not spring from underlying and positive structural laws dominating the whole of the historical process, but from the latter's dislocations which determine an unevenness that cannot be grasped by any structure. The schema is so daunting, however, that Trotsky himself hesitates; it is the point where he does not dare – at this stage of his theoretical evolution, at least – to step outside and draw the conclusions that can be logically deduced from his own analysis. While the revolution begun in Russia must move in a socialist direction to achieve consolidation, Trotsky does not believe – and nor do any of the Russian Social Democratic leaders either – that it can be consolidated without the triumph of a proletarian revolution in the West. Stagism still dominates the vision of 'world history' and the unevenness of the historical process merely intervenes to explain the dynamics of the seizure of power in a specific case.

> It is at the end of the 1920s and the beginning of the 1930s that Trotsky's theoretical vision broadens and that the permanent revolution logic comes to hegemonize his global view of contemporary history. The global dimension of capitalism as a world system and its uneven character tend to overlap.

> Capitalism ... prepares and in a certain sense realizes the universality and permanence of man's development. By this a repetition of the forms of development by different nations is ruled out. Although compelled to follow after the advanced countries, a backward country does not take things in the same order. ... Unevenness, the most general law of the historic process, reveals itself most sharply and complexly in the destiny of the backward countries. Under the whip of external necessity, their backward culture is compelled to make leaps. From the universal law of unevenness thus derives another law which, for the lack of a better name, we may call the law of *combined development* – by which we mean a drawing together of the different stages of the journey, combining of separate steps, an amalgam of archaic with more contemporary forms.
>
> (L. Trotsky, History of the Russian Revolution, quoted in Löwy 1981, pp. 87–88)

Referring to the previous passages, Michel Löwy aptly comments:

> Thus the amalgam of backward and advanced socio-economic conditions becomes the structural foundation for the fusion or combination of democratic and socialist tasks in a process of permanent revolution. Or, to put it differently, one of the most important political consequences of combined and uneven development is the unavoidable persistence of unresolved *democratic tasks* in the peripheral capitalist countries. Despite the claims of his critics, Trotsky never denies the democratic dimension of revolution in backward countries nor did he ever pretend that the revolution would be 'purely socialist'; what he did repudiate, however, was the dogma of bourgeois-democratic revolution as a *separate historical stage* that has to be completed before the proletarian struggle for power can commence.
>
> (Löwy 1981, p. 88)

In this generalization of the theory it is important to observe that the two terms of Trotsky's formula – unevenness and combination – are strictly incompatible with each other. For if unevenness is the 'most general law of the historic process', then the 'drawing together of the different stages of the journey' which characterizes combination loses all meaning. If unevenness is *absolutely* radical (and it must be if it is the most general law of history), then the elements of combination cannot be assigned to stages established *a priori*. On the contrary, what we have are elements whose combination depends on contingent hegemonic articulations and not on any structurally necessary stage. Either there is uneven development – in which case the element of combination disappears – or the combination of different stages is a superficial historical phenomenon which necessarily refers to a deeper structural stratum in which the dominance of stagism is unchallenged – in which case unevenness cannot have the function of a ground attributed to it by Trotsky's text.

Trotsky does not perceive the problem, and the conclusions he draws from his own lucid analysis are limited as a result. In fact, the very unity of Trotsky's text depends entirely on maintaining that hidden inconsistency: only at that price can he simultaneously introduce the possibility of absolutely original political articulations in relation to the Marxist tradition and maintain a conception of social agency which is characteristic of the most traditional Marxism. But in order to draw completely new political and theoretical conclusions, let us fully accept his thesis of the primacy of unevenness (in other words, dislocation) and take to the limit its concomitant deconstructive effects on stagism.

Firstly, an uneven structure cannot have objective and positive laws of movement, the action of each of the uneven elements will collide with the others and limit their action. Moreover, if unevenness really does have the character of a ground, such collisions and limitations cannot be reduced to a supergame whose rules would 'spatialize' them.

Secondly, the very fact that the notion of 'structural stage' has dissolved, means that the unevenness in question cannot result from the synchronic presentation of elements that should have appeared as a succession, but must be thought of differently. As far as the combination of stages is concerned, one structural arrangement is as possible as another. But if we are faced with elements that, considered in isolation, are indifferent to the various structural ensembles with which they can be articulated, where is the unevenness? The solution is suggested by Trotsky's own examples. As we saw, he proclaims, speaking of the backward countries, that 'under the whip of *external* necessity, their backward culture is *compelled* to make leaps' (our emphasis). This reference to compulsion and externality is fundamental, because it clearly implies that the unevenness results from the *disruption* of a structure by forces operating *outside* it. This is exactly what we have called dislocation. The unevenness of development is the result of the dislocation of an articulated structure, not the combination of elements which essentially belong to different 'stages'.

Thirdly, the structural dislocation particular to unevenness and the external nature of that dislocation mean that the structure does not have in itself the conditions for its possible future rearticulation. And the very fact that the dislocated elements are not endowed with any kind of essential unity outside their contingent forms of articulation means that a dislocated structure is an open structure in which the crisis can be resolved in the most varied of directions. It is strict *possibility* in the sense we defined earlier. As a result, the structural rearticulation will be an eminently *political* rearticulation. The field of unevenness is, in the strict sense of the term, the field of politics. Moreover, the more points of dislocation a structure has, the greater the expansion of the field of politics will be.

Fourthly, the subjects constructing hegemonic articulations on the basis of dislocation are not internal but external to the dislocated structure. As we stated above, they are condemned to be subjects by the very fact of dislocation. In this sense, however, efforts to rearticulate and reconstruct the structure also entail the constitution of the agents' identity and subjectivity. It is this point which clearly shows the limits of Trotsky's 'permanentist' approach. For Trotsky, the identity of social agents – classes – remains unaltered throughout the whole process. It is to make that result possible that stagism, while shaken, had to be maintained. But if the constitutive nature of unevenness makes any fixing of identities impossible in terms of stages, it means that the elements articulated by social agents come to form part of the latter's identity. It is not a question of whether the *same* subject – the working class – can take on democratic tasks or not, but of whether, having assumed them, a new subject is constituted on the basis of articulating working class identity and democratic identity. And this articulation changes the meaning of both identities. As we have argued elsewhere, this decisive step is not taken by Trotsky or by the Leninist tradition considered as a whole. It is only with the Gramscian notion of 'collective will' that the barrier of class essentialism begins to dissolve.

Fifthly, the greater the dislocation of a structure is, the more indeterminate the political construction emerging from it will be. In this sense, Leninism represented an advance from the orthodox Marxism of the Second International, in spite of its limitations. No wonder the International's most representative leaders hurled accusations of 'voluntarism' and 'adventurism' against Leninist political practice. To base political intervention on the opportunities opened up by the *indetermination* of a historical juncture went right against a vision of politics which saw the latter as lacking all autonomy, since it was merely the result of an *entirely* determined process. Once again, it is only by radicalizing this dimension of indetermination that the field of politics can be extended, and this requires a deepening of the dialectic implicit in the dislocation—possibility relationship.

Let us examine this relationship in a case which has been traditionally put forward as an example of capitalism's growing control of social relations: the phenomenon of commodification. In its most frequent description, capitalism has an inherent tendency to dissolve previous social relations and to transform all objects of private life previously outside its control into commodities. The human beings produced by this growing expansion of the market would be completely dominated by capitalism. Their very needs would be created by the market and through the manipulation of public opinion by the mass media controlled by capital. We would thus be moving in the direction of increasingly regimented societies dominated by the major centres of economic power. Given that the working class would be increasingly incorporated into the system at the same time, no radically anti-capitalist sector would exist and future prospects would appear more and more bleak. Hence the deep pessimism of an Adorno. But this picture does not at all correspond with reality. It is without doubt true that the phenomenon of commodification is at the heart of the multiple dislocations of traditional social relations. But this does not mean that the only prospect thrown up by such dislocations is the growing passive conformity of all aspects of life to the laws of the market.

The response to the negative effects of the commodification process can be a whole variety of struggles which attempt to subject the activities of the market to social regulation. This does not necessarily have to be state regulation; numerous forms of local and national organization – consumer organizations, for example – can be given the power to participate. Only a nostalgia for traditional social relations can maintain an exclusively pessimistic vision of this process. And it is worth remembering that the world broken up by capitalist expansion was far from idyllic and was the source of many relations of subordination. More crucially still, a world organized round traditional social relations is one in which the possibilities of variation and transformation are strictly limited: human beings cannot choose and build their own life because it has already been organized for them by a pre-existent social system. The dislocation of social relations, on the other hand – generated by a phenomenon such as commodification – provokes acts of resistance which launch new social actors into the historical arena; and the new actors, precisely because they are moving on a dislocated terrain, must constantly reinvent their own social forms.

The pessimism of the Frankfurt School stems from the fact that in its approach two central assumptions of Marxist theory remain unchanged: (a) that the capitalist system constitutes a self-regulating totality and (b) that the transformation of the system, as in any self-regulating totality, can only take place as a result of the development of the internal logic of the system itself. Since this vision accepts that the internal logic of the system does not lead to the emergence of an agent capable of overthrowing it, the only thing left intact is the system's character as a self-regulating totality, as a result of which it can now expand limitlessly. But it is with this conception of a self-regulating totality that the dislocation—possibility dialectic breaks. Since the dislocation is radical, the movements of the system cannot just be internally determined. Among other things, this means that there is no system in the strong sense of the term. As a result of this externality, and to the very extent that it prevents the social from closing into a systematic whole, the prospects created by a historical juncture expand. In this way, I believe a much more optimistic vision is gained of the prospects opening up for contemporary social struggles. The latter start from the reality of the commodification phenomenon and attempt to control it socially, not to wage a merely defensive struggle against an apparently self-regulating and inexorable structure. The problem, then, is how to articulate the presence and functioning of the market with a democratic and socialist society. But this requires a break, both with a vision of socialism as an absolutely planned society in which all market mechanisms have been suppressed, and with a conception of the market's functioning in which it is presented as having an internal logic that leads automatically to capitalism.

We can refer to the problem of the growing bureaucratic unification and control of social relations in contemporary societies in the same way. The obligatory reference here, of course, is Max Weber. Unlike traditional societies in which social relations appear dominated by customary practices, under modern conditions there is a growing rationalization of social endeavour by bureaucratic power. Just a step away is the assertion that we are moving increasingly towards regimented societies in which the concentration of administrative power is becoming almost total. But what this vision ignores, on the one hand, is that the administrative standardization in a single power centre is increasingly questioned by the internationalization of political and economic relations, and, on the other, that bureaucratization produces resistance by those suffering its effects. The Weberian theory of bureaucracy was elaborated in an age which believed firmly in the ability of the centralized national state to regulate economic activity and to intervene effectively in the management of social and political relations. Not in vain was the theory of 'organized capitalism' (organized within the framework of the national state, that is) formulated at that time. But the rapid internationalization of political and economic relations in recent decades has rendered the national framework obsolete – or rather, has transformed it into just one of the forces to be taken into account in the determination of any structural change. The conditions for bureaucratic efficiency and rationality thus appear constantly placed in question.

The phenomenon of bureaucratization thus gives rise to a double liberating effect. On the one hand, bureaucratic rationalization dislocates the old structural power relations. In this sense, the first *positive* effect of bureaucratization (even if it presents itself in an 'alienated' form) is that it constitutes a victory for conscious political intervention in the sedimented practices of tradition. The 'alienated' character of the bureaucratic decision stems from its origin in a 'universal class' (Hegel) – that is, an absolute power that springs from society, but at the same time takes a controlling distance from it. But inasmuch as that absolute power is resisted by antagonistic social forces and limited by the international framework in which the bureaucratic state is operating, the omnipotent nature of bureaucracy is questioned and demystified. Bureaucratic power is thus revealed as *one more* power along with the rest. But in that case – and this is the second liberating effect – it is not possible to return to the traditional social relations prior to bureaucratic rationalization. The struggle between bureaucracy and the social forces opposing it takes place entirely in the field opened by the bureaucratic transformation. The latter is confronted, not with a return to customary repetitive practices, but with a range of alternative forms of rationalization. These rationalizations will not now start from a single power centre, but from a multiplicity of power centres; and they will be more democratic in that the decisions adopted will come through negotiation between those multiple powers. But in any case, such democratic planning would have been impossible without (a) the dislocation of traditional social structure by bureaucratic power and (b) the historical agents' new awareness of their capacity to transform their social relations, also conferred by bureaucratic intervention. In this way, bureaucracy – the opposite of democracy – is the historical condition for it. Let us recall de Tocqueville's thesis on the symmetry between the *ancien régime* and the Revolution: the Revolution was only possible on the basis and as a continuation of the administrative unification and rationalization carried through by the *ancien régime*. As with commodification, the result of bureaucracy would just be a totally administered society if it was guaranteed an absolute *a priori* power but if that is not the case, the prospects opened by the bureaucratic revolution are much broader than anything it can control in terms of its own logic.

Finally, it is the same if we go on to consider the organization of the production process itself. Marx has pointed to the radical revolutionary nature of the transition from manufacture to large-scale industry: while in the first the worker found, in spite of having to concentrate all his labour effort in a partial task, that his body and skill still imposed limits on and determined technical progress, in the second these limits are broken. Referring to such an analysis by Marx, Lefort comments:

> Of what does the radical newness of the era of large-scale industry consist? From now on, the production process becomes autonomous; the mode of the division of labour obeys the technical necessities of mechanical fabrication such as they are made known by the natural sciences, instead of remaining bound to the range of individual aptitudes. In the language of Marx, the subjective principle of the division of labour is substituted by an objective principle. In manufacturing, the worker certainly had to adapt himself to a specific operation before entering the production process; but the operation was accommodated in advance to the worker. In other words, the organic constitution of the worker determined the division and combination of gestures required for a given production process. A corporeal schema continued to determine how the workshop was structured. In mechanical production, by contrast, the principle of the division of labour ceases to be subjective.
>
> (*Lefort 1986, p. 159*)

In other words, while the limits of technical transformation possible under manufacture were set by the worker's body and skill, in the case of large-scale industry they were transgressed by a process completely dominated by the internal logic of technical change. And here we find ourselves in the same situation as with commodification and bureaucracy. On the one hand, the existing situation of large-scale industry could be described in terms of alienation, as the direct producer ceases to be the centre of reference and meaning of the production process. But on the other, the situation can be seen in exactly the opposite way: with large-scale industry the limits are no longer biologically determined and the organization of the production process is freed from any dependence on the direct producer. If this is not fully visible from the way the problem is dealt with by Marx, it is because of the contrast he makes between the division of labour in manufacture – where it is a subjective principle – and in large-scale industry – where it is an objective principle. Behind this conception of the objective nature of the organizational and technological transformation of large-scale industry, of course, is the naturalist vision of the economic process as a self-generating process, subject to the same necessary laws as nature. But if we abandon this objectivist outlook, we are offered a completely new vision. Hidden behind the apparent objectivity of the changes in the division of labour are the decisions of the capitalist, which are no longer subject to the constraints imposed by the 'organic constitution' of the worker. And in the event of the economic process passing from private capitalist ownership to some form of social management, the capitalist's liberation from the limitations of direct production is transferred to the community as a whole. What the direct producer loses in individual autonomy, s/he more than gains as a member of a community.

In one sense, our analysis keeps within the field of Marxism and attempts to reinforce what has been one of its virtues: the full acceptance of the transformations entailed by capitalism and the construction of an alternative project that is *based on* the ground created by those transformations, not on *opposition to* them. Commodification, bureaucratization and the increasing dominance of scientific and technological planning over the division of labour should not necessarily be resisted. Rather, one should work within these processes so as to develop the prospects they create for a non-capitalist alternative. In another sense, however, our analysis departs from Marxism. From a Marxist perspective, the development of social alternatives to capitalism is a process which fully accepts the historical ground it has created, but which must nevertheless be conceived as the internal development of the contradictions belonging to capitalist forms themselves. We are thus dealing with a process whose basic dimensions are entirely predetermined and where the question of *power* as a political construction is removed. For if the analysis assumes that any non-capitalist alternative is merely the result of the *internal* contradictions of capitalism, then the question of the power that capitalism could have to impose its *diktats* in a given juncture is eliminated. Not in vain can politics only be a superstructure in this approach. In our analysis, on the other hand, the problem of the resolution of power relations is never taken for granted. Any transformation of capitalism opens up a range of possibilities that are not just determined by the endogenous logic of capitalist forms, but also by the latter's constitutive outside and by the whole historical situation in which those logics operate. Inasmuch as capitalism always had a constitutive outside, its domination can never be merely imposed through the internal development of its logic, but must be imposed through the hegemonization of something radically exterior to itself. In which case, capitalism must be seen, in terms of its most fundamental and constitutive features, as a system of power. And to this we must add something that can be deduced from our analysis above. The more dislocated is the ground on which capitalism operates, the less it can rely on a framework of stable social and political relations and the more central this political moment of hegemonic construction will be; but for that very reason, the more extensive the range of alternative political possibilities opposed to capitalist hegemonization will also be.

Let us consider the crucial breaking points of the vision of capitalism as a force generating its transformation from its own internal logic. The peak moment of this image corresponds to the age of so-called liberal capitalism. The processes of accumulation at the level of civil society are considered sufficient to guarantee the self-reproduction of the system as a whole. This autonomy was largely a myth, of course, but one which did have a certain historical foundation: insofar as social reproduction appeared as immanent in traditional social relations, the idea of it being consciously regulated was completely unthinkable. In such circumstances the image of the self-regulating market – and of capitalist accumulation, which was only the extension of market relations to the field of production – was imposed as an alternative to traditional society but nevertheless retained one of the latter's essential features. The objective nature of the laws of the market, their operation outside the will and awareness of the producers, constituted an intelligible principle of social functioning (which made the existence of political economy possible as a science), but one which, like all pre-capitalist mechanisms of social reproduction, escaped the conscious intervention of the agents and did not therefore give space for alternative possibilities.

It is with the transition to what Hilferding dubbed 'organized capitalism' that the element of conscious regulation – and thus an eminently political regulation – begins to take on a new centrality. The characteristics of organized capitalism are well known: the rapid concentration and centralization of industrial, commercial and finance capital; the growing dependency of industries on bank credit; the growing separation between ownership and control of enterprises and the consequent expansion of managerial bureaucracies; imperialist expansion; the growing interrelation between the state and capitalist monopolies; the corporatization of economic and social power based on a tripartite agreement between the state, a few monopolistic enterprises and national trade union organizations; the concentration of industry in a few cities and in particular regions of the world; the growth in the number of employees in large-scale enterprises and the parallel growth of the big cities, etc.

It is worth concentrating a moment on the most conspicuous features of the organized capitalism theory. Firstly, it recognizes that regulation by the market is not enough to guarantee the conditions of capitalist reproduction. It must be supplemented by the conscious regulation imposed by monopolistic agreements, banking control, state intervention and corporatist agreements. This conscious intervention thus allows the regulation of the increasingly dislocated reality of the market. But secondly, if the element of conscious intervention becomes autonomous from the blind mechanisms of the market, then there is no logic for the latter to be necessarily imposed on the former. In this sense, conscious intervention can be oriented in various directions, and this means that the system of possible alternatives arising at a given juncture expands. Take the various forms of 'planism' that proliferated in the 1920s and 1930s, or later, the project of a welfare state as a redistributive effort within the framework of a corporatist agreement. Whether planning takes one direction or another, then, appears to be an eminently political decision that depends on existing power relations. Thirdly, the theory of organized capitalism assumes, both in its left-wing and right-wing forms, that the national state constitutes the framework of all economic planning. The conception of state power as the locus and source of all economic decisions and planning is one of the cornerstones of the welfare state.

This second mode of capitalist operation – between the theory and practice of which there are profound differences, of course – has gone into crisis in recent decades. We have entered what some authors have called 'disorganized capitalism' (Lash and Urry 1987; Offe 1985). Lash and Urry characterize its main features as follows: the internationalization of capital has led to nationally based enterprises having less control over domestic markets. There has been a deconcentration of capital and a general decline in cartels. A growing separation has also occurred between financial and industrial capital. The number of manual workers in manufacturing industry has dropped in absolute and relative terms; and a shift has taken place from Taylorism to more flexible forms of organization which no longer involve the concentration of the workforce in large plants. In industrial relations, this has led to a decline in collective bargaining at the national level, while the growing independence of the monopolies from the state has reduced the importance of corporatist agreements. In terms of social structure, there has been a rapid development in the services sector, in particular, and thus of the professional class. Such transformations have been accompanied by a new international division of labour: the Third World countries have seen successive investments in basic extractive and manufacturing industries and this has produced a change in the occupational structure in the First World, where employment is now oriented towards the service occupations. Finally, the new spatial division of labour has weakened the regional concentration of industry, and accentuated the export of labour-intensive industries to the Third World. At the same time, it has led to the emergence of rural spaces in the metropolitan countries, as well as to a decline in towns and cities, both in terms of size and their domination of the surrounding area.

As can be seen, we are faced with an absolute and relative decline in the decision-making power of the national state as a centre of regulation of economic life. This decline, however, is just that: a decline. We are not facing a collapse in which a once absolute power has suddenly been transferred *in toto* to the multinational corporations. A break must be made with the simplistic vision of an ultimate, conclusive instance of power. The myth of liberal capitalism was that of a totally self-regulating market from which state intervention was completely absent. The myth of organized capitalism was that of a regulatory instance whose power was disproportionately excessive and led to all kinds of wild expectations. And now we run the risk of creating a new myth: that of the monopoly corporations' limitless capacity for decision-making. There is an obvious symmetry in all three cases: one instance – be it the immanent laws of the economy, the state or monopoly power – is presented as if it did not have conditions of existence, as if it did not have a constitutive outside. The power of this instance does not therefore need to be hegemonically and pragmatically constituted since it has the character of a ground.

On the other hand, if we abandon this metaphysical hypothesis of the ultimate instance and accept, according to our previous analysis, that all power is contingent and depends on conditions of existence that are contingent themselves, then the problem of power is decisively displaced: the construction of a popular power does not mean transferring an absolute power from one instance to another, but taking advantage of the opportunities offered by the new dislocations characterizing disorganized capitalism to create new forms of social control. The response to the decline in the regulatory capacity of the national state cannot therefore be to abandon political struggle with a sense of impotency, nor to call up the myth of an impossible autarchy, but to open up new spaces for popular struggle on the real ground on which economic regulation will have to take place in an era of disorganized capitalism: that of supranational communities (the European Community, for example).

The novelty of the present situation, then, lies in the fact that the nodal point around which the intelligibility of the social is articulated does not now tend to be displaced from one instance to another in society, but to dissolve. The plurality of dislocations generates a plurality of centres of relative power, and the expansion of all social logic thus takes place on a terrain that is increasingly dominated by elements external to it. Accordingly, articulation is constitutive of all social practice. But in that case, to the very extent that dislocations increasingly dominate the terrain of an absent structural determination, the problem of *who* articulates comes to occupy a more central position. It is this problem of who the subjects of historical transformations are – or, more fundamentally, what being a subject entails – that we must now consider.

Social imaginary and democratic revolution

Our approach to the problem of the social agent/structure alternative can be clearly gathered from the development of our argument above. Let us recapitulate the main points, (l) The opposition between a society that is completely determined in structural terms and another that is entirely the creation of social agents is not an opposition between different conceptions of the social, but is inscribed in social reality itself. As we said earlier, the subject exists because of dislocations in the structure. (2) Dislocation is the source of freedom. But this is not the freedom of a subject with a *positive* identity – in which case it would just be a structural locus; rather it is merely the freedom of a structural fault which can only construct an identity through acts of *identification*. (3) But as these acts of identification – or of decision – are based on a radical structural undecidability, any decision presupposes an act of power. Any power is nevertheless ambiguous: to repress something entails the *capacity* to repress, which involves power; but it also entails the *need* to repress, which involves limitation of power. This means that power is merely the trace of contingency, the point at which objectivity reveals the radical alienation which defines it. In this sense, objectivity – the being of objects – is nothing but the sedimented form of power, in other words a power whose traces have been erased. (4) However, since there is no original *fiat* of power, no moment of radical foundation at which something beyond any objectivity is constituted as the absolute ground on which the being of objects is based, the relationship between power and objectivity cannot be that of the creator and the *ens creatum*. The creator has already been partially created through his or her forms of identification with a structure into which s/he has been thrown. But as this structure is dislocated, the identification never reaches the point of a full identity: any act is an act of reconstruction, which is to say that the creator will search in vain for the seventh day of rest. And as the creator is not omniscient, and has to create within an open range of possibilities that reveal the radical contingency of any decision, power and objectivity become synonymous. (5) On the one hand, then, we have decision – that is, identification as opposed to identity; and on the other, the discernible marks of contingency in the decision, that is power. The ensemble of these marks cannot therefore be objective; it must be the location of an absence. This location is precisely that of the subject. Subject equals the pure form of the structure's dislocation, of its ineradicable distance from itself. An examination of the subject's forms of presence in the structure must therefore be an exploration of *contingency's discursive forms of presence in the field of objectivity* – or more precisely, the ways in which objectivity is subverted by contingency. Or in a third formulation, which amounts to the same, it must analyse the emergence of the subject as the result of the collapse of objectivity.

When we speak of politics here, we are not referring to any regional category. 'Politics' is an ontological category: there is politics because there is subversion and dislocation of the social. This means that *any* subject is, by definition, political. Apart from the subject, in this radical sense, there are only *subject positions* in the general field of objectivity. But the subject, as understood in this text, cannot be objective: it is only constituted on the structure's uneven edges. Thus, to explore the field of the subject's emergence in contemporary societies is to examine the marks that contingency has inscribed on the apparently objective structures of the societies we live in.

Let us begin by identifying the basic dimensions of this antithetical relationship between subject and structure.

(1) *Any subject is a mythical subject.* By myth we mean a space of representation which bears no relation of continuity with the dominant 'structural objectivity'. Myth is thus a principle of reading of a given situation, whose terms are external to what is representable in the objective spatiality constituted by the given structure. The 'objective' condition for the emergence of myth, then, is a structural dislocation. The 'work' of myth is to suture that dislocated space through the constitution of a new space of representation. Thus, the effectiveness of myth is essentially hegemonic: it involves forming a new objectivity by means of the rearticulation of the dislocated elements. Any objectivity, then, is merely a crystallized myth. The moment of the myth's realization is consequently the moment of the subject's eclipse and its reabsorption by the structure – the moment at which the subject is reduced to 'subject position'. If the condition for the mythical character of a space is its distance *vis-à-vis* what is representable in the space of the dominant structural objectivity (a distance which is only made possible by the latter's dislocation), the subject is only subject insofar as s/he mediates between both spaces – a mediation which is not itself representable since it has no space of its own.

(2) *The subject is constitutively metaphor.* The condition for any representation (and hence for any literality) is the presence of two spaces that can be mutually related through a one to one correlation of their constitutive elements. And the condition of possibility of this one to one correlation is that there should

be something identical constituting the ultimate reality of both the represented space and the space of representation. It is in this sense that the Wittgenstein of the *Tractatus* sustained that the possibility of language referring to reality depended on both sharing the same logical form. But what happens when the subject is exactly the opposite? The mythical space constituted by the subject does not have the same 'logical form' as the structure whose principle of reading the subject becomes. On the contrary, it is the critique and substitution of this 'form' which characterizes the mythical operation. The mythical space is presented as an alternative to the logical form of the dominant structural discourse. However, for reasons mentioned earlier, the mythical space cannot function as a critical alternative to another space if the latter is fully constituted, as if it were simply a question of choosing between the two. Between two fully constituted spaces lacking any common foundation, there is not the slightest criterion for a choice. It is only if one of the spaces is dislocated that the other can appear as its inverted image. But, one could ask, does not this inverted image keep (as its negative reverse) the same logical form of the structural space? The answer is clearly negative. If the mythical space was opposed to a full 'logical form' of the dominant structural space, then we would indeed be faced with an inverted image. But it is not the 'structurality' of the dominant structure to which the mythical space is opposed, but its destructuring effects. The mythical space is constituted as a critique of the lack of structuration accompanying the dominant order. In this sense, however, the mythical space has a dual function and a split identity: on the one hand, it is its own literal content – the proposed new order; but on the other, this order symbolizes the very principle of spatiality and structurality. The critical effects of the mythical space on the dominant structural space will therefore increase the latter's destructuration: (1) the mythical space will appear as pure positivity and spatiality, and to this end it will present that to which it is opposed as a non-space, a non-place where a set of dislocations are added together, (2) in order to conceive of itself as a space – as the point of a fully realized objectivity – it will have to present those dislocations as equivalent, but as systematic, nonetheless. But as this systematic character cannot be that of a structure, it must be referred back to a transcendent point, to an initial non-place of the dislocations that will be conceived as the *source* of the latter. The transcendent *origin* of the structural dislocations is thus opposed to the *objective* immanence of the mythical space. The metaphorical nature of mythical space thus stems from the fact that the concrete or literal content of myth represents something different from itself: the very principle of a fully achieved literality. The fascination accompanying the vision of a promised land or an ideal society stems directly from this perception or intuition of a fullness that cannot be granted by the reality of the present. Myth only springs forth as a metaphor on a ground dominated by this peculiar absence/presence dialectic. But as we have seen, this dialectic between absence (dislocation of the structure) and presence (identification with an unachieved fullness) is nothing but the space of the subject. The subject (lack within the structure) only takes on its specific form of representation as the metaphor of an absent structure.

(3) *The subject's forms of identification function as surfaces of inscription.* As we have seen, if the subject is the metaphor of an absent fullness, it means that the concrete content of its forms of identification will function as the very representation of fullness, of all possible fullness. But this means that once myth – or, what amounts to the same thing, the forms of identification giving the subject its only discursive presence possible – has achieved a certain social acceptance, it will be used as an inverted form of representation of all possible kinds of structural dislocation. Any frustration or unsatisfied demand will be compensated for or offset by the myth of an achieved fullness. This indetermination of myth – as the means of expression by which specific dislocations might be overcome – is a direct consequence of its metaphorical nature, of the possibility it opens for the expression of the form of fullness itself, beyond any concrete dislocation. This means that myth functions as a surface on which dislocations and social demands can be inscribed. The main feature of a surface of inscription is its incomplete nature: if the inscription process was complete, there would be an essential symmetry between the surface and the inscription left on it, thus eliminating any distance between the act of expression and what is expressed by it. But if the process is never complete, the symmetry is broken and our view is displaced from what is inscribed to the process of inscription itself. In this sense, social myths are essentially incomplete: their content is constantly reconstituted and displaced.

(4) *The incomplete character of the mythical surfaces of inscription is the condition of possibility for the constitution of social imaginaries.* The relation between the surface of inscription and what is inscribed on it is therefore essentially unstable. There are two extreme possibilities here. The first is the complete hegemonization of the surfaces of inscription by what is inscribed on them. As we mentioned earlier the moment of inscription is eliminated in favour of the literality of what is inscribed. The other possibility is symmetrically opposite: the moment of representation of the very form of fullness dominates to such an extent that it becomes the unlimited horizon of inscription of *any* social demand and *any* possible dislocation. In such an event, myth is transformed into an imaginary. The imaginary is a horizon: it is not one among other objects but an absolute limit which structures a field of intelligibility and is thus the condition of possibility for the emergence of any object. In this sense, the Christian millennium, the Enlightenment and positivism's conception of progress, and communist society are all imaginaries: as modes of representation of the very form of fullness, they are located beyond the precarious-ness and dislocations typical of the world of objects. Put another way, it is only because there are 'failed' objects, quasi-objects, that the very form of objectivity must free itself from any concrete entity and assume the character of a horizon.

With these considerations as our starting point, we can determine the collective imaginaries' pattern of constitution and dissolution. The condition for the emergence of an imaginary is the metaphorization of the literal content of a particular social demand. Let us suppose that a particular social group is suffering a range of dislocations in its customary practices and proposes a series of measures to overcome them. This body of measures constitutes a certain spatial model – an ideal model in this sense: the mythical space of a possible social order. From the beginning, the duality of this space – literal content and metaphorical representation of fullness – is present, but insofar as the mythical space is directly linked to a specific dislocation, the possibilities for the expansion and autonomization of the moment of metaphorical representation are severely limited. Yet the very fact that this mythical order is from the beginning something more than the terrain of the original dislocation entails the possibility – which may or may not be realized – of radicalizing the metaphorical moment of the representation. Thus, it only needs other dislocations and demands to be added to the fullness that the mythical space must represent for the metaphorical moment to become autonomous from the literality of the original dislocation, and for the mythical space to be transformed into an imaginary horizon. Gramsci saw this process as the transition from a *corporatist class* to a *hegemonic class*, which for him involved the 'universalization' of the demands of a particular group. What our analysis adds to the Gramscian conception is the idea that this transition is only possible because the duality of the representation has been present from the start, because all mythical space is external to the dislocation it purports to suture; and because any group, from this point of view, is exterior to its own demands. This also shows us what the logic of the dissolution of collective imaginaries is: insofar as a mythical space begins to absorb less social demands, and an increasing number of dislocations that cannot be integrated into that space of representation coexist, the space is, so to speak, re-literalized; its power of metaphorization is reduced, and its dimension of horizon is thus lost.

There is therefore a double movement governing the constitution of collective identities. On the one hand, no collective imaginary appears essentially linked to a literal content. As a collective imaginary represents the very form of 'fullness', the latter can be 'embodied' by the most diverse of contents. In this sense, the imaginary signifiers forming a community's horizon are tendentially empty and essentially ambiguous. On the other hand, however, it would be fundamentally incorrect to suppose that such ambiguity might be offset by the literality of the various social demands giving content to the imaginary in every historical juncture. This would mean assuming that the demands are self-transparent discourses, when in actual fact we know that their very constitution requires the intervention of mythical spaces and imaginary horizons. The process is considerably more complex and involves a constant interpenetration between these two dimensions. It is important to point out that there is no necessary relation between the dislocation as such (which, as we have seen, is pure *temporality*) and the discursive *space* that is to constitute its principle of reading and its form of representation. That is to say that the imaginary horizon on which a particular dislocation is inscribed – which thus transforms it into a demand and introduces a principle of intelligibility into the situation as an ensemble – is external to the dislocation as such and cannot be deduced from the latter. There is therefore no common measure between the dislocated structure and the discourse aiming to introduce a new order and a new articulation.

Consider the German economic crisis of the 1920s, for example, and its devastating effects on the middle classes. All routine expectations and practices – even the sense of self-identity – had been entirely shattered. There was thus a generalized dislocation of traditional patterns of life. That National Socialist discourse emerged as a possible response to the crisis and offered a principle of intelligibility for the new situation is not something that stemmed *necessarily* from the crisis itself. That the crisis was resolved in favour of Nazism cannot be deduced *from the terms* of the crisis themselves. What occurred was something different: it was that Nazi discourse was the only one in the circumstances that addressed the problems experienced by the middle classes as a whole and offered a principle for their interpretation. Its victory was the result of its *availability* on a terrain and in a situation where no other discourse presented itself as a real hegemonic alternative. From our previous analysis, it can be clearly gathered why mere availability is on occasion enough to ensure the victory of a particular discourse: for if the mythical space has the dual function of expressing its concrete content and representing 'fullness' as such – and since there is no common measure between the dislocation and the forms of its discursive 'spatialization' – then the mere fact that it presents itself as the embodiment of fullness is enough to ensure its acceptance. The discourse of a 'new order' is often accepted by several sectors, not because they particularly like its content but because it is the discourse of *an* order, of something that is presented as a credible alternative to a crisis and a generalized dislocation.

This does not mean, of course, that *any* discourse putting itself forward as the embodiment of fullness will be accepted. The acceptance of a discourse depends on its credibility, and this will not be granted if its proposals clash with the basic principles informing the organization of a group. But it is important to point out that the more the objective organization of that group has been dislocated, the more those 'basic principles' will have been shattered, thereby widening the areas of social life that must be reorganized by a mythical space. The collapse of liberal and rationalist convictions among widespread sectors of the population with the emergence of the totalitarianisms of the twentieth century is just one extreme example of this process. There is therefore a dual movement. On the one hand mythical space, as the incarnation of the form of fullness as such, metaphorically transfers this embodying function to its concrete content and thus manages hegemonically to impose a particular social order. It is only through this overdetermination of functions that this social order is imposed and consolidated. But this overdetermination, which is the source of its strength, is also – and this is the second movement – the source of its weakness: for if the very form of fullness has a space of representation, then the latter will be the locus to which *any* specific demand will be referred and where *any* specific dislocation will find the inverted form of its expression. The relation between the literal content of the mythical space and its function of representing the general form of fullness is a *radically* hegemonic and unstable relation; one that is exposed to an 'outside' that it is *essentially* incapable of mastering. This opens either the possibility that the moment of the general form of fullness might predominate – in which case the literal content will be deformed and transformed through the addition of an indefinite number of social demands – or that the literal content of the mythical space might predominate – in which case its ability to hegemonize the general form of fullness will be reduced; a growing coexistence will exist between unexpressed demands and a *supposed* universality that is incapable of delivering the goods; and the mythical space will lose its dimension of imaginary horizon. In practice, mythical spaces move on an unstable balance between these extremes: for longer or shorter periods they have a certain relative elasticity beyond which we witness their inexorable decline.

In speaking of 'mythical spaces' and their possible transformation into imaginary horizons, it is important to point out that we are not referring to anything that is essentially 'primitive' and whose re-emergence in contemporary societies would constitute an outbreak of irrationalism. On the contrary, myth is constitutive of any possible society. As we have seen, any space formed as a principle for the reordering of a dislocated structure's elements is mythical. Its mythical character is given by its radical discontinuity with the dislocations of the dominant structural forms. The welfare state, for example, was a myth aimed at reconstructing the operation of capitalist societies following the Great Depression. A society from which myth was radically excluded would be either an entirely 'spatial' and 'objective' society – where any dislocation had been banished, like the model for the operation of a perfect machine – or one in which dislocations lacked any space for representation and transcendence. In other words, either the cemetery or the lunatic asylum.

But it is not just that myth is not absent from the functioning of contemporary societies: it is also that the latter are required by their very dynamics to become increasingly mythical. This is linked to the proliferation of dislocations peculiar to advanced capitalism – the era, as we saw, of disorganized capitalism. The combined effects of commodification, of bureaucratic rationalization and of the increasingly complex forms of division of labour – all require constant creativity and the continuous construction of spaces of collective operation that can rest less and less on inherited objective, institutional forms. But this means that in contemporary societies the (mythical) space of the subject is widened at the expense of structural objectivity. We live today in societies that are in many ways less 'alienated' than in the past: that is to say societies in which there is a greater indeterminacy of our position within them and in which we are more free to decide our movements and identity. They are also societies in which social reproduction depends less and less on repetitive practices and requires the constant production of social myths. In one sense we can say that the duality between subject and object is being overcome: the classical problem of knowledge as the adequation between knowing and being disappears in that myth constitutes the subject and being of objects at the same time. But the transparency – if it can be called transparency – of myth is very different from that presupposed by the Hegelian abolition of the knowing/being duality found, for example, in Lukács. While for Lukács this abolition involves the consummation of a fullness that makes the alienated existence of the subject in relation to the being of the object impossible (a consummation which thus entails the radical reduction of the real to the rational), in the case of myth the opposite occurs. It is insofar as any fullness is denied to both subject and object that myth can establish the reality of both, thus transcending the division from which epistemological discourse emerges.

But this is the point at which a decisive question is posed for our discourse. Does not the *recognition* of the mythical – or contingent – character of the spatial configurations making us up as subjects already involve a certain exteriority to that mythical space and, by extension, to any space? As the ground of the subject (extended at the cost of the structure) must pay the concomitant price of its dissolution as a *locatable* ground, does not the transcendence of epistemological discourse give rise to a paradox? If any representation involves spatiality, does not the recognition of the mythical nature of any space entail forgoing any intelligibility of the *place* from which such a recognition is verified? These are crucial questions which should be answered, in our view, by drawing up close to what constitutes the specificity, in its most radical sense, of the societies in which we live. Reformulated in different, but equivalent terms, it is the question of the very possibility of a *community* in an era of generalized politics. In the following pages, we will deal with this issue from a particular angle: the way in which the discourses constituting community spaces have dealt with those realities denied the dignity of spatial representation.

Politics and space are antinomic terms. Politics only exist insofar as the spatial eludes us. Or – and this amounts to the same thing – political victory is equivalent to the elimination of the specifically political nature of the victorious practices. That is why any revolution must cultivate the myth of 'origins'; in order to establish itself as the source of all positivity, it must rub out the contingent traces of its 'ignoble' beginnings. As we know, spatiality means coexistence within a structure that establishes the positive nature of all its terms. Dislocation, on the other hand, means the impossibility of that coexistence: particular elements only manage to obtain positivity (i.e. objectivity) at the expense of the elimination of others. The representation of both as positive differential realities in the same space is therefore impossible. Only if the antagonistic elements are presented as anti-space, as anti-community, do they manage to obtain a form of discursive presence. This discourse of dislocation and antagonism, however, will not only be non-spatial but the very negation of space as such; and as we saw, the mythical space will therefore appear as the realization of the principle of pure spatiality. This offers us two starting points: an analysis of the forms of exclusion that have historically provided the conditions for the construction of a pure spatiality, and the forms of discursive presence that have been granted to the non-spatial.

Let us start by considering two historical approaches to the problem of politics which display the common characteristic of making impossible – strictly unthinkable – the political dimension of all social practice. The first is Plato's text on the possibility and limits of community. (If I do not attempt to unify the different approaches under a term like 'political philosophy' it is because this would assume the unity of an object of reflection, which is precisely what is in question.) For Plato, politics cannot be a radical construction based on the experience of dislocation, since an ideal objectivity of the community *previous to any experience* tells us what the community *is*. Any maladjustment between empirically existent communities and the form of community as such is therefore reduced to a problem of knowledge. The statesman is not an 'ideologist' – a builder of myths; nor is he even the possessor of a wisdom or 'know-how' like the Aristotelian *phronimos:* rather he is a philosopher – the possessor of a knowledge in the rigorous sense of the term. Platonic thought addresses the *problem* of politics – the issue of dislocation – but is a non-political response to that problem. If dislocation involves contingency, and contingency power, the absence of dislocation leads in the Platonic schema to a radical communitarian essentialism that eliminates the very question of power and thus the possibility of politics.

In Plato's scheme, there was no power to share; what was 'shareable' was the Form of the Good written into the structure of the community. The results of this line of argument were two-fold: the idea of citizenship was severed from the idea of meaningful participation in the making of political decisions; and the idea of political community, that is, a community that seeks to resolve its internal conflicts through political methods, is replaced by the idea of the virtuous community devoid of conflict and, therefore, devoid of 'polities'. Plato did not deny that each member of the community, no matter how humble his contribution, had a right to share the benefits of the community; what he did deny was that this contribution could be erected into a claim to share in political decision-making (Wolin 1960, p. 57).

This communitarian schema was so absolutely spatial that nothing in it could be left to the discretion of a temporal intrusion – dislocation. Everything, including the number of the community's inhabitants, had to be mastered by a simultaneity in which being and knowledge entered into strict correspondence. And yet how is it not possible to note that the essentialism of the Platonic republic can only constitute itself starting from its *other* – from a radical contingency which is its very condition of possibility? For the incarnation of the philosopher in the actual ruler, to the *empirical* search for which Plato dedicated a great part of his life, is a fortuitous fact which escapes all intelligibility. But if the tyrant of Syracuse refused, as the King of Prussia would do many centuries later, to play the august role of incarnating the rationality prepared for him by philosophy, then this revealed much more than an empirical circumstantial *fault*. It showed that rationality, if it must be embodied in a contingent historical force, is itself mere contingency and that to be achieved it must therefore be constituted as power. The simultaneity or pure spatiality of the constitutive moments of the Platonic community thus require as their condition of possibility the purely temporal, dislocated instance of an irrational incarnation. It is not necessary to go over all the forms through which ancient thought attempted to reduce temporal dislocation to spatiality: it is enough to recall the efforts to write all historical change into a theory of cyclical sequence that

Polybius would dream of having overcome definitively through the perfect balance of the Roman constitution.

Our second example of an approach which makes politics unthinkable can be found in Hobbes, where the element of dislocation, of the impossibility of an order, represents much more than the dimension of impurity and contingency found in all empirical reality: it is the very definition of the state of nature. The important thing from the point of view of our problem is that if the state of nature is conceived as dislocation pure and simple, and as absence of any order in the generalized struggle of everyone against everyone else, then its antithetical opposite is not an order with a specific content, but order *tout court,* the very form of order independent of any content. Let us recall the point we made earlier, the more a system of norms and beliefs constituting a community has been shattered by dislocations, the less the new order's relation and continuity with that system will be; and the more its specific content will represent the order's abstract and general principle. This indifference to the specific content of the order, which grows insofar as its point of departure is an increasingly deep dislocation, finds its logical culmination in Hobbes's theory: as the initial state is defined as a state of nature which makes *any* organization of the community impossible, its antithesis (the principle of order) will be identified with the will of the ruler, *whatever* the content of that will might be. On the one hand, it could be said that we are faced here with the same elimination of politics as in Plato: both the Hobbesian monarch and the Platonic philosopher-king concentrate the whole of power in their hands, and the moment of argumentation, dissension and antagonism characterizing politics is equally eliminated. But on the other hand, we could say that the ruler of Hobbes is the antithesis of Plato's; while the legitimacy of the Platonic ruler depends on his *knowledge* of what the community *essentially is,* Hobbes's monarch must *invent* and *construct* the communitarian order, since the community, outside the order constituted by the ruler, is merely the chaos peculiar to the state of nature. The Platonic communitarian space is never mythical, since it is what it has always essentially been, and its corruption is associated with the close interpenetration between evil and ignorance, which bases the legitimacy of power on knowledge. The Hobbesian communitarian space is mythical through and through in the sense we defined earlier, it is based on an act of radical creation. There is therefore something fundamentally modern in Hobbes: while in Plato power stems from the recognition of a pre-existent objectivity, in Hobbes socio-political objectivity stems from power.

This contrast between Plato and Hobbes thus shows us how politics is impossible in both cases. But it also shows us, as its reverse side, the conditions that a community must meet to be a wholly political community. Let us dwell on this problem. As we saw, politics is impossible in Plato because community has a being prior to any decision; and in Hobbes because decision excludes all plurality and deliberation. But in that case a political community must necessarily be an essentially incomplete community in which its being must be constanrly redefined and recreated. And this constitutive incompletion has two dimensions: (l) it is an incompletion of the community for which the decisions are taken – in other words, the community has no being other than that derived from those decisions: and (2) it must also be an incompletion of those taking the decisions. For if political actors were not contingent and limited, they would be omnipotent, in which case their decisions would endow the community with a complete being, thus eliminating incompletion. Thus, if the first dimension distances us from Plato, the second does the same with Hobbes. A history of the presence of the political moment in the representation of communitarian spaces in Western thought must therefore be a history of the ways in which incompletion – or dislocation, which amounts to the same thing – has been given a discursive presence. This history could be conceived as an account of the long process by which the community has come to terms with its political nature.

As we have seen, any representation of a dislocation involves its spatialization. The way to overcome the temporal, traumatic and unrepresentable nature of dislocation is to construct it as a moment in permanent structural relation with other moments, in which case the pure temporality of the 'event' is eliminated. As we said, diachrony is one of the forms of synchrony. The main form of this spatial domesticization of time in ancient thought was the theory of the cycle: the succession of different kinds of government in relation to the constitutive excesses of each is a process that always recommences. Thus, while there is no form of government that does not produce dislocatory effects – and contain the seeds of its own dissolution – the cycle does not dissolve and is therefore constituted as a pure space providing the means of representation of any possible dislocation. This circular reduction of time to space is the limit that thought on historicity and contingency reached in classical antiquity. (As we pointed out earlier, the only exception is Polybius, for whom the Roman conquest effectively breaks the cycle, but in order to constitute an even purer spatiality that eliminates not just the representation of structural dislocations, but their very *possibility*.)

The dominant figure of thought on dislocation in classical antiquity was *corruption*. Corruption is essentially inherent to political forms and leads to their decline and replacement in the cyclical succession. And the boundary of essence establishing the eidetic purity of these forms only allows corruption to be conceived as non-being. In the case of ancient thought it would be totally senseless to speak of a 'fullness of time', since the incorruptible is intemporal. Any 'apocalypse' is excluded from this perspective. It is Judaeo-Christian thought that is to introduce a radical diachrony, thus providing a new discursive surface for the insertion of dislocations. In the first place the latter are no longer conceived in terms of corruption, but *evil*. There is nothing inherent in social forms which internally generates their decline; rather it is the intervention of perverse powers.

> And I stood upon the sand of the sea and saw a beast rise up out of the sea, having ... ten horns. ... And it was given to him to make war with the saints, and to overcome them: and power was given to him over all kindreds, and tongues, and nations. And all that dwell upon the earth shall worship

him, whose names are not written in the book of life—And I beheld another beast coming up out of the earth ... And he doeth great wonders ... and deceiveth them that dwell upon the earth by means of those miracles which he had power to do.

(Book of Revelation, quoted by Cohn 1970, p. 24)

Dislocation here is merely an event, a sudden intervention originating from an absolute outside that bears no relation whatsoever to the previous situation. It is also the intervention of a new and identifiable force, rather than the result of the deterioration of a pre-existent reality. Diachrony is not therefore dominated by any regularity, be it cyclical or of any other kind. But neither is diachronic succession the recording of a series of unstructured events, as apocalyptic discourse is organized around a promise. If the radicality of thought on dislocation requires the absolute unintelligibility of evil – and, as a result, its reduction to a mere event and its personification as a malign power – the final victory of God is assured, and the advent of the pure space of a fullness guaranteed. As divine plans are inscrutable, none of the phases of apocalyptic diachrony can be explained in terms of a necessary or logical succession: in this way the nature of pure dislocated event of each of the moments of this history is maintained, but at the same time they are endowed with a surface of discursive inscription. But in the second place, the hinge of the transition to the kingdom of God on earth cannot consist of just another moment in the series of events recorded by diachrony. If all previous historical actors have been limited in their inability to prevail over the powers of evil, the actor who has the strength to objectively suppress evil and to impose divine justice must himself be divine, or at least have been transformed by God into the incarnation of his omnipotence. He must therefore be a limitless actor.

> Then the heavens shall be opened in a tempest, and Christ shall descend with great power; and a fiery brightness shall go before him, and a countless host of angels; and all that multitude of godless shall be annihilated, and torrents of blood shall flow. ... When peace has been brought about and every evil suppressed, that righteous and victorious King will carry out a great judgement on the earth of the living and the dead, and will hand over all heathen peoples to servitude under the righteous who are alive, and will raise the [righteous] dead to eternal life, and will himself reign with them on earth, and will found the Holy City, and this kingdom of the righteous shall last for a thousand years.
>
> (Lactantius, quoted by Cohn 1970, p. 28)

In the third and final place, an apocalyptic reading of the real creates the conditions for a permanent gap between eschatological identities and the empirical actors embodying them. This means, on the one hand, that knowledge is based on an operation of recognition: it is a question of detecting behind limited empirical agents the limitless and universal actors that they embody (hence assertions such as 'the Pope is the Antichrist'). And on the other hand, the very idea that the relation between empirical agent and eschatological actor must be conceived as an incarnation assumes that a rigid separation exists between both – eschatological reality does not give rise to any contamination by empirical appearances. The price that the apocalyptic inscription of dislocations has had to pay is therefore clear: the emergence of a permanent zone of friction between the universal/necessary and the contingent.

In his admirable book, *The Legitimacy of the Modern Age,* Hans Blumenberg (1983) has introduced the concept of 'reoccupations'. By this he means the process by which particular notions, associated with the advent of a new vision and new problems, have the function of replacing ancient notions that had been formed on the ground of a different set of issues, with the result that the latter end up imposing their demands on the new notions and inevitably deforming them. Something like this happens with the arrival of modern ideologies of radical social transformation which 'reoccupy' a ground that had been formed, in its essential structural determinations, by the medieval millenialist apocalypse. As we saw, the latter had a dual function; on the one hand it affirmed dislocation's character as 'mere event'; but on the other it gave it a discursive presence by conceiving it as a moment in the march towards the realization of the millennium (with the inscrutability of divine plans – which only become manifest in revelation – constituting the key point that kept the two dimensions together). But it only needed the eclipse of God from the scene, while at the same time maintaining the image of a necessary transition to the chiliastic world of a homogeneous, reconciled (and therefore non-dislocated) society for all the intrinsic tensions of apocalyptic discourse to be fully manifested.

The first requirement of a rationalist and naturalist discourse presenting itself as an attempt to radically reconstruct society is for all transitions to be intramundane. In that case the achievement of the universality peculiar to a transparent society can only be the result of the transference of the omnipotence of the Creator to the *ens creatum*. But with inexorable logic it then follows that there can be no dislocation possible in this process. If everything that happens can be explained *internally* to this world, nothing can be a mere event (which entails a radical temporality, as we have seen) and everything acquires an absolute intelligibility within the grandiose scheme of a pure spatiality. This is the Hegelian—Marxist moment. As we have pointed out from the very start of this chapter, the moment of negativity – of evil (in the apocalyptic discourse), of dislocation – becomes mere appearance in the general movement of reason. Modern rationalism thus adapted badly to the ground of medieval eschatology in its 'reoccupation' of the latter. Its maintenance of a radical representability of the real – which is what the Middle Ages attempted in opposition to the characteristic 'non-being' of the corruption of classical thought – thus depends on eliminating any thought of dislocation. But this equally opens the symmetrically opposite possibility: that of maintaining dislocation's nature as pure event or temporality, in which case its representation becomes impossible. Dislocation cannot therefore be conceived as the corruption and non-being of a pure *eidos,* but nor can it be inscribed as the manifestation of the fierce struggle with the forces of evil. What remains, then, is the mere temporality and incompletion of something that has become essentially unrepresentable. The Enlightenment, the 'great narratives' of the nineteenth century and the totalitarianisms of the twentieth were clearly oriented in the direction of the first alternative (combining it – inconsistently in many cases – with a quasi-eschatological reiteration of the image of the struggle against evil forces). By contrast, our age – the age of the democratic revolution – is beginning to explore the possibilities of historical action that the second alternative opens.

At the time of writing [1989] – a year that has seen Tiananmen Square, the collapse of the regimes in Eastern Europe and the beginning of a process of political transformation with unpredictable results in the Soviet Union – it is obviously easy to indulge in facile teleologies and present the whole process from the Enlightenment to the Russian Revolution as a continuum, or rather a progression, that was to culminate in the Peking massacres or the execution of Ceausescu. But such images are superficial and absurd. The very notion of 'reoccupation' that we invoked above conspires against them: if new ideas, new discourses, new social demands adapt badly to the ground they reoccupy, it is this tension that must provide a starting point, not the supposed teleological unity of a single field embracing the whole of its contents.

But this should not allow us to forget the reality and operativeness of the reoccupied ground, as well as the way in which some basic dimensions of the medieval millennium have continued to determine fundamental structures of radical thought right up to the present. All such dimensions can be summed up in a single fact: the *universal* nature of the history of the millennium – which is the condition of the limitless representability made possible by such a history. This also requires the universality of the actors and society in which the millennium is finally realized. In secularist versions of the millennium this universality is maintained in all its force, but as it is not easy for them to establish the distinction between concrete agents and the eschatological universality they embody, there is a constant process of metaphorical – or rather metonymical – transference between both. The logics of 'incarnation' are thus fundamentally ambiguous. Let us give a couple of examples. The very notion of socialism as *social* management of the production process was conceived in opposition to a mode of reproduction based on the search for individual profit. If the 'social' of 'social management' acquired meaning simply through opposition to the 'individual', such meaning was reduced to the abstract universality of the community. Who is the subject of *social* management then? The sociological hypothesis of communitarian universality being ultimately self-transparent – through the growing homogenization of society – has not been realized in any concrete experience, since the agents meant to *embody* 'the social' (the state or the party, for example) were always limited agents. This is the point where the metonymical transference takes place: just as gold has the dual function of having its own use value and of embodying the general form of value, the concrete particularity of an institution or social force takes on the function of representing universality itself. As we have seen, this operation is not impossible; and we can even assert that it is inherent to any process of political construction. The implicit duality of any mythical space means that *any* concrete content can also come to express the very form of fullness – that is to say universality. The ground of that duality is *a priori* undecidable in either direction. All depends on how the process of universalization is conceived. If communitarian universality establishes a relation of total equivalence with the social order advocated by a particular group, the incarnation will not be contingent, in fact there will be no incarnation at all, since the 'idea' and the 'body' in which it is to be incarnated have a relation of indissoluble necessity between them. An objective process has guaranteed positions from which a knowledge of the social proves possible. The dictatorship of the proletariat bases its legitimacy on the same privileged access to knowledge as the Platonic philosopher-king, with the difference that in the latter the unity between monarchical power and knowledge was fortuitous, while in the case of the dictatorship of the proletariat there is a millennialist—naturalist theory of history explaining why the latter incarnation of the universal has an objective and necessary character. In this case, (1) the social imaginary is totally reduced to mythical space in the sense that myth loses its character as a *limitless* surface of inscription; and (2) myth denies its own character as such, since on presenting itself as a necessary social order, it establishes a relation of essential continuity with the social demands that it determines as legitimate from its own inside, thus annulling any distance between the dislocations of the structure and the mythical surface on which they are to be inscribed. This obviously means that any other social demand is excluded from the pure space of the transparent society.

It is this closed nature of a space denying its mythical character that allows the indivisible unity between empirical actors and their universal 'functions' or 'tasks' to be welded together. It is perfectly clear that this fusion between empiricity and universality/rationality is at the root of the totalitarian potentialities of the 'social management' advocated by socialism. But it is important to add that this fusion is the result of the 'reoccupation' by socialist discourse of the ground of the universalist diachrony that is inherent to the Christian apocalypse. This point is crucial. For the current crisis of socialism is to a large extent that of the long-term effects of this reoccupation; and in order for the demands on which the socialist myth has been based to regain validity and acquire new historical possibilities, it only needs them to be inscribed in a discourse different from that of 'social management' – by which we mean an abstract universality that must be embodied. But this means moving in the opposite direction to the discourse of eschatological universality. We shall return to this point shortly.

The second example refers to the agent leading the historical emergence of the reconciled society. The reconciled society is the realization of the essence of humankind. It is therefore the full realization of a pure universality. How is it then possible for limited, partial and contingent agents to constitute historically something that patently transcends their powers? We have already seen how the Christian apocalypse solved this problem: by advocating the divine exteriority of the saviour from those to be saved. But this solution was not possible for a rationalist/naturalist eschatology. It thus asserted, firstly, that contingent limitations were not really limitations, but the necessary steps of reason towards self-awareness; and secondly, that the advent of the reconciled society required the emergence of a social actor whose own particularity would express the pure essence of humanity. Once again, the moment of incarnation dissolves: the proletariat, on liberating itself, liberates humanity as a whole. How this process worked in practice is well known. The supposed abolition of the subject's mythical nature crashed against a contingency unyielding to any rationalist reduction. And this meant that increasingly tortuous expedients and formulas were resorted to. Universality did not correspond to the proletariat, but to its historical interests which had to be expressed through a party, etc. What had originally been put forward as the abolition of any contingent embodiment gave way in practice to a migration of the universal through successive bodies – from class to party, from the party to the autocrat, etc. The same eschatological ambition automatically gave way to this authoritarian escalation, once the contingency of the concrete social actors rebelled against the role that 'Reason' had reserved for them. A considerable part of the tragic history of our time is contained in this game of hide and seek between 'Reason' and its various embodiments.

We must now go on to question ourselves on the second alternative to the eclipse of God. This is not based on the advocacy of an intrinsic positive logic of the intramundane, which necessarily leads to the elimination of all dislocation, but on the assertion of the latter's constitutive nature, which leads to the crisis of all spatiality and the ultimate impossibility of all representation. The development of this second line of historical action is the specific ground of the democratic revolution (or rather, it is the strictly political *mode* through which democracy operates, since democracy is the very placing in question of the notion of *ground*). Let us recall the duality of mythical space, which constitutes a concrete 'order' and represents the very form of order (or fullness) at the same time. The more this second dimension predominates, the more the mythical space will become an imaginary horizon. But this means two things. The first is that the manifestation of the very form of fullness can only take place through the growing emancipation of this form from any concrete content. In other words, this emancipation can only take place insofar as the representation of the very possibility of inscription and the representation of the materiality of the inscribed become increasingly distanced. This can only mean that the general form of fullness is exactly equivalent to the general form of possibility. That is to say that the fullness of the social does not manifest itself in any concrete social order but in the possibility of representing its radical indeterminacy, in other words its nature as a mere possibility. The second thing is that radical indeterminacy does not manifest itself through a *cancellation* of all determinations – this would consist of an operation that could only be conceivable on the basis of the fullness of the category of 'determination' and would thus leave the latter intact – but through a subversion of all determination, that is through the assertion of its presence in a context that destroys its own possibility.

That is precisely what we have termed dislocation. But as we have seen, dislocation destroys all space and, as a result, the very possibility of representation.

Let us dwell for a moment on this point, however. The impossibility of representation cannot consist of the *presence* of *something* that does not have access to the space of representation. Such duality would merely be that of an exclusion, and the exclusion of the unrepresentable would precisely aid the constitution of the space of that which can be represented. Rather it is a question of an all-embracing subversion of the space of representability in general, which is the same as the subversion of spatiality itself. Let us give an example which is frequent in the constitution of political imaginaries in the Third World. Migrants from rural areas to the expanding cities bring with them a range of values, discourses and symbols, etc. from their places of origin. In the new urban environment a fresh set of antagonisms and dislocations occur in relation to their traditional way of life. A frequent reaction in such circumstances is to reaffirm traditional symbols and values of rural life as a means of creating a culture of resistance: in other words, those symbols and values operate as surfaces for the inscription of the *new* urban antagonisms and dislocations. Once the symbols' circulation has reached a certain level of generalization in the representation of a vast range of antagonisms, they become the necessary surface for the inscription of any new demand. It is for that reason that, when social groups different from those that were their original bearers – the urban middle sectors, for example – attempt to construct forms of resistance to their specific dislocations, they will increasingly invoke the symbols of resistance of internal migrants: for such symbols are the only ideological raw material expressing anti-establishment protest in that society. This constant extension of the area of the representable in the discursive surfaces formed by anti-establishment symbols has a dual effect, of course: on the one hand, it consolidates that surface as the representation of the very *form* of the anti-establishment, but on the other, if it can perform this function of representing *any* demand and social protest, it is because it has been emptied of any concrete content by the very fact of its consolidation as a necessary discursive surface. The fullness of the community thus becomes an empty form and its relation with the concrete demands of the different groups is therefore essentially hegemonic and unstable.

We can see, then, the new type of link between 'particularity' and 'universality' that this kind of emptying entails. None of the problems we saw arise with the reoccupation of the space of the millennialist apocalypse disappears, but their meaning is essentially displaced; and this displacement leads us from the reoccupation of a ground to its radical deconstruction. The 'universal' does not disappear but has lost the transparency of a positive and closed world: the community 'universalizes' its values through the circulation of symbols that are stripped of any specific content to the very extent that that circulation encompasses a growing number of social demands. No universality exists other than that which is built in a pragmatic and precarious way by that process of circulation which establishes an equivalence between an increasingly wide range of demands. But this means that the problem of the tension implicit in any 'embodiment' disappears, since the essential asymmetry between the particularity of the demands and the universality of the values never gives rise to a reconciliation in which any particularity would be finally reabsorbed into a universal and transparent order. There is no *Pax Romana* for the social 'order'. But for that very reason the problem of 'embodiment' does not simply reoccupy the ground of the apocalypse in its teleological or naturalist—rationalist forms; rather, in its new form, it makes that ground impossible. It is no longer a question of a necessary universality 'searching' for the historical force that might embody it. On the contrary, since all universality is only built through the overdetermination of an indefinite and open range of concrete demands, it is a question of the force intended to embody such 'relative universalities' being indeterminate; and such a force will only be the result of a hegemonic struggle. This is exactly what politics consists of.

There are two aspects here: on the one hand, since no force is the incarnation of the universal in and by itself, a 'collective will' will only consolidate its hegemony if it manages to appear to other groups as the force capable of providing the best social arrangement possible to secure and expand a universality that transcends it. The asymmetry between 'relative universality' and the force embodying it thus paves the way for a democratic competition between groups, as the 'universal' is not commensurate with any of the forces that might momentarily embody it. On the other hand, however, the 'universal' does not have, independently of the successive forces embodying it, a fixed existence and meaning either. There is no longer a definable *eidos* outside of its corrupt forms, nor a Kingdom of God that can be apprehended through revelation. This means that the question of power, the intrinsic impurity of antagonisms and struggles, penetrates the field of the universal itself. Recognition of the historical limitation of social agents is the very condition for democracy, but for the same reason, power is paradoxically the very condition for freedom.

A reflection on a limited historical case – that of internal migrants in Third World countries – has provided the point of departure for our presentation of such theoretical developments. Yet it would be a mistake to think that the validity of the analysis is limited to this and similar cases alone. On the contrary, both the fragmentation and growing limitation of social actors, and the permanent dissociation between social imaginaries and the mythical spaces capable of embodying them, are a process that is deeply rooted in the democratic revolution of the last two centuries, as well as in the overall state of contemporary societies. In relatively stable societies there is no distancing between inscription surfaces and what is inscribed on them. 'Order' is immanent in social relations; and in all forms of counter-society, the *content* of mythical space absorbs any possible dimension of horizon. There is therefore no room for the constitution of the duality of mythical space and social imaginary. But the situation changes in societies that have gone through the experience of capitalism and the uneven and combined development inherent to it.

Let us pick up on several points of our analysis. The fragmentation and growing limitation of social actors is linked to the multiplication of the dislocations produced by 'disorganized capitalism'. It follows from this that more and more areas of social life must become the product of *political* forms of reconstruction and regulation. But the very abundance of such dislocations and their intrinsic antagonisms means that the limitation and fragmentation of the social actors they give rise to also increase. This fragmentation, however, does not mean atomization: isolated demands are overdetermined in the constitution of social imaginaries, and mythical spaces – which compete for the hegemonization of the imaginaries – articulate demands in various ways. In turn, the role of those spaces and imaginaries in transforming dislocations into demands is absolutely central. There is thus no longer any room for the base/superstructure dichotomy: any social level – if we can speak of levels to refer to something that is essentially non-spatial – can be the location of mythical rearticulations and imaginary aggregations. Society, then, is ultimately unrepresentable: any representation – and thus any space – is an attempt to constitute society, not to state what it is. But the antagonistic moment of collision between the various representations cannot be reduced to space, and is itself unrepresentable. It is therefore mere event, mere temporality. For reasons we have explained, this final incompletion of the social is the main source of our political hope in the contemporary world: only it can assure the conditions for a radical democracy.

Let us draw the final conclusions. The state of social struggles in the contemporary world offers several grounds for political optimism. They at least create the preconditions for a radicalization of democracy, which is increasingly becoming the reference point for the construction of a new left. We are faced with a growing fragmentation of social actors, but this, far from being the cause for any nostalgia for the lost 'universal class', must be the source for a new militancy and a new optimism. One of the consequences of fragmentation is that the issues, which are the rallying point for the various social struggles, acquire greater autonomy and face the political system with growing demands. They thus become more difficult to manipulate and disregard. The self-evidence and homogeneity of the subject of *social* control in traditional socialist discourse has disappeared. Instead, a plurality of subjects exercise a democratic and negotiated control of the productive process on the basis of this fragmentation, thus avoiding any form of dictatorship, whether by the market, the state or direct producers. The indeterminacy of the relations between the different demands of the social actors certainly does open the possibility for their articulation by the right, but insofar as such articulations are not *necessary,* the field of possibilities for historical action is also widened, as counter-hegemonic struggles become possible in many areas traditionally associated with the sedimented forms of the status quo. The future is indeterminate and certainly not guaranteed for us; but that is precisely why it is not lost either. The current expansion of democratic struggles in the international arena gives cause for cautious optimism.

Two final points. The first is concerned with the relation between reason and emancipation that we referred to at the beginning of this chapter. To what extent does placing in question the rationalism characterizing the project of modernity not mean undermining the foundations of the emancipatory project linked to it? From the earlier development of our argument it is clear what our reply will be. In our perspective it is a question of historically constituting the subject to be emancipated – indeed, emancipation and constitution are part of the same process. But in that case, why prefer one future over another? Why choose between different types of society? There can be no reply if the question is asking for a kind of Cartesian certainty that pre-exists any belief. But if the agent who must choose is someone who *already* has certain beliefs and values, then criteria for choice – with all the intrinsic ambiguities that a choice involves – can be formulated. Such an acceptance of the facticity of certain strata of our beliefs is nothing but the acceptance of our contingency and historicity. We could even go so far as to say that it is the acceptance of our 'humanity' as an entity to be constructed; while in the case of rationalism, we *have been given* 'humanity' and are merely left with the secondary task of realizing it historically. For the reasons we have identified, this recognition of our limitation and contingency, of the precarious and pragmatic construction of the universality of our values – a pragmatism that leaves the perverse dialectics of 'necessary embodiments' behind – is the very condition for a democratic society. To reformulate the values of the Enlightenment in the direction of a radical historicism and to renounce its rationalistic epistemological and ontological foundations, then, is to expand the democratic potentialities of that tradition, while abandoning the totalitarian tendencies arising from its reoccupation of the ground of apocalyptic universalism.

This leads us to the final question concerning the current debate over the 'end of history'. Does this formula have any purchase in providing an adequate name for our present social and political experience? If the 'end of history' is understood as the end of a conceptually graspable object encompassing the whole of the real in its diachronic spatiality, we are clearly at the end of 'history'. But from that perspective, 'history' is a quasi-transcendental category, an attempt to inscribe the totality of events and dislocations in conceptual forms transcending them. In another sense, however, we can say that we are at the *beginning* of history, at the point where historicity finally achieves full recognition. For insofar as any 'transcendentality' is itself vulnerable, any effort to spatialize time ultimately fails and space itself becomes an event. In this sense history's ultimate unrepresentability is the condition for the recognition of our radical historicity. It is in our pure condition of event, which is shown at the edges of all representation and in the traces of temporality corrupting all space, that we find our most essential being, which is our contingency and the intrinsic dignity of our transitory nature. In one of the most crucial passages of his work Ortega y Gasset recalls that a proverb can be heard in the thirsty deserts of Libya saying: 'Drink from the well and leave the place to your neighbour.'

Note

1 See the excellent book by Löwy (1981), where this and other texts by Marx and Engels on the class base of the democratic revolution are exhaustively discussed.

Bibliography

Blumenberg, H. 1983. *The Legitimacy of the Modern Age*. Cambridge, MA: MIT Press.
Cohn, N. 1970. *The Pursuit of the Millennium*. London: Maurice Temple Smith.
Lash, S. and Urry, J. 1987. *The End of Organized Capitalism*. Cambridge: Polity Press.
Lefort, C. 1986. *The Political Forms of Modern Society*. Cambridge: Polity Press.
Löwy, M. 1981. *The Politics of Combined and Uneven Development*. London: Verso.
Marx, K. 1973. *The Revolutions of 1848*. Harmondsworth: Penguin.
Marx, K. and Engels, F. 1953. *The Russian Menace to Europe*. London: George Allen & Unwin.
Offe, C. 1985. *Disorganized Capitalism*. Cambridge, MA: MIT Press.
Wolin, S. 1960. *Politics and Vision*. Boston: Little, Brown.

3

WHY DO EMPTY SIGNIFIERS MATTER TO POLITICS? (1994)

An empty signifier is, strictly speaking, a signifier without a signified. This definition is also, however, the enunciation of a problem. For how would it be possible that a signifier is not attached to any signified and remains, however, an integral part of a system of signification? An empty signifier would be a sequence of sounds, and if the latter are deprived of any signifying function the term 'signifier' itself would become excessive. The only possibility for a stream of sounds being detached from any particular signified while still remaining a signifier is if, through the subversion of the sign which the possibility of an empty signifier involves, something is achieved which is internal to signification as such. What is this possibility?

Some pseudo-answers can be discarded quite quickly. One would be to argue that the same signifier can be attached to different signifieds in different contexts (as a result of the arbitrariness of the sign). But it is clear that in that case the signifier would not be *empty* but *equivocal*: in each context the function of signification would be fully realised. A second possibility is that the signifier is not *equivocal* but *ambiguous:* that either an overdetermination or an underdetermination of signifieds prevents from fully fixing it. Yet this floating of the signifier still does not make of it an empty one. Although the floating takes us one step towards the proper answer to our problem, the terms of the latter are still avoided. We do not have to deal with an excess or deficiency of signification, but with the precise theoretical possibility of something which points, from within the process of signification, to the discursive presence of its own limits.

An empty signifier can, consequently, only emerge if there is a structural impossibility in signification as such, and if this impossibility can only signify itself as an interruption (subversion, distortion, etc.) of the structure of the sign. That is, that the limits of signification can only announce themselves as the impossibility of realising what is within those limits—if the limits could be signified in a direct way, they would be internal to signification and, *ergo,* would not be limits at all.

An initial and purely formal consideration can help to clarify the point. We know, from Saussure, that language (and, by extension, all signifying systems) is a system of differences, that linguistic identities—values—are purely relational and that, as a result, the *totality* of language is involved in each single act of signification. Now, in that case, it is clear that the totality is essentially required—if the differences did not constitute a system, no signification at all would be possible. The problem, however, is that the very possibility of signification is the system, and the very possibility of the system is the possibility of its limits. We can say, with Hegel, that to think of the limits of something is the same as thinking of what is beyond those limits. But if what we are talking about are the limits of a *signifying system*, it is clear that those limits cannot be themselves signified, but have to *show* themselves as the *interruption* or *breakdown* of the process of signification. Thus, we are left with the paradoxical situation that what constitutes the condition of possibility of a signifying system—its limits—is also what constitutes its condition of impossibility—a blockage of the continuous expansion of the process of signification.

A first and capital consequence of this is that true limits can never be neutral limits but presuppose an exclusion. A neutral limit would be one which is essentially continuous with what is at its two sides, and the two sides are simply different from each other. As a signifying totality is, however, precisely a system of differences, this means that both are part of the same system and that the limits between the two cannot be the limits of the system. In the case of an exclusion we have, instead, authentic limits, because the actualisation of what is beyond the limit of exclusion would involve the impossibility of what is this side of the limit. True limits are always antagonistic. But the operation of the logic of exclusionary limits has a series of necessary effects which spread to both sides of the limits and which will lead us straight into the emergence of empty signifiers.

(1) A first effect of the exclusionary limit is that it introduces an essential ambivalence within the system of differences constituted by those limits. On the one hand, each element of the system has an identity only as far as it is different from the others. Difference = identity. On the other hand, however, all these differences are equivalent to each other as far as all of them belong to this side of the frontier of exclusion. But, in that case, the identity of each element is constitutively split: on the one hand, each difference expresses itself *as* difference; on the other hand, each of them *cancels* itself as such by entering into a relation of equivalence with all the other differences of the system. And, given that there is only system as far as there is radical exclusion, this split or ambivalence is constitutive of all systemic identity. It is only insofar as there is a radical impossibility of a system as pure presence, beyond all exclusions, that actual *systems* (in the plural) can exist. Now, if the systematicity of the system is a direct result of the exclusionary limit, it is only that exclusion that grounds the system as such. This point is essential because it results from it that the system cannot have a positive ground and that, as a result, it cannot signify itself in terms of any positive signified. Let us suppose for a

moment that the systematic ensemble was the result of all its elements sharing a positive feature (e.g., that they all belonged to a regional category). In that case that positive feature would be different from other differential positive features, and they would all appeal to a deeper systematic ensemble within which their differences would be thought of as differences. But a system constituted through radical exclusion interrupts this play of the differential logic: as what is excluded from the system, far from being something positive, is the simple principle of positivity—pure Being. This already announces the possibility of an empty signifier—i.e., a signifier of the pure cancellation of all difference.

(2) The condition, of course, for this operation to be possible is that what is beyond the frontier of exclusion is reduced to pure negativity—i.e., to the pure threat that that beyond poses to the system (constituting it that way). If the exclusionary dimension was eliminated, or even weakened, what would happen is that the differential character of the 'beyond' would impose itself and, as a result, the limits of the system would be blurred. Only if the beyond becomes the signifier of pure threat, of pure negativity, of the simply excluded, can there be limits and system (i.e., an objective order). But in order to be the signifiers of the excluded (or, simply, of exclusion), the various excluded categories have to cancel their differences through the formation of a chain of equivalences of that which the system demonises in order to signify itself. Again, we see here the possibility of an empty signifier announcing itself through this logic in which differences collapse into equivalential chains.

(3) But, we could ask ourselves, why does this pure being or systematicity of the system, or—its reverse—the pure negativity of the excluded require the production of empty signifiers in order to signify itself? The answer is that as we are trying to signify the limits of signification—the Real, if you want, in the Lacanian sense—there is no direct way of doing so except through the subversion of the process of signification itself. We know, through psychoanalysis, how what is not directly representable—the unconscious—can only find as a means of representation the subversion of the signifying process. Each signifier constitutes a sign by attaching itself to a particular signified, inscribing itself as a difference within the signifying process. But if what we are trying to signify is not a difference but on the contrary a radical exclusion which is the ground and condition of all differences, in that case no production of *one more* difference can do the trick. As, however, all the means of representation are differential in nature, it is only if the differential nature of the signifying units is subverted, only if the signifiers empty themselves of their attachment to particular signifieds and assume the role of representing the pure being of the system—or, rather, the system as pure Being—that such a signification is possible. What is the ontological ground of such a subversion, what makes it possible? The answer is: the split of each unit of signification that the system has to construct as the undecidable locus in which both the logic of difference and the logic of equivalence operate. It is only by

privileging the dimension of equivalence to the point that its differential nature is almost entirely obliterated—that is, emptying it of its differential nature—that the system can signify itself as a totality.

Two points have to be stressed here. The first is that the being or systematicity of the system which is represented through the empty signifiers is not a being which has not been *actually* realised, but one which is constitutively unreachable, for whatever systematic effects would exist there will be the result, as we have seen, of the unstable compromise between equivalence and difference. That is, that we are faced with a constitutive lack, with an impossible object which, as in Kant, shows itself through the impossibility of its adequate representation. Here we can give a full answer to our initial question: there can be empty signifiers within the field of signification because any system of signification is structured around an empty place resulting from the impossibility of producing an object which, however, is required by the systematicity of the system. So, we are not dealing with an impossibility without location, as in the case of a logical contradiction, but with a *positive* impossibility, with a *real* one to which the χ of the empty signifier points.

However, if this impossible object lacks the means of its adequate or direct representation, this can only mean that the signifier which is emptied in order to assume the representing function will always be constitutively inadequate. What, in that case, does determine that one signifier rather than the other assumes in different circumstances that signifying function? Here we have to move to the main theme of this chapter: the relation between empty signifiers and politics.

Hegemony

Let me go back to an example that we discussed in detail in *Hegemony and Socialist Strategy* (Laclau and Mouffe 1985): the constitution, according to Rosa Luxemburg, of the unity of the working class through an overdetermination of partial struggles over a long period of time. Her basic argument is that the unity of the class is not determined by any *a priori* consideration about the priority of either the political struggle or the economic struggle but by the accumulated effects of the internal split of all partial mobilisations. In relation to our subject, her argument amounts to approximately the following: in a climate of extreme repression any mobilisation for a partial objective will be perceived not only as related to the concrete demand or objectives of that struggle but also as an act of opposition against the system. This last fact is what establishes the link between a variety of concrete or partial struggles and mobilisations—all of them are seen as related to each other, not because their *concrete* objectives are intrinsically related, but because they are all seen as equivalent in confrontation with the repressive regime. It is not, consequently, something positive that all of them share which establishes their unity, but something negative: their opposition to a common enemy. Luxemburg's argument is that a revolutionary mass identity is established through the overdetermination, over a whole historical period, of a plurality of separate struggles. These traditions fused, at the revolutionary moment, in a ruptural point.

Let us try to apply to this sequence our previous categories. The meaning (the signified) of all concrete struggle appears, right from the beginning, internally divided. The concrete aim of the struggle is not only that aim in its concreteness; it also signifies opposition to the system. The first signified establishes the differential character of that demand or mobilisation *vis-à-vis* all other demands or mobilisations. The second signified establishes the equivalence of all these demands in their common opposition to the system. As we can see, any concrete struggle is dominated by this contradictory movement that at the same time asserts and abolishes its own singularity. The function of representing the system as a totality depends, consequently, on the possibility of the equivalential function neatly prevailing over the differential one; but this possibility is simply the result of every single struggle being always already, originally, penetrated by this constitutive ambiguity.

It is important to observe that, as we have already established, if the function of the differential signifiers is to renounce their differential identity in order to represent the purely equivalential identity of a communitarian space as such, they cannot construct this equivalential identity as something belonging to a differential order. For instance: we can represent the Tsarist regime as a repressive order by enumerating the differential kinds of oppressions that it imposes on various sections of the population as much as we want; but such enumeration will not give us the specificity of the repressive moment, that which constitutes—in its negation—what is peculiar to a repressive relation between entities. Because in such a relation each instance of the repressive power counts as pure bearer of the negation of the identity of the repressed sector. Now if the differential identity of the repressive action is in that way 'distanced' from itself by having itself transformed into the mere incarnating body of the negation of the being of another entity, it is clear that between this negation and the body through which it expresses itself there is no necessary relation—nothing predetermines that one particular body should be the one predestined to incarnate negation as such.

It is precisely this which makes the relation of equivalence possible: different particular struggles are so many bodies which can indifferently incarnate the opposition of all of them to the repressive power. This involves a double movement. On the one hand, the more the chain of equivalences is extended, the less each concrete struggle will be able to remain closed in a differential self—in something which separates it from all other differential identities through a difference which is exclusively its own. On the contrary, as the equivalential relation shows that these differential identities are simply indifferent bodies incarnating something equally present in all of them, the longer the chain of equivalences is, the less concrete this 'something equally present' will be. At the limit it will be pure communitarian being independent of all concrete manifestation. And, on the other hand, that which is beyond the exclusion delimiting the communitarian space—the repressive power—will counter less as the instrument of particular differential repressions and will express pure anti-community, pure evil and negation. The community created by this equivalential expansion will be, thus, the pure idea of a communitarian fullness which is absent—as a result of the presence of the repressive power.

But at this point the second movement starts. This pure equivalential function representing an absent fullness which shows itself through the collapse of all differential identities is something which cannot have a signifier of its own—for in that case the 'beyond all differences' would be one more difference and not the result of the equivalential collapse of all differential identities. Precisely because the community as such is not a purely differential space of an objective identity but an absent fullness, it cannot have any form of representation of its own, and has to borrow the latter from some entity constituted within the equivalential space—in the same way as gold is a particular use value which assumes, as well, the function of representing value in general. This emptying of a particular signifier of its particular, differential signified is, as we saw, what makes possible the emergence of 'empty' signifiers as the signifiers of a lack, of an absent totality. But this leads us straight into the question with which we closed the previous section: if all differential struggles—in our example—are equally capable of expressing, beyond their differential identity, the absent fullness of the community; if the equivalential function makes all differential positions similarly indifferent to this equivalential representation, if none is pre-determined *per se* to fulfil this role; what does determine that one of them rather than the other incarnates, at particular periods of time, this universal function?

The answer is: the unevenness of the social. For if the equivalential logic tends to do away with the relevance of all differential location, this is only a tendential movement which is always resisted by the logic of difference which is essentially non-equalitarian. (It comes as no surprise that Hobbes's model of a state of nature, which tries to depict a realm in which the full operation of the logic of equivalence makes the community impossible, has to presuppose an original and essential equality between men.) Not any position in society, not any struggle is equally capable of transforming its own contents in a nodal point that becomes an empty signifier. Now, is this not to return to a rather traditional conception of the historical affectivity of social forces, one which asserts that the unevenness of structural locations determines which one of them is going to be the source of totalising effects? No, it is not, because these uneven structural locations, some of which represent points of high concentration of power, are themselves the result of processes in which logics of difference and logics of equivalence overdetermine each other. It is not a question of denying the historical effectivity of the logic of differential structural locations but, rather, of denying to them, as a whole, the character of an infrastructure which would determine, out of itself, the laws of movement of society.

If this is correct, it is impossible to determine at the level of the mere analysis of the *form* difference/equivalence which particular difference is going to become the locus of equivalential effects—this requires the study of a particular conjuncture, precisely because the presence of equivalential effects is always necessary, but the relation equivalence/difference is not intrinsically linked to any particular differential content. This relation by which a particular content becomes the signifier of the absent communitarian fullness is exactly what we call a *hegemonic relationship*. The presence of empty signifiers—in the sense that we have defined them—is the very condition of hegemony. This can be easily seen if we address a very well-known difficulty which has a recurring stumbling block in most theorisations of hegemony—Gramsci's included. A class or group is considered to be hegemonic when it is not closed in a narrow corporatist perspective but presents itself as realising the broader aims either of emancipating, or ensuring order, for wider masses of the population. But this faces us with a difficulty if we do not determine precisely what these terms 'broader aims', 'wider masses' refer to. There are two possibilities: first, that society is an addition of discrete groups, each tending to their particular aims and in constant collision with each other. In that case 'broader' and 'wider' could only mean the precarious equilibrium of a negotiated agreement between groups, all of which would retain their conflicting aims and identity. But 'hegemony' clearly refers to a stronger type of communitarian unity than such an agreement evokes. Second, that society has some kind of pre-established essence, so that the 'broader' and 'vaster' has a content of its own, independent of the will of the particular groups, and that 'hegemony' would mean the realisation of such an essence. But this would not only do away with the dimension of contingency which has always been associated with the hegemonic operation, but would also be incompatible with the consensual character of 'hegemony': the hegemonic order would be the *imposition* of a pre-given organisational principle and not something emerging from the political interaction between groups. Now, if we consider the matter from the point of view of the social production of empty signifiers, this problem vanishes. For in that case the hegemonic operation would be the presentation of the particularity of a group as the incarnation of that empty signifier which refers to the communitarian order as an absence, an unfulfilled reality.

How does this mechanism operate? Let us consider the extreme situation of a radical disorganisation of the social fabric. In such conditions—which are not far away from Hobbes's state of nature—people need *an* order, and the actual content of it becomes a secondary consideration. 'Order' as such has no content, because it only exists in the various forms in which it is actually realised, but in a situation of radical disorder 'order' is present as that which is absent; it becomes an empty signifier, as the signifier of that absence. In this sense, various political forces can compete in their effort to present their particular objectives as those which carry out the filling of that lack. To hegemonise something is exactly to carry out this filling function. (We have spoken about 'order', but obviously 'unity', 'liberation', 'revolution', etc., belong to the same order of things. Any term which in a certain political context becomes the signifier of the lack plays the same role. Politics is possible because the constitutive impossibility of society can only represent itself through the production of empty signifiers.)

This explains also why any hegemony is always unstable and penetrated by a constitutive ambiguity. Let us suppose that a workers' mobilisation succeeds in presenting its own objectives as the signifier of 'liberation' in general. (This, as we have seen, is possible because the workers' mobilisation, taking place under a repressive regime, is also seen as an anti-system struggle.) In one sense this is a hegemonic victory, because the objectives of a particular group are identified with society at large. But, in another sense, this is a dangerous victory. If 'workers' struggle' becomes the signifier of liberation as such, it also becomes the surface of inscription through which *all* liberating struggles will be expressed, so that the chain of equivalences which are unified around this signifier tend to empty it, and to blur its connection with the actual content with which it was originally associated. Thus, as a result of its very success, the hegemonic operation tends to break its links with the force which was its original promoter and beneficiary.

Hegemony and democracy

Let us conclude with some reflections on the relation between empty signifiers, hegemony and democracy.

Consider for a moment the role of social signifiers in the emergence of modern political thought—I am essentially thinking of the work of Hobbes. Hobbes, as we have seen, presented the state of nature as the radically opposite of an ordered society, as a situation only defined in negative terms. But, as a result of that description, the order of the ruler has to be accepted not because of any intrinsic virtue that it can have, but just because it is *an* order, and the only alternative is radical disorder. The condition, however, of the coherence of this scheme is the postulate of the equality of the power of individuals in the state of nature—if the individuals were uneven in terms of power, order could be guaranteed through sheer domination. So, power is eliminated twice: in the state of nature, as all individuals equally share in it, and in the Commonwealth, as it is entirely concentrated in the hands of the ruler. (A power which is total or a power which is equally distributed among all members of the community is no power at all.) So, while Hobbes implicitly perceives the split between the empty signifier 'order as such' and the actual order imposed by the ruler, as he reduces—through the covenant—the first to the second, he cannot think of any kind of dialectical or hegemonic game between the two.

What happens if, on the contrary, we reintroduce power within this picture—i.e., if we accept the unevenness of power in social relations? In that case, civil society will be partially structured and partially unstructured and, as a result, the total concentration of power in the hands of the ruler ceases to be a logical requirement. But in that case the credentials of the ruler to claim total power are much less obvious. If partial order exists in society, the legitimacy of the identification of the empty signifier of order with the will of the ruler will have the further requirement that the content of this will does not clash with something the society *already* is. As society changes over time this process of identification will be always precarious and reversible and, as the identification is no longer automatic, different hegemonic projects or wills will try to hegemonise the empty signifiers of the absent community. The recognition of the constitutive nature of this gap and its political institutionalisation is the starting point of modern democracy.

Bibliography

Laclau, E. and Mouffe, C. 1985. *Hegemony and Socialist Strategy: Towards a Radical Democratic Politics*. London: Verso.

4

THE DEATH AND RESURRECTION OF THE THEORY OF IDEOLOGY (1996)

I

In a recent essay on theories of ideology Slavoj Žižek (1994, pp. 1–33) describes contemporary approaches by distributing them around the three axes identified by Hegel: *doctrine, belief* and *ritual,* that is,

> ideology as a complex of ideas (theories, convictions, beliefs, argumentative procedures); ideology in its externality, that is, the materiality of ideology, Ideological State Apparatus; and finally, the most elusive domain, the 'spontaneous' ideology at work at the heart of social 'reality' itself.
> (Žižek 1994, p. 9)

He gives as an example the case of liberalism:

> liberalism is a doctrine (developed from Locke to Hayek) materialised in rituals and apparatuses (free press, elections, markets, etc) and active in the 'spontaneous' (self-)experience of subjects as 'free individuals'.
> (Žižek 1994, p. 9)

In the three cases Žižek finds an essential symmetry of development: at some stage the frontier dividing the ideological from the non-ideological is blurred, and, as a result, there is an inflation of the concept of ideology which loses, in that way, all analytical precision. In the case of ideology as a 'system of ideas', the unity of that system depends on the possibility of finding a point external to itself from which a critique of ideology could proceed—e.g. by showing through a symptomal reading the true interests to which a given ideological configuration responded. But, as Žižek points out, with examples taken from the works of Barthes, Paul de Man, Ducrot, Pêcheux and myself, it is precisely the assumption of this 'zero level' of the ideological of a pure extra-discursive reality, which constitutes the ideological misconception *par excellence*. In the case of 'Ideological State Apparatuses'—or, in the Foucauldian version, the disciplinary procedures operating at the level of micro-power—we find symmetrical versions of the same *petitio principio*: does not the unity of the state apparatuses require the very cement of the ideology they supposedly explain; or, in the case of the disciplinary techniques: does not their dispersion itself require the constant recomposition of their articulation, so that we have to appeal to a discursive medium which makes the very distinction between the ideological and the non-ideological collapse? And the case is even clearer when we move to the realm of beliefs: here, from the very beginning, we are confronted with a supposedly 'extra-ideological' reality whose very operation depends on mechanisms belonging to the ideological realm.

> The moment we take a closer look at these allegedly extra-ideological mechanisms that regulate social reproduction, we find ourselves knee-deep in the already mentioned obscure domain in which reality is indistinguishable from ideology. What we encounter here, therefore, is the third reversal of non-ideology into ideology: all of a sudden we become aware of a For-itself of ideology at work in the very In-itself of extra-ideological actuality.
>
> (Žižek 1994, pp. 14–15)

Here Žižek correctly detects the main source of the progressive abandonment of 'ideology' as an analytical category:

> this notion somehow grows 'too strong', it begins to embrace everything, inclusive of the very neutral, extra-ideological ground supposed to provide the standard by means of which one can measure ideological distortion. That is to say, is not the ultimate result of discourse analysis that the order of discourse as such is inherently 'ideological'?
>
> (Žižek 1994, p. 16)

We see, thus, the logic governing the dissolution of the terrain classically occupied by the theory of ideology. The latter died as a result of its own imperialistic success. What we are witnessing is not the decline of a theoretical object as a result of a narrowing of its field of operation but rather the opposite: its indefinite expansion, consequent to the explosion of the dichotomies which—within a certain problematic—confronted it with other objects. Categories such as 'distortion' and 'false representation' made sense as long as something 'true' or 'undistorted' was considered to be within human reach. But once an extra ideological viewpoint becomes unreachable, two effects necessarily follow:

(1) discourses organising social practices are both incommensurable and on equal footing with all others;
(2) notions such as 'distortion' and 'false representation' lose all meaning.

Where does this leave us, however? Are we supposed to put aside entirely notions such as 'distortion', 'false consciousness', etc? The difficulty is that if we simply do so, we enter into a vicious circle whereby the conclusions of our analysis negate its premises. Let us for a moment consider the reasons for the decline of the 'critique of ideology' approach—as expressed in its purest terms by classical Marxism, and prolonged today by Habermas' regulative ideal of undistorted communication. The bedrock of such a critique is to postulate access to a point from which—at least tendentially—reality would speak without discursive mediations. The full positivity and graspability of such a point gives a rationale to the whole critical operation. Now, the critique of this approach starts from the negation of such a metalinguistic level, from showing that the rhetorico-discursive devices of a text are irreducible and that, as a result, there is no extra-discursive ground from which a critique of ideology could proceed. (This does not mean, of course, that ideological critique is impossible—what is impossible is a critique of ideology *as such;* all critiques will necessarily be intra-ideological.)

What is not, however, usually perceived is that this critique of the 'critique of ideology' can advance in two different directions which lead to contradictory results. The first leads to what we could call a new positivism and objectivism. If we entirely do away with the notion of 'distortion' and assert that there are only incommensurable 'discourses', we merely transfer the notion of a full positivity from an extra-discursive ground to the plurality of the discursive field. This transference retains entirely the idea of a full positivity. In the same way that we have a naturalistic positivism we can have a semiotic or a phenomenological one. If, on the other hand, what we are asserting is that the very notion of an extra-discursive viewpoint is the ideological illusion *par excellence,* the notion of 'distortion' is not abandoned but is instead made the cornerstone of the dismantling of any metalinguistic operation. What is new in the latter is that what now constitutes a distorted representation is the very notion of an extra-discursive closure. We will discuss later the ways in which the concept of 'distortion' has to be reformulated in order to fulfil this new role. Let us just say for the time being that this reformulation is the starting point for a possible re-emergence of a notion of ideology which is not marred by the stumbling blocks of an essentialist theorisation.

Let us concentrate for a moment on the Althusserian theory of ideology. Ideology is, for Althusser, *eternal.* The mechanisms producing the subject through misrecognition are inscribed in the very essence of social reproduction. We have no hope of escaping the mirroring game involved in ideological interpellation. For him, however, ideology constitutes itself as an object through its opposition to science: the determination of the distortion brought about by ideological representations, the alienated character of the subject, depend on the analyst's knowledge of what social reproduction actually is—a knowledge which includes understanding the mirroring mechanism. We know that history is a process without a subject, precisely because we are able to go scientifically beyond subjective alienation.

This leaves us, however, with an apparently intractable problem. Everything depends on what is being misrecognised or, rather, on the nature and extent of the misrecognition. If what is misrecognised is a particular type of social relation, we could easily imagine a different one in which no misrecognition at all occurs. This is what was assumed by the classical notion of emancipation. But what Althusser argues is different: it is that we are dealing with a necessary misrecognition which is independent of any type of social configuration. In this case, however, what is misrecognised is the principle of social structuration as such, the closure operated by any symbolic system. This launches us into a new problem: if closure *as such* requires misrecognition (i.e. its opposite) it is the very idea of closure that constitutes the highest form of misrecognition. Either misrecognition is reducible to an objective function by a neutral gaze, or that gaze is not neutral but part of the universal misrecognition—in which case what presents itself as the opposite of misrecognition belongs to the essence of the latter. I can keep a strong frontier between closure (the auto-reproduction of social relations) and the necessary forms of misrecognition accompanying it only insofar as there is a metalinguistic vantage point from which closure shows itself without any subjective passage through misrecognition. But if that vantage point proves to be illusory, misrecognition contaminates closure; and, given that misrecognition, distortion is universal, its other (closure, self-transparency) becomes the main form of misrecognition. In that case, distortion is constitutive of social objectivity. What can, however, be a form of distortion which remains such while the distinction between the distortion and what is distorted is obliterated? This is the next problem that we have to address.

II

The notion of a constitutive distortion is apparently a *contradictio in adjecto*. A distortion, it seems, cannot be constitutive; it is only if there is a more primary meaning which is not itself distorted, that a distortive effect could become visible at all. Does this conclusion exhaust, however, all the logical possibilities that a relation of distortion opens? Let us consider the matter carefully. It is certainly inherent to all distortion that a 'primary' meaning is presented under a 'false' light. What operation this presentation involves—concealment, deformation, etc.—is something that we could leave indeterminate for the time being. What is essential to distortion is:

(1) that a primary meaning is presented as something different from what it is;
(2) that the distortive operation—not only its results—have to be somehow visible.

This last point is crucial: if the distortive operation does not leave any traces in its result, it would fully succeed in constituting a new meaning. What we are dealing with, however, is a constitutive distortion. That is, we are positing both an originary meaning (for this is required by any distortion) and withdrawing it (for the distortion is constitutive). In that case, the only logical possibility of pulling together these two apparently antinomic dimensions is if the original meaning is illusory and the distortive operation consists in precisely creating that illusion—that is, to project into something which is essentially divided the illusion of a fullness and self-transparency that it lacks. Let us say something about what is being projected, and about the visibility of the projection as such.

In our previous discussion we have used three necessarily interrelated notions—'originary meaning', 'self-transparency' and 'closure'. It is time to say something more about the nature of this link. Something is originary insofar as it does not have to go outside itself in order to constitute what it is; it is self-transparent insofar as its internal dimensions are in a relation of strict solidarity between themselves; and it is closed in itself as far as the ensemble of its 'effects' can be determined without going beyond its original meaning. As we see, each of these notions (without exactly being synonymous with the other two), requires the latter's presence in order to actualise its own meaning. And it is precisely this full meaning that is dislocated by the postulation of a constitutive distortion: in the first and third cases both the 'originarity' and internality of the 'effects' are upset by discursive mediation, and the opacity of the internal dimensions of the self-enclosed entity interrupts its self-transparency.

This would only show, however, that *dislocation* is constitutive, that the very notion of a metaphysical closure has to be put into question.[1] But the notion of *distortion* involves something more than mere dislocation: namely, that a concealment of some sort takes place in it. Now, as we have seen earlier, what is concealed is the ultimate dislocation of what presents itself as a close identity, and the act of concealment consists in projecting on to that identity the dimension of closure that it ultimately lacks. This has two capital consequences:

(1) The first is that that dimension of closure is something that is actually absent—if it was ultimately present there would be *revelation* rather than *projection* and no concealment would be involved. In that case what we are dealing with is the presence of an absence and the ideological operation *par excellence* consists of attributing that impossible role of closure to a particular content that is radically incommensurable with it. In other words: the operation of closure is impossible but at the same time necessary; impossible because of the constitutive dislocation which lies at the heart of any structural arrangement, necessary because without that fictitious fixing of meaning there would not be meaning at all.[2] Here we can start seeing in what way ideology as 'misrepresentation' could be eternal: not, as Althusser thought, because the alienation of the subject is the necessary complement of an objective history whose meaning could be located elsewhere, but because the notion of that 'objective meaning' is itself the very form of misrepresenting that through which any identity acquires its fictitious coherence. The crucial point is to realise that it is this dialectics between necessity and impossibility that gives ideology its terrain of emergence.

(2) This dialectics creates in any ideological representation—and at this stage it should be clear that ideology is one of the dimensions of any representation—an insurmountable split which is strictly constitutive. On the one hand closure

as such, being an impossible operation, cannot have a content of its own and only shows itself through its projection in an object different from itself. On the other hand this particular object, which at some point assumes the role of incarnating the closure of an ideological horizon, will be deformed as a result of that incarnating function. Between the particularity of the object which attempts to fulfil the operation of closure and this operation, there is a relationship of mutual dependency in which each of the two poles is required, and at the same time, each partially limits the effects of the other. Let us suppose that at some point, in a Third World country, nationalisation of the basic industries is proposed as an economic panacea. Now, this is just a technical way of running the economy and if it remains so it will never become an ideology. How does the transformation into the latter take place? Only if the particularity of the economic measure starts incarnating something more and different from itself; for instance, the emancipation from foreign domination, the elimination of capitalist waste, the possibility of social justice for excluded sections of the population, etc. In sum: the possibility of constituting the community as a coherent whole. That impossible object—the fullness of the community—appears here as depending on a particular set of transformations at the economic level. This is the ideological effect *stricto sensu:* the belief that there is a particular social arrangement which can bring about the closure and transparency of the community.[3] There is ideology whenever a particular content shows itself as more than itself. Without this dimension of horizon we would have ideas or systems of ideas, but never ideologies.

With this we have answered our first question: what an ideological distortion projects on a particular object is the impossible fullness of the community.[4] In order to address the second—how the operation of distortion becomes visible—we have to explore further the dialectics of incarnation/deformation to which we have just alluded. Let us start with deformation. If what we have said above is correct, the deformation inherent in a process of ideological (mis)representation consists of making a certain content equivalent to a set of other contents. In our example: an economic measure becomes equivalent to other historical transformations leading to a process of global human emancipation. Let us be clear that equivalence does not mean identity; each of these transformations retains something of its own identity and, however, the purely privative character of the identity is weakened through its participation in the equivalential chain. This is so because, as far as the equivalential chain is concerned, each of these transformations—without entirely dropping its own particularity—is an equivalent name for the absent fullness of the community. The only thing we can say is that the relationship between particular and equivalential identities is unstable; everything depends on what function—representing a content within the community or representing the latter as an absent fullness—will prevail. And the same applies to the dimension of incarnation: representing the fullness of the community cannot entirely do away with the particularity of the content through which the incarnation takes place, for in the case that such a doing away was complete we would arrive at a situation in which incarnated meaning and incarnating body would be entirely commensurable with each other—which is the possibility that we are denying *ex hypothesi*. We see here what it is that makes possible the visibility of the distortive operation: the fact that neither of the two movements in which it is based can logically reach its *ad quem* term.

We have so far spoken—largely for analytic reasons—of two dimensions that we have called 'incarnation' and 'deformation'. The distinction is certainly valid from an analytic point of view, for 'incarnation' refers to an absent fullness using an object different from itself as a means of representation, while 'deformation' refers to a relation of equivalence between particular objects. The relevance of the distinction is, however, limited by the fact that an incarnation in the sense that we have described can only proceed through equivalential deformation. To assume the opposite—that is, the incarnation of an impossible object in a particular body, which did not pass through an equivalential relationship between particularities—would involve attributing a new meaning arbitrarily to an old term—with the result that between the two meanings there would be a simple relation of equivocality, in the Aristotelian sense. But in that case, as the new meaning would be fully constituted and entirely independent of the old, the absent fullness would have found a direct form of representation, a presence of its own and, as a result, would not be absent after all but very much present. This would make any relation of incarnation impossible.[5] If the relation of incarnation *is*, to the contrary, possible, and if what is to be incarnated is an impossible object, the incarnating body cannot be the transparent medium through which a fully constituted meaning receives expression. The dilemma is clear: the incarnating body has to express something different from itself but as, however, this 'something different' lacks an identity of its own, its only means of constitution are the contents belonging to the incarnating body. It is clear that these two requisites can only be made compatible if some deformation of those contents takes place. Now this is exactly what happens in an equivalential relation. The specificity of equivalence is the destruction of meaning through its very proliferation. Let us suppose that I try to define the meaning of a term through equivalential enumeration—e.g. 'welfare of the people'. I can say that health, housing, education, etc. constitute an equivalential chain giving us a notion of what people's welfare is. It is clear that such a list can be indefinitely expanded. This expansion consists, apparently, of an enrichment of meaning, but what is achieved through this enrichment is its exact opposite: if I have to specify what all the links of the equivalential chain have in common, the more the chain expands, the more differential features of each of the links will have to be dropped in order to keep alive what the equivalential chain attempts to express.

We could put this in slightly different terms by saying that each of the links of the equivalential chain names something different from itself, but that this naming only takes place as far as the link belongs to the chain. And for the reasons previously mentioned, the more extended the chain, the more that naming will prevail over the particularistic references of the individual links. It is for this reason that we have spoken of destruction of meaning through its very proliferation. This allows us to understand the precise relationship between 'empty' and 'floating' signifiers, two terms which have had a considerable currency in contemporary semiotic and post-structuralist literature. In the case of a floating signifier we would apparently have an overflowing of meaning while an empty signifier, on the contrary, would ultimately be a signifier without a signified. But if we analyse the matter more carefully, we realise that the floating character of a signifier is the only phenomenic form of its emptiness. A signifier like 'democracy', for instance, is certainly a floating one; its meaning will be different in liberal, radical anti-fascist and conservative anti-communist discourses. How is this floating structured, however? In the first place, for the floating to be possible the relationship between signifier and signified has already to be a loose one—if the signifier was strictly attached to one and only one signified no floating could take place. So, the floating requires a tendential emptiness. But, in the second place, the pattern of the floating requires:

(1) that the floating term is differently articulated to opposed discursive chains (otherwise there would be no floating at all);
(2) that within these discursive chains the floating term functions not only as a differential component but as an equivalential one *vis-à-vis* all the other components of the chain.

If 'democracy' is presented as an essential component of the 'free world', the fixing of the meaning of the term will not occur purely by constructing for it a differential position, but by making of it one of the names of the fullness of society that the 'free world' attempts to achieve, and this involves establishing an equivalential relation with all the other terms within that discourse. 'Democracy' is not synonymous with 'freedom of the press', 'defence of private property' or 'affirmation of family values'. But what gives its specific ideological dimension to a discourse of the 'free world' is that each of these discursive components is not closed in its own differential particularity but functions also as an alternative name for the equivalential totality which their relations constitute. So, floating a term and emptying it are two sides of the same discursive operation.

All this leads to an inevitable conclusion: understanding the workings of the ideological within the field of collective representations is synonymous with understanding this logic of simplification of the social field that we have called 'equivalence', and its two central operations; 'floating' and 'emptying'. We will illustrate these propositions with three historical examples of the configuration of ideological spaces and then conclude with more general considerations on the contradictory movements which govern the operation of ideological closures.

III

My first example comes from Michael Walzer's (1994) *Thick and Thin*. He begins the book by recalling having seen on TV news in 1989 the picture of a demonstration in Prague. It is a picture of people marching in the streets of Prague; they carry signs, some of which say, simply, 'Truth' and others 'Justice'. When I saw the picture, I knew immediately what the signs meant—and so did everyone else who saw the same picture. Not only that, I also recognised and acknowledged the values that the marchers were defending—and so did (almost) everyone else. Is there any recent account, any post-modernist account, of political language that can explain this understanding and acknowledgement? How could I penetrate so quickly and join so unreservedly in the language game or the power play of a distant demonstration? The marchers shared a culture with which I was largely unfamiliar; they were responding to an experience I had never had. And yet, I could have walked comfortably in their midst. I could carry the same signs (Walzer 1994, p. 1).

It is on the basis of this experience that Walzer distinguishes between thick[6] and thin morality. The first represents the complete set of moral principles of a group and is embedded in the totality of its cultural practices. It varies from time to time and from place to place. Thin morality, on the contrary, constitutes an ultimate core of moral principles which make possible transcultural evaluations and understanding—as in the case of the Prague demonstration. Walzer's problem is: how do we account for this transcultural core?

Walzer's treatment of the problem is highly illuminating. He rejects all easy solutions that would transform thin morality into an *a priori* core to be specified independently of more comprehensive moral frameworks. Thus, he rejects the Habermasian view, according to which '[m]inimal morality consists in the rules of engagement that bind all the speakers; maximalism is the never-finished outcome of their arguments' (Walzer 1994, p. 12, n. 11). As he shows, this view presupposes rules of engagement which are far from minimal, and also it assumes that minimalism would be an initial core out of which maximalism would later grow. But this view for Walzer is wrong: morality always starts from being thick. 'Morality is thick from the beginning, culturally integrated, and it reveals itself thinly only on special occasions, when moral language is turned to special purposes' (Walzer 1994, p. 4). If this is so, it follows that minimalism is not an Esperanto embedded in maximalism; that it cannot substitute for maximalism; and that it can never be foundational for, thin morality not being a content specifiable *a priori*, 'it is not the case that different groups of people discover that all of them are committed to the same set of ultimate values' (Walzer 1994, p. 18). This, however, does not mean that thin morality is shallow: on the contrary, its principles constitute a morality 'close to the bone'. 'In moral discourse thinness and intensity go together, whereas with thickness comes qualification, compromise, complexity and disagreement' (Walzer 1994, p. 6).

In that case, what is the actual content of thin morality? Walzer thinks he can give an answer to that question. I quote his answer in full:

> It is possible, nonetheless, to give some substantial account of the moral minimum. I see nothing wrong with the effort to do that so long as we

understand that it is necessarily expressive of our own thick morality. There is no neutral (unexpressive) moral language. Still, we can pick out from among our values and commitments those that make it possible for us to march vicariously with the people in Prague. We can make a list of similar occasions (at home, too) and catalogue our responses and try to figure out what the occasions and the responses have in common. Perhaps the end product of this effort will be a set of standards to which all societies can be held—negative injunctions, most likely, rules against murder, deceit, torture, oppression, and tyranny.

(Walzer 1994, pp. 9–10)

Now I find this answer disappointing. It looks as if Walzer, in spite of his insightful argumentation, has not finally resisted the temptation of giving to thin morality a positive content—something against which the whole movement of his thought militates. For the problem that remains unanswered is the following: if the whole operation depends on picking out from our commitments and values those which are to be the content of thin morality, the meaning of the operation depends upon who does the picking. If Walzer's argument is correct—as I think it is—and there is no neutral picking out, the distinction between thin and thick morality can only be internal to a particular thick culture and is likely to be different in different cultures. The problem is, however, partly obscured by the deceptive obviousness of terms such as 'deceit', 'torture', 'oppression' and 'tyranny'—to which we could add 'truth' and 'justice'. It seems evident that nobody would favour 'tyranny', 'deceit' and 'injustice'. *Ergo,* the universality of the agreement apparently makes it the ideal candidate to give to thin morality a content. It is here that the misunderstanding lies. What I will attempt to show is that by agreeing to oppose 'injustice', 'deceit' or 'tyranny', we have not agreed about anything whatsoever. At this point our argument dovetails with previous remarks on floating and empty signifiers.

Let us go back to the Prague demonstration. People carried signs saying 'Truth' and 'Justice'. Before asking ourselves about an ultimate thin core, an anterior question has to be answered: does either of the terms assert anything different from the other? Two terms can be within a discursive structure in two opposite types of relation: a relation of *combination* if they are constituted through differentiation from each other, and a relation of *substitution* if they can replace each other within the same signifying context. As we have seen, the latter is a case of a relation of equivalence. Although in an equivalence the differential meaning of its components does not entirely collapse, all the terms of the equivalence point, through their differential bodies, to something other than themselves—what we have called an absent fullness. What we have to decide is the meaning of 'truth' and 'justice' in the placards of the demonstrators: were they primarily interested in differentiating 'truth' from 'justice', or were they using them as equivalent terms to express the good of the community, denied by the fallen regime? I think there can be no doubt: they were doing the latter. But in that case, if the only content of the demonstrators' discourse was 'truth' and 'justice'—as these are empty signifiers pointing to the absent fullness of the community—agreeing with them about the positive value of those signifiers would be the same as agreeing about nothing. The Chinese invasion of Tibet was called by its perpetrators 'the peaceful liberation', and it is clear that agreeing with them that 'liberation' and 'peace' are good things does not involve any support for their action.

But, of course, the discourse of the demonstrators was not only about 'truth' and 'justice'. The chain of equivalences through which the empty signifier 'justice' circulated was far more complex and included, as Walzer rightly points out, things such as 'an end to arbitrary arrests, equal and impartial law enforcement, the abolition of the privileges and prerogatives of the party elite—common, garden variety justice' (Walzer 1994, p. 2). The crucial question, however, is whether we can move to all these specifications without abandoning the terrain of thin morality, or whether by entering into that terrain we are moving towards contextual, thick morality. In other words: what is the relation, for instance, between 'arbitrary arrests' and 'injustice'? Can we deduce the injustice of arbitrary arrests from a mere analysis of the category of 'injustice'? Or, does the construction of 'arbitrary arrests' as unjust require some further contextual specifications? I think that the latter is the case, that irrespective of how much we want arbitrary arrests to be seen as unjust, historical and contextual conditions have to coalesce for the articulation between the two terms to be established, and that these conditions are not just thrown up by the mere circulation of 'justice' as an empty signifier within a discursive content. If this is so, and if thin morality must have a richer content than mere agreement about the positive character of some empty terms, thin morality is as contextual as thick (although, of course, the contexts are different). This morality is not a core to be isolated analytically, but the result of a historical construction. It requires the prolongation of equivalential logics beyond the limits of given communitarian contexts. This, of course, means that the contents of thin morality, far from being permanent, are permanently renegotiated.

The crucial point is that, if our argument is accepted, we are not dealing with a stable and minimal content—with some sort of 'original position' *à la* Rawls—but with attributing to a particular content the function of representing (or incarnating) the absent fullness of the community—one of whose names is 'justice'. As we know, however, this incarnation—which involves making that particularity the expression of something different from itself—is possible only to the extent that a particular content enters into a relation of equivalence with other particularities. As we know, the effect of the logic of equivalence is to impoverish meaning: this explains how thinness can proceed out of thickness. In a world in which processes of globalisation constantly transgress the limits of particular communities, the historical conditions are created for the development of ever more extended chains of equivalence and, in this way, for thinness to expand. The production of social identities is the result, in the contemporary world, of the crossing of contradictory logics of contextualisation and decontextualisation: if the crisis of stable universal values opens the way for an increasing social diversity (contextualisation), then thin morality (decontextualisation) too also becomes increasingly more important.

But this operation of attributing the function of representing the absent fullness of the community to a chain of particular contents is ideological in the strict sense of the term (and it should be clear from everything we have said that this assertion does not involve any pejorative connotation). A chain of particular contents represents an impossible object—this is a first distortion, what we have called incarnation; but this incarnation is only possible (second distortion) insofar as an equivalential relation weakens the differential character of each link of the chain. We can also see clearly why the distortion has to be constitutive: because the object to be represented is, at the same time, impossible and necessary. The illusion of closure is something we can negotiate with, but never eliminate. Ideology is a dimension which belongs to the structure of all possible experience.

IV

In order to clarify our argument, let us take some examples from an entirely different historical experience, but one which depends on extending to its extreme limit the logic of equivalence: I am referring to mysticism. We have spoken about the need for representing an object—a fullness—which, by definition, transcends all representation. Now, this is, at its purest, the problem of the mystic. He aspires to give expression to direct contact with God, i.e. with something which is strictly ineffable because it is incommensurable with anything existing. He is the *deus absconditus,* a mystical Nothing. For the great monotheistic religions there is an unsurpassable abyss between the Creator and the *ens creatum.*

> Mysticism does not deny or overlook the abyss; on the contrary, it begins by realising its existence, but from there it proceeds to a quest for the secret that will close it in, the hidden path that will span it.
>
> *(Scholem 1995, p. 8)*

The mystical Nothing is not an empty place, in some sense it is the fullest of all places, although that fullness, precisely for being so, transcends the limits of the sayable. It is on this basis that Gershom Scholem establishes a distinction between allegory and symbol.

> If allegory can be defined as the representation of an expressible something by another expressible something, the mystical symbol is an expressible representation of something which lies beyond the sphere of expression and communication, something which comes from a sphere whose face is, as it were, turned inward and away from us. ... The symbol 'signifies' nothing and communicates nothing, but makes something transparent which is beyond all expression. Where deeper insight into the structure of the allegory uncovers fresh layers of meaning, the symbol is intuitively understood all at once—or not at all ... It is a 'momentary totality' which is perceived intuitively in a mystical *now*—the dimension of time proper to the symbol.
>
> *(Scholem 1995, p. 27)*

Now, how is it possible to express the inexpressible? Only if a certain combination of terms is found in which each of them is divested of its particular meaning—if each of them does not express but destroys the differential character of that meaning. We already know the way in which this can be achieved: through the equivalence. I will take as an example one of the cases studied by Scholem: the litany *haadereth vehaemunah lehay olamim,* to be found in the 'Greater Hekhaloth' and included in the liturgy of the High Holidays. I quote its beginning:

> Excellence and faithfulness—are His who lives forever Understanding and blessing—are His who lives forever Grandeur and greatness—are His who lives forever Cognition and expression—are His who lives forever Magnificency and majesty—are His who lives forever Counsel and strength—are His who lives forever, etc.
>
> *(Scholem 1995, p. 58)*

The other attributes of Him who lives forever are lustre and brilliance, grace and benevolence, purity and goodness, unity and honour, crown and glory, precept and practice, sovereignty and rule, adornment and permanence, mystery and wisdom, might and meekness, splendour and wonder, righteousness and honour, invocation and holiness, exultation and nobility, song and hymn and praise, and glory.

The analysis of this prayer by Scholem is revealing. He stresses the fact that the mystical effect of the prayer is obtained by an equivalential reiteration which destroys any differential meaning of the attributes of the Lord. He asserts:

> the climax of sublimity and solemnity to which the mystic can attain in his attempt to express the magnificence of his vision is also the *non plus ultra* of vacuousness. Philipp Bloch, who was the first to be deeply impressed by the problem presented by these hymns, speaks of their 'plethora of purely pleonastic and unisonous words which do not in the least assist the process of thought but merely reflect the emotional struggle'. But at the same time he shows himself aware of the almost magical effect of this vacuous and yet sublime pathos on those who are praying when, for example, hymns composed in this spirit are recited on the Day of Atonement.
>
> *(Scholem 1995, p. 58)*

And referring to the litany quoted above, he says that it 'is a classic example [in its original language] of an alphabetical litany which fills the imagination of the devotee with splendid concepts clothed in magnificent expression; the particular words do not matter' (Scholem 1995, p. 59).

It cannot be clearer. The enumeration does not enrich our conceptual knowledge of the attributes of God, for the only meaning that each of these attributes keeps in the enumeration is the positive value that those terms have in ordinary language—and from this point of view they are all strictly equivalent. The addition of them all in a way that destroys their differentiated meanings is the means of expressing the inexpressible. As in the case of 'truth' and 'justice' in the placards of the Prague demonstrators, each of the terms is an alternative name for something which lacks any direct form of representation. The difference is, of course, that in the Prague case the enumeration was not indefinite because there was an attempt to link the empty signifiers 'truth' and 'justice' to contents like the 'end of arbitrary arrests', etc. which retain their particular meanings; while the mystical discourse attempts to go beyond all particular meaning, expanding the enumeration indefinitely.[7]

In the literature on mysticism there is a frequent distinction between introvertive and extrovertive experiences, the first being purely internal experiences of a going beyond all differences and multiplicity, while the extrovertive mystic, in the words of W.T. Stace, 'using his physical senses, perceives the multiplicity of external material objects—the sea, the sky, the houses, the trees—mystically transfigured so that the One, or the Unity, shines through them' (Stace 1960, p. 61). Let us quote three passages from Eckhart, taken from Stace's book. The first illustrates an experience of the introvertive type, while the second and third refer us back to extrovertive mystical experiences. The first is as follows:

> the human spirit scales the heaven to discover the spirit by which the heavens are driven ... Even then ... it presses on further into the vortex, the source in which spirit originates. There the spirit in knowing has no use for number, for numbers are of use only in time, in this defective world. No one can strike his roots into eternity without being rid of the concept of number ... God leads the human spirit into the desert, into his own unity which is pure One.
>
> (Stace 1960, p. 99)

The extrovertive texts assert the following:

> All that a man has here externally in multiplicity is intrinsically One. Here all blades of grass, wood and stone, all things are One. This is the deepest depth.
>
> (Stace 1960, p. 63)

> Say Lord, when is a man in mere understanding? I say to you 'when a man sees one thing separated from another'. And when is he above mere understanding? That I can tell you: 'When he sees all in all, then a man stands above mere understanding'.
>
> (Stace 1960, p. 64)

Extrovertive mysticism presents no problem for us: we are confronted with a pure relation of equivalence. Blades of grass, wood and stone cancel out their differences and become alternative names of something which is beyond them but which can only be named through them. But introverted mysticism is apparently different, for it looks as if the passage through equivalence was not necessary, and as if a pure beyond, although ineffable, could be experienced in a direct way. In that case closure could finally take place, not evidently at the level of representation but at the level of an ineffable experience. I would suggest, however, that this conclusion is deceptive. Although I cannot entirely prove the point here, my hypothesis is that even in introspective mysticism, the experience of the One requires the appeal to something particular which is less than the Absolute. As we have seen, for Eckhart no one 'can strike his roots into eternity without being rid of the concept of number'. The decisive question is whether once we have got rid of that concept, the One is experienced as unmediated fullness, as undistorted presence, or whether that which we have got rid of is an internal component of the experience of the One. In that case what is less than the Absolute contaminates the very experience in which the Absolute discloses itself. I think the second to be the case, that in order to be experienced as Absolute, the Absolute requires the constant reference to what is less than itself. Now, the concept of number enters into this picture not in its own specific particularity, but as an instance of a being which is 'other than the One'. And this 'being other than the One' is something which only shows itself insofar as they are all equated in their contraposition to the Absolute. So the relation of equivalence between particularities is required for the experience of even an introvertive mysticism.

V

The thesis I am trying to defend is that this double movement found in its most extreme form in mysticism—that is, incarnation and deformation of particular contents through the expansion of equivalential logics is at the root of *all* ideological processs conception of myth is structured.

Sorel's work takes place in the period of the so-called 'crisis of Marxism' at the turn of the century—that is in a historical climate where the conviction that the operation of the inevitable laws of capitalism was leading to a proletarian revolution had been seriously eroded. Croce's rejection of historical positivism, for instance, had led him to assert the inanity of any unifying interpretation of the historical process and, consequently, the impossibility of grounding social action in any kind of scientific certitude. Any action was for him, as a result, the effect of a subjective conviction.

These two themes—the impossibility of unifying historical events by conceptual means, and the grounding of historical action in conviction and will—are certainly present in Sorel, but he gives to them a new twist and invests them with a new meaning, viewing them in terms of a far more radical historical possibility. Here we find the cornerstone of Sorel's thought in its mature stage: social processes do not involve only displacements in the relation of forces between classes because a more radical and constitutive possibility is always haunting society—the dissolution of the social fabric and the implosion of society as a totality. Society not only suffers domination and exploitation: it is also threatened with decadence, with the only too real possibility of its radical non-being. This distinctive possibility opens the way to a new and peculiar logic in the relation between groups. There are three capital moments in this logic.

(1) The first is that the opposition which dominates Sorel's vision of the social is not primarily the one between bourgeoisie and proletariat but, rather, that between decadence and the full realisation of society. If the proletariat as a social force receives historical priority this is because it is seen as the main instrument to confront decadence. But—and this is a crucial point—it is not the actual victory of the proletariat against the bourgeoisie that will bring about 'grandeur' and will arrest decadence, but the very fact of the open confrontation between the two groups. Without confrontation there is no identity; social identities require conflict for their constitution. Sorel thus sees in Marxism not a scientific doctrine explaining the objective laws of capitalism, but a finalistic ideology of the proletariat, grounded in class struggle. Social relations, left to themselves, are simply a *'mélange'*. Only the will of determined social forces gives a consistent shape to social relations, and the determination of that will depends on the violent confrontations between the groups.

(2) But if the historical justification of the action of the proletariat is given by its being the only force capable of opposing the decadence of civilisation, that justification is indifferent to the contents of the proletarian programme and depends entirely on the contingent ability of those contents to bring about an effect which is external to themselves. There is no ethical justification intrinsic to socialism. This has two capital consequences. The first, that all social identity or social demand is constitutively split. It is, on the one hand, a particular demand; but, on the other hand, it can also be the bearer, the incarnation of social 'grandeur', as opposed to decadence. Between particular contents and the absent fullness of society the same relation is established that has been discussed throughout this chapter. 'Grandeur' and 'decadence' do not have intrinsic contents of their own, but are the empty signifiers of a fullness of society (or its opposite, its corruption or non-being) which could be actualised by the most different social forces. So—and this is the second consequence—it is enough that the working class shows itself as a limited historical actor, closed in its corporative demands and incapable of incarnating the will to fullness of society, for its claims to lose all legitimacy. The political trajectory of Sorel is a living example of the contingency of the relation between working class demands and 'grandeur': he passed from being a theoretician of revolutionary syndicalism to allying himself with a faction of the monarchist movement, and ended his career by supporting the Third International. The diffusion of Sorelian themes in antagonistic social movements, from bolshevism to fascism, is an even more telling example of the ambiguous possibilities that his *démarche* opened.

(3) But there is something more—and more important in the logic of Sorel's critique of bourgeois society. If it is the moment of violence as such and not the victory of either of the two poles of the confrontation that enables the prevention of social decadence, it is the reproduction of violence as an end in itself

that constitutes the real objective. This means, on the one hand, that proletarian violence can become an instrument of the regeneration of the bourgeoisie itself, insofar as the latter will develop its own violence in order to respond to that of the proletariat. But, on the other hand, proletarian violence will be a non-violent violence, one addressed to nothing in particular, having become its own end. Aristotle distinguished between actions which are mere instruments for the achievement of an end (i.e. walking to the corner to buy a newspaper) and those who constitute their own end (i.e. walking to promenade oneself). Now, this distinction can easily be deconstructed—even the most instrumental of actions develops abilities in the actor that become part of his identity, and whose reproduction becomes partly its own end. In Sorel this logic is taken to its ultimate conclusion: the action (violence) is increasingly separated from its own contents and exclusively judged by the effect it has on the identity of the actors.

This split in the signification of any historical action can be seen at work in the three basic contrapositions that structure Sorel's thought: force/violence; utopia/myth; general political strike/general proletarian strike. The important point is that the second term of each of these contrapositions differs from the first because of the equivalential relation that each of its internal components establishes with the others. Let us examine force/violence in the first place. Force is always concrete; it is *particular* force as developed, for instance, in class-dominated societies. And the dominated groups also use force when they try either to obtain concessions or to displace from power the ruling elites, in order to establish a new system of domination. A force is always concrete, it is entirely absorbed by its own differentiated particularity. Violence is, on the contrary, addressed not to this or that system of domination but to the form of domination as such. It is the (impossible) event bringing about the reconciliation of society with itself. Each instance of violence against domination *as such* is equivalent to all the others; the particularity of each struggle expresses, through that particularity, a content strictly differentiated from each particular instance.

> Utopia/myth: While a Utopia is an intellectual construction, the blueprint of a fully achieved (and in principle achievable) society, myth is an ensemble of equivalential images capable of galvanising the imaginary of the masses, thus launching them into collective action.
>
> (M)en who are participating in a great social movement always picture their coming action as a battle in which their cause is certain to triumph. These constructions, knowledge of which is so important for historians, I propose to call myths; the syndicalist 'general strike' and Marx's catastrophic revolution are such myths … I now wish to show that we should not attempt to analyse such groups of images in the way that we analyse a thing into its elements, but that they must be taken as a whole, as historical forces, and that we should be especially careful not to make any comparison

between accomplished fact and the picture people had formed for themselves before action.

(Sorel 1925, p. 22)

That is, the contraposition between utopia and myth is not only grounded in the different nature of their particular contents—neater and *intellectualiste* in one case, more imprecise and diffuse in the other—but in their entirely different functions: the contents of the myth are substitutable by each other (that is why they have to be taken as a whole) as they all symbolise an absent fullness, and their efficacy has to be measured by their equivalential mobilising effects, not by the success of their differentiated literal contents. For Croce, the impossibility of a full rational action meant that an ungrounded decision was at the root of the constitution of a historical will. The absent rationality had to be substituted by an emotional identification which explains the creative role of passion in History. This is exactly the function of myth in Sorel, for whom passion played the central role in the constitution of the will.

Finally, the two types of strike. Here the same duality is repeated. While the political strike aims at particular objectives within a system of domination, the proletarian's strike target is the abolition of domination as such. But again, the proletarian strike being a myth, it is not an actual event, separated from actual political strikes, but a dimension which unifies, in an equivalential way, a variety of struggles and actions over a whole historical period. Whether a concrete event belongs to either the political or to the proletarian action is something which is, in the last instance, undecidable and always open to a plurality of readings and strategico-discursive interventions.

As we can see the same duality resulting from the equivalential logics operating in both the Prague demonstration and in mysticism is to be found at the root of these Sorelian distinctions. While in the case of force the particularity of the aim gives the struggle its entire meaning, with violence the concrete struggle is just the occasion for a more general confrontation which shows itself through the equivalence of that concrete struggle with others, governed by different aims. While in the case of Utopia each of its dimensions can be analytically distinguished by its particular function within the whole, with myth each of its distinctive features becomes the equivalential symbol of all the others. Finally, while in the case of the political strike the struggle is entirely exhausted when its aim is achieved, with the proletarian strike each of the partial confrontations is the pretext for keeping alive and training the proletariat as a revolutionary agency. In the case of the second term of each of the distinctions the particularity is the means of representation for something transcending it.

VI

Let us now generalise these conclusions, and bring them to bear upon a theory of ideology. The crisis of the notion of 'ideology' was linked to two interconnected processes: the decline of social objectivism and the denial of the possibility of a metalinguistic vantage point which allows the unmasking of ideological distortion. From the first point of view 'ideology' had been considered as a level of the social whole—as in the Marxist trinity of the economic, the political and the ideological. This conception, however, declined, once it was understood that ideological mechanisms were essential to the structuration of both the political and the economic levels. This led to an inflation of the concept of ideology, referred to at the beginning of this chapter, and finally to its abandonment when it was perceived that it had lost all analytic value. Other terms, such as 'discourse', were less ambiguous and better adapted to express a conception of the social link which transcended both objectivism and naturalism.

The history of the second conception of ideology, that related to notions such as false or distorted consciousness, has been different for although the metalinguistic operation of unmasking was no longer considered possible, distorting mechanisms, as we have seen, were given increasing attention as far as they were linked to the creation of the illusion of closure indispensable to the constitution of the social link. It is the study of the mechanisms which make this illusion possible that constitutes the specific field of a contemporary theory of ideology.

We have said before that these mechanisms turn around the forms of representation of an object that is simultaneously necessary and impossible. This is at the root of the constitutive distortion which explains the ideological operation. It consists, as we have seen, in a double process according to which, between closure as an impossible operation and the particularity of the object incarnating it, there is a mutual dependency in which each pole partially limits the effects of the other. We have said enough about the way in which equivalence deforms and weakens the particularity of each of its links. What we have to add now is what happens from the other angle: the effects, on the structuration of the chain, of what remains of those particularities. These remainders are absolutely essential for any equivalence for if they were to vanish, the chain would collapse into simple identity.

Let us take as an example the particular demands which, according to Walzer, give content to 'justice' for the Prague demonstrators: the end of arbitrary arrests, equal and impartial law enforcement, etc. As we have seen, justice', as an empty signifier is not necessarily associated with any of these demands. But, as it has no form of representation of its own, once incarnated in certain demands it becomes in some way imprisoned by them, and is not able to circulate freely. The remainders of particularity (of the links of the chain) limit its possible displacements. Even more: a chain of equivalences can in principle expand indefinitely, but once a set of core links has been established, this expansion is limited. Some new links would simply be incompatible with the remainders of particularity which are already part of the chain. Once the 'end of arbitrary arrests' has become one of the names of 'justice', the 'prevalence of the will of the people over all legal restrictions' could not without difficulty enter into the same system of equivalences. This does not mean that the particularistic remainder of the 'end of arbitrary arrests' will be always the same—on the contrary, new equivalential links can modify the meaning of 'arbitrariness' or of 'arrest'—but the important point is that deformation does not operate unimpeded. There is a resistance of meaning which operates in the opposite direction.

It is through the operation of this double and contradictory movement that the illusion of closure is discursively constructed. This shows us the theoretical (and impossible) conditions under which the end of the ideological could take place. It could only happen if either of the two movements that we have specified could reach its ultimate extreme and fully eliminate the operativity of the other. It would occur if the distortion became actual dissolution, and the equivalence, identity: in that case everything would become an undifferentiated One, and the project of the mystic would have succeeded. But it would also happen if the equivalential logic was eliminated and the remainder of particularity grew to dominate the totality of the object. This is the dream of the different versions of the 'end of ideology', generally associated with the ideal of pure, non-political, administrative practices. In both cases closure would not be an illusion but an actual reality. But both are impossible dreams, ensuring that we will continue living in an ideological universe.

Notes

1 This is what many currents of contemporary thought have shown, from Wittgensteinian later philosophy to deconstruction. My own contributions to this task can be found in *New Reflections on the Revolution of Our Time* (London: Verso, 1990) and in several of the essays collection in *Emancipation(s)* (London: Verso, 1996).
2 Closure is the condition of meaning in so far as all identities, being purely differential, need the system to constitute themselves as identities.
3 But let us remember that this illusion is a necessary one. The argument should be understood as presenting ideology as a dimension of society which cannot be suppressed, not as a critique of ideology.
4 This communitarian reference only applies, of course, to social and political ideologies, which are the ones with which we are primarily concerned. But in other types of ideology the pattern is similar. A scientific paradigm, for instance, can present itself as incarnating the fullness of the pure principle of scientificity. A scientific theory becomes, thus, an ideology, when it becomes a horizon. Darwinism would be a good example.
5 If this is, however, possible in the Christian conception of incarnation it is because what is incarnated is not an absent fullness but an object entirely constituted previous to the act of incarnation, as different from one which depends on that act for its constitution.
6 Walzer takes his notion of 'thickness' from C. Geertz, *The Interpretation of Cultures* (New York: Basic Books, 1973).
7 The question which remains is to see whether the mystical discourse really succeeds in carrying out this universal weakening of meaning through equivalence. It is perhaps possible that, after all, it remains a residual element of particularism which cannot be eliminated. We will return to this question later.

Bibliography

Scholem, G. 1995. *Major Trends in Jewish Mysticism*. New York: Schocken Books.
Sorel, G. 1925. *Reflections on Violence*. London: Allen & Unwin.

Stace, W.T. 1960. *Mysticism and Philosophy*. Philadelphia and New York: J. B. Lippincott.
Walzer, M. 1994. *Thick and Thin: Moral argument at home and abroad*. Notre Dame, IN and London: University of Notre Dame Press.
Žižek, S. 1994. The Spectre of Ideology: Introduction. In *Mapping Ideology*, ed. S. Žižek. London and New York: Verso.

5

IDEOLOGY AND POST-MARXISM (2007)

The editor [Michel Freeden] has asked me to provide an account of the theoretical approach which I have developed in a variety of publications over the last twenty years. In attempting to do so I intend to present an articulation as systematic as possible of the main categories associated with discourse theory in the way in which it has been conceived by myself and by a series of other scholars. It is in the global architectonics of this articulation, rather than in the particular theses composing it, that the contribution of this chapter is to be found.

The starting point of our reflection was an ambiguity to be found in the Marxist conception of history, which had been pointed out very often but which, in our view, had not received the systematic treatment that it deserved. It was the following: history was for Marx, in the first place, an entirely objective process dominated by the contradiction between the development of productive forces and the successive systems of relations of production constitutive of social organisation. The epitome of this objectivist vision was the 'Preface' to the [*Contribution to the*] *Critique of Political Economy,* where social antagonisms play a clearly secondary role, being only the distorted reflection of an underlying necessary logic. On the other hand, however, Marxism also asserted that the history of humanity was the history of class struggle, to quote the famous formulation of the *Manifesto*. How to bring these two visions into unity? My increasing conviction became that this was an impossible task, and that the so-called 'crisis of Marxism' was, to a large extent, the result of this impossibility. By the 1970s this objectivist vision was entirely discredited. The labour theory of value, on which it was grounded, was shown to be plagued by all kinds of theoretical inconsistencies; the key prediction of an increasing simplification of the social structure under capitalism was entirely disproved; and the complexity of social and political identities in a globalised world challenged any narrow, 'class based' perspective.

What, however, about the second vision, the one that challenged a petrified notion of social relations by asserting the centrality of social antagonisms—'class struggle', in Marx's terms? Although the 'class' limits of that vision could certainly be equally put into question, the centrality of the antagonistic moment had lost none of its relevance. It required, it is true, a new awareness of what is involved in an antagonistic relation and, especially, a thinking of that relation which did not subordinate it to the precise locations assigned to it by the objectivist conception. This is the starting point of our post-Marxism.

So how to conceive the nature of an antagonistic relation? For the objectivist conception this was an entirely secondary issue, because the logic of history *passed through* but was not *constituted by* antagonisms. But if the latter are seen as primarily constitutive of the social fabric, the determination of their ontological status becomes a central theoretical issue. We [Ernesto Laclau and Chantal Mouffe] started, in *Hegemony and Socialist Strategy* (1985), by referring to the Kantian distinction between real opposition and contradiction, none of which we saw as being able to grasp what is involved in a social antagonism. Contradiction, as Kant pointed out, can only take place between concepts. This is why an idealist philosophy like Hegel's, which reduces the real to the concept, could conceive of antagonisms as contradictions; but, as the Della Volpian school in Italy pointed out, this is incompatible with a materialist philosophy like Marxism, which asserts the extra-mental character of the real. However, although we agreed on this point with the Della Volpians, we could not follow them in their second thesis, according to which social antagonisms should be conceived in terms of the Kantian real opposition *(Realrepugnanz)*, for the simple reason that real oppositions are not in the least antagonistic. There is nothing antagonistic in the clash between two stones. In that case, however, if neither contradiction nor real opposition has the right credentials to intellectually grasp what is involved in an antagonism, how could we conceive of the latter?

This was the point in which our approach took a radical turn. While both contradiction and real opposition are objective relations—between conceptual objects in the first case, between real objects in the second—antagonisms, for us, are not objective relations but a kind of relation in which the limits in the constitution of any objectivity are shown. How so? From the viewpoint of each of the two antagonistic forces, its opponent is not an objective presence, completing the fullness of one's own identity, but represents, on the contrary, that which makes impossible reaching such a fullness. This means that, as far as we remain within the perspective of each of the two antagonistic forces, the moment *stricto sensu* of the clash, far from being objective, indicates the impossibility of society reaching a full objectivity. To conceive of antagonisms as objective would require the viewpoint of an objective observer, who would see in them an expression of a deeper objectivity escaping the consciousness of the two forces in conflict. This is the task performed by the Hegelian 'cunning of Reason'. But it is exactly the temptation that we have to resist if we are going to see antagonisms as *constitutive* and not *derivative*.

The notion of antagonism as a *limit* of objectivity is, however, only a starting point. A set of issues connected with the notion of 'limit' immediately arises. Let us refer to some of them. Firstly, how exactly to conceive of a limit? If what is beyond the limit is in *pari materia* with what is this side of it, the limit would be a sham, it would just be an internal differentiation within a single space of representation. So a *true* limit should interrupt that space, it should be radically *heterogeneous* with it. We have thus introduced the notion of 'heterogeneity' which, however, is far from transparent and whose true implications can only be approached through a series of steps attempting to unveil its true implications. We could start with a transcendental question: How has an entity to be so that its limits are really heterogeneous—i.e. that they imply a radical interruption of a space of representation? There is a precondition for such an interruption, which is that the gap that it involves should not be the one taking place between regional fields of representation—whose differentiation would itself be fully representable—but should be rather an *aporia* internal to the principle of representation as such. This precondition already excludes a set of candidates as possible paradigms of the basic ontological terrain. All notions of a limit as grounded in *positive* differences are, of course, incompatible with the idea of a radical limit (positive differences presuppose a ground within which they are constituted, so they cannot apprehend what a *radical* limit is). But, for the same reason, dialectical contradictions should be excluded: as in any dialectical contradiction (A—not A) the precondition is that I have in 'A' everything I need to make the transition to 'not A', dialectics has to postulate a single space of representation within which that transition is to take place. Heterogeneity in the radical sense that we are postulating is incompatible with both dialectics (based on contradiction) and with simple opposition (based on contrariety). With this we reach again the conclusion at which we had already arrived: neither contradiction nor real opposition are compatible with the notion of 'limit' that antagonism, as based on radical heterogeneity, requires. So what we need is an ontological terrain in which the failure inherent to representability (the moment of clash present in antagonism which, as we have said, escapes direct representation) becomes itself representable, even if only through the traces of non-representability within the representable (as in Kant's *noumenon*: an object which shows itself through the impossibility of its adequate representation).

Let us enumerate more precisely the transcendental conditions of a terrain in which the notion of antagonism as limit of objectivity can be inscribed. The first and more important one is that what is inscribable within such a terrain should be wider than the field of objective relations (otherwise we would be confined to the exclusive alternative real opposition/dialectical contradiction). Second, what is actually inscribable within that terrain should not be just what is representable, but also the ultimate inner impossibility of representability as such (otherwise we would not have transcended the field of objectivity). Third, the 'entities' constructed around the limit of objectivity could not be *conceptually* graspable (if they were there would be, again, positive objects). Fourth, whatever primacy any entity has over the others, it cannot be the one inherent to a hierarchy within a specifiable differential universe (which necessarily presupposes objective relations other than the non-relational relations that we are looking for). The first condition is met by the notion of *discourse:* the second by that of *empty signifier;* the third by the concept of the *name* as the ground of the thing; the fourth by the notions of *unevenness* and *radical investment,* best shown by the Lacanian notion of object *a* and by the logic of hegemony, which are ultimately identical. Let us summarise the argument around these four conditions.

What does a non-relational relation mean? One that is not inscribable within the field of objectivity because its function is, precisely, to subvert that field. Or, what is the same, one that destabilises the givenness of entities. A clash between two social forces, if we remain at the level of their physical materiality, would entirely belong within the field of the ontically given. This means that the negation of the fullness of being resulting from antagonism expresses itself *through* that field but consists of something beyond it. The presence of the antagonistic other prevents me from fully being myself. So what is necessary is an ontological terrain within which that distance from myself resulting from antagonism could be inscribed. This terrain is what we have called *discourse* and, as we have pointed out several times, it is not restricted to speech and writing but embraces all systems of signification. It is, in that sense, coterminous with social life. The notion of 'language games' in Wittgenstein, which covers both the use of words and the actions which are associated with it, is close to what we understand by 'discourse'. Our project differs, however, from Wittgenstein's as far as we try to explore the ontological implications of linguistic categories—such as 'signifier/signified', 'paradigm/syntagm', etc.—which cease in that way to be merely regional categories of a linguistics conceived in a narrow sense. In some respects we could say that, if we are searching for a terrain in which the subversion of identities resulting from antagonistic relations could be represented, rhetoric should be a privileged field for our inquiry, given that it consists, precisely, in the distancing of all literal meaning as a result of the tropological movement. This is undoubtedly true, but we must add the crucial proviso that rhetoricity is not a literary adornment, external to language, but an internal part of linguistic functioning. Roman Jakobson, for instance, in a decisive turn, has associated metaphor and metonymy with the paradigmatic and syntagmatic poles of language respectively, grounded in relations of substitution and combination. This turn is crucial for our attempt at presenting the discursive terrain as the primary ontological one.

This first step in the direction of a discursive/rhetorical ontology is a necessary one but not, however, sufficient. If we remained at this point we would have simply replaced a dialectic or positivist ontology by a semiotic one, but such replacement would have not made much headway in the direction of explaining antagonistic relations. Language is, according to Saussure, a system of differences, and the latter are, in their interconnections, as objective as the relations of contradiction and real opposition that we have discarded. Something more is needed for our purpose. Let us go back for a moment to rhetorics. According to Cicero, we must appeal to figural language because there are more objects in the world to be named than words at our disposal. This is for him, of course, an empirical deficiency, but if it could be shown that there is in the structure of signification something of the nature of a *constitutive* impossibility, if signification requires the presence of something which cannot be signified as its essential precondition, we would have moved a step further towards the solution of our riddle (the antagonistic clash, which cannot be directly represented as an objective moment, could perhaps be signified in a different way if language has other modes of signification than a direct, objective representation).

The arsenal of rhetoric has a mode of signification which does away with the complementarity literal/figural. It is what is called *catachresis* (a figural term to which no literal one corresponds). Obliqueness is constitutive of catachrestical signification. For reasons I cannot elaborate now there are grounds to think that catachresis is not a specific trope but the mark of rhetoricity as such, present in all tropes. The literal would simply be a term which conceals the traces of its own rhetoricity, so that rhetoricity would be constitutive of language.

Why so? Because for reasons that I have given elsewhere[1] no system of signification can close itself otherwise than through catachrestical displacements. The whole argument is developed in that essay and I will not repeat it here. I will just enumerate its logical steps. They are as follows:

(1) language (and by extension all systems of signification) being essentially differential, its closure is the precondition of signification being possible at all.
(2) Any closure, however, requires the establishment of limits, and no limit can be drawn without, simultaneously, positing what is beyond it.
(3) But as the system is the system of *all* differences, what is beyond the limit can only be of the nature of an exclusion.
(4) The exclusion operates, nonetheless, in a contradictory way: it is, on the one hand, that which makes possible the system of differences as a totality; but, on the other, *vis-à-vis* the excluded element, the differences are no longer merely differential but equivalential to each other. This tension being logically unavoidable, the systemic totality is an object which is, at the same time, impossible and necessary. Impossible: the tension between equivalence and difference being insurmountable, there is no literal object corresponding to that totality. Necessary: without that object there would be no signification.
(5) Conclusion: the impossible object would have to be represented, but this representation would have to be *essentially* distorted and figural. This is the point at which catachresis enters the scene. The possible means of this distorted communication are only the particular differences. So one of them, without ceasing to be particular, has to incarnate that impossible totality. Seen from a certain angle, this is the production of an *empty signifier:* it signifies a totality which is literally impossible. Seen from another angle, this is a *hegemonic* operation (or the construction of a master signifier in the Lacanian sense): a certain particularity transforms its own body in the representation of an incommensurable totality.

We have now all the necessary elements to define what is involved in an antagonistic relation. The moment of the antagonistic clash, which cannot be directly represented, can however be signified—positivised, if you want—through the production of an empty signifier (or two, rather; one at each side of the antagonistic frontier). The camp belonging to one's own identity, which cannot close itself around its ontic particularity because of the presence of the antagonistic force, has to signify itself through a chain of equivalences between its internal contents and through the production of an empty signifier with no signified, for it represents the impossible fullness of the community. And what each of the forces in conflict will see at the other side of the antagonistic frontier will not be a purely ontic content either; that content would just be a means of representation of something different from itself: the anti-community. This gap between ontic *means* of representation is pregnant of a multiplicity of political consequences, the most important being the essential instability of any equivalential chain: no empty signifier can fully control which are the links that will be part of that chain. We see now clearly how the limit of objectivity that the antagonistic clash represents can be signified. Such signification will involve a permanent catachrestical movement. Although the clash has no direct, objective representation, it will show itself through its subversion of the field of objectivity. We are not far away from Lacan's notion of the subversion of the Symbolic by the Real.

There are two other transcendental conditions that the antagonistic relation has to fulfil if it is going to be theoretically perspicuous. The first concerns the theoretical status of the empty signifier. The answer to this question would normally be quite simple: we are dealing with a concept. If the question was concerned with the position of the notion of 'empty signifier' within a theoretical structure, there is no doubt that, whatever that position would be, we would be referring to an entity of a conceptual nature. But the question is not that. The question is about the relation of an empty signifier to the objects it groups under its denomination. We know that any conceptual grouping should be conceived as a *subsumption*. There is something that the concept expresses which is reproduced without alteration in each of the instances of its application. The concept cannot be anything but a universal, and the instances realising it must necessarily reproduce something identical in all of them, a hard common positive core beyond their particularistic variations. Now, what happens if that common core is absent, if the ground of an equivalential relationship is not given by any positive feature underlying the various individual social demands but by their common opposition to something that negates all of them? Here we reach the kernel of an antagonistic relation: the components of each pole of the antagonism are not united by any shared positive feature (in that case we would be dealing with a purely *objective* unity), but by the opposition of all of them to the force with which they are confronted. So the empty signifier—the term which unifies the ensemble of those components—cannot be a concept, for the relation it establishes with the instances it regroups is not one of *conceptual* subsumption. As we know, what is essential in a conceptual subsumption (Kant's determinative judgement would be a typical expression) is that the rule should precede the instances of its application. But the subsumption of a plurality of equivalential links under an empty signifier cannot be a conceptual operation, because of the heterogeneity of those links, whose only common feature is of a negative nature. In that case, if the connection of the empty signifier with the instances it covers is not of a conceptual nature, of what nature is it?

It is a *name*. Let me briefly explain how I see the difference between a nominal and a conceptual order. The central issue is: how do names refer to objects? In my book (*On Populist Reason*)[2] I have addressed this issue, arguing that the two main approaches—descriptivism and anti-descriptivism—part their ways on the crucial issue of whether or not that reference involves a conceptual mediation. The classical descriptivist position—in its various formulations, from John Stuart Mill to Bertrand Russell—asserts that any objective reference involves a conceptual mediation: every name is associated with a set of descriptive features, so that when I find an object in the world showing those features, I apply that name to it. So we are fully within the realm of the Kantian determinative judgement: without the descriptive features functioning as a rule for assigning a name to an object, that assignation would be entirely arbitrary. The second perspective is the anti-descriptivist approach, linked to the work of Saul Kripke and his followers: here the conceptual mediation is absent; naming is a primal baptism, not grounded on any universal rule. Needless to say, our view, which definitely moves away from the notion of conceptual subsumption, clearly locates itself within the anti-descriptivist camp. With one proviso, however. If primal baptism involves assigning a name to an object without any kind of conceptual mediation, a problem, however, persists: is the unity of the object something *given,* so that the name rubber-stamps something already achieved before the process of naming it, or, instead, does the unity of the object result from the act of naming it? Everything we have said about 'empty signifiers' already announces that only the second is, for us, a valid alternative. To put it in Lacanian terms: the unity of the object is only the retroactive effect of naming it. And we can easily see why. If the various determining components of an object shared some essential features preceding the act of naming it, the act of naming would be ancillary to a conceptual mediation. But if those features are heterogeneous and, as a result, radically contingent, the unity of the object has no other ground than the act of naming it. This explains our thesis that *the name is the ground of the thing.* And shows also why no conceptual subsumption can account for the type of unity achieved by an empty signifier within a discursive terrain.

One more structural moment of our approach requires stressing. We have so far indicated how the Real subverts a symbolic fabric, how the limit of objectivity acts retroactively over the latter, distorting its internal coherence. The key of this distortion is to be found in the production of empty signifiers. They—this is a key feature—have an irradiation effect which goes beyond any determinable structural location. This means that the investment they receive cannot be one more structural determination for in that case it would be fully objective and the disruptive effect that they bring about would be lost. It is because of that that we speak of *radical investment*. It is 'radical' because it fully comes from outside and it is 'investment'—almost in a financial sense—because you endow one structural element with a value which does not derive from its location within the structure. This is the reason why all attempts at privileging one structural element over the other—the famous 'determination in the last instance' by the economy, for instance—entirely miss the point. That determination could only be an objective effect, and could not explain the limitation of objectivity which results from an antagonistic presence.

In that case, what is the nature of an investment which is truly radical? In our view, it can only be of an *affective* nature. This assertion requires, however, a precautionary warning. It would be wrong to think that signification would be on the side of objectivity while the affective investment would be a force entirely alien to the signifying process. As I have tried to show in my work[3] this would be a fallacious division because, first, signification requires affect, as far as the paradigmatic pole of language—which Saussure, revealingly, called 'associative'—requires substitutions only possible in terms of an individual experience; and, second, affect is not a force fully constituted outside signification, but only exists through the differential cathexis of a signifying chain. This is the point at which I have tried to link the logic of hegemony to that of the object *a* in Lacanian theory, especially in the way in which it has been presented in the work of Joan Copjec[4]. According to Lacan, sublimation is to elevate an object to the dignity of the Thing (of the Freudian Thing, of course). This means that a certain partial object ceases to be a partiality within a totality—which would reduce it to mere moment within a global structure—and becomes a partiality which *is* the totality. But this is nothing else than the role that we have attributed to the 'empty signifier' in the constitution of a hegemonic formation. So the logics of the object *a* and that of hegemony are not simply homologous: they are identical, as both show how structural effects are possible which, however, are not structurally determined. It is important to fully realise the consequences of this last assertion. In order to have a full overlap between structural determination and structural effects, the structure should be *causa sui*; it should be, in other terms, some kind of Spinozean eternity. And, indeed, that is what is presupposed by all theories which made the mode of production the *fundamentum inconcussum* of the social. As soon, however, as we subvert this self-determination through the presence of a heterogeneous other—as is the case in antagonism—structural effects tend to distance themselves from structural determination—which is the same as saying that the latter is a system of power which, like all power, is exercised over something external to itself. In other terms: once self-determination is over, any structural configuration is going to have conditions of existence that are not generated by itself. In the case of the mode of production this means that, as those conditions of existence are not themselves the result of any determination in the last instance, they are going to be internal to the articulated whole that they help to constitute. This is the reason why the notion of 'mode of production' has to be replaced by that of 'hegemonic formation'.

We can, at this point, return to the question of the transition from Marxism to post-Marxism. The starting point was, as we have indicated, the ultimate incompatibility between the two premises which constituted the terrain of classical Marxism: the vision of history as a story unified by the contradiction between development of productive forces and the various systems of relations of production—a development which was centred in necessary laws; and the notion of a centrality of class struggle—which opened, at least potentially, the possibility of contingent outcomes. If the contradictory nature of these two premises remained concealed for a long time, it was because of the way in which they were articulated in Marxist discourse: the objectivist component had the upper hand and established limits to the full expansion of the logic implicit in the notion of social antagonism. One can only think of the role that the category of 'historical necessity' played in the Marxism of the Second International to see the limits that it put on political creativity and imagination. Once, however, the faith in that historical necessity was weakened, the dams represented by Marxist dogmas were breached in every direction. One has, however, to point out that this was not a collapse but, rather, an orderly overflow: it was simply the development of the potential contained in the centrality of class struggle as motor of historical change once it was no longer limited by the premise of an objectively determined limit. The movement from Marxism to post-Marxism is, to a large extent, the story of this transition.

It is, perhaps, paradoxical, that the first casualty in this transition was the very notion which had made it possible: the centrality of 'class struggle'. How so? The reason is to be found in the inner heterogeneity which we have found as inhabiting the notion of social antagonism. If antagonism could have been explained in a dialectical manner (A—not A), there would have been no problem: both the clash and the agents of the clash would have been determined in the same movement. But we have already explained the reasons why a dialectical transition is radically impotent to explain what goes on in an antagonistic confrontation. If we move, however, to the heterogeneity that we have found at the heart of this antagonistic relation, if its two poles do not belong to the same space of representation, in that case there is no way to root the notion of struggle to a particular social category such as 'class'.

Let us see the true dimensions of a heterogeneous relation. As I have pointed out elsewhere, there is no way of finding the moment of radical heterogeneity in a dialectical transition. Let us see, for instance, the notion that capitalist relations of production are inherently antagonistic. For a dialectical conception which reduces antagonism to contradiction, the first task should be to find a homogeneous terrain within which the contradiction could emerge. To do this I have to reduce the capitalist to an economic category—buyer of labour power—and the same in the case of the worker—seller of labour power. The conclusion was that this relation is intrinsically antagonistic because the capitalist extracts surplus value from the worker. But this conclusion is unwarranted. The relation only becomes antagonistic if the worker *resists* the extraction of surplus value, but I can analyse the category of 'seller of labour power' as much as I like and I will still be unable to logically derive from it the category of 'resistance'. So the very reduction of capitalist and worker to economic categories that the construction of a homogeneous space of dialectical mediation requires makes it impossible to think of the specifically antagonistic moment of the relation. Why could an antagonism, however, exist between workers and capitalists? Because of the way the worker is constituted *outside* the relations of production (the fact that below a certain level of wages he/she cannot live a decent life, etc.). But in that case the conflict is not *inherent* to the relations of production but *between* the relations of production and the way social agents are constituted outside them. The conclusion is clear: the two spaces of representation (the worker's and the capitalist's) are radically heterogeneous, so that the terrain within which a dialectical mediation would have been possible has broken up.

From here the consequences rapidly follow. Once we have concluded that an antagonism presupposes two heterogeneous spaces of representation which are not dialectically mediated there is no reason to assume that locations within the relations of production are going to be privileged points to antagonistic confrontation. Capitalist development creates many others: ecological crises, imbalances between different sectors of the economy, imperialist exploitation, etc. In that case, the subjects of an 'anti-capitalist' struggle are many and cannot be reduced to a category as simple as that of 'class'. We are going to have a plurality of struggles. Struggles in our society tend to proliferate the more we move into a globalised era, but they are less and less 'class' struggles. Could we argue that, however, there is in capitalist societies—as Marx believed in the 19th century—an inner tendency to the simplification of social structure, so that we are advancing towards a situation in which we would have, as the final showdown of history, a simple confrontation between workers and capitalists? To take a brief glance at what goes on in contemporary societies is enough to brush aside this objection without further ado.

One consequence of our analysis is that we have to assert the primacy of politics in the structuration of social spaces. No question any longer of infrastructural logics which, at our backs, would determine the future of our societies. The *political*—the world of contingent articulations—is, it is true, limited by the *social*—the field of sedimented social practices—but the social automatisms of the latter have a decreasing influence in determining the structuration of our communities. The effects, again, of globalisation are clearly visible in this area.

A second consequence is that political actors are *always* going to be, to some extent, *popular* actors. We understand by a 'people' a collective actor resulting from the equivalential reaggregation of a plurality of demands around a nodal point or empty signifier (we have already explained this last category). There are two limits to the constitution of popular actors that we should briefly consider. The first is linked to the sectorialisation of social demands. The heterogeneity linked to social antagonisms can never generate unlimited equivalential chains except at periods of organic crises. In that way the 'populistic' inscription of a demand is always going to find limits which, however, conjuncturally vary. We have thus a tension between the ability of a group to act hegemonically over other sectors and its objective location in a system of relations which puts limits to this hegemonic opening. A trade union, for instance, can act as a rallying point for a variety of other social demands, but the fact that it has to defend the interest of the workers within a very precise institutional framework can act as a fetter to its hegemonic ambitions. The whole Gramscian dialectic between 'corporative' and 'hegemonic' class is the best representation of this tension. (When we are speaking of the structural limitations imposed by a certain framework we are not going back to the 'objectivist' infrastructure that we have criticised. We are not saying that those structural limitations are a bedrock of history whose contradictions would explain the course of the latter, but that any social situation is the result of a negotiation between a symbolic framework and a heterogeneous other that undermines it.)

We have been referring so far to the possibilities and obstacles in creating an anti-system mobilisation. Our second consequence concerns the opposite movement: the reaction to antagonistic mobilisations from those in power. Their general politics can be summarised in one formula: to demobilise the underdog. The anti-political move *par excellence* consists in obtaining, as much as possible, a situation in which all interests become corporative, preventing the formation of a 'people'. The Saint-Simonian formula: 'from the government of men to the administration of things' is a clear expression of this trend. In my book on populism (2005) I have mentioned that in Mexico during the rule of the Institutional Revolutionary Party (PRI), the government was relatively flexible when confronted with individual demands. What it did not tolerate is what they called *'el paquete'* (the parcel)—that is, a global set of demands equivalentially articulated, which would have implied a major political turn. However, there is also possible a populism from power, whenever a major initiative involving drastic changes in the institutional system requires popular mobilisation.

We can, at this point, turn for the last time to the history of Marxism to see how the 'institutionalist' and the 'populist' moments were combined in producing ambiguous political effects. To start with, Marxism was the epitome of the refusal to endorse any kind of populistic reaggregation. The revolutionary perspective was, however, maintained, because just concentrating on the defence of the interests of the workers and letting the 'necessary laws of history' do the rest, they would end up representing the vast mass of the population once the process of proletarianisation had reached a certain level. The combination between the illusory character of this prognostic and the actual politics which made it possible—the defence of the corporative interests of the workers—had paralysing political effects. The trade union location, far from being some kind of 'free territory', was part of the institutional system of the country, so that when the latter was threatened, as happened in 1914, 'national' solidarity prevailed over 'class' ideology. With the division of the working class movement and the emergence of the Comintern, the poverty of pure 'classism' was shown even more clearly: a zigzag oscillation between ultra-leftist adventurism and opportunistic accommodation with the status quo was the trade mark of Communist politics. The 'bolshevisation' of the Communist parties in the 1920s sealed the destiny of this essentially anti-hegemonic orientation. It was only in the few cases in which Stalinist control was relaxed and some Communist movements managed to transform themselves in nodal points of a wider national and popular collective will that the outcome was other than a disastrous defeat. Mao's Long March and Tito's partisan war were perhaps the two main victorious experiences which constructed wider popular identities and showed the limitations of a pure 'class struggle' strategy. Gramsci's theorisation, centred on the notions of 'hegemony' and 'collective will', was the main expression of an alternative strategy which found, however, few followers.

There is a last point to which we have to refer. What about 'ideology', which appears in the title of this chapter? Within the Marxist terrain, there have been two main notions of ideology and both, in my view, should be rejected. The first is the notion of 'false consciousness'; the second, that of ideology as a necessary level of any social formation. The first is linked with the possibility of a 'true' consciousness by a humanity reconciled with itself—and in some of its versions, ideology is opposed to science. The essentialism of this vision has entirely discredited it. As for the second, it is too much linked to the notion of a naturalistic infrastructure being reflected in distorted ideas in the mind of people to have any purchase for contemporary theorisation. We are however, reluctant to entirely abandon the notion of ideology. I think it can be maintained if its meaning is given a particular twist. As we have seen, there is something essentially catachrestical in any precarious stabilisation of meaning. Any 'closure' is necessarily tropological. This means that those discursive forms that construct a horizon of all possible representation within a certain context, which establish the limits of what is 'sayable', are going to be necessarily figurative. They are, as Hans Blumenberg called them, 'absolute metaphors', a gigantic *as if*. This closing operation is what I would still call *ideological* which, in my vocabulary, as should be clear, has not the slightest pejorative connotation.

Notes

1 See my essay 'Why do Empty Signifiers Matter to Politics?', *Emancipation(s)* (London: Verso, 1996). (And this volume Chapter 3.)
2 E. Laclau, *On Populist Reason* (London: Verso, 2005), ch. 4.
3 E. Laclau, 'Glimpsing the Future', in S. Critchley and O. Marchart (eds), *Laclau: A Critical Reader* (London: Routledge, 2004).
4 J. Copjec, *Imagine There's No Woman* (Cambridge, MA: MIT Press, 2002).

Bibliography

Copjec, J. 2002. *Imagine There's No Woman*. Cambridge, MA: MIT Press.
Laclau, E. 1996. *Emancipation(s)*. London: Verso.
——2004. Glimpsing the Future. In *Laclau. A Critical* Reader, ed. S. Critchley and O. Marchart. London: Routledge.
——2005. *On Populist Reason*. London: Verso.
Laclau, E. and Mouffe, C. 1985. *Hegemony and Socialist Strategy: Towards a Radical Democratic Politics*. London: Verso.

PART II
Analysing populism

6

TOWARDS A THEORY OF POPULISM (1977)

'Populism' is a concept both elusive and recurrent. Few terms have been so widely used in contemporary political analysis, although few have been defined with less precision. We know intuitively to what we are referring when we call a movement or an ideology populist, but we have the greatest difficulty in translating the intutition into concepts. This has often led to an *ad hoc* kind of practice: the term continues to be used in a merely allusive way and any attempt to ascertain its content is renounced. David Apter, for example, referring to the new political regimes of the Third World, states:

> What we are witnessing in the world today is a range of accommodated political systems. Even the toughest of them is weak. Even the most monolithic in forms tends to be divided in its practices and diluted in its ideas. Few are totalitarian. Almost all are populist and, in a real sense, mainly *pre*democratic rather than *anti*democratic.
>
> *(Apter 1969, p. 2)*

Throughout his book, despite the fact that the 'populism' of these new regimes plays an important role in their characterisation, Apter nowhere seriously tries to determine the content of the concept he uses.

To the obscurity of the concept is linked the indeterminacy of the phenomenon to which it alludes. Is populism a type of movement or a type of ideology? What are its boundaries? In some conceptions it is limited to certain precise social bases; in others, 'populism' indicates a trait common to political phenomena as disparate as Maoism, Nazism, Peronism, Nasserism or Russian *Narodnichestvo*. The result is a vagueness which contributes little to a scientific analysis of any political phenomenon. The main object of this chapter will be to put forward some propositions that may help us to overcome the traditional imprecision. Our objective, then, will be an essentially theoretical one; reference to concrete 'populist' movements will be made only for purposes of illustration. *Although the concepts to be employed have been developed basically with Latin American experience in mind, their validity is not limited to a determinate historical or geographical context.* We will first discuss various theories of populism, especially functionalist accounts – for these have been the most influential and conceptually refined. We will then present an alternative theoretical schema centred upon the concept of *popular-democratic interpellation.* Finally, we will comment on some characteristics of the historical process experienced by Latin American political systems after 1930, which has made them particularly prone to populist mobilisation.

I

We can single out four basic approaches to an interpretation of populism. *Three of them consider it* simultaneously *as a movement and as an ideology. A fourth reduces it to a purely ideological phenomenon.*

For the first approach populism is the typical expression of a determinate social class and characterises, therefore, both the movement and its ideology. Populism is deemed to be typical of a distinct social class, whatever the concrete example selected. Thus, for those whose focus of study is 19th century Russian *Narodnichestvo,* populism will be presented essentially as a peasant ideology, or an ideology elaborated by intellectuals that exalts peasant values. If the object of analysis is North American populism, it will be considered an ideology and mobilisation typical of a society of small farmers opposed to urban life and big business. Finally, in Latin America, where the mobilisation of urban masses has often acquired populist connotations, it will be seen as the political and ideological expression either of a petty-bourgeoisie, of marginal sectors or of a national bourgeoisie seeking to mobilise the masses for a partial confrontation with the local oligarchies and imperialism. The problems of this kind of interpretation are obvious: it evades the phenomenon it sets out to explain. If one is to maintain that there is at least *one* common element between Varguismo, the movement of William Jennings Bryan and *Narodnichestvo,* and that this element is populism, it is obvious that its specificity must be sought *outside,* not within the social bases of those movements, since they are totally dissimilar. If, on the other hand, the use of the concept is restricted to movements with a similar social base, the area of analysis is illegitimately displaced: the object of explanation is now another phenomenon – the 'something in common' present in many different social movements. Yet it was the definition of this specificity which constituted the original problem. As we shall see, this has been typical procedure by which the specificity of populism has been conjured out of existence. The operation is normally carried out in three steps:

(1) an initial intuitive perception of populism as constituting a common feature shared by quite distinct political movements, which then determines *a priori* that this feature must find its explanation in the social bases of those movements;

(2) concrete populist movements are therefore studied and in the course of research a peculiar transfer of meaning occurs: populism ceases to be considered *a common feature* of various movements and is transformed into a synthetic concept which defines or symbolises the *complex of features* characteristic of the concrete movement under investigation;

(3) henceforth, when it is necessary to provide a definition of what is specific about populism, the analyst – rather than isolating a common feature of various movements – is driven to compare these movements *as such* and to try and determine what they have in common via a typically empiricist procedure of abstraction/generalisation. But, as we said, this attempt cannot get very far, since the so-called populist movements differ fundamentally from each other. Consequently what is generally done in such cases is to continue talking of populism without defining it – which brings us back to our starting point.

The difficulties of establishing the class connotations of populism have often led to a second conception which we might call a kind of theoretical *nihilism*. According to this, 'populism' is a concept devoid of content. It should therefore be eliminated from the vocabulary of the social sciences, and replaced by a direct analysis of the movements which up to now have been called populist – according to their class nature. Hence an analysis of the class bases of any movement is the key to a discovery of its nature. But, we may ask, is that all? Does class analysis really eliminate the problem of populism? It is surely obvious that this is not so. Because at least one unresolved enigma remains: for 'populism' is not just an analytical category but a datum of experience. It is that 'something in common' which is perceived as a component of movements whose social bases are totally divergent. Even if it were a pure illusion or appearance, we would still have to explain the 'illusion' or 'appearance' as such. Peter Worsley has formulated the problem exactly, in the following terms:

> It may well be, then, that to speak of populism as a genus is to assume what needs to be demonstrated: that movements with very different features, separated in time, space and culture, do possess certain crucial attributes which justify our subsuming them consciously and analytically under the same rubric, "populist", despite variations in their other characteristics. If such a term is to be used, we need to specify just what these crucial attributes are, and not simply assume that the arbitrary bandying about of a word implies any resemblances at all, sociologically speaking, between the activities to which it has become attached. Such resemblances may not exist. But since the word *has* been used, the existence of the verbal smoke might well indicate a fire somewhere.
>
> *(Worsley 1970, p. 219)*

We can even accept the argument that populism is insufficient to define the concrete specificity of a certain kind of political movement. But can we deny that it constitutes an abstract element of it? These are questions that a mere stance of nihilism cannot answer. Hence the inadequacies of this type of approach. Despite its conceptual indefinition, populism continues to enjoy a good health in the social sciences.

A third conception tries to overcome these difficulties by restricting the term 'populism' to the characterisation of an ideology and not a movement. The typical features of this ideology are deemed to be hostility to the status quo, mistrust of traditional politicians, appeal to the people and not to classes, anti-intellectualism and so on. The ideological complex thus formed can then be adopted by social movements with different bases, according to concrete historical conditions about which it is impossible to formulate any *a priori* generalisation. But this type of analysis, although it can enrich – in fact has enriched – the study of the *forms* in which populism has appeared, contains two major inadequacies.

(1) The characteristic features of populist ideology are presented in a purely descriptive way, that is, incapable of constructing their peculiar unity.
(2) Nothing is said of the role played by the strictly populist element in a determinate social formation.

Finally, there is the functionalist conception of populism. For the latter, populism is an aberrant phenomenon produced by the asynchronism of the processes of transition from a traditional to an industrial society. The functionalist account is by far the most consistent and developed of all the conceptions we have mentioned so far. In order to discuss it, let us take as an example the well-known model of Gino Germani, together with the derivative analyses of Torcuato Di Tella.

The process of economic development is conceived by Germani (1965), following a well-established sociological tradition, as a transition from a traditional to an industrial society. This transition involves three basic changes: (1) modification of the type of social action: shift from a predominance of prescriptive to elective actions; (2) passage from an institutionalisation of tradition to that of change; (3) evolution from a relatively undifferentiated complex of institutions to an increasing differentiation and specialisation of them. These three basic changes are accompanied by profound modifications in the predominant type of social relations and personality. (For example, he suggests that modernisation of the attitude of children towards parents and wives towards husbands will provoke changes in the attitudes of parents towards children and husbands towards wives. However, these latter attitudes, reflecting the dominant element in the relationship, will not necessarily be modern in themselves.) In this model, transitional stages are considered in the form of *asynchronism* –that is to say a coexistence of elements belonging respectively to the two poles of traditional and industrial society. This asynchronism may be *geographical* (dual society; central and peripheral countries or regions); *institutional* (coexistence of institutions corresponding to different phases); *sociological* ('the "objective" characteristics – e.g. occupation, position in the socio-economic structure – and "subjective" characteristics – attitudes, social character, social personality – of certain groups correspond to "advanced" stages, while those of other groups correspond to a "backward" stage'); or *motivational* ('because the same individual belongs to multiple different groups and institutions, asynchronism affects the individual himself. There coexist in his psyche attitudes, ideas, motivations, beliefs corresponding to successive "stages" of the process'). The fit or correspondence between these heterogeneous elements, however, is not reduced to a mere coexistence. The modernisation of one of them will provoke changes in the others, although not necessarily in a modern direction.

Two of these forms of symbiosis appear particularly important to Germani: the *demonstration effect* and the *fusion effect*. In the case of the first, habits and mentalities that correspond to the more advanced stages of developments are diffused in backward areas (such as consumption habits which bear no relation to low levels of production). In the case of the second, ideologies and attitudes corresponding to an advanced stage, on being reinterpreted in a backward context, tend to reinforce traditional features themselves. Two other concepts of key importance in Germani's analysis are those of *mobilisation* and *integration*. By *mobilisation*[1] is understood the process whereby formerly passive groups acquire *deliberative* behaviour (i.e. intervention in national life, which may oscillate between inorganic protest movements and legalised activity channelled through political parties). By *integration* is understood that type of mobilisation:

(1) which is carried out through existing politico-institutional channels and is thus legalised by the regime in power;
(2) in which the regime's framework of legitimacy is implicitly or explicitly accepted by the mobilised groups, such that the rules of the game of the existing legality are accepted.

Using this conceptual system, Germani develops a theoretical framework for an understanding of the emergence of populist movements – or national and popular movements, as he calls them. This theoretical framework is established by a comparison between the historical experience of the transition in Europe and in Latin America. In Europe a clear distinction can be registered between two stages: democracy with limited participation and democracy with total participation. During the first stage the foundations of a rational State with a bureaucratic type of authority are established; there is individual liberty and a liberal State, but political rights are reserved for the bourgeoisie, while popular classes remain shackled to a traditional mentality and unintegrated into the new forms of society; 'capitalist asceticism' predominates, and an ethic of production takes precedence over that of consumption. In the second stage the masses become integrated into political and urban life: but what is important is that this mobilisation occurs by way of a process of integration, which avoids great traumas or profound ruptures in political apparatus of the State.

> The difference between the example of England and other Western countries and the case of Latin America lies, then, in the different degree of

correspondence between the gradual mobilisation of an increasing proportion of the population (and eventually all of it) and the emergence of multiple mechanisms of integration – trade unions, education, social legislation, political parties, mass consumption – capable of absorbing these successive groups, providing them with means for adequate self-expression, both academically and lyrically, as well as other basic aspects of modern culture'

(Germani 1965, p. 154).

To these changes were added, in European countries, the transition to a new capitalism of big corporations and the predominance of consumer society and the welfare state.

In present-day [1977] underdeveloped societies, and especially in Latin America where Germani concentrates his analysis, the demonstration effect, the fusion effect and asynchronisms far greater than those known in the process of European transition, unite to produce a characteristic political consequence: the impossibility of a *mobilisation* carried out through *integration*. Consequently, mobilisation takes place in aberrant and anti-institutional ways, which constitute the matrix from which emerge the national-popular movements. At the same time the new historical climate of the 20th century, characterised by the decline of liberal democracy and the rise of fascist and communist totalitarianisms, has contributed to this result. This is typically reflected in the ideologies of industrialisation, whose essential characteristics seem to be authoritarianism, nationalism and one or other form of socialism, collectivism or State capitalism, that is to say, movements which combine in various ways ideological contents corresponding to opposed political traditions. The result was authoritarianism of the left, nationalism of the left, socialism of the right and a multiplicity of hybrid, even paradoxical, formulas from the point of view of the right-left dichotomy (or continuum). It is precisely these forms, despite their diverse and in many ways opposed variants, that we can subsume beneath the generic label of "national-popular" movements, and which seem to represent the peculiar form of intervention into political life of those strata in the course of rapid mobilisation in countries with delayed industrialisation (Germani 1965, p. 157).

Germani's explanation of populism, then, boils down to this: the premature incorporation of the masses into Latin American political life created a pressure which went beyond the channels of absorption and participation which the political structures were able to provide. Consequently, mass integration on the model of 19th century Europe could not be carried out, and various elites, influenced by the new historical climate of the 20th century, manipulated the newly-mobilised masses to serve their own ends. The mentality of these masses, because of their insufficient integration, was characterised by the coexistence of traditional and modern features. Hence populist movements constitute a haphazard accumulation of fragments corresponding to the most dissimilar paradigms. Note the following paragraph of Germani, reminiscent of the 'chaotic enumeration' of surrealist poetry:

We have here something difficult to understand within the experience of 19th century Europe. Quite different political groups, nationalists of the extreme right, fascists or Nazis, Stalinist communists, all the variations of Trotskyism – and the most diverse sectors – intellectuals, modernised workers, professionals and politicians of petty-bourgeois origin, military men, sectors of the old landowning "oligarchy" in economic and political decline, no less than the most bizarre combinations between them, have tried (sometimes successfully) to base themselves upon this human support in order to achieve their political aims. Obviously, these aims do not always coincide with the aspirations of the mobilised layers themselves, although there can sometimes be an identity of aspirations and objectives between elites and masses.

(Germani 1965, p. 158)

A more detailed analysis of populism and its variants, in a similar theoretical perspective to that of Germani, is to be found in a well-known essay by Torcuato Di Tella (1970, pp. 47–74). Populism is defined here as

a political movement which enjoys the support of the mass of the urban working class and/or peasantry, but which does not result from the autonomous organisational power of either of these two sectors. It is also supported by non-working class sectors upholding an anti-status quo ideology.

(Di Tella 1970, p. 47)

In other words, social classes are present in populism but not as classes; a peculiar distortion has separated the *class nature* of these sectors and their forms of political expression. Like Germani, Di Tella associates this distortion with an asynchronism between processes of economic, social and political development. In the case of populism, it is the 'revolution of rising expectations' and the 'demonstration effect' that is responsible for the asynchronism.

The mass media raise the levels of aspirations of their audience, particularly in the towns and among the educated. This is what has been aptly called the "revolution of rising expectations". ... Radio, the cinema, the ideals of the Rights of Man, and written constitutions – all tend to produce effects greater than those produced in the European experience. Yet economic expansion lags behind, burdened by demographic explosion, by lack of organisational capacity, by dependence on foreign markets and capital, or by premature efforts at redistribution. A bottleneck necessarily develops, with expectations soaring high above the possibilities of satisfying them.

(Di Tella 1970, p. 49)

It is precisely this distortion which makes it impossible for the political system to function in the Western style and consequently leads to the emergence of populism.

In these conditions, it is difficult for democracy to function properly. In Western experience democracy was traditionally based on the principle of no taxation without representation. In the developing countries, the revolution of rising expectations generates a desire to have representation without ever having been taxed. Groups lacking sufficient economic or organisational national power demand a share in both the goods and decision-making process of society. They no longer "know their place" as European workers knew theirs until recently. They form a disposable mass of supporters, larger and more demanding than any Louis Napoleon would have dreamed of.
(Di Tella 1970, p. 49)

However, a further element is necessary for this mass to be mobilised in a populist direction: the appearance of an élite committed to the process of mobilisation. Di Tella explains the emergence of an élite to lead the populist movement by a new aberrant phenomenon: the existence among these sectors of a status incongruence between aspirations and 'job satisfaction'. The essential features of populism must therefore be sought: (1) in an élite imbued with an anti-status quo ideology; (2) in a mobilised mass generated by a 'revolution of rising expectations'; (3) in an ideology with a widespread emotional appeal. Within this theoretical framework, Di Tella develops a classification of populist movements according to whether or not the leading élite belongs to the upper levels of the social stratification system, and to the degree of acceptance or rejection which these élites experience in their groups of origin.

As we can see, Di Tella's conception is as teleological as that of Germani. At one pole is traditional society; at the other, fully developed industrial society. The roots of populism are to be sought in the asynchronism between the processes of transition from one to the other. Populism thus constitutes the form of political expression of popular sectors when they are unable to establish an autonomous organisation and class ideology. To a higher degree of development would correspond more of a 'class' and less of a 'populist' organisation. Peronism, for example, occupies an intermediate position on this continuum. From the point of view of the working class, Western-style trade unionism would constitute the paradigmatic form of representation of its interests congruent with a highly developed society. (Note that the conception of populism as an aberrant expression of asynchronism in development processes does not necessarily – although frequently it may – imply a negative evaluation of its role in the historical contexts where it appears. Di Tella, for example, considers that populism, although a transitional phenomenon, is an important and positive instrument of reform and change.)

The first objection that the Germani-Di Tella analysis prompts is whether populism can be assigned to a transitional stage of development. Populist experiences have also taken place in 'developed' countries: think of Qualunquismo in Italy or Poujadisme in France, even the fascist experience, which most conceptions consider as a *sui generis* form of populism. To link populism to a determinate *stage* of development is to make the same mistake as many interpretations in the

1920s – including that of the Comintern – which regarded fascism as an expression of Italy's agrarian underdevelopment, which could not therefore be repeated in advanced industrialised countries such as Germany. It is true that populist experiences in the capitalist metropoles are less frequent than in peripheral countries, but can we therefore conclude that this is due to the different *levels of development* of the two? The argument implies highly questionable assumptions:

(1) the greater the level of economic development, the less likelihood of populism;
(2) after a certain threshold, when the asynchronisms of the development process have been overcome, industrial societies are immune from the populist phenomenon;
(3) 'backward' societies which are today undergoing populist experiences – whether regarded positively or negatively – will necessarily advance towards more 'modern' and 'class' forms of channelling popular protest.

These assumptions constitute a set of perfectly arbitrary ideological axioms. What is more, the theory does not provide us with the instruments necessary to ascertain its validity. For the concept of 'industrial society' has not been theoretically constructed – it is the result of an *ad quem* extension of certain features of advanced industrial societies and the simple descriptive addition of those features; while the concept of 'traditional society' is merely the antithesis of each of the features of industrial society taken individually. Within this schema, transitional stages can only consist of the coexistence of features belonging to both poles. Hence 'populist' phenomena can only appear as a confused and motley assortment of 'traditional' and 'modern' characteristics. Hence, too, the appearance of modernising elites appealing to populist mass mobilisation is not satisfactorily explained. (Unless we consider as an explanation what is in reality the reproduction of the problem in different terms – such as the status-incongruence hypothesis; or we accept, with Germani, explanations such as the demonstration effect of the new historical climate created by the crisis of liberal democracy – which appears to be more of an infection than a demonstration effect.) Hence, finally, the misuse of explanations in terms of *manipulation,* which either regress to pure moralism (deceit, demagogy) or, in trying to explain what made the 'manipulation' possible, return to the terms of the traditional society/industrial society dichotomy; masses with traditional features are suddenly incorporated into urban life, and so on. The conclusion is unavoidable that in this conception, populism is never defined in itself but only in counterposition to a prior paradigm.

The second criticism to be made of the theory is this. Given that the concepts of the two types of society have not been theoretically constructed but are the result of a simple descriptive addition of their characteristic features, there is no way of understanding the significance of a phenomenon apart from indicating its relative degree of progress: that is, its location on the continuum which leads from traditional society to industrial society. This degree of progress is, in turn, reduced to the respective proportion of 'traditional' and 'modern' elements which enter into the definition of the phenomenon under analysis. Germani would no doubt object that he not only takes into account the presence of isolated elements but also their *functions,* in as much as the bulk of his analysis is devoted *precisely* to studying the particular forms assumed by the combination of elements belonging to the various stages – such as the demonstration and fusion effects – and the real function of those combinations in society as a whole. Let us consider this problem for a moment. In studying the fusion effect, Germani clearly appreciates – and this is certainly a merit – that certain forms of 'modernisation' are not only compatible with but tend to reinforce traditional forms (the modernisation of consumption patterns of traditional oligarchic sectors, for example, can in his analysis contribute to the strengthening of a precapitalist consumption ethic and the maintenance of traditional patterns in the sphere of production). So far there would be no objection; indeed, the chosen word, 'fusion', aptly describes the fact that the 'traditional' and 'modern' elements lose their identity as such in the resulting mélange. But if the logic of the case is developed, it comes to negate the premises on which the whole reasoning is based. Let us follow this line of argument:

(1) If we accept that the modernisation of certain aspects of society is not necessarily an indicator of the modernisation of that society as a whole – on the contrary, the modernisation of partial aspects can result in a strengthening of a traditional social pattern – we must admit that one society can be more 'traditional' than another from the point of view of some or most of its features, and nevertheless be more 'modern' from the point of view of its structure. This means, on one hand, that the structure cannot be reduced to the mere descriptive addition of its features, and on the other, that the variable relationship between these features and the whole is such that the former, considered in themselves, lack any specific meaning.
(2) Henceforth a structural element is introduced into the analysis, from it follows a need to abandon the analysis of transition in terms of a *continuum* of features and attitudes, and to confront it as a *discontinuous* series of structures.
(3) Consequently, if the elements considered in isolation lose significance in themselves, to unite them in the paradigms of a 'traditional society' and 'industrial society' is meaningless. Any assertion that the isolated elements have an essence 'in themselves' that is separate from the structures and consists of their insertion into a prior paradigm is a metaphysical statement without legitimacy.

It follows that the categories that enable us to conceptualise concrete societies are analytical ones devoid of any historical dimension (if by the latter we are to understand that the notion of stage is present in the very definition of the concept). Consequently, the concepts of *modernisation, asynchronism* and in general all those which introduce a teleological perspective into scientific analysis, also lose validity. Germani has incorporated a structural dimension into his analysis with concepts like 'demonstration effect' and 'fusion effect', but he has not taken the consequence of this incorporation to its logical conclusion. For he has retained a teleological approach to the analysis of political phenomena. The elements which 'fuse' are either absolutely 'traditional' or absolutely 'modern'. In what, then, does this process of 'fusion' consist? On this point Germani avoids constructing a concept that would enable us to understand it – 'fusion' is an allusive or metaphorical name, but not a concept – and he substitutes for this construction an explanation in terms of origins: fusion is the result of asynchronism. That is to say, the fusion effect only explains what is intelligible within the terms of our two paradigms: the elements which fuse. As generally occurs with explanations in terms of paradigms, all we know at the end of the analysis is what we already knew at the beginning. Paradigms only explain themselves.

Whether or not a teleological perspective and an explanation in terms of paradigms is retained has important consequences for the analysis of concrete political processes. Let us take a common example in the literature on populism: that of the new migrant. This is often cited in order to explain why social sectors coming from backward rural areas, on entering the labour force of newly expanding urban industries, have difficulty in developing European-style trade unionism and are easily won over by mobilisations of a populist kind. Germani and others tend to explain this phenomenon as essentially the result of two processes:

(1) politically inexperienced masses bring with them from rural areas a traditional type of mentality and ideology, which they have not had time to surpass towards a modern ideology and style of political action similar to that of the European working class;
(2) asynchronisms in the development process prematurely throw these masses into political action, whereupon the absence of a developed 'class consciousness' yields deviant forms of mobilisation and does not result in an autonomous organisational activity of the class as such.

It is obvious that recently-arrived migrants bring with them a rural type of mentality. It is also obvious that this mentality is transformed in contact with an urban milieu and industrial activity. The problems begin when we try to measure the degree of 'modernity' of these ideologies according to a paradigm constituted by the experience of the European working class; they are multiplied if we consider that any deviation from this paradigm is an expression of the perpetuation of traditional elements. Let us look at this more closely. Having arrived at an urban centre, the migrant starts to experience a complex of pressures: class exploitation in new places of work, transforming him into a proletarian; multiple pressures of urban society – problems of housing, health, education – through which he enters into a dialectical and conflictual relationship with the State. Under these circumstances, a natural reaction would be to assert the symbols and ideological values of the society from which he has come, in order to express his antagonism towards the new society which exploits him. Superficially this would seem to be the *survival* of old elements, but in reality, behind this survival is concealed a *transformation*:

these 'rural elements' are simply the raw materials which the ideological practice of the new migrants transforms in order to express new antagonisms. In this sense, the resistance of certain ideological elements to their articulation in the dominant discourse of older urban sectors *can* express exactly the opposite of traditionalism: a refusal to accept capitalist legality which in this sense – reflecting the most radical of class conflicts – expresses a more 'advanced' and 'modern' attitude than European-style trade unionism. The scientific study of ideologies presupposes precisely the study of this kind of transformation – which consists in a process of articulation and disarticulation of discourses – and of the *ideological terrain* which gives them meaning. But this process is unintelligible so long as ideological elements are pre-assigned to essential paradigms.

The conclusion to be drawn from the foregoing analysis is unequivocal: the meaning of the ideological elements identified with populism must be sought in the structure of which they are a moment, and not in ideal paradigms. These structures seem to refer – again unmistakably – to the class nature of populist movements, to their roots in modes of production and their articulation. Therewith, however, our exploration of theories of populism seems to become circular: we started by pointing out the impossibility of linking the strictly populist element to the *class* nature of a determinate movement; we then analysed theories which present it as the expression of situations in which classes cannot fully express themselves as such; now we conclude that the ideological features which result from these situations only make sense if we refer them to the structures of which they are part, that is to class structures.

II

There would appear to be no way out of a vicious circle. On the one hand, the strictly 'populist' element only finds its specificity if we leave aside consideration of the class nature of concrete populist movements. Yet on the other hand, we must refer to class contradictions as a fundamental structural moment in order to discover the principle of unity of various isolated political and ideological features. However, if we look more closely at the problem, we can see that this vicious circle is in reality the result of a confusion. This confusion arises from a failure to differentiate two aspects: the general problem of *class determination* of political and ideological superstructures, and the *forms of existence* of classes at the level of these superstructures. Note that these are two distinct problems: to assert the class determination of superstructures does not mean establishing the *form* in which this determination is exercised. (Or, to put it in another way, the form in which classes as such are present in them.) To regard these two problems as identical can be justified only if social classes at the ideological and political level are conceived by way of a process of *reduction*. In effect, if every ideological and political element has a *necessary* class belonging, it is obvious that a class is also expressed *necessarily* through each such element; therewith, the political and ideological forms of existence of a class are reduced, as necessary moments, to an unfolding of its essence.

Classes then no longer *determine* political and ideological *superstructures,* but *absorb* them as a necessary moment in their process of self-unfolding. This kind of interpretation can, as is well known, be lent an economist perspective – common in the Marxism of the Second or Third Internationals – that theorises superstructures as a *reflection* of relations of production, or a 'superstructuralist' perspective (Lukács or Korsch) that makes 'class consciousness' the basic, constitutive moment of class as such. In both cases, however, the relationship between *class* and *superstructure* is conceived in equally reductionist terms. Similarly, this conception leads to an identification between classes as such and empirically observable social groups. Because if every feature of any given group can be reduced – at least in principle – to its class nature, there is no way of distinguishing between the two. The relation between the insertion of the group in the process of production – its class nature – and its 'empirical' features would be of the kind that medieval philosophy established between *natura naturans* and *natura naturata*. It is easy to see, then, why a conception which makes *class reduction* the ultimate source of intelligibility of any phenomenon has met with particular difficulties in the analysis of populism, and has oscillated between reducing it to the expression of class interests – or of the immaturity of a class – and continuing to use the term in an undefined and purely allusive way.

Let us, however, follow a different line of argument. Let us abandon the reductionist assumption and define classes as the poles of antagonistic production relations which have no *necessary*[2] form of existence at the ideological and political levels. Let us assert, at the same time, the determination in the last instance of historical processes by the relations of production, that is to say, by classes. Three basic consequences follow from this change in emphasis:

(1) *It is no longer possible to think of the existence of classes, at the ideological and political levels, by way of a process of reduction*. If classes are present at the ideological and political levels – since relations of production maintain the role of determination in the last instance – and if the *contents* of ideology and of political practice cease to be the *necessary* forms of existence of classes at these levels, the only way of conceiving this presence is to say that the class character of an ideology is given by its *form* and not by its *content*. What does the form of an ideology consist of? The answer is in the principle of articulation of its constituent interpellations. The class character of an ideological discourse is revealed in what we could call its *specific articulating principle*. Let us take an example: nationalism. Is it a feudal, bourgeois or proletarian ideology? Considered in itself it has no class connotation. The latter only derives from its specific articulation with other ideological elements. A feudal class, for example, can link nationalism to the maintenance of a hierarchical-authoritarian system of a traditional type – we need only think of Bismarck's Germany. A bourgeois class may link nationalism to the development of a centralised nation-state in fighting against feudal particularism, and at the same time appeal to national unity as a means of neutralising class conflicts – think of the case of

France. Finally, a communist movement can denounce the betrayal by capitalist classes of a nationalist cause and articulate nationalism and socialism in a single ideological discourse – think of Mao, for example. One could say that we understand by nationalism something distinct in the three cases. This is true, but our aim is precisely to determine where this difference lies. Is it the case that nationalism refers to such diverse contents that it is not possible to find a common element of meaning in them all? Or rather is it that certain common nuclei of meaning are connotatively linked to diverse ideological-articulatory domains? If the first solution were accepted, we would have to conclude that ideological struggle as such is impossible, since classes can only compete at the ideological level if there exists a common framework of meaning shared by all forces in struggle. It is precisely this background of shared meanings that enables antagonistic discourses to establish their difference. The political discourses of various classes, for example, will consist of antagonistic efforts of articulation in which each class presents itself as the authentic representative of 'the people', of 'the national interest', and so on. If, therefore, the second solution – which we consider to be the correct answer – is accepted, it is necessary to conclude that *classes exist at the ideological and political level in a process of articulation and not of reduction.*

(2) Articulation requires, therefore, the existence of non-class contents[3] – interpellations and contradictions – which constitute the raw material on which class ideological practices operate. These ideological practices are determined not only by a view of the world consistent with the insertion of a given class in the process of production, but also by its relations with other classes and by the actual level of class struggle. The ideology of a dominant class does not merely consist of a *Weltanschauung* which ideologically expresses its essence, but is a functioning part of the system of rule of that class. The ideology of the dominant class, *precisely because it is dominant,* interpellates not only the members of that class but also members of the dominated classes. The concrete form in which the interpellation of the latter takes place is a partial absorption and neutralisation of those ideological contents through which resistance to the domination of the former is expressed. The characteristic method of securing this objective is to eliminate antagonism and transform it into a simple difference. A class is hegemonic not so much to the extent that it is able to impose a uniform conception of the world on the rest of society, but to the extent that it can articulate different visions of the world in such a way that their potential antagonism is neutralised. The English bourgeoisie of the 19th century was transformed into a hegemonic class not through the imposition of a uniform ideology upon other classes, but to the extent that it succeeded in articulating different ideologies to its hegemonic project by an elimination of their antagonistic character: the aristocracy was not abolished, in the Jacobin style, but was reduced to an increasingly subordinate and decorative role, while the demands of the working class were partially absorbed – which resulted in reformism and trade unionism. The particularism and *ad hoc*

nature of dominant institutions and ideology in Great Britain does not, therefore, reflect an inadequate bourgeois development but exactly the opposite: the supreme articulating power of the bourgeoisie.[4] Similarly, ideologies of dominated classes consist of articulating projects which try to develop the potential antagonisms constituting a determinate social formation. What is important here is that the dominant class exerts its hegemony in two ways: (1) through the articulation into its class discourse of non-class contradictions and interpellations; (2) through the absorption of contents forming part of the ideological and political discourses of the dominated classes. The presence of working-class demands in a discourse – the eight-hour day, for example – is insufficient to determine the class nature of that discourse. The political discourse of the bourgeoisie also came to accept the eight-hour day as a 'just' demand, and to adopt advanced social legislation. This is a clear proof that it is not in the presence of determinate *contents* of a discourse but in the articulating principle which unifies them that we must seek the class character of politics and ideology.

Can a dominant class, through the successive accumulation of elements from ideological discourses of dominated classes, reach a point at which its very class articulating principles are called into question? This is the thesis argued by C.B. Macpherson, for example. He wrote of the dilemmas of liberal-democratic theory in the 20th century, that 'It must continue to use the assumptions of possessive individualism, at a time when the structure of market society no longer provides the necessary conditions for deducing a valid theory of political obligation from those assumptions' (1972, p. 65). Class struggle determines changes in the ideological-articulating capacity of classes. When a dominant class has gone too far in its absorption of contents of the ideological discourse of the dominated classes, it runs the risk that a crisis may reduce its own neutralising capacity and that the dominated classes may impose their own articulating discourse within the State apparatus. That is the case today in Western Europe, where the expansion of monopoly capital is becoming more and more contradictory to the liberal democratic institutions created by the bourgeoisie in its competitive stage, and where consequently the defence and extension of democratic liberties are becoming more and more linked to an alternative socialist discourse. Another more classic example, is the transformation, described by Lenin, of democratic banners into socialist banners in the course of a revolutionary process.

(3) The third conclusion that follows from the analysis is that if classes are defined as the antagonistic poles of a mode of production, and if the relation between the levels of production and the levels of political and ideological superstructures must be conceived in the form of articulation and not of reduction, classes and empirically observable groups do not necessarily coincide. Individuals are the bearers and points of intersection of an accumulation of contradictions, not all of which are class contradictions. From this follows:

(a) Although class contradictions take priority in this accumulation of contradictions, and although any other contradiction exists articulated to class discourses, it cannot be concluded – since we have eliminated the reductionist assumption – that the class which articulates these other contradictions is necessarily the class to which the individual belongs. This is the phenomenon of 'alienation' or 'false consciousness' – terms with which subjectivist theories have tried to explain the ideological colonisation of one class by another and which, since they assigned a class belonging to every ideological element, they could only conceive as a collapse or an inadequate development of 'class consciousness'. Within our theoretical framework, on the contrary, this kind of phenomenon would correspond to those situations where the non-class interpellations and contradictions in which the individual participates are subjected to the articulating principle of a class distinct from that to which the individual belongs.

(b) If classes constitute themselves as such at the level of production relations, and if the articulating principle of a discourse is always a class principle, it follows that those sectors – such as the middle classes – which do not participate in the relations of production that are basic to a society will lack an articulating principle of their own and the unification of their ideology will depend on other classes. They can never constitute themselves, therefore, as hegemonic classes.

(c) If the hegemony of a class consists in the articulation into its own discourse of non-class interpellations, and if classes only exist at the political and ideological level as articulating principles, it follows that a class only exists as such at those levels to the extent that it struggles for its hegemony.

It follows from the previous analysis that it is possible to assert the class belonging of a movement or an ideology and, at the same time, to assert the non-class character of some of the interpellations which constitute it. At this point we can start to perceive where the enigma of 'populism' lies and to glimpse a possible way out of the vicious circle into which analysis of various theories of populism led us. If we can prove that the strictly 'populist' element does not lie in the movement as such, nor in its characteristic ideological discourse – for these always have a class belonging – but in a specific non-class contradiction articulated into that discourse, we will have resolved the apparent paradox. Our next task, therefore, must be to determine whether or not this contradiction exists.

Let us begin by asking if there is a common nucleus of meaning in all the uses to which the term 'populism' has been put. It is evident that the term is ambiguous, but the problem is to determine what kind of ambiguity. Aristotle distinguished between three kinds of terms: those which only permitted one meaning he called *univocal;* those which admitted two meanings but with no relation between them apart from the verbal unity of the name he called *equivocal;* finally, he called *analogical* those terms which have quite distinct meanings, but in which we can find reference to a common element which constitutes the analogic basis of all possible uses of the term (for example, 'healthy', which can be applied to a person, a walk, a climate, a meal, but which throughout its different uses retains a common reference to *health* – which is thus the analogical basis of all the possible uses of the term 'healthy'). Now, is the ambiguity we observe in the term 'populism', equivocal or analogical? The answer must be that it is the second, because despite the wide diversity in the uses of the term, we find in all of them the common reference to an analogical basis which is *the people*. According to a widely-known theory, populism is characterised by its appeal to the people above class divisions. This definition fails both by excess and by default: by default, since a populist discourse can refer *both* to the people *and* to classes (presenting, for example, a class as the historical agent of the people's interests); and by excess since, as we will see, not all reference to 'the people' automatically transforms a discourse into a 'populist' one. But in any case, it is certainly true that reference to 'the people' occupies a central place in populism. This is where we find the basic source of the ambiguity surrounding 'populism': *the people* is a concept without a defined theoretical status; despite the frequency with which it is used in political discourse, its conceptual precision goes no further than the purely allusive or metaphorical level. We said at the outset of this chapter that 'populism' is both an elusive and a recurrent concept. Now we understand why it is elusive: all the uses of the term refer to an analogical basis which, in turn, lacks conceptual precision. The recurrence of the term remains to be explained. Some light may be thrown on why it continues to be used, if we could show that the notion of 'the people' is linked to a specific contradiction which, although not theoretically defined, is of decisive importance in the analysis of any political conjuncture.

This is the point at which our previous analysis may clarify matters. 'The people' is not merely a rhetorical concept but an objective determination, one of the two poles of the dominant contradiction at the level of a concrete social formation. Let us recall the main conclusions of our analysis:

(1) the 'people'/power bloc contradiction is an antagonism whose intelligibility depends not on the relations of production but the complex of political and ideological relations of domination constituting a determinate social formation;
(2) if the dominant contradiction at the level of the mode of production constitutes the specific domain of class struggle, the dominant contradiction at the level of a concrete social formation constitutes the specific domain of the popular-democratic struggle;
(3) however, as class struggle takes priority over popular-democratic struggle, the latter only exists articulated with class projects. But, in turn, as political and ideological class struggle takes place on a terrain constituted by non-class interpellations and contradictions, this struggle can only consist of antagonistic projects for the articulation of those non-class interpellations and contradictions.

This perspective opens up the possibility for understanding a phenomenon which has not received an adequate explanation in Marxist theory: *the relative continuity* of popular traditions, in contrast to the historical discontinuities which characterise class structures. Marxist political discourse – like any radical popular discourse – abounds in references to 'the secular struggle of the people against oppression', 'popular traditions of struggle', to the working class as 'the agent of uncompleted popular tasks', and so on. As we know, these traditions are crystallised in symbols or values in which the subjects interpellated by them find a principle of identity. One could say that we have here symbols of merely emotional value and that appeal to them has only a rhetorical significance. But this kind of explanation – apart from not making clear why the emotional appeal is effective – does not succeed in resolving a real dilemma. If we accept the universality of the class criterion, and at the same time speak of the *secular* struggle of the people against oppression, the ideology in which that secular struggle is crystallised can only be that of a class other than the working class – since the latter only arises with modern industrialism. But in that case, the appeal to this tradition in socialist discourse would constitute crass opportunism, since it taints the ideological purity of proletarian ideology with the injection of ideological elements characteristic of other classes. If we take the opposite course and accept that these traditions do not constitute class ideologies, we are confronted with the problem of determining their nature. The theoretical perspective previously outlined enables us to overcome this impasse. 'Popular traditions' constitute the complex of interpellations which express the 'people'/power bloc contradiction as distinct from a class contradiction. This enables us to explain two things. In the first place, in so far as 'popular traditions' represent the ideological crystallisation of resistance to oppression in general, that is, *to the very form of the State,* they will be longer lasting than class ideologies and will constitute a structural frame of reference of greater stability. But in the second place, popular traditions do not constitute consistent and organised discourses but merely *elements* which can only exist in articulation with class discourses. This explains why the most divergent political movements appeal to the same ideological symbols. The figure of Tupac Amaru can be evoked by various guerrilla movements and by the present military government in Peru; the symbols of Chinese nationalism were conjured up by Chiang Kai-Shek and by Mao Tse Tung; those of German nationalism by Hitler and by Thälmann. But even though they constitute mere elements, popular traditions are far from being arbitrary and they cannot be modified at will. They are the residue of a unique and irreducible historical experience and, as such, constitute a more solid and durable structure of meanings than the social structure itself. This dual reference to the people and to classes constitutes what we could call the *double articulation of political discourse.*

Let us take a particularly illustrative example: the recent and excellent analysis of Engels's *Peasant Wars in Germany* by Alain Badiou and François Balmès. These two authors arrive at conclusions similar to ours in some respects, albeit from a theoretical and political perspective with which I am far from concurring. As they point out, Engels's text constitutes a perfect example in which we can see the limits of a mere class analysis. Engels says:

> At that time [15th and early XVIth 16th century] the plebeians were the only class that stood outside the existing official society. ... They had neither privileges nor property: they did not even have the kind of property the peasant or petty burgher had, weighed down as it was with burdensome taxes. They were unpropertied and rightless in every respect; their living conditions never even brought them into direct contact with the existing institutions, which ignored them completely. ... This explains why the plebeian opposition even then could not stop at fighting only feudalism and the privileged burghers; why, in fantasy at least, it reached beyond the then scarcely dawning modern bourgeois society; why, an absolutely propertyless faction, it questioned the institutions, views and conceptions common to all societies based on class antagonisms. ... The anticipation of communism nurtured by fantasy became in reality an anticipation of modern bourgeois conditions. ... Only in the teachings of Münzer did these Communist notions express the aspirations of a real fraction of society. It was he who formulated them with a certain definiteness, and they are since observed in every great popular upheaval, until they gradually merge with the modern proletarian movement.
>
> (Engels 1956, pp. 59–60)

The terms of the problem are clear. We find in Münzer a communist programme which will persist as an ideological theme in all the great popular uprisings of the mercantilist epoch, until they fuse with the programme of the modern proletariat. (Engels goes as far as to assert that the communist sects of the 19th century, on the eve of the March Revolution, were no better equipped theoretically than the followers of Münzer.) The problem, as Badiou and Balmès point out, is to determine the class practice of which this programme was an expression. Engels's answer on this point is hesitant. On one hand he tries to resolve the problem within a strictly class framework: a communist programme can only be the programme of the proletariat, and in that sense, the Münzerite plebeians of the 16th century were an embryonic proletariat which expressed itself ideologically through a kind of mass communism. But, according to Badiou and Balmès, this is not a convincing response, since all the evidence shows that this was a communist ideology which reflected and unified a peasant revolt. Peasant insurrections generate ideas of an egalitarian and communist kind, and it was these ideas which Thomas Münzer systematised. Consequently, it is necessary to favour an alternative solution. Basing themselves on other passages of the same text of Engels, Badiou and Balmès suggest the following:

> "Communist resonances" are a constant in popular uprisings, partially autonomous from the "modern proletarian movement" which is the historical agent

of them. Here in the ideological sphere is opened up a dialectic between the *people* and the *proletariat,* to which Maoism has given its fullest expression.

(Badiou and Balmès 1976, p. 66)

Badiou and Balmès then derive the following theoretical conclusions:

All the great mass revolts of successive exploited classes (slaves, peasants, proletarians) have as their ideological expression egalitarian, anti-property and anti-State formulations which form the features of a communist programme. ... These elements of the general position taken by insurgent producers we call *communist constants:* ideological constants of a communist kind, continually regenerated by the process of unification of great popular revolts at all times. Communist constants do not have a defined class character: they synthesise the universal aspiration of the exploited, which is to overthrow the whole principle of exploitation and oppression. *They come into existence on the terrain of the contradiction between masses and the State.* Naturally, this contradiction is itself structured in class terms, for the State is always that of a particular dominant class. However, there is a general form of the State, organically linked to the very existence of classes and of exploitation, and it is against this that the masses invariably arise, as bearers of its dissolution and of the historic movement which "will relegate the whole apparatus of the State where it will henceforward belong in the museum of antiquities, along with the spinning-wheel and the bronze axe".

(Badiou and Balmès 1976, p. 67)

This analysis has the indubitable merit of isolating 'the people' as the pole of a contradiction which is not that of class, and of positing this contradiction as the opposition of the masses to the State. The difficulty with the formulation of Badiou and Balmès, however, is that it confuses the form of logical resolution of the contradiction they analyse – that is, the suppression of the State – with the concrete and historical forms of existence of that contradiction. Neither of the two terms of what they call 'communist constants' can be justified without qualification. Communism does not represent the normal form of existence of an 'egalitarian, anti-property and anti-state' ideology of the masses, but a particular articulation of it: that which precisely permits the development of all the potential antagonism of that ideology. Normally, the antagonism inherent in this contradiction is neutralised and partially absorbed in the discourse of the dominant classes. Macpherson, for example, has studied the way in which popular-democratic ideology was progressively separated from those antagonistic elements which at the beginning of the 19th century were identified with government by 'underlings' and with a hated Jacobinism, such that it could be absorbed and neutralised by dominant liberal ideology. He comments:

By the time democracy came, in the present liberal-democratic countries, it was no longer opposed to the liberal society and the liberal state. It was, by then, not an attempt by the lower classes to overthrow the liberal state or the competitive market economy; it was an attempt by the lower class to take their fully and fairly competitive place within those institutions and that system of society. Democracy had been transformed. From a threat to the liberal state it had become a fulfilment of the liberal state. ... The liberal state fulfilled its own logic. In so doing, it neither destroyed nor weakened itself; it strengthened both itself and the market society. It liberalised democracy while democratising liberalism.

(Macpherson 1975, pp. 10–11)

Just as popular-democratic ideology could be articulated with liberalism, so it can be articulated also with socialism and other class ideologies. In his book, Macpherson studies some of these articulations. The conclusion is clear: democracy only exists at the ideological level in the form of elements of a discourse. There is no popular-democratic discourse as such. In this sense, democracy is not spontaneously communist for the simple reason that there is no democratic spontaneity. Popular-democratic struggle is subordinate to class struggle and democratic ideology only exists articulated as an abstract moment in a class discourse. I think that it is necessary to establish a distinction here: (1) *spontaneous* mass ideology, articulated as a whole, will always be a class ideology; (2) however, democratic ideological elements can *potentially* lead to communism to the extent that the logical development of the 'people'/power bloc contradiction leads to the suppression of the State. But the antagonistic potentialities of a contradiction and its actual form of existence – which is what spontaneity consists of – are very different. The transformation of the antagonistic potential of democracy into concrete mass spontaneity depends on a historical condition which goes beyond the domain of popular-democratic struggle: on the rise *as a hegemonic force* of a class whose own interests carry it to a suppression of the State. In that sense, only socialism represents the possibility of full development and supersession of the 'people'/power bloc contradiction.

This may help us see why it is mistaken to call popular ideologies *constants*.[5] If we are referring to ideologies articulated as a whole, it is obvious that they are not 'constants' but that they change according to the rhythm of the class struggle. If we refer, on the other hand, to the popular-democratic elements of a discourse, the transformation process is more complex but, in any case, we still cannot talk of constants. Let us take an example to illustrate our argument. Let us imagine a semi-colonial social formation in which a dominant fraction of landowners exploits indigenous peasant communities. The ideology of the dominant bloc is liberal and Europeanist, while that of the exploited peasantry is anti-European, indigenist and communitarian. This second ideology – the sole opponent of the power bloc – has, therefore, a clear peasant origin. In that society develops a growing urban opposition of middle and working classes who challenge the hegemonic landowning fraction's monopoly of power. In these circumstances, the organic intellectuals of these new groups, trying to make their political opposition consistent and systematic, increasingly appeal to the symbols and values of peasant groups, *because they constitute the only ideological raw materials which, in this social formation, express a radical confrontation with the power bloc.* But in the urban reformulation of those symbols and values, they become transformed: they lose their reference to a concrete social base and are transformed into the ideological expression of the 'people'/power bloc confrontation. Henceforth they have lost all class reference and can, therefore, be articulated into the ideological discourses of the most divergent classes. What is more, no political discourse can do without them: dominant classes to neutralise them, dominated classes to develop their potential antagonism, these ideological elements are always present in the most varied articulations. (Think of the metamorphoses of Mexican nationalism, of the omnipresence of indigenism as an ideological symbol in Peru or of the opposing reformulations of the ideological symbols of Peronism by its left and right fractions.) This explains why these ideological elements *qua* elements change more slowly than the class structure: because they represent simple abstract moments of a discourse and express a contradiction inherent in any class society, which is not linked exclusively to a determinate mode of production. But, as we have seen, they also become transformed, even though they move more slowly and obey different laws from those which govern class discourses.

We have, then, determined the theoretical status of the concept of 'the people' and the specific contradiction of which it constitutes a pole. However, we still have not defined the specificity of populism. Can we consider as populist that type of discourse where popular-democratic interpellations predominate? Obviously not. Numerous ideological discourses make reference to 'the people' which we would not think of calling 'populist'. *If, therefore, it is not the mere presence of popular-democratic interpellations in a discourse which transforms it into a species populism and if, however, we know that populism is directly linked to the presence of 'the people' in this discourse, we must conclude that what transforms an ideological discourse into a populist one is a peculiar form of articulation of the popular-democratic interpellations in it. Our thesis is that populism consists in the presentation of popular-democratic interpellations as a synthetic-antagonistic complex with respect to the dominant ideology.* Let us look at this in detail. As we have seen, the ideology of dominant classes not only interpellates dominant subjects but also dominated classes, with the effect of neutralising their potential antagonism. As we have also said, the basic method of this neutralisation lies in a transformation of all antagonism into simple difference. The articulation of popular-democratic ideologies within the dominant discourse consists in an absorption of everything in it which is a simple differential particularity and a repression of those elements which tend to transform the particularity into a symbol of antagonism. (The clientelism of rural districts, for example, exalts everything that is folklore in mass ideology, at the same time as it presents the *caudillo* as the intermediary between the masses and the State, tending to suppress the antagonistic elements in it.) It is in this sense that the presence of popular elements in a discourse is not sufficient to transform it into a populist one. Populism starts at the point where popular-democratic elements are presented as an antagonistic option against the ideology of the dominant bloc.

Note that this does not mean that populism is *always* revolutionary. It is sufficient for a class or class fraction to need a substantial transformation in the power bloc in order to assert its hegemony, for a populist experience to be possible. We can indicate in this sense a populism of the dominant classes and a populism of the dominated classes:

(1) When the dominant bloc experiences a profound crisis because a new fraction seeks to impose its hegemony but is unable to do so within the existing structure of the power bloc, one solution can be a direct appeal by this fraction to the masses to develop their antagonism towards the State. As I have pointed out elsewhere, this was the case with Nazism. Monopoly capital could not impose its hegemony within the existing institutional system – as it had done in England or France – nor could it base itself on the army which constituted an enclave under the feudal influence of the Junkers. The only solution was a mass movement which would develop the potential antagonism of popular interpellations, but articulated in a way which would obstruct its orientation in any revolutionary direction, Nazism constituted a populist experience which, like any populism of the dominant classes, had to appeal to a set of ideological distortions – racism, for example – to avoid the revolutionary potential of popular interpellations from being reoriented towards their true objectives. The populism of the dominant classes is always highly repressive because it attempts a more dangerous experience than an existing parliamentary regime: whilst the second simply *neutralises* the revolutionary potential of popular interpellations, the first tries to *develop* that antagonism but to keep it within certain limits.

(2) For the dominated sectors, ideological struggle consists in an expansion of the antagonism implicit in democratic interpellations and in an articulation of it with their own class discourses. The struggle of the working class for its hegemony is an effort to achieve the maximum possible fusion between popular-democratic ideology and socialist ideology. In this sense a 'socialist populism' is not the most backward form of working-class ideology but the most advanced – the moment when the working class has succeeded in condensing the ensemble of democratic ideology in a determinate social formation within its own ideology. Hence the unequivocally 'populist' character adopted by victorious socialist movements: think of Mao, think of Tito and think even of the Italian Communist Party – which has come the closest in Western Europe to a hegemonic position – and has frequently been called populist.

So we see why it is possible to call Hitler, Mao and Peron simultaneously populist. Not because the social bases of their movements were similar; not because their ideologies expressed the same class interests but because popular interpellations appear in the ideological discourses of all of them, presented in the form of antagonism and not just of difference. Opposition to dominant ideology may be more or less radical, and therefore the antagonism will be articulated in the discourses of the most divergent classes, but in any case it is always present, and this presence is what we intuitively perceive as the specifically populist element in the ideology of the three movements.

Finally, let us recall what our study of fascism remarked of *Jacobinism*. After indicating the way in which popular interpellations are articulated into discourses of a clientelist type and in those of popular parties, we pointed out that in Jacobinism the autonomy of popular-democratic interpellations reaches its maximum degree compatible with a class society. We also said that this was only a transitory moment which, sooner or later, must dissolve with the reabsorption of popular interpellations by class ideological discourses. What is important is that this reabsorption can be effected in two ways: either the popular-democratic elements are kept at the level of *mere* elements in so far as the existing ideological framework is increasingly accepted, or a crystallisation of the Jacobin inflexion occurs – an organisation of popular-democratic interpellations into a synthetic totality which, united with other interpellations which adapt Jacobinism to the interests of the classes which express themselves through it, presents itself as an antagonist of the existing ideological framework. The first solution signifies a reconversion of the phase of *Jacobinism* to the phase of *popular parties*. The second solution is populism. It is clear, then: (1) that what is populist in an ideology is the presence of popular-democratic interpellations in their specific antagonism; (2) that the ideological complex of which populism is a moment consists in the articulation of this antagonistic moment within divergent class discourses. It cannot therefore be said that concrete populist ideologies are above classes, but neither can the strictly populist moment be linked to the discourse of a determinate social class.

If the argument so far is correct, *the emergence of populism is historically linked to a crisis of the dominant ideological discourse which is in turn part of a more general social crisis.* This crisis can either be the result of a fracture in the power bloc, in which a class or class fraction needs, in order to assert its hegemony, to appeal to 'the people' against established ideology as a whole; or of a crisis in the ability of the system to neutralise the dominated sectors – that is to say, a crisis of transformism. Naturally, an important historical crisis combines both ingredients. What should be clear, however, is that the 'causes' of populism have little to do with a determinate *stage of development,* as functionalist theses suppose. It is true that the long process of expansion of the forces of production which characterised Europe in the stage of monopoly capitalism increased the system's ability to absorb and neutralise its contradictions. But it is also true that each time the capitalist system has experienced a serious crisis in Western Europe, various forms of populism have flourished. We need only think of the crisis after the First World War which produced the triumph of fascism, the world economic crisis which led to the ascent of Nazism and the world recession today that is accompanied by the multiplication of regionalisms that tend to be expressed in ideologies which make of populism a central moment.

III

Let us take, as an example of a populist articulation of democratic interpellations, a case which is particularly illustrative because of the multiple metamorphoses which it underwent: Peronism. No other Latin American populist movement was constituted from the articulation of more disparate interpellations; no other achieved such success in its attempt to transform itself into the common denominator of mass popular-democratic language; no other, finally, was articulated into such varied class discourses.

Peronism – together with Varguism – has been considered one of the two typical examples of a Latin American populist movement. From the previous argument we may deduce that this expression – 'populist movements' – contains an ambiguity which needs clarification. It is certainly inexact if we wish to characterise the nature of those movements, but it is correct if we use it to allude to the presence of 'populism' as a moment in their ideological structure. An ideology is not 'populist' in the same sense that it is 'conservative', 'liberal' or 'socialist', for the simple reason that, whilst these three terms allude to the articulating principles of the respective ideologies considered as a whole, 'populism' alludes to a kind of contradiction which only exists as an abstract moment of an ideological discourse. Hence the problem of the reasons for the proliferation of populist movements in Latin America after 1930 can be more exactly reformulated in the following terms: why did the ideological discourses of political movements with quite distinct orientations and social bases have to have increasing recourse to populism, that is to say, to develop the potential antagonism of popular-democratic interpellations?

A fairly generalised opinion tends to link 'populism' with import substitution industrialisation. Francisco Weffort and Octavio Ianni[6] have produced the best studies of Latin American populism from this perspective. It follows from what has been said that we cannot share this criterion: 'populism' is not the *necessary* superstructure of any social or economic process. Populist phenomena can present themselves in the most varied contexts to the extent that certain conditions for them are met. If, therefore, we try to explain why movements with populist ideologies flourished in Latin America between 1930 and 1960, this explanation must show how the conditions necessary for the emergence of populist phenomena were united in this period and were, on the other hand, much less frequent before and after it. We have already established what these conditions are: a particularly serious crisis of the power bloc which results in a fraction of it seeking to establish its hegemony through mass mobilisation, and a crisis of transformism.

To understand the specificity of the populist rupture, from which Peronism emerged, it is necessary to understand the nature of the previous dominant ideological system in Argentina, and its characteristic articulating principles. We must note two things in this respect: (a) that the principle of unity of an ideological discourse is provided not by the development of the logical implications of a determinate interpellation but by the power of condensation it has in a specific connotative domain; (b) that class hegemony consists not only in an ability to impose a 'conception of the world' upon other classes, but also, and especially, in an ability to articulate different 'conceptions of the world' in such a way as to neutralise their potential antagonism.

In Argentina before the crisis of 1930, the hegemonic class in the power bloc was the landowning oligarchy, and the basic articulating principle of its ideological discourse was liberalism. The reasons for this are to be found in a double circumstance common to all Latin America from the mid-19th century to 1930: if, on the one hand, the full incorporation of the Latin American economies into the world market necessitated the constitution of nation-states, which created the conditions of political stability and institutional continuity necessary for economic activity to develop, on the other hand, political power remained in the hands of local landowning oligarchies. Now, if in Europe these two constellations were contradictory – since the liberal State arose largely in the struggle against feudal particularism – in Latin America they were complementary, since it was the landowning oligarchies who were seeking to maximise their production for the world market and who, therefore, sought to organise a central State. The emergent Latin American political systems sought to give expression to this dual situation: centralised States were formed in which the representation of local oligarchical interests predominated. The formula most adapted to this situation was a parliamentary liberal State with a strong predominance of the legislative over the executive. The degree of decentralisation of power varied greatly in the different Latin American countries. In some cases the executive was reduced to a mere arbitrator – think of the old Republic in Brazil or of the constitutional reorganisation of Chile after the revolution of 1891. In other cases, such as Argentina, where the ensemble of power and wealth was concentrated in a relatively limited area of territory, the decentralisation was less and the Executive enjoyed greater autonomy. But in all cases, whatever the form, the central State was conceived as a federation of local oligarchies. Parliamentary power and landowning hegemony became synonymous in Latin America.

The very historical process of the implantation and consolidation of the oligarchic State in Argentina explains the specific connotative domain with which liberal ideology was articulated. *In the first place,* liberalism initially had little ability to absorb the democratic ideology of the masses and integrate it into its discourse. Democracy and liberalism were opposed to each other. Imperialist penetration and the incorporation of the country into the world market in the second half of the 19th century necessitated the dissolution of previous forms of social organisation and precapitalist relations of production. This involved a violent and repressive policy towards the dominated classes. The struggles between the interior of the country and Buenos Aires, the Montonero Rebellion of the 1860s, the uprising of Lopez Jordan in the early 1870s were episodes in this struggle through which the liberal State was imposed. *In the second place,* liberalism was throughout this period connotatively articulated to economic development and material progress as positive ideological values. (Note that this is not a necessary articulation: after 1930 liberalism and developmental ideology were definitively to lose any capacity for mutual implication.) *In the third place,* liberal ideology was articulated to 'Europeanism', that is to say, to a defence of the European way of life and ideological values as representing 'civilisation'. There was a radical rejection of popular national traditions, considered to be synonymous with backwardness, obscurantism and stagnation. *In the fourth place,* Argentinian liberalism was consequently anti-personalist. The emergence of national political leaders with direct contact to the masses, which could take precedence over the local political machines with their clientelistic base, was always viewed with mistrust by oligarchic power.

These four ideological elements, of which liberalism was the articulating principle, constituted the system of coordinates defining the ideological domain of oligarchic hegemony. Positivism was the philosophical influence which systematised these distinct elements into a homogeneous whole. Popular ideologies – that is to say, that complex of interpellations constituting popular subjects in their opposition to the power bloc – exhibited the opposite features. It was therefore natural for popular resistance to be expressed in anti-liberal ideologies; for it to be nationalist and anti-European; for it to defend popular traditions against the corrosive effects of capitalist expansion; for it to be, therefore, *personalist* and to lend support to popular leaders who represented a politics hostile to the status quo. How were the ideological symbols of this popular resistance elaborated? As we have already said, ideological practice always works with raw materials constituted by prior interpellations which, on being disarticulated from the class discourses into which they were formerly integrated, lose any necessary class belonging. In the Andean countries popular resistance was increasingly expressed through indigenist symbols, which originally represented the resistance to the dissolution of peasant communities but which, reinterpreted by urban sectors, lost any necessary rural connotation and came to be symbols of popular resistance in general. In Argentina, by contrast, where there were no peasant traditions and where massive immigration had radically modified the social structure of the country, anti-liberal popular resistance utilised the traditions of the 19th century Montoneros, the ideological symbols of the federalism that had opposed the Europeanising unitarism of Buenos Aires.[7]

The problem is then: to what extent did the dominant oligarchic bloc during this period succeed in neutralising its contradictions with 'the people' and in articulating popular-democratic interpellations into liberal discourse? This is exactly the problem discussed by Macpherson, as we mentioned before: to what extent was democracy liberalised and liberalism democratised? To what extent was the ideological discourse of the dominated classes neutralised and its protest maintained at the stage of *popular parties,* and to what extent did it become Jacobinised and lead to populism?

The answer to this question leaves no room for doubt: the landowning oligarchy was completely successful in neutralising democratic interpellations, and in no case did popular resistance reach the point of populist radicalisation. The reason lies in the success of the incorporation of Argentina into the world market and the great redistributive capacity of the landowning oligarchy during the expansive cycle of differential rent. I have discussed economic aspects of this process elsewhere.[8] What is important for the present purpose is that two basic consequences followed from this process: (1) the power bloc was highly cohesive, since no sector of it either opposed the agricultural and livestock orientation of the country or was in a position to dispute oligarchic hegemony; (2) the re-distributive capacity of the oligarchy enabled it to include nascent middle and working classes within its expansive cycle and to co-opt their respective leaderships into the power bloc. That is to say, there took place neither a crisis at the level of the power bloc nor a collapse of transformism – both of which are, as we have seen, preconditions for the emergence of populism.

It remains however, important to describe the ideological forms through which oligarchic hegemony was imposed. As we have said, this hegemony was secured in two ways: the absorption of popular interpellations into its discourse and the articulation of the ideologies which were formally in opposition to it in a peculiar form which neutralised them. Let us consider four ideological ensembles: (a) oligarchic ideology as such; (b) the ideology of the Radical Party; (c) ideologies of non-liberal oligarchies; (d) working-class ideologies.

(a) *The ideology of the oligarchy as such*. To the extent that liberalism, as the oligarchic ideology, progressively asserted its hegemony, it increased its capacity for absorbing within its discourse popular-democratic interpellations which had initially been completely excluded from it. The most complete ideological expression of liberalism in its pure State, that is to say, in so far as it presented only the four previously defined coordinates and included no mass popular-democratic interpellations in its discourse, was *Mitrism*. This was the political discourse of the Buenos Aires oligarchy at a stage when its ideological hegemony over the rest of the country was minimal, when it had to assert its power by means of straightforward repression. (This was the epoch of the Paraguayan War, the confrontations with Urquiza and the federalism of Entre Rios, and the final Montonero rebellions of the interior.) Later, when the country was pacified and its economic transformation was under way, liberalism asserted its hegemony via a constant widening of the social basis of the power bloc and an increasing absorption and neutralisation of the popular democratic ideology of the masses. The first stage of this broadening of its social base was the co-option into the power bloc of the oligarchies of the interior of the country. This process culminated in 1880 with the accession of Roca to the presidency of the Republic. It is significant that Roca, in his partial confrontation with the Mitrism of Buenos Aires, had to incorporate into his discourse elements of the federal ideological tradition in order to differentiate himself from the latter. 'I have my traces of federalism', he said. This is a constant that was to persist throughout the history of liberal Argentina: each time the social bases of the system were widened, the new sectors co-opted into the power bloc asserted their relatively more 'democratic' character, through ideological symbols deriving from popular federal tradition.[9] Liberalism, precisely because of its increasing hegemony, could present itself as an articulating alternative to those popular interpellations it originally had excluded. Finally, the installation of electoral machines with a clientelist base definitively consecrated the new method of incorporating the masses into the system: popular traditions were accepted as a specific subculture of the dominated classes, as a *sermo humilis* disconnected from the language of power. The link between the two was provided by the local caudillo, who, presenting himself as the intermediary between the masses and the State, established at once the unity and the chasm between them.

(b) *The ideology of the Radical Party.* The experience of Roquism presents us with this apparent paradox: liberalism was the more hegemonic to the extent that the ideological discourse of which it constituted the articulating principle was less *exclusively* liberal. The reason is, as we have said, that hegemony does not consist in the imposition of a uniform ideology but in the articulation of dissimilar ideological elements. This is even clearer in the case of Irigoyen and the Radical Party, in which there was a perfect synthesis between liberalism and democracy. With their co-option into the power bloc – the highest point of oligarchic transformism – popular-democratic interpellations ceased to be a subculture mediated by clientelistic machines and became incorporated into national political life. The *sermo humilis* took possession of the language of power. It was precisely this violation of the rule of the separation of styles that oligarchic liberalism felt as an outrage; hence the numerous invectives against Irigoyen which ranged from derogatory references to the 'bully-boy of Balvanera' to 'mazorquero' (member of Rosas' death squads) or even 'fascist'. Was this, therefore, a populist experience? It seems clear that it was not. The most noticeable feature of Irigoyen's political discourse, in common with other middle-class reformers in Latin America during this period – Batlle y Ordoñez in Uruguay, Alessandri in Chile, Madero in Mexico, Ruy Barbosa in Brazil and Alfonso Lopez in Colombia – was undoubtedly the increasing presence within it of popular-democratic elements; but these elements remained at the emotional or rhetorical level and were never articulated as a coherent totality in opposition to liberal ideology. As we have seen, it is only this kind of articulation which gives a populist character to the presence of democratic interpellations in any given discourse. The general proposals of the middle-class reformers of this period, on the contrary, never went beyond institutional demands that accepted the liberal framework of the regime: 'my programme is the National Constitution' (Irigoyen); 'effective suffrage and no re-election' (Madero). This kind of articulation of democratic ideology is characteristic of the stage of *popular parties* and in no circumstance does it lead to populist Jacobinisation.[10]

(c) *Non-liberal oligarchic ideologies.* What existed in this period in the way of a systematic attempt to create a coherent anti-liberal ideology was the very opposite of populism: it was a right-wing nationalism, emphasising whatever was authoritarian, elitist, clerical and anti-popular in the anti-liberal tradition. This ideological trend reflected, from an opposite perspective, the very high degree of fusion between democracy and liberalism in Argentina: because its exponents despised democracy and the 'radical scum', *and saw them as an inevitable result of liberalism,* they defended an authoritarian State which found its source of inspiration in Maurras. Later, on the eve of the 1930 Revolution, a new element was incorporated into this tradition: *militarism* – for the role of the Army was now to transform itself, in the theories of right-wing nationalism, into the historical agent of an anti-liberal revolution. Where did this anti-liberal oligarchic ideology find its raw materials? Obviously, in the same federal traditions from which had grown popular-democratic ideologies. But, whilst the latter represented a transformation of those traditions, reducing them to a complex of symbols and ideological elements expressing the resistance of the masses to the State, oligarchic anti-liberalism effected a transformation in the opposite direction: it reduced those traditions to the ideological forms which articulated the discourse of the dominant classes before the expansion of the liberal State: clericalism, hispanicism, the continuity of colonial values and authoritarianism.

(d) *Working-class ideologies.* The most notable feature of the ideological structure of the working class of the epoch was that it made not the slightest effort to articulate popular-democratic interpellations into its political discourse. Three reasons combine to explain this phenomenon: (1) Due to the principally agrarian character of Argentina, the working class was confined to small enclaves in the big coastal cities. During this period workers were therefore marginal to the broader confrontations in which 'the people' as such was constituted. (2) The working class of this period was recruited overwhelmingly from European immigrants. This had two consequences: firstly, the fusion between their class ideology and the popular-democratic ideology of the country to which they had come could not but be a slow process; secondly, those aspects of their new country which seemed most comprehensible in terms of their European experience were precisely the liberal State and its institutions. Hence their tendency to interpret any incomprehensible element in terms of European paradigms as the residue of a more primitive cultural stage which material progress, the expansion of the liberal State and the progressive Europeanisation of the country would finally eliminate. The condensation of these three elements – Europeanism, liberalism and material progress – into a unified ideological discourse reproduced the kind of articulation which, as we have seen, characterised oligarchic liberalism. (3) To this it is necessary to add the specific way in which the strictly populist element was integrated into this ideology. As we know, the most characteristic structural feature of socialist ideology at the end of the 19th century and the beginning of the 20th was class reductionism, which confined the proletariat to a pure class ideology that viewed any popular interpellation as the ideology of a class enemy. Naturally this obstructed any form of socialist populism. *What is important is that this class reductionism, applied by the immigrant working class in Argentinian society, came to identify the diffuse democratic ideology of the masses as pre-capitalist residues which the progressive Europeanisation of Latin American societies would finally eliminate.* Hence the close and increasing unity between hegemonic liberal ideology and socialist ideology. The Socialist Party reasoned in the following way: the full development of a capitalist society is the precondition for the full development of the working class; therefore, the expansion of the liberal State – considered as the necessary political superstructure of capitalism – was a progressive process and must be supported. In turn it was thought that the immigration process was casting onto Argentinian shores an ever greater number of immigrants, who would in the end eliminate the ideological residues of federal and Montonera Argentina. In this way, socialist ideology accepted the articulative ensemble characteristic of liberal discourse and added only one element: working-class reductionism. This element did not significantly alter the picture, however, since the working class was regarded as the social force which would carry liberal society to its democratic consummation. The Communist Party, for its part, effected an equally liberal reading of Argentinian politics – if with a different terminology. During the period of the Popular Fronts it was to measure the progressive character of different bourgeois political forces according to the degree of their adherence to liberal ideology, while denouncing as fascist any attempt to incorporate elements of popular nationalist tradition into political discourse. If we compare Argentinian socialism and communism we have to conclude, therefore, that the alternative of reform/revolution did not provide a measure of the degree of progressiveness of either ideology, since all variants of that alternative occurred within an ideological discourse which accepted all the constitutive articulations of oligarchic liberalism.

An analysis of these four ideological ensembles – which of course were not the only ones present – enables us to understand the system of ideological alternatives in pre-Peronist Argentina: an increasing unity between liberalism and democracy in the dominant discourse, a marginal authoritarian ideology, *both* anti-democratic *and* anti-liberal; class reductionism in working-class ideologies. These three aspects, *taken as a whole,* expressed oligarchic hegemony.

The decade of the 1930s saw important changes in this ideological crystallisation, presaging the decline of oligarchic hegemony and the emergence of new contradictions in the power bloc. In the first place, the power bloc experienced a deep crisis: the world depression led to a process of import-substituting industrialisation that created new antagonisms between nascent industrial sectors and the landowning oligarchy. Secondly, there was a crisis of transformism. As a result of the economic depression, the oligarchy could no longer tolerate the generous redistributive policies characteristic of the Radical governments, and had to ban the middle classes from access to political power. In order to do this, it established a parliamentary system based on electoral fraud. The democratic demands of the masses and the ideological symbols which represented them were less and less absorbed by the liberal regime, to a point where the scission between liberalism and democracy became complete. This was reflected in an increasing division within the Radical Party: the official party leadership, in the hands of Alvear, hoped for an impossible return of the unity between liberalism and democracy, and to this end negotiated with the now fraudulent liberal regime; it accepted subordinate positions within it to such a point that, towards the end of the period, official Radicalism was to all intents and purposes indistinguishable from the conservative coalition in power. On the other hand, a minority nationalist current tried to develop within Radicalism all the antagonism implicit in popular interpellations, to accentuate the incompatibility of liberalism and democracy, and to indict the liberal regime as a whole. English imperialism was denounced for the first time as a dominant structural force in Argentinian history; liberalism was perceived as the political superstructure necessary for the subjection of the country to the agrarian oligarchy and foreign interests; the basis was laid for a popular and anti-liberal revisionism of Argentinian history. The decade of the 1940s thus challenged Radicalism with the disarticulation of its tradition of political discourse: it now had to opt for liberalism *or* democracy. The perfect synthesis between the two that had characterised Irigoyenism was dissolved.

Right-wing nationalism also underwent important changes. The implantation of an oligarchic liberal regime, which had buried their corporativist hopes, made right-wing nationalists think increasingly of an alternative military solution; the corrupt character of the conservative regime and its servile subjection to Great Britain led them to denounce imperialism; while the need to break imperialist links and to transform Argentina into an independent power led some nationalist sectors to demand an industrialist reorientation of the economy. These two new components of authoritarian nationalism-anti-imperialism and industrialism implied a growing confrontation with oligarchic liberalism. It also presented right-wing nationalism in the 1940s with a clear alternative: either to accentuate the anti-imperialist and industrialist character of its programme which – given the increasing opposition to the latter on the part of the oligarchy – could only lead to a quest for support from a mass movement, and a consequent renunciation of the elitist and anti-popular elements in its ideology; or to retain those elements but at the cost of diluting the radicalism of the anti-oligarchic programme.

Finally, working-class ideologies also underwent a process of crisis in this period. Internal migrations had incorporated into industrial activity a new proletariat from the interior of the country, whose ideology was not based on the class reductionism of the old proletariat of European origin, but on a particular type of discourse in which popular-democratic interpellations were central. Meanwhile industrialisation was now transforming the role of the proletariat in the political process; from being a relatively marginal sector – as it had been in the Argentina of agriculture and livestock – it came to be the most concentrated social sector, and the backbone of all those forces interested in the expansion of the internal market and opposed to the continuation of oligarchic rule.

We can see, then, the extent to which the decline of oligarchic hegemony was reflected in a crisis of the dominant political discourse. This – as in any ideological crisis – consisted of a progressive disarticulation of the constitutive elements of that discourse. Liberalism and democracy ceased to be articulated; democratic interpellations could less and less be integrated into liberal ideology. For authoritarian nationalism, the possibility of a simultaneous anti-democratic and anti-liberal posture became increasingly problematic; there arose, particularly after anti-imperialist and industrial components had been incorporated into its discourse, a possibility previously nonexistent: democratic authoritarianism. Finally, class reductionism and proletarian ideology ceased to be necessarily correlated and the possibility arose of a working-class populism. This disarticulation meant, among other things, that the power bloc's ability to neutralise its contradictions with the people had diminished; in the mirror of liberal ideological forms, now broken and murky, new and unforeseen combinations were possible. This was a breach opened at the ideological level, and with it the possibility of populism. For populism in Argentina was to consist precisely in a reunification of the ensemble of interpellations that expressed opposition to the oligarchic power bloc – democracy, industrialism, nationalism, anti-imperialism; their condensation into a new historical subject; and a development of their potential antagonism towards a confrontation with the principle of oligarchic discourse itself – liberalism. The whole effort of Peronist ideology at this stage was bent towards the aim of detracting liberalism from its last links with a democratic connotative domain and presenting it as a straightforward cover for oligarchic class interests. Peron declared, in a revealing speech during the electoral campaign of 1946:

> 'I am, then, much more democratic than my adversaries, because I seek a real democracy whilst they defend an appearance of democracy, the external form of democracy. I seek a higher standard of living to protect the workers, even the poorest, from capitalist coercion; while the capitalists want the misery of the proletariat and its abandonment by the State to enable them to carry on their old tricks of buying and usurping ballot-papers. ... In conclusion: Argentina cannot stagnate in the somnolent rhythm of activity to which so many who have come and lived at her expense have condemned her; Argentina must recover the firm pulse of a healthy and clean-living youth. Argentina needs the young blood of the working class.[11]

This attempt to distinguish between liberal ideological forms and real democracy dominated the whole of Peronist discourse. Look at this claim:

> For the truth is this: in our country the real problem is not a conflict of "liberty" against "tyranny", Rosas against Urquiza, "democracy" against "totalitarianism". What lies at the root of the Argentinian drama is a contest between "social justice" and "social injustice". The fraud and corruption to which we have come is simply repugnant: it represents the greatest possible treachery against the working masses. The Communist and Socialist parties, which hypocritically present themselves as workers' parties whilst serving

capitalist interests, have no qualms about carrying out electoral propaganda with the aid of cash handed over by the bosses. ... To use a word of which they are very fond, we could say that they are the true representatives of continuism; but a continuism in the policy of workers' slavery and misery.[12]

It is not our intention to study the evolution of Peronism as a movement, since we wish only to point out how the strictly populist moment in its ideology was constituted. But in any case we should note certain significant facts. Firstly, if the strictly populist element in Peronist ideology was the radicalisation of anti-liberal popular interpellations, Peronist discourse consisted not only of these interpellations but also of their articulation within a discourse which sought to confine any confrontation with the liberal oligarchy within limits imposed by the class project that defined the regime: the development of a national capitalism. Hence the antagonism of popular interpellations was permitted to develop only up to a certain point. Peronism sought to limit their explosive potential by presenting them always in articulation with other ideological elements which were anti-liberal, but were not popular — military or clerical ideology, for example. Secondly, if Peronism was undeniably successful in constituting a unified popular-democratic language at the national level, this was due to the social homogeneity of Argentina, exceptional in the Latin American context: lack of a peasantry, overwhelming predominance of the urban population, substantial development of the middle classes, development of trade unionism throughout the country. Thirdly, the massive presence of the working class in Peronism gave it an exceptional ability to persist as a movement after the fall of the regime in 1955. Whilst other Latin American populist movements did not survive the fall of their regimes, the fact that Peronism was rooted in the working class enabled it to continue as a political force and even to extend its influence into the middle classes, radicalised in the last two decades as a result of the contradictions created by the expansion of monopoly capital. Fourthly, if the antagonism of popular interpellations developed only within the limits tolerated by the Peronist regime while it existed, it was impossible to impose these limits once Peronism was proscribed and started to reorganize its cadres from below. To the extent that Argentinian liberalism, restored in 1955, demonstrated its complete inability to absorb the democratic demands of the masses and resorted more and more to repression, the potential antagonism of popular interpellations could develop to the full. Popular ideology became increasingly anti-liberal, and in the most radicalised sectors increasingly fused with socialism. 'National socialism' was the formula coined in the course of this process. The return to power of Peronism in 1973 proved that the change was irreversible: successive attempts to turn the clock back and to articulate popular-democratic ideology in a form assimilable by the bourgeoisie all failed. The regime of Isabel Peron collapsed into repressive chaos without having achieved any stable form of articulation between popular interpellations and bourgeois ideology.

The singularities of Peronism can be more clearly seen if we compare it with the other major populist experience in Latin America of this period, to which it is often likened: Varguism. Let us recall its origins. The Brazilian revolution of 1930 was the product of an accumulation of contradictions which, in the Argentinian experience, had been successively resolved. Inter-regional conflicts had ceased to be of decisive political importance in Argentina after the federalisation of Buenos Aires in 1880. The accession to power of the middle classes with their redistributive projects within the agro-exporting system had occurred with the electoral victory of Radicalism in 1916. The new contradictions between the agrarian and industrial sectors only became important after 1930. We find in Brazil, on the contrary, that these contradictions had not been resolved and that they accumulated in the revolutionary process of 1930. Inter-regional conflicts, in which less influential States opposed the increasing predominance of São Paulo, played a decisive role in the alliance which carried Vargas to power. The Brazilian middle classes, due to the extreme regionalisation of the country, had not been able to create a political party with national dimensions as Irigoyen had done in Argentina. The result was that they could not prevail against the political machines of the local oligarchies – witness the fruitless attempt of Ruy Barbosa in the presidential elections of 1910 – and no internal democratisation of the liberal regime took place, as had occurred in Argentina or Uruguay. These frustrated liberal-democratic tendencies – perfectly represented by the Democratic Party in Sao Paulo – also played an important part in the revolution. Finally, the *tenentes* were of prime importance in the seizure of power – radicalised sectors of the Army which sought to carry out a programme of democratisation and modernisation of the country, via a complete break from the oligarchical political system and the liberal State. It was in these sectors that we can find the first traces of a populist ideology.

Vargas had to manoeuvre amidst a highly complex coalition of contradictory forces, and only in 1937 was he able to establish full political control through the Estado Novo. But even then, and throughout his entire political career, Vargas was never able to become the leader of a unified and homogeneous movement like that of Peron: on the contrary, he was always to be an articulator of heterogeneous forces over which he established his personal control through a complicated system of alliances. If in the more industrialised areas of the country he was able to establish firm bases of independent support in the working class and vast sectors of the middle classes, in the interior of the country he had to seek his support from traditional political machines. This fragmentation of his political support was reflected in his inability to form a unified political party: the forces which rallied to him were organised in two parties. The Social Democratic Party (PSD) grouped the conservative forces in his coalition; the Brazilian Labour Party (PTB) was based on urban sectors, especially the working class, and attempted to develop a populist Jacobinism. The dual face of Varguism – accentuated by the fact that the importance of the working class in Brazil was incomparably less than in Argentina – was reflected in an inadequate and fragmented populism, which did not succeed in constituting a political language of national dimensions. Varguism was never, therefore, genuinely populist. On the contrary, it oscillated in a pendular movement: at moments of stability its political language tended to be paternalistic and conservative; at moments of crisis, on the other hand, when the conservative elements abandoned the coalition, it swung in a 'populist' direction – that is to say, one that developed the antagonism latent in democratic interpellations. But precisely in these crises an elementary political logic imposed itself: the social bases for a populist discourse have always so far been insufficient in Brazil to guarantee political power. This was to be demonstrated by the fate of Vargas in 1945, 1954 and finally by the fall of Goulart in 1964.

We may conclude this section by indicating why populist experiences have been less frequent in Latin America in the last two decades. I think the reasons lie in the following factors:

(a) Transformism has entered into a definitive crisis. The capacity of Latin American power blocs restructured under the hegemony of monopoly capital to absorb the democratic demands of the masses is extremely limited. I will not enter into an analysis of the economic origins of this phenomenon, which I have explored elsewhere.[13] Its consequence, in any case, is that today the dominant blocs do not even attempt to take popular initiatives – that is to say, to articulate popular-democratic ideology into the discourse of power. On the contrary, the new type of military regime in contemporary Latin America tends to rest more and more exclusively upon its repressive apparatuses. The result has been to throw into crisis not only the various populist experiences, but also the limited transformism needed for the minimal subsistence of a liberal regime. This also explains why despite the increasing authoritarianism of Latin American military regimes, they have not been able to assume a fascist orientation for, as we have seen, the ideological base of fascism was a peculiar articulation of popular ideologies, whilst the orientation of current military dictatorships in Latin America seem to preclude *any* such articulation in its discourse.

(b) In the past a crisis of transformism led, as we have seen, to the creation of various forms of populism by dissident fractions of the dominant power bloc. Any development in this direction now, however, seems improbable for the following reasons. In the 1930s and 1940s, the power blocs were deeply divided due to the crisis of oligarchic hegemony, and at least a fraction of them was ready to move in the direction of a national independent capitalism and to seek mass support to this end.

Today [1977], on the contrary, the nationalist experiences have collapsed and the power blocs have been reunited under the control of monopoly capital. In these conditions, there are no antagonisms sufficiently deep for a fraction of the power bloc to reorient in a populist direction. The second reason for thinking that a new populism of the dominant classes is unlikely is that, in the course of the experiences of the last twenty-five years, the Latin American masses have developed the antagonism inherent in democratic interpellations to a point where it is very difficult for any fraction of the bourgeoisie to absorb and neutralise them. This has led, in turn, to a consolidation of the power blocs and an accentuation of their repressive policies towards the dominated classes. For the latter, however, a new, long-term ideological perspective is opening up: to develop the radicalisation of popular-democratic ideology and increasingly fuse it with socialist ideology, at a stage when the bourgeoisie as a whole is more and more engulfed in repression and barbarism.

IV

Finally, let us point out some conclusions which follow from our analysis. 'Populism' arises in a specific ideological domain: that constituted by the double articulation of political discourse. The dialectical tension between 'the people' and classes determines the *form* of ideology, both among dominant and dominated sectors. The *metamorphoses* of 'the people' consist in its various forms of articulation with classes. To the extent that 'the people' and classes constitute poles of contradictions which are different but equally constitutive of political discourse, they are both present in it. But whilst the class contradiction determines the articulating principle of that discourse, lending it its specific singularity in a determinate ideological domain, the first contradiction represents an abstract moment which can be articulated to the most divergent class discourses. 'Populism', as a particular inflexion of popular interpellations, can never constitute the articulating principle of a political discourse – even when it constitutes a feature present in it. It is precisely this abstract character of 'populism' which permits of its presence in the ideology of the most varied of classes. The same can be said of a concept such as 'market economy', which does not define the articulating principle of an economic system – this always lies in its dominant mode of production – but which is an abstract element present in many modes of production, from slavery to capitalism, that yet constitute an indispensible component for understanding the functioning of the system as a whole.

It might be asked why, if popular-democratic ideologies do not exist separately from but are articulated within class discourses, we cannot proceed directly to a study of the latter as such, and leave aside an analysis of the former. The answer is that such an emphasis would eliminate what is most specific to the ideological class struggle – the attempt to articulate the same interpellations in antagonistic discourses. It is precisely because 'the people' can never be totally absorbed by any class discourse, because there is always a certain openness in the ideological domain, whose structuring is never complete, that the class struggle can also occur as an ideological struggle. To suppose, on the contrary, that class ideologies constitute a closed and perfectly consistent bloc is to reduce the conflict between them to a purely mechanical clash which could hardly be characterised as 'ideological struggle'. To deny the dialectic between 'the people' and classes would be, then, to deny the ideological class struggle.

Let us consider more closely this characteristic dialectic between 'the people' and classes. Classes only exist as hegemonic forces to the extent that they can articulate popular interpellations to their own discourse. For the dominant classes this articulation consists, as we have seen, in a neutralisation of 'the people'. For the dominated classes to win hegemony, they must precipitate a crisis in the dominant ideological discourse and reduce its articulating principles to vacuous entelechies without any connotative power over popular interpellations. For this, they must develop the implicit antagonism of the latter to the point where 'the people' is completely unassimilable by any fraction of the power bloc. But, to present popular interpellations in the form of antagonism is, as we know, a characteristic of populism. If therefore a dominated class is to impose its hegemony through a confrontation with the power bloc, and if this confrontation necessitates the development of the antagonism implicit in popular interpellations, it can be deduced that the more radical is its confrontation with the system, the less possible will it be for that class to assert its hegemony without 'populism'. Populism is therefore not an expression of the ideological backwardness of a dominated class but, on the contrary, an expression of the moment when the articulating power of this class imposes itself hegemonically on the rest of society. This is the first movement in the dialectic between 'the people' and classes: *classes cannot assert their hegemony without articulating the people in their discourse; and the specific form of this articulation in the case of a class which seeks to confront the power bloc as a whole, in order to assert its hegemony, will be populism.*

Now let us look at the process from the other angle. The 'people'/power bloc contradiction cannot be developed without classes. If classes cannot be hegemonic without articulating 'the people', 'the people' only exist articulated to classes. The degree of 'populism', therefore, will depend on the nature of the antagonism existing between the class which is struggling for hegemony and the power bloc. Let us begin by posing an extreme case: that of a class which, in order to assert its hegemony, demands the *full* development of the antagonism inherent in popular-democratic interpellations. What does this *full* development mean? As we have argued here – and as Badiou and Balmès have noted from a different viewpoint – to the extent that popular resistance exerts itself against a power external and opposed to 'the people', that is to say, *against the very form of the State,* the resolution of 'the people'/power bloc contradiction can only consist in the suppression of the State as an antagonistic force with respect to the people. Therefore, the only social sector which can aspire to the full development of the people'/power bloc contradiction, that is to say, *to the highest and most radical form of populism,* is that whose *class interests* lead it to the suppression of the State as an antagonistic force. *In socialism, therefore, coincide the highest form of 'populism' and the resolution of the ultimate and most radical of class conflicts.* The dialectic between 'the people' and classes finds here the final moment of its unity: there is no socialism without populism, and the highest forms of populism can only be socialist. This is the profound intuition present from Mao to Togliatti in all those trends within Marxism which, from very diverse political positions and cultural traditions, have tried to go beyond class reductionism. The advance towards socialism can only consist, in that sense, in a long series of struggles through which socialism asserts its popular identity and 'the people' its socialist objectives. Socialist hegemony does not mean the pure and simple destruction of the previous society, but the absorption of its elements into a new articulation. It is only when socialism has developed this articulating capacity that it comes to be hegemonic.

Let us consider the opposite situation: that in which populism is developed by a class whose antagonism against the power bloc is less radical and which does not lead to the suppression of the State as an antagonistic force with regard to 'the people'. The dialectic between the people and classes leads in this case to different forms of articulation. The feature common to them all is that populist radicalisation of democratic interpellations must be linked to a connotative domain of such a kind as to contain the antagonism implicit in popular-democratic interpellations within the limits necessary for the confrontation of the new dominant class with the traditional power bloc. We already know how this neutralisation was achieved in the case of fascism: popular interpellations were linked to contents such as racism and corporativism which obstructed their radicalisation in a socialist direction. We also know that the maintenance of these limits necessitates a high degree of ideological homogenisation which was made possible only by repression. Hence the 'totalitarian' character of fascism. In the case of Bonapartist regimes – such as Peronism – the method of neutralisation was different: it consisted essentially in allowing the persistence of various 'elites' which based their support of the regime upon antagonistic articulating projects, and in confirming State power as a mediating force between them. There was thus a coexistence in Argentina between groups basing their support for the regime upon an articulation of 'populism' and clerical anti-liberalism, 'populism' and Nazism, 'populism' and trade-unionist reformism, 'populism' and democratic anti-imperialism and, finally, 'populism' and socialism. The Bonapartist State exerted a mediating power between these opposed bases of support and coalesced very few ideological symbols. The renowned ideological poverty and lack of official doctrine of Peronism is to be explained precisely by this mediating character of the State and Peron himself. Fascism, on the other hand, could develop a more precise official doctrine and a more defined ideological structure to the extent that it was a less 'mediating' and more 'totalitarian' experience. Bonapartist régimes, by definition, do not seek a unification or assimilation of ideological apparatuses, since it is precisely in their mediating capacity between opposing forces that their source of power is to be found. It is for this reason that, as we have pointed out, the radicalisation of Peronist political language beyond the limits tolerable to Bonapartism was a process that occurred after the fall of Peronism in 1955.

To conclude, we must answer the following question: why not limit the use of the term 'populism' to the second case we have analysed, and adopt a different terminology to refer to those experiences where radicalised popular interpellations have been articulated with socialism? This would apparently be the most sensible course, given the pejorative connotations generally associated with the term 'populism'. I do not think, however, that such a decision would be appropriate for it would obscure the universality of the basic premise constituted by the dual articulation of political discourse, and could lead to the illusion that popular interpellations within socialist discourse were *created* by this discourse and were absent from the ideology of dominant classes. This would be the surest way of falling into class reductionism. On the contrary, to assert the relative continuity of popular interpellations by contrast with the discontinuous articulations of class discourses is the only valid starting point for a scientific study of political ideologies.

Notes

1. The concept of mobilisation has been widely developed in modern political science literature. Cf. especially the works of J. P. Nettl, *Political Mobilisation. A Sociological Analysis of Methods and Concepts,* London, 1967; Apter 1969; Karl Deutsch, 'Social Mobilisation and Political Developments', in H. Eckstein and D. Apter, *Comparative Politics,* New York, 1963, pp. 582–603.
2. The conception of ideology and politics as *levels* presents a series of difficulties which we cannot pursue here. We will continue, therefore, to use the current term, 'class'.
3. Practices are, of course, always embodied in ideological apparatuses.
4. On this point we disagree with Perry Anderson's view that the persistence of British institutional and ideological particularism is the expression of an incompletely consummated bourgeois revolution. Cf. Perry Anderson, 'Origins of the Present Crisis', *New Left Review,* I/23, January–February, 1964.
5. Badiou and Balmès might object that they do not call popular ideologies themselves constants, only the communist elements in them. This does not affect our criticism, however, because as we have argued, communism is not a constant but one of the possible articulations of popular-democratic elements.
6. Cf. especially F. Weffort, 'Gases sociales y desarrollo social (Contribución al estudio del populismo)' in A. Quijano y F. Weffort, *Populismo, margin-alidad y dependencia,* Costa Rica, 1973; O. Ianni, *La Formación del Estado populista en America Latina,* Mexico, 1975.
7. This does not mean that the federal groups from the interior counterposed an alternative programme of economic development based on industrial sovereignty to the programme of capitalist expansion based on the penetration of imperialist capital and the full incorporation of Argentina in the world market. This fictive picture was the result of a reading of Argentinian history by nationalist writers after 1930, who thereby projected into the 19th century the connotative domain to which anti-liberalism was linked in their own epoch.
8. 'Modos de Producción, Sistemas Económicos y Población Excedente. Aproximación Histórica a los Casos Argentino y Chileno', *Revista Latino-Americana de Sociologia,* 1969, No 2.
9. This does not mean that Roca was not a perfect liberal, as much as, or more than Mitre. The difference was that Roca represented a more advanced moment of liberalism, when its increasing hegemony enabled it to begin partially absorbing elements of the federal tradition and integrating them into its discourse. But of course, it would be utterly mistaken to suppose that for this reason Roca embodied a more nationalist economic policy or a greater degree of resistance to imperialist penetration.
10. By contrast, in some cases where it was more difficult for the power bloc to co-opt the middle classes and transformism operated inadequately, there occurred a Jacobinisation of democratic interpellations and the emergence, even in this period, of populism. This was the case in Chile, where the collapse of Alessandri's attempts during the 1920s to carry out his programme of democratic reforms within the framework of the liberal State, led to the popular dictatorship of General Ibanez, which did carry it out within a clearly nationalist and populist ideological framework. It was also the case in Peru, where the inability of oligarchic liberalism to incorporate and neutralise middle-class demands led to their increasing fusion with an indigenist ideology in the American Popular Revolutionary Alliance (APRA). Finally, it was the case too in Mexico, where the contradiction

between the peasant communities and the expansion of agrarian capitalism prevented the revolution against the Porfiriato from being kept at the mere level of reforms within the liberal State, and led on the contrary to the collapse of the Madero regime and to the long process of the Mexican Revolution
11 J.D. Peron, speech proclaiming his candidature, 12 February 1946. Reproduced in M. Peña, *El Peronismo, Selección de Documentos para la Historia,* Buenos Aires, 1972, p. 10.
12 *Ibid.*, p. 12.
13 Cf. Ernesto Laclau, 'Argentina: Imperialist Strategy and the May Crisis', *New Left Review,* No 62, July–August, 1970.

Bibliography

Apter, D. 1969. *The Politics of Modernisation*. London: University of Chicago Press.
Badiou, A. and Balmès, F. 1976. *De l'Idéologie*. Paris.
Deutsch, K. 1963. Social Mobilisation and Political Developments. In *Comparative Politics,* eds H. Eckstein and D. Apter. New York.
Di Tella, T. 1970. Populism and Reform in Latin America. In *Obstacles to Change in Latin America,* ed. C. Véliz. London.
Germani, G. 1965. *Politicay Sociedad en una epoca de transition*. Buenos Aires.
Macpherson, C.B. 1975. *The Real World of Democracy*. Oxford: Oxford University Press.
Nettl, J.P. 1967. *Political Mobilisation. A Sociological Analysis of Methods and Concepts*. London.
Worsley, P. 1970. The Concept of Populism. In *Populism,* ed. G. Ionescu and E. Gellner. London: Weidenfeld & Nicolson.

7

POPULISM

What's in a name? (2005)

Any definition presupposes a theoretical grid giving sense to what is defined. This sense – as the very notion of definition asserts – can only be established on the basis of differentiating the defined term from something else that the definition excludes. This, in turn, presupposes a *terrain* within which those differences as such are thinkable. It is this terrain which is not immediately obvious when we call a movement (?), an ideology (?), a political practice (?) populist. In the first two cases – movements or ideologies – to call them populist would involve differentiating that attribute from other characterisations at the same defining level, such as 'fascist', 'liberal', 'communist', etc. This engages us immediately in a complicated and ultimately self-defeating task: finding that ultimate redoubt where we would find 'pure' populism, irreducible to those other alternative characterisations. If we attempt to do so we enter into a game in which any attribution of a social or ideological content to populism is immediately confronted with an avalanche of exceptions. Thus we are forced to conclude that when we use the term some actual meaning is presupposed by our linguistic practices, but that such a meaning is not, however, translatable in any definable sense. Furthermore, we can even less, through that meaning, point to any identifiable referent (which would exhaust that meaning).

What if we move from movements or ideologies as units of analysis, to political practices? Everything depends on how we conceive of that move. If it is governed by the unity of a subject constituted at the level of the ideology or the political movement, we have not, obviously, advanced a single step in the determination of what is specifically populist. The difficulties in determining the populistic character of the subjects of certain practices cannot but reproduce themselves in the analysis of the practices as such, as far as the latter simply *expresses* the inner nature of those subjects. There is, however a second possibility – namely, that the political practices do not *express* the nature of social agents but, instead, *constitute* the latter. In that case the political practice would have some kind of ontological priority over the agent – the latter would merely be the historical precipitate of the former. To put it in slightly different terms: practices would be more primary units of analysis than the group – that is, the group would only be the result of an articulation of social practices. If this approach is correct, we could say that a movement is not populist because in its politics or ideology it presents actual *contents* identifiable as populistic, but because it shows a particular *logic of articulation* of those contents – whatever those contents are.

A last remark is necessary before we enter into the substance of our argument. The category of 'articulation' has had some currency in theoretical language over the last thirty or forty years – especially within the Althusserian school and its area of influence. We should say, however, that the notion of articulation that Althusserianism developed was mainly limited to the *ontic* contents entering into the articulating process (the economic, the political, the ideological). There was some *ontological* theorisation as far as articulation is concerned (the notions of 'determination in the last instance' and of 'relative autonomy'), but as these formal logics appeared as necessarily derived from the ontic content of some categories (for example, the determination in the last instance could *only* correspond to the economy), the possibility of advancing an ontology of the social was strictly limited from the very beginning. Given these limitations, the political logic of populism was unthinkable.

In what follows, I will advance three theoretical propositions: (1) that to think the specificity of populism requires starting the analysis from units smaller than the group (whether at the political or at the ideological level); (2) that populism is an ontological and not an ontic category – i.e. its meaning is not to be found in any political or ideological content entering into the description of the practices of any particular group, but in a particular *mode of articulation* of whatever social, political or ideological contents; (3) that that articulating form, apart from its contents, produces structuring effects which primarily manifest themselves at the level of the modes of representation.

Social demands and social totality

As we have just asserted, our starting point should be the isolation of smaller units than the group and the consideration of the social logics of their articulation. Populism is one of those logics. Let us say, to start with, that our analysis postulates an asymmetry between the community as a whole ('society') and whatever social actor operates within it. That is, there is no social agent whose will coincides with the actual workings of society conceived as a totality. Rousseau was perfectly aware that the constitution of a general will – which was for him the condition of democracy – was increasingly difficult under the conditions of modern societies, where their very dimensions and their heterogeneity make the recourse to mechanisms of representation imperative; Hegel attempted to address the question through the postulation of a division between civil and political society, where the first represented particularism and heterogeneity (the 'system of needs') and the second the moment of totalisation and universality; and Marx reasserted the utopia of an exact overlapping between communitarian space and collective will through the role of a universal class in a reconciled society. The starting point of our discussion is that no attempt to bridge the chasm between political will and communitarian space can ultimately succeed, but that the attempt to construct such a bridge defines the specifically political articulation of social identities.

We should add, to avoid misunderstanding, that this non-overlapping between the community as a totality and the actual and partial wills of social actors does not lead us to adopt any kind of methodologically individualistic approach to the question of agency. The latter presupposes that the individuals are meaningful, self-defined totalities; it is only one step from there to conclude that social interaction should be conceived in terms of negotiations between agents whose identities are constituted around clear-cut interests. Our approach is, on the contrary, entirely holistic, with the only qualification that the promise of fullness contained in the notion of an entirely self-determined social whole is unachievable. So the attempt at building communitarian spaces out of a plurality of collective wills can never adopt the form of a contract – the latter presupposing the notions of interests and self-determined wills that we are putting into question. The communitarian fullness that the social whole cannot provide cannot be transferred either to the individuals. Individuals are not coherent totalities but merely referential identities which have to be split up into a series of localised subject positions. And the articulation between these positions is a social and not an individual affair (the very notion of 'individual' does not make sense in our approach).

So what are these smaller units from which our analysis has to start? Our guiding thread will be the category of 'demand' as the elementary form in the building-up of the social link. The word 'demand' is ambiguous in English: it has, on the one hand, the meaning of *request* and, on the other, the more active meaning of *imposing* a request – a claim – on somebody else (as in 'demanding an explanation'). In other languages, like Spanish, there are different words for the two meanings: the word corresponding to our second meaning would be *reivindicación*. Although when in our analysis we use the term 'demand' we clearly put the stress on the second meaning, the very ambiguity between both is not without its advantages, because the theoretical notion of demand that we will employ implies a certain undecidability between the two meanings – in actual fact, as we will see, they correspond to two different forms of political articulation. Let us also add that there is a common hidden assumption underlying both meanings: namely that the demand is not self-satisfied but has to be addressed to an instance different from that within which the demand was originally formulated.

Let us give the example of a straightforward demand: a group of people living in a certain neighbourhood want a bus route introduced to transport them from their places of residence to the area in which most of them work. Let us suppose that they approach the city hall with that request and that the request is satisfied. We have here the following set of structural features: (1) a social need adopts the form of a *request* – i.e. it is not satisfied through self-management but through the appeal to another instance which has the power of decision; (2) the very fact that a request takes place shows that the decisory power of the higher instance is not put into question at all – so we are fully within our first meaning of the term demand; (3) the demand is a punctual demand, closed in itself – it is not the tip of an iceberg or the symbol of a large variety of unformulated social demands. If we put these three features together we can formulate the following important conclusion: requests of this type, in which demands are punctual or individually satisfied, do not construct any chasm or frontier within the social. On the contrary, social actors are accepting, as a non-verbalised assumption of the whole process, the legitimacy of each of its instances: nobody puts into question either the right to present the request or the right of the decisory instance to take the decision. Each instance is a part (or a differential point) of a highly institutionalised social immanence. Social logics operating according to this institutionalised, differential model, we will call *logics of difference*. They presuppose that there is no social division and that any legitimate demand can be satisfied in a non-antagonistic, administrative way. Examples of social utopias advocating the universal operation of differential logics come easily to mind: the Disraelian notion of 'one nation', the welfare state or the Saint-Simonian motto: 'From the government of men to the administration of things'.

Let us now go back to our example. Let us suppose that the request is rejected. A situation of social frustration will, no doubt, derive from that decision. But, if it is only *one* demand that is not satisfied, that will not alter the situation substantially. If, however, for whatever reason, the variety of demands that do not find satisfaction is very large, that multiple frustration will trigger social logics of an entirely different kind. If, for instance, the group of people in that area who have been frustrated in their request for better transportation find that their neighbours are equally unsatisfied in their claims at the levels of security, water supply, housing, schooling and so on, some kind of solidarity will arise between them all: all will share the fact that their demands remain unsatisfied. That is, the demands share a *negative* dimension beyond their positive differential nature.

A social situation in which demands tend to reaggregate themselves on the negative basis that they all remain unsatisfied is the first precondition – but by no means the only one – of that mode of political articulation that we call populism. Let us enumerate those of its structural features that we can detect at this stage of our argument.

(1) While the institutional arrangement previously discussed was grounded on the logic of difference, we have here an inverse situation, which can be described as a *logic of equivalence* – i.e. one in which all the demands, in spite of their differential character, tend to reaggregate themselves, forming what we will call an *equivalential chain*. This means that each individual demand is constitutively split: on the one hand, it is its own particularised self; on the other, it points, through equivalential links, to the totality of the other demands. Returning to our image: each demand is, actually, the tip of an iceberg,

because although it only shows itself in its own particularity, it presents its own manifest claim as only one among a larger set of social claims.
(2) The subject of the demand is different in our two cases. In the first, the subject of the demand was as punctual as the demand itself. The subject of a demand conceived as differential particularity we will call *democratic subject*. In the other case the subject will be wider, for its subjectivity will result from the equivalential aggregation of a plurality of democratic demands. A subject constituted on the basis of this logic we will call *popular subject*. This shows clearly the conditions for either the emergence or disappearance of a popular subjectivity: the more social demands tend to be differentially absorbed within a successful institutional system, the weaker the equivalential links will be and the more unlikely the constitution of a popular subjectivity; conversely, a situation in which a plurality of unsatisfied demands and an increasing inability of the institutional system to absorb them differentially co-exist, and thus creates the conditions leading to a populist rupture.
(3) It is a corollary of the previous analysis that there is no emergence of a popular subjectivity without the creation of an internal frontier. The equivalences are only such in terms of a lack pervading them all, and this requires the identification of the source of social negativity. Equivalential popular discourses divide, in this way, the social into two camps: power and the underdog. This transforms the nature of the demands: they cease to be simple requests and become fighting demands *(reivindicaciones)* – in other words we move to the second meaning of the term 'demand'.

Equivalences, popular subjectivity, dichotomic construction of the social around an internal frontier. We have apparently all the structural features to define populism. Not quite so, however. A crucial dimension is still missing, which we have now to consider.

Empty and floating signifiers

Our discussion so far has led us to recognise two conditions – which structurally require each other – for the emergence of a populist rupture: the dichotomisation of the social space through the creation of an internal frontier, and the construction of an equivalential chain between unfulfilled demands. These, strictly speaking, are not two conditions but two aspects of the same condition, for the internal frontier can only result from the operation of the equivalential chain. What is important, in any case, is to realise that the equivalential chain has an *anti-institutional* character: it subverts the particularistic, differential character of the demands. There is, at some point, a short-circuit in the relation between demands put to the 'system' and the ability of the latter to meet them. What we have to discuss now are the effects of that short-circuit on both the nature of the demands and the system conceived as a totality.

The equivalential demands confront us immediately with the problem of the representation of the specifically equivalential moment. For, obviously, the demands are always particular, while the more universal dimension linked to the equivalence lacks any direct, evident mode of representation. It is our contention that the first precondition for the representation of the equivalential moment is the totalisation (through signification) of the power which is opposed to the ensemble of those demands constituting the popular will. This should be evident: for the equivalential chain to create a frontier within the social it is necessary somehow to represent the other side of the frontier. There is no populism without discursive construction of an enemy: the *ancien régime,* the oligarchy, the Establishment or whatever. We will later return to this aspect. What we will now concentrate on is the transition from democratic subject positions to popular ones on the basis of the frontier effects deriving from the equivalences.

So how does the equivalence *show* itself? As we have asserted, the equivalential moment cannot be found in any positive feature underlying all the demands, for – from the viewpoint of those features – they are entirely different from each other. The equivalence proceeds entirely from the opposition to the power beyond the frontier, which does not satisfy any of the equivalential demands. In that case, however, how can the chain as such be represented? As I have argued elsewhere (Chapter 3, this volume) that representation is only possible if a particular demand, without entirely abandoning its own particularity, starts also functioning as a signifier representing the chain as a totality (in the same way as gold, without ceasing to be a particular commodity, transforms its own materiality into the universal representation of value). This process by which a particular demand comes to represent an equivalential chain incommensurable with it is, of course, what we have called *hegemony*. The demands of Solidarnoś?, for instance, started by being the demands of a particular working-class group in Gdansk, but as they were formulated in an oppressed society, where many social demands were frustrated, they became the signifiers of the popular camp in a new dichotomic discourse.

Now there is a feature of this process of constructing a universal popular signification which is particularly important for understanding populism. It is the following: the more the chain of equivalences is extended, the weaker will be its connection with the particularistic demands which assume the function of universal representation. This leads us to a conclusion which is crucial for our analysis: the construction of a popular subjectivity is possible only on the basis of discursively producing *tendentially* empty signifiers. The so-called 'poverty' of the populist symbols is the condition of their political efficacy – as their function is to bring to equivalential homogeneity a highly heterogeneous reality, they can only do so on the basis of reducing to a minimum their particularistic content. At the limit, this process reaches a point where the homogenising function is carried out by a pure name: the name of the leader.

There are two other important aspects that, at this point, we should take into consideration. The first concerns the particular kind of distortion that the equivalential logics introduce into the construction of the 'people' and 'power' as antagonistic poles. In the case of the 'people', as we have seen, the equivalential logic is based on an 'emptying' whose consequences are, at the same time, enriching and impoverishing. Enriching: the signifiers unifying an equivalential chain, because they must cover all the links integrating the latter, have a wider reference than a purely differential content which would attach a signifier to just one signified. Impoverishing: precisely because of this wider (potentially universal) reference, its connection with particular contents tends to be drastically reduced. Using a logical distinction, we could say that what it wins in *extension* it loses in *intension*. And the same happens in the construction of the pole of power: that pole does not simply function through the materiality of its differential content, for that content is the *bearer* of the negation of the popular pole (through the frustration of the latter's demands). As a result, there is an essential instability which permeates the various moments that we have isolated in our study. As far as the particular demands are concerned nothing anticipates, in their isolated contents, the way in which they will be differentially or equivalentially articulated – that will depend on the historical context – and nothing anticipates either (in the case of the equivalences) the extension and the composition of the chains in which they participate. And as for the two poles of the people/power dichotomy, their actual identity and structure will be equally open to contestation and redefinition. France had experienced food riots since the Middle Ages but these riots, as a rule, did not identify the monarchy as their enemy. All the complex transformations of the eighteenth century were required to reach a stage in which food demands became part of revolutionary equivalential chains embracing the totality of the political system. And the American populism of farmers, at the end of the nineteenth century, failed because the attempt at creating chains of popular equivalence unifying the demands of the dispossessed groups found a decisive obstacle in a set of structural *differential* limits which proved to be stronger than the populist interpellations: namely, the difficulties in bringing together black and white farmers, the mutual distrust between farmers and urban workers, the deeply entrenched loyalty of Southern farmers to the Democratic Party and so on.

This leads us to our second consideration. Throughout our previous study, we have been operating under the simplifying assumption of the *de facto* existence of a frontier separating two antagonistic equivalential chains. This is the assumption that we have now to put into question. Our whole approach leads us, actually, to this questioning, for if there is no a priori reason why a demand should enter into some particular equivalential chains and differential articulations rather than into others, we should expect that antagonistic political strategies would be based on different ways of creating political frontiers, and that the latter would be exposed to destabilisations and transformations.

If this is so, our assumptions must, to some extent, be modified. Each discursive element would be submitted to the structural pressure of contradictory articulating attempts. In our theorisation of the role of the empty signifiers, their very possibility depended on the presence of a chain of equivalences which involves, as we have seen, an internal frontier. The classical forms of populism – most of the Latin American populisms of the 1940s and 1950s, for instance – correspond to this description. The political dynamic of populism depends on this internal frontier being constantly reproduced. Using a simile from linguistics we could say that while an institutionalist political discourse tends to privilege the syntagmatic pole of language – the number of differential locations articulated by relations of combination – the populist discourse tends to privilege the paradigmatic pole, i.e. the relations of substitution between elements (demands, in our case) aggregated around only two syntagmatic positions.

The internal frontier on which the populist discourse is grounded can, however, be subverted. This can happen in two different ways. One is to break the equivalential links between the various particular demands, through the individual satisfaction of the latter. This is the road to the decline of the populist form of politics, to the blurring of the internal frontiers and to the transition to a higher level of integration of the institutional system – a transformist operation, as Gramsci called it. It corresponds, broadly speaking, to Disraeli's project of 'one nation', or to the contemporary attempts by theoreticians of the Third Way and the 'radical centre' at substituting administration for politics.

The second way of subverting the internal frontier is of an entirely different nature. It does not consist in *eliminating* the frontiers but in *changing their political sign*. As we have seen, as the central signifiers of a popular discourse become partially empty, they weaken their former links with some particular contents – those contents become perfectly open to a *variety* of equivalential rearticulations. Now, it is enough that the empty popular signifiers keep their radicalism – that is, their ability to divide society into two camps – while, however, the chain of equivalences that they unify becomes a different one, for the political meaning of the whole populist operation to acquire an opposite political sign. The twentieth century provides countless examples of these reversals. In America, the signifiers of popular radicalism, which at the time of the New Deal had a mainly left-wing connotation, were later reappropriated by the radical Right, from George Wallace to the 'moral majority'. In France the radical 'tribunicial function' of the Communist Party has, to some extent, been absorbed by the National Front. And the whole expansion of fascism during the inter-war period would be unintelligible without making reference to the right-wing rearticulation of themes and demands belonging to the revolutionary tradition.

What is important is to grasp the pattern of this process of rearticulation: it depends on partially keeping in operation the central signifiers of popular radicalism while inscribing in a different chain of equivalences many of the democratic demands. This hegemonic rearticulation is possible because no social demand has ascribed to it, as a 'manifest destiny' any a priori form of inscription – everything depends on a hegemonic contest. Once a demand is submitted to the articulatory attempts of a plurality of antagonistic projects it lives in a no-man's-land *vis-à-vis* the latter – it acquires a partial and transitory autonomy. To refer to this ambiguity of the popular signifiers and of the demands that they articulate we will speak of *floating signifiers*. The kind of structural relation that constitutes them is different from the one that we have found operating in the empty signifiers: while the latter depend on a fully fledged internal frontier resulting from an equivalential chain, the floating signifiers are the expression of the ambiguity inherent to all frontiers and of the impossibility of the latter acquiring any ultimate stability. The distinction is, however, mainly analytic, for in practice empty and floating signifiers largely overlap: there is no historical situation where society is so consolidated that its internal frontier is not submitted to any subversion or displacement, and no organic crisis so deep that some forms of stability do not put limits on the operativity of the subversive tendencies.

Populism, politics and representation

Let us put together the various threads of our argument so as to formulate a coherent concept of populism. Such a coherence can only be obtained if the different dimensions entering into the elaboration of the concept are not just discrete features brought together through simple enumeration, but part of a theoretically articulated whole. To start with, we only have populism if there is a series of politico-discursive practices constructing a popular subject, and the precondition of the emergence of such a subject is, as we have seen, the building up of an internal frontier dividing the social space into two camps. But the logic of that division is dictated, as we know, by the creation of an equivalential chain between a series of social demands in which the equivalential moment prevails over the differential nature of the demands. Finally, the equivalential chain cannot be the result of a purely fortuitous coincidence, but has to be consolidated through the emergence of an element which gives coherence to the chain by signifying it as a totality. This element is what we have called *empty signifier*.

These are all the structural defining features which enter, in my view, into the category of populism. As can be seen, the concept of populism that I am proposing is a strictly *formal* one, for all its defining features are exclusively related to a specific mode of articulation – the prevalence of the equivalential over the differential logic – independently of the actual *contents* that are articulated. That is the reason why, at the beginning of this chapter, I asserted that 'populism' is an ontological and not an ontic category. Most of the attempts at defining populism have tried to locate what is specific to it in a particular ontic content and, as a result, they have ended in a self-defeating exercise whose two predictable alternative results have been either to choose an empirical content which is immediately overflowed by an avalanche of exceptions, or to appeal to an 'intuition' which cannot be translated into any conceptual content.

This displacement of the conceptualisation, from contents to form, has several advantages (apart from the obvious one of avoiding the naïve sociologism which reduces the political forms to the preconstituted unity of the group). In the first place, we have a way of addressing the recurrent problem of dealing with the ubiquity of populism – the fact that it can emerge from different points of the socio-economic structure. If its defining features are found in the prevalence of the logic of equivalence, the production of empty signifiers and the construction of political frontiers through the interpellation of the underdog, we understand immediately that the discourses grounded in this articulatory logic can start from *any* place in the socio-institutional structure: clientelistic political organisations, established political parties, trade unions, the army, revolutionary movements and so on. 'Populism' does not define the actual politics of these organisations, but is a way of articulating their themes – whatever those themes may be.

Secondly, we can grasp better, in this way, something which is essential for the understanding of the contemporary political scene: the circulation of the signifiers of radical protest between movements of entirely opposite political signs. We have made reference before to this question. To give just one example: the circulation of the signifiers of Mazzinism and Garibaldianism in Italy during the war of liberation (1943–45). These had been the signifiers of radical protest in Italy, going back to the Risorgimento. Both fascists and communists tried to articulate them to their discourses and, as a result, they became partially autonomous *vis-à-vis* those various forms of political articulation. They retained the dimension of radicalism, but whether that radicalism would move in a right or in a left direction was at the beginning undecided – they were floating signifiers, in the sense that we have discussed. It is obviously an idle exercise to ask oneself what social group expresses itself through those populist symbols: the chains of equivalence that they formed cut across many social sectors, and the radicalism that they signified could be articulated by movements of entirely opposite political signs. This migration of signifiers can be described if populism is conceived as a formal principle of articulation; not if that principle is concealed behind the particular contents that incarnate it in different political conjunctures.

Finally, approaching the question of populism formally makes it possible to address another, otherwise intractable issue. To ask oneself if a movement *is* or *is not* populist is, actually, to start with the wrong question. The question that we should, instead, ask ourselves, is the following: *to what extent* is a movement populist? As we know, this question is identical to this other one: to what extent does the logic of equivalence dominate its discourse? We have presented political practices as operating at diverse points of a continuum whose two *reductio ad absurdum* extremes would be an institutionalist discourse, dominated by a pure logic of difference, and a populist one, in which the logic of equivalence operates unchallenged. These two extremes are actually unreachable: pure difference would mean a society so dominated by administration and by the individualisation of social demands that no struggle around internal frontiers – i.e. no politics – would be possible; and pure equivalence would involve such a dissolution of social links that the very notion of 'social demand' would lose any meaning – this is the image of the 'crowd' as depicted by the nineteenth-century theorists of 'mass psychology' (Taine, Le Bon, Sighele, etc.).

It is important to realise that the impossibility of the two extremes of pure difference or pure equivalence is not an empirical one – it is logical. The subversion of difference by an equivalential logic does not take the form of a total elimination of the former through the latter. A relation of equivalence is not one in which all differences collapse into identity, but one in which differences are still very active. The equivalence eliminates the *separation* between the demands, but not the demands themselves. If a series of demands – transport, housing, employment and so on, to go back to our initial example – are unfulfilled, the equivalence existent between them – and the popular identity resulting from that equivalence – requires very much the persistence of the demands. So equivalence is still definitely a particular way of articulating differences. Thus between equivalence and difference there is a complex dialectic, an unstable compromise. We will have a variety of historical situations which presuppose the *presence* of both, but at the same time, their *tension*. Let us mention some of them:

(1) An institutional system becomes less and less able to differentially absorb social demands, and this leads to an internal chasm within society and the construction of two antagonistic chains of equivalences. This is the classic experience of a populist or revolutionary rupture, which results generally from the types of crisis of representation that Gramsci called 'organic crises'.

(2) The regime resulting from a populist rupture becomes progressively institutionalised, so that the differential logic starts prevailing again and the equivalential popular identity increasingly becomes an inoperative *langue de bois* governing less and less the actual workings of politics. Peronism, in Argentina, attempted to move from an initial politics of confrontation – whose popular subject was the *descamisado* (the equivalent of the *sans-culottes*) to an increasingly institutionalised discourse grounded in what was called 'the organised community' (*la comunidad organizada*). We find another variant of this increasing asymmetry between actual demands and equivalential discourse in those cases in which the latter becomes the *langue de bois* of the state. We find in them that the increasing distance between actual social demands and dominant equivalential discourse frequently leads to the repression of the former and the violent imposition of the latter. Many African regimes, after the process of decolonisation, followed this pattern.

(3) Some dominant groups attempt to constantly recreate the internal frontiers through an increasingly anti-institutional discourse. These attempts generally fail. Let us just think of the process, in France, leading from Jacobinism to the Directoire and, in China, the various stages in the cycle of the 'Cultural Revolution'.

A movement or an ideology – or, to put both under their common genus, a discourse – will be more or less populistic depending on the degree to which its contents are articulated by equivalential logics. This means that no political movement will be entirely exempt from populism, because none will fail to interpellate to some extent the 'people' against an enemy, through the construction of a social frontier. That is why its populist credentials will be shown in a particularly clear way at moments of political transition, when the future of the community is in the balance. The degree of 'populism', in that sense, will depend on the depth of the chasm separating political alternatives. This poses a problem, however. If populism consists in postulating a radical alternative within the communitarian space, a choice at the crossroads on which the future of a given society hinges, does not populism become synonymous with politics? The answer can only be affirmative. Populism means putting into question the institutional order by constructing an underdog as an historical agent – i.e. an agent which is an *other* in relation to the way things stand. But this is the same as politics. We only have politics through the gesture which embraces the existing state of affairs as a system and presents an alternative to it (or, conversely, when we defend that system against existing potential alternatives). That is the reason why the end of populism coincides with the end of politics. We have an end of politics when the community conceived as a totality, and the will representing that totality, become indistinguishable from each other. In that case, as I have argued throughout this chapter, politics is replaced by administration and the traces of social division disappear. Hobbes' *Leviathan* as the undivided will of an absolute ruler, or Marx's universal subject of a classless society, represent parallel ways – although, of course, of an opposite sign – of the end of politics. A total, unchallengeable state and the withering away of the state are both ways of cancelling out the traces of social division. But it is easy, in that sense, to see that the conditions of possibility of the political and the conditions of possibility of populism are the same: they both presuppose social division; in both we find an ambiguous *demos* which is, on the one hand, a section within the community (an underdog) and, on the other hand, an agent presenting itself, in an antagonistic way, as *the whole* community.

This conclusion leads us to a last consideration. As far as we have politics (and also, if our argument is correct, its derivative which is populism) we are going to have social division. A corollary of this social division is that a section within the community will present itself as the expression and representation of the community as a whole. This chasm is ineradicable as far as we have a *political* society. This means that the 'people' can only be constituted in the terrain of the relations of representation. We have already explained the representative matrix out of which the 'people' emerges: a certain particularity which assumes a function of universal representation; the distortion of the identity of this particularity through the constitution of equivalential chains; the popular camp resulting from these substitutions presenting itself as representing society as a whole. These considerations have some important consequences. The first is that the 'people', as operating in populist discourses, is never a primary datum but a construct – populist discourse does not simply *express* some kind of original popular identity; it actually *constitutes* the latter. The second is that, as a result, relations of representation are not a secondary level reflecting a primary social reality constituted elsewhere; they are, on the contrary, the primary terrain within which the social is constituted. Any kind of political transformation will, as a result, take place as an internal displacement of the elements entering the representation process. The third consequence is that representation is not a second best, as Rousseau would have had it, resulting from the increasing chasm between the universal communitarian space and the particularism of the actually existing collective wills. On the contrary, the asymmetry between community as a whole and collective wills is the source of that exhilarating game that we call politics, from which we find our limits but also our possibilities. Many important things result from the impossibility of an ultimate universality – among others, the emergence of the 'people'.

8

WHY CONSTRUCTING A PEOPLE IS THE MAIN TASK OF RADICAL POLITICS (2006)

I have been rather surprised by Slavoj Žižek's critique of my book *On Populist Reason*.[1] Given that the latter is strongly critical of Žižek's approach, I was expecting, of course, some reaction on his part. He has chosen for his reply, however, a rather indirect and oblique road; he does not answer a single of my criticisms of his work and formulates, instead, a series of objections to my book that only make sense if one fully accepts his theoretical perspective—which is, precisely, what I had questioned. To avoid continuing with this dialogue of the deaf I will take the bull by the horns, reasserting what I see as fundamentally wrong in Žižek's approach and, in the course of this argument, I will also refute Žižek's criticisms.

Populism and class struggle

I will leave aside the sections of Žižek's essay dealing with the French and Dutch referenda—a matter on which my own views are not far from his[2]—and will instead concentrate on the theoretical parts, where he states our divergences. Žižek starts by saying that I prefer populism to class struggle (see p. 554). This is a rather nonsensical way of presenting the argument. It suggests that populism and class struggle are two entities actually existing in the world, between which one would have to choose, such as when one chooses to belong to a political party or to a football club. The actual fact is that my notion of the people and the classical Marxist conception of class struggle are two different ways of conceiving the construction of social identities, so that if one is correct the other has to be dismissed—or, rather, reabsorbed and redefined in terms of the alternative view. Žižek gives, however, an accurate description of the points where the two outlooks differ:

> Class struggle presupposes a particular social group (the working class) as a privileged political agent; this privilege is not itself the outcome of

hegemonic struggle, but grounded in the "objective social position" of this group—the ideologico-political struggle is thus ultimately reduced to an epiphenomenon of "objective" social processes, powers, and their conflicts. For Laclau, on the contrary, the fact that some particular struggle is elevated into the "universal equivalent" of all struggles is not a predetermined fact but itself the result of the contingent political struggle for hegemony. In some constellation, this struggle can be the workers' struggle, in another constellation, the patriotic anticolonialist struggle, in yet another constellation, the antiracist struggle for cultural tolerance. There is nothing in the inherent positive qualities of some particular struggle that predestines it for such a hegemonic role as the "general equivalent" of all struggles.

(p. 554)

Although this description of the contrast is obviously incomplete, I do not object to the general picture of the basic distinction between the two approaches that it provides. To this, however, Žižek proposes a further feature of populism that I would not have taken into account. While I would have rightly pointed out the empty character of the master signifier embodying the enemy, I would not have mentioned the *pseudoconcreteness* of the figure incarnating such an enemy. I must say that I do not find any substance in this charge. My whole analysis is precisely based upon the assertion that any politico-discursive field is always structured through a reciprocal process by which emptiness weakens the particularity of a concrete signifier, but, conversely, that particularity reacts by giving to universality a necessary incarnating body. I have defined hegemony as a relationship by which a certain particularity becomes the name of an utterly incommensurable universality. So the universal, lacking any means of direct representation, obtains only a borrowed presence through the distorted means of its investment in a certain particularity.

But let us leave this issue aside for the time being, for Žižek has a far more fundamental addition to propose to my theoretical notion of populism. According to him, one needs also to consider the way in which populist discourse displaces the antagonism and constructs the enemy. In populism, the enemy is externalized or reified into a positive ontological entity (even if this entity is spectral) whose annihilation would restore balance and justice; symmetrically, our own—the populist political agent's—identity is also perceived as preexisting the enemy's onslaught (p. 555).

Of course, I never said that populist identity preexists the enemy's onslaught, but exactly the opposite: that such an onslaught is the precondition of any popular identity. I have even quoted, to describe the relation I had in mind, Saint-Just as saying that the unity of the Republic is only the destruction of what is opposed to it. But let us see how Žižek's argument unfolds. He asserts that reifying antagonism into a positive entity involves an elementary form of ideological mystification and that, although populism can move in a variety of political directions (reactionary, nationalist, progressive nationalist, and so on), "insofar as, in its very notion, it displaces the immanent social antagonism into the antagonism between the unified people and its external enemy, it harbors in the last instance a long-term protofascist tendency" (p. 557). To this he adds his reasons to think that communist movements can never be populistic, that while in fascism the Idea is subordinated to the will of the leader, in communism Stalin is a *secondary leader*—in the Freudian sense—because he is subordinated to the Idea. A beautiful compliment to Stalin! As everybody knows, he *was not* subordinated to *any* ideology but manipulated the latter in the most grotesque way to make it serve his pragmatic political agenda. For example, the principle of national self-determination had pride of place in the Stalinist ideological universe; there was, however, the proviso that it had to be applied "dialectically," which meant that it could be violated as many times as was considered politically convenient. Stalin was not a particularity subsumable under a conceptual universality; instead, conceptual universality was subsumed under the name Stalin. From this point of view, Hitler was not lacking in political ideas either—the Fatherland, the race, and so on—which he equally manipulated for reasons of political expediency. I am not saying that the Nazi and the Stalinist regimes were indistinguishable, of course, but, instead, that whatever differences between them one can find they are not grounded in a different ontological relationship between the Leader and the Idea.[3] (As for the actual relationship between populism and communism I will come back to that presently.)

But let us go back to the logical steps through which Žižek's analysis is structured—that is, how he conceives of his supplement to my theoretical construct. His argument is hardly anything more than a succession of *non sequitur* conclusions. The sequence is as follows: (1) he starts by quoting a passage from my book in which, referring to the way popular identities were constituted in British Chartism, I show that the evils of society were not presented as deriving from the economic system, but from the abuse of power by parasitic and speculative groups;[4] (2) he finds that something similar happens in fascist discourse, where the figure of the Jew becomes the concrete incarnation of everything that is wrong with society (this concretization is presented by him as an operation of reification); (3) he concludes that this shows that in all populism (why? how?) there is "a long-term protofascist tendency"; (4) communism, however, would be immune to populism because, in its discourse, reification does not take place, and the leader safely remains as a secondary one. It is not difficult to perceive the fallacy of this whole argument. First, Chartism and fascism are presented as two species of the genus populism; second, one of the species' (fascism's) *modus operandi* is conceived as reification; third, for no stated reasons (at this point the Chartist example is silently forgotten) that makes the *modus operandi* of the species become the defining feature of the whole genus; fourth, as a result, one of the species becomes the teleological destiny of all the other species belonging to that genus. To this we should add, fifth, as a further unwarranted conclusion, that if communism cannot be a species of the genus populism, it is *presumably* (the point is nowhere explicitly made) because reification does not take place in it. In the case of communism we would have an unmediated universality; this would be the reason why the supreme incarnation of the concrete, the Leader, has to be entirely subordinated to the Idea.

Needless to say, this last conclusion is not grounded on any historical evidence but on a purely a prioristic argument.

More important, however, than insisting on the obvious circularity of Žižek's whole reasoning, is to explore the two unargued assumptions on which the latter is based. They are as follows: (1) any incarnation of the universal in the particular should be conceived as reification; (2) such an incarnation is inherently fascist. To these postulates we will oppose two theses: (1) that the notion of reification is entirely inadequate to understand the kind of incarnation of the universal in the particular that is inherent in the construction of a popular identity; (2) that such an incarnation—rightly understood—far from being a characteristic of fascism or of any other political movement, is inherent to any kind of hegemonic relation—that is, to the kind of relation inherent to the political as such.

Let us start with *reification*. This is not a common-language term but has a very specific philosophical content. It was first introduced by Lukács, although most of its dimensions were already operating *avant la lettre* in several of Marx's texts, especially in the section of *Capital* concerning commodity fetishism. The omnipotence of exchange-value in capitalist society would make impossible access to the viewpoint of totality; relations between men would take an objective character and, while individuals would be turned into things, things would appear as the true social agents. Now if *we* take a careful look at the structure of reification one salient feature becomes visible immediately: it essentially consists in an operation of *inversion*. What is derivative appears as originary; what is appariential is presented as essential. The inversion of the relationship subject/predicate is the kernel of any reification. It is, in that sense, a process of ideological mystification through and through, and its subjective correlatum is the notion of false consciousness. The categorial ensemble reification/false consciousness only makes sense, however, if the ideological distortion can be reversed; if it was constitutive of consciousness we could not speak of distortion. This is the reason Žižek, in order to stick to his notion of false consciousness, has to conceive of social antagonisms as grounded in some kind of *immanent* mechanism that has to see the consciousness of social agents as merely derivative—or rather, in which the latter, if it is admitted at all, is seen as a transparent expression of the former. The universal would speak in a direct way, without needing any mediating role from the concrete. In his words: populism "displaces the immanent social antagonism into the antagonism between the unified people and its external enemy." That is, the discursive construction of the enemy is presented as an operation of distortion. And indeed, if the universal inhabiting antagonism had the possibility of an unmediated expression, the mediation through the concrete could only be conceived of as reification.

Unfortunately for Žižek, the kind of articulation between the universal and the particular that my approach to the question of popular identities presupposes is radically incompatible with notions such as reification and ideological distortion. We are not dealing with a false consciousness opposed to a true one—which would be waiting for us as a teleologically programmed destiny—but with the contingent construction of a consciousness *tout court*. So what Žižek presents as his supplement to my approach is not a supplement at all but the putting into question of its basic premises. These premises result from an understanding of the relation between the universal and the particular, the abstract and the concrete, which I have discussed in my work from three perspectives—psychoanalytic, linguistic, and political—and which I want briefly to summarize here to show its incompatibility with Žižek's crude false-consciousness model.

Let us start with psychoanalysis. I have attempted to show in *On Populist Reason* (2005) how the logic of hegemony and that of the Lacanian *objet a* largely overlap and refer to a fundamental ontological relation in which fullness can only be touched through a radical investment in a partial object—which is not a partiality *within* the totality but a partiality which *is* the totality. In this point my work has drawn a great deal from the analysis of Joan Copjec, who has made a serious exploration of the logical implications of Lacanian categories, without distorting them à la Žižek with superficial Hegelian analogies. The most relevant point for our subject is that fullness—the Freudian Thing—is unachievable; it is only a retrospective illusion that is substituted by partial objects embodying that impossible totality. In Lacan's words: sublimation consists in elevating an object to the dignity of the Thing. As I have tried to show, the hegemonic relation reproduces all these structural moments; a certain particularity assumes the representation of an always receding universality. As we see, the reification/distortion/false-consciousness model is radically incompatible with the hegemony/*objet a* one; while the former presupposes the achievement of fullness through the reversion of the process of reification, the latter conceives of fullness (the Thing) as unachievable because it is devoid of any content; and while the former sees incarnation in the concrete as a distorted reification, the latter sees radical investment in an object as the only way in which a certain fullness is achievable. Žižek can maintain his reification/false consciousness approach only at the price of radically eradicating the logic of the *objet a* from the field of political relations.

Next step: signification. (What I have called the linguistic perspective refers not only to the linguistic in the strict sense but to all systems of signification. As the latter are coterminous with social life, the categories and relations explored by linguistic analysis do not belong to regional areas, but to the field of a general ontology.) Here we have the same imbrication between particularity and universality that we have found in the psychoanalytic perspective. I have shown elsewhere that the totalization of a system of differences is impossible without a *constitutive* exclusion.[5] The latter, however, has, as a primary logical effect, the split of any signifying element between an equivalential and a differential side. As these two sides cannot be logically sutured, the result is that any suture will be *rhetorical;* a certain particularity, without ceasing to be particular, will assume a certain role of universal signification. Ergo, unevenness within signification is the only terrain within which a signifying process can unfold. Catachresis = rhetoricity = the very possibility of meaning. The same logic that we found in psychoanalysis between the (impossible) Thing and the *objet a* we find again as the very condition of signification. Žižek's analysis does not directly engage with signification, but it is not difficult to draw the conclusion that would derive, in this field, from his reification approach: any kind of rhetorical substitution that stops short of a fully fledged signifying reconciliation would amount to false consciousness.

Finally, politics. Let us take an example that I have used at several points in *On Populist Reason* (2005): *Solidarnosc* in Poland. We have there a society where the frustration of a plurality of demands by an oppressive regime had created a spontaneous equivalence between them, which, however, needed to be expressed by some form of symbolic unity. We have here a clear alternative: either there is an ultimately *conceptually* specifiable content that is negated by the oppressive regime—in which case that content can be directly expressed, in its *positive* differential identity—or the demands are radically heterogeneous and the only thing they share is a *negative* feature—their common opposition to the oppressive regime. In that case, it is not a question of a *direct* expression of a positive feature underlying the different demands; because what has to be expressed is an irreducible negativity, its representation will necessarily have a symbolic character.[6] The demands of *Solidarnosc* will become the symbol of a wider chain of demands whose unstable equivalence around that symbol will constitute a wider popular identity. This constitution of the symbolic unity of the popular camp—and its correlatum: the symbolic unification of the oppressive regime through similar discursive/equivalential means—is what Žižek suggests that we should conceive as reification. But he is utterly wrong. In reification we have, as we have seen, an inversion in the relation between true and distorted expression, while here the opposition true/distorted does not make any sense; given that the equivalential link is established between radically heterogeneous demands, their "homogenization" through an empty signifier is a pure *passage à l'acte,* the construction of something essentially new and not the revelation of any underlying "true" identity. That is the reason why in my book I have insisted that the empty signifier is a pure name that does not belong to the conceptual order. So there is no question of true or false consciousness. As in the case of the psychoanalytic perspective—the elevation of an object to the dignity of the Thing, as in the case of signification—where we have the presence of a figural term that is catachrestical because it names and, thus, gives discursive presence to an essential void within the signifying structure, we have in politics also a constitution of new agents—peoples, in our sense—through the articulation between equivalential and differential logics. These logics involve figural embodiments resulting from a *creatio ex nihilo* that is not possible to reduce to any preceding or ultimate literality. So forget reification.

What we have said so far already anticipates that, in our view, the second thesis of Žižek, according to which symbolic representation—which he conceives as reification—would be essentially or, at least, tendentially fascist, does not fare any better. Here Žižek uses a demagogic device: the role of the Jew in Nazi discourse, which immediately evokes all the horrors of the Holocaust and provokes an instinctive negative reaction. Now it is true that fascist discourse employed forms of symbolic representation, but there is nothing specifically fascist in doing so, for there is no political discourse that does not construct its own symbols in that way. I would even say that this construction is the very definition of what politics is about. The arsenal of possible ideological examples different from the one Žižek has chosen is inexhaustible. What, rather than a symbolic embodiment, is involved in a political discourse that presents Wall Street as the source of all economic evils? Or in the burning of the American flag by Third World demonstrators? Or in the rural, antimodernist emblems of Gandhi's agitations? Or in the burning of Buenos Aires cathedral by the Peronist masses? We will identify with some symbols while rejecting others, but that is no reason to assert that the matrix of a symbolic structure varies according to the material content of the symbols. That assertion is not possible without some notion of reification à la Žižek, which would make it possible to ascribe some contents to true consciousness and others to a false one. But even this naïve operation would not succeed without the further postulate that any form of symbolic incarnation will be an expression of false consciousness, while true consciousness would be totally exempt from symbolic mediation. (This is the point at which Lacanian theory becomes Žižek's nemesis; to do away entirely with symbolic mediation and have a pure expression of true consciousness is the same as to claim that there is a direct access to the Thing as such, while *objects a* will only be granted the status of distorted representations.)

Demands: between requests and claims

The minimal unit in our social analysis is the category of demand. It presupposes that the social group is not an ultimately homogeneous referent but that its unity should rather be conceived as an articulation of heterogeneous demands. Žižek has formulated two main objections to this approach: the first, that the notion of demand does not grasp the true confrontational nature of the revolutionary act ("Does the proper revolutionary or emancipatory political act not move beyond this horizon of demands? The revolutionary subject no longer operates at the level of demanding something from those in power; he wants to destroy them" [p. 558]); the second, that there is no correlation between the plurality implicit in the notion of an equivalential chain of demands and the actual aims of a populist mobilization because many populist movements are structured around one-issue objectives

> (A more general remark should be made here about one-issue popular movements. Take, for example, the 'tax revolts' in the U.S. Although they function in a populist way, mobilizing the people around a demand that is not met by the democratic institutions, it does *not* seem to rely on a complex chain of equivalences, but remains focused on one singular demand.
>
> [p. 560])

Žižek's two objections have utterly missed the point. Let us start with the first. Although Žižek refers to the tension request/claim around which our notion of demand is explicitly constructed, he is entirely unaware of its theoretical consequences. In our view, any demand starts as a *request;* institutions of local power, for instance, are asked to meet the grievances of people in a particular area—for example, housing. This is the only situation that Žižek envisages; those in power are asked to graciously acquiesce to the request of a group of people. From this perspective, the situation would be utterly uneven; granting the demand would be a *concession* from those in power. But to reduce the issue to that case is to ignore the second dimension of our analysis, the social process through which a request is transformed into a *claim*. How does this mutation take place? As I have argued, it happens through the operation of the equivalential logic. People whose demands concerning housing are frustrated see that other demands concerning transport, health, security, schooling, and so on are not met either. This triggers a process that I have described *in extenso* in my book. It boils down to the following: the frustration of an *individual* demand transforms the request into a claim as far as people see themselves as bearers of rights that are not recognized. These claims are, however, limited, for the referential entity to which they are addressed is perfectly identifiable—in our example of housing, the town hall. But if the equivalence between claims is extended—in our example: housing, transport, health, schooling, and so on—it becomes far more difficult to determine which is the instance to which the claims are addressed. One has to discursively construct the enemy—the oligarchy, the establishment, big money, capitalism, globalization, and so on—and, for the same reason, the identity of the claimers is transformed in this process of universalization of both the aims and the enemy. The whole process of the Russian revolution started with three demands: "peace, bread, and land." To whom were these demands addressed? The more the equivalence expanded, the more clear it became that it was not just to the tsarist regime. Once we move beyond a certain point, what were requests *within* institutions became claims addressed *to* institutions, and at some stage they became claims *against* the institutional order. When this process has overflown the institutional apparatuses beyond a certain limit, we start having the people of populism.

We could ask ourselves, Why should social actions always be conceived as demands? The reason, as I have explained in *On Populist Reason* (2005), is that the subject is always the subject of lack; it always emerges out of an asymmetry between the (impossible) fullness of the community and the particularism of a place of enunciation. That also explains why the names of fullness will always result from a radical investment of universal value in a certain particularity—again: the elevation of a particular object to the dignity of the Thing. But it is important to realize that this investment does not leave the particular object unchanged. It "universalizes" that object through its inscription within an infrastructure of equivalential relations. That is why this can never be a pure matter of reification, as Žižek argues. (Reification involves, as we have said, an *inversion* by which particularity and universality exchange places without changing their identities, while the hegemonic relation presupposes contamination between the particular and the universal.)

This situation, by which a certain particularity is never *mere* particularity because it is always crisscrossed by equivalential relations that "universalize" its content, is enough to answer the second of Žižek's objections, namely, that one-issue mobilizations, having particularistic aims, cannot constitute wider political identities. This is a complete illusion. The ostensive issue could be particular, but it is only the tip of the iceberg. Behind the individual issue, a much wider world of associations and affects contaminate it and transform it into the expression of much more general trends. To take the one-issue character of mobilization at face value would be the same as reducing the analysis of a dream to its manifest content. The French and Dutch referenda are good examples. The issue was a punctual one but, as Žižek himself shows, a whole world of frustrations, fears, and prejudices found its expression in the No. And everybody knows that what is at stake in the tax referenda in the U.S. are deep political displacements of communitarian common sense. The conclusion is that the latent meaning of a mobilization can never be read off its literal slogans and proclaimed aims; a political analysis worthy of its name only starts when one probes the overdetermination that sustains that literality.

So what general conclusions can be derived from this complex set of interconnections between popular identities and demands and within demands themselves, between requests and claims? The most important one is that each of the possible articulations within this structural matrix leads to a different way of constituting social identities and to different degrees in the universalization of their claims. At one extreme, when the demands do not go beyond the stage of mere requests, we have a highly institutionalized arrangement. Social actors have an "immanent" existence within the objective locations delineating the institutional order of society. (Of course this is a purely ideal extreme; society is never so structured that social agents are entirely absorbed within institutions.) The second scenario is one in which there is a more permanent tension between demands and what the institutional order can absorb. Here requests tend to become claims, and there is a critique of institutions rather than just a passive acceptance of their legitimacy. Finally, when relations of equivalence between a plurality of demands go beyond a certain point, we have broad mobilizations against the institutional order as a whole. We have here the emergence of the people as a more universal historical actor, whose aims will necessarily crystallize around empty signifiers as objects of political identification. There is a radicalization of claims that can lead to a revolutionary reshaping of the entire institutional order. This is probably the kind of development that Žižek has in mind when he speaks of not demanding anything from those in power, but wanting to destroy them instead. The difference between his approach and mine is, however, that for me the emergence of emancipatory actors has a logic of its own, which is anchored in the structure of the demand as the basic unit of social action, while for Žižek there is no such logic; emancipatory subjects are conceived as fully fledged creatures, who emerge without any kind of genetic process, as Minerva from Jupiter's head. The section in my book that deals with Žižek's work has as a title, "Žižek: Waiting for the Martians." There is, indeed, something extraterrestrial about Žižek's emancipatory subjects; their conditions as revolutionary agents are specified within such a rigid geometry of social effects that no empirical actor can fit the bill. In his recent writings, however,

Žižek deploys a new strategy in naming revolutionary agents, consisting in choosing some actually existing social actors to whom he attributes, however, so many imaginary features that they become Martians in everything but name. We will later return to Žižek's strategy of "Martianization."

Heterogeneity and social practices

We should now move to a set of remarks that Žižek makes concerning the status of Marxist theory. The most important one refers to Marxian political economy. According to him, my basic reproach to the latter would be that it is

> a positive "ontic" science that delimits a part of substantial social reality, so that any direct grounding of emancipatory politics in CPE [critique of political economy] (or, in other words, any privilege given to class struggle) reduces the political to an epiphenomenon embedded in substantial reality.
>
> (p. 565)

After that, in order to refute the claims that he attributes to me, Žižek embarks on a long tirade in which he tries to show that commodity fetishism is an internal effect of the capital form as such and that this form is not abstract, for it determines actual social processes:

> this abstraction ... [is] real in the precise sense of determining the structure of the very material social processes. The fate of whole strata of population and sometimes of whole countries can be decided by the solipsistic speculative dance of capital, which pursues its goal of profitability in a blessed indifference with regard to how its movement will affect social reality.
>
> (p. 566)

Having so detected the central systemic violence of capitalism, Žižek concludes:

> Here we encounter the Lacanian difference between reality and the Real: reality is the social reality of the actual people involved in interaction and in the productive processes, while the Real is the inexorable abstract spectral logic of capital that determines what goes on in social reality.
>
> (p. 566)

The last remark is, purely and simply, a misrepresentation of the Lacanian notion of the Real—a good example of how Žižek systematically distorts Lacanian theory to make it compatible with a Hegelianism that is, in most respects, its very opposite. The Real cannot be an inexorable spectral logic and even less something that determines what goes on in social reality for the simple reason that the Real is not a specifiable object endowed with laws of movement of its own but, on the contrary, something that only exists and shows itself through its disruptive effects within the Symbolic.[7] It is not an *object* but an internal *limit* preventing the ultimate constitution of any objectivity. To identify the Real with the logic of capital is a nice example of that reification to which Žižek always returns. His mistake is similar to Kant's, who after having said that categories apply only to phenomena and not to things in themselves, asserted that the latter are the external cause of appearances, thus applying a category—cause—to something that cannot legitimately be subsumed under *any* category. The reason why Žižek has to distort the notion of the Real in this way is clear: only if the logic of capital is self-determined can it operate as an infrastructure determining what goes on in social reality. But the Real, in the Lacanian sense, does exactly the opposite; it establishes a limit that prevents any self-determination by the Symbolic. All this cheap metaphoric use of the reality/Real duality to refer to something that is no more than the old base/superstructure distinction is entirely out of place; it is evident that the logic of capital is as symbolic as the social reality that it is supposed to determine. The consequence is that, if the logic of capital and social reality are in *pari materia*—both of them are symbolic—the holes and disruptions created in social reality by the presence of the Real will also be present within the very logic of capital self-development (which, as a result, will be contaminated by something heterogeneous with itself; it will not be pure self-development).

What I am saying is not that the Real is not relevant for the issues that we are discussing but that Žižek has looked for it in all the wrong places. To conceive the Real as an objective, conceptually specifiable logic does not make any sense. However, before attempting to give to the Real its precise ontological location—if we can use these terms in connection with something whose presence, precisely, subverts all locations—I want to refer to Žižek's assertion that I have "reproached" Marxian political economy for being an ontic science delimiting a region of social reality and reducing the political to an epiphenomenal position. This "reproach" attributed to me is a pure invention of Žižek's. I have never asserted that Marx's political economy is a regional science, for the simple reason that, whatever its merits or deficiencies, it is a discourse concerning social totality ("the anatomy of civil society is political economy"). So the only two possible ways of criticizing it are either to prove that there are logical inconsistencies in the sequence of its categories or to show that there is a heterogeneous outside preventing political economy from closing itself around its internal categories and thus constituting *the fundamentum inconcussum* of the social. Now the first criticism is possible, and—although I have not engaged in formulating it myself—it has been repeatedly made over the last century to the point where little remains of the labor theory of value the way it was presented by Marx. It is enough to mention the names of Eugen von Böhm-Bawerk, Ladislaus Bortkiewicz, Joan Robinson, or Piero Sraffa.[8] The whole discussion about the transformation of values into prices at the beginning of the twentieth century was a first stage in this critical analysis. Žižek totally ignores this literature and continues asserting Marx's version of the labor theory of value as an unchallengeable dogma.

But let's not waste time with this sterile dogmatism, and let's go to the second possible criticism of Marxian economics, which is far more relevant for our subject. The alternative is as follows. A first possible scenario would be one in which there would be no outside to the process described by the succession of the economic categories; history would just be their endogenous unfolding. So the ontic—to use Žižek's terms—story that they depict would, at the same time, be ontological. Thus we would have a purely internal process not interrupted by any outside. The logical succession would also have a metaphysical value. What, however, about the forces *opposing* capitalism? In this model, they can only be an internal effect of capitalism itself. It is well known how class struggle features in this objectivist perspective: capitalism creates its own grave diggers. The second scenario results from the opposite assumption: forces opposing capitalism are not just the result of capitalist logic, but they *interrupt* it from the outside, so that the story of capitalism cannot result from the unfolding of its internal categories. To give just one example: as several studies have shown, the transition from absolute to relative surplus value is not only the result of movements in the logic of profit in a conflict-free space but also a response to workers' mobilizations. If this is so, there is no purely internal history of capitalism, as the one described by the preface to the *Critique of Political Economy,* but a conflict-ridden history that cannot be apprehended by any kind of conceptually graspable development. I want to insist on this point because it will lead us straight onto the notion of people as presented in *On Populist Reason* (2005).

Needless to say, of the two options within this alternative, we definitely choose the second. In actual fact, *On Populist Reason* (2005) is, to a large extent, the attempt to unfold the theoretical consequences following from this choice. Žižek, however, thinks that he knows better and opts for denying that the alternative exists. Thus: "Marx distinguishes between working class and proletariat: working class effectively is a particular social group, while proletariat designates a subjective position" (p. 564). Now, to start with, Marx *never* made such a distinction. Perhaps he should have done, but he did not. On the contrary, all his theoretical effort was to show that the riddle of history could only be solved as far as revolutionary subjectivity was firmly rooted in an objective position, resulting itself from a process governed by immanent and necessary laws. Has Žižek ever read the *Communist Manifesto*? If he had, he would have known that for Marx and Engels "not only has the bourgeoisie forged the weapons that bring death to itself; it has also called into existence the men who are to wield those weapons—the modern working class, the proletarians."[9] Has he read *The Holy Family* where, against Bruno Bauer, they argue for the inevitability of communism based precisely in the dehumanization of the proletariat (working class) brought about by the logic of private property? Has he read *The German Ideology,* where they oppose true socialism and present division of labor—that is, a structured ensemble of objective social positions—as the root and source of human alienation? And what are *Capital* and *Grundrisse* but a sustained attempt to root exploitation in an objective process whose necessary counterpart is working-class struggle? Enough. There is no point in continuing to refer to an argument that any undergraduate knows. Moreover, it is plainly clear what

Marx would have thought about a taxonomic distinction between the subjective and the objective; he would have said that, from the point of view of social totality, what matters is not the distinction as such but the logic and topography of the interconnections between its two terms; and the preface to the [*Contribution to the*] *Critique of Political Economy* makes perfectly clear what such an interconnection was for him.

The alternative that we have presented is, actually, reflected in a contradictory way in Žižek's thought. The distinction between the subjective and the objective, on the one hand, is vital for Žižek for, following Alain Badiou's duality between situation and event,[10] he wants to establish a radical discontinuity between the revolutionary break and what had preceded it. The corollary is that the revolutionary act should have nothing in common with the situation within which it takes place. Žižek has also insisted, on the other hand, *ad nauseam,* on the centrality of the anticapitalist *economic* struggle, which means that something in the existing situation—the economic as particular location within a social topography—has a transcendental structuring role of sorts, determining a priori the events that can actually take place. So the situation would have ontological primacy over the event, whose chasm with that situation could not, as a result, be radical. So Žižek is confronted with an *exclusive* alternative, and it is rather comic that he does not realize it and continues asserting both options in a perfectly contradictory way.

Let us leave Žižek to enjoy his contradiction, and let us, instead, move to the way in which the alternative is dealt with in Marx's work. There is no doubt that, for Marx, the objective side has the upper hand. History is a coherent story because the development of productive forces establishes its underlying meaning. Technological progress leads to increasing exploitation, so the workers' struggle helps to hasten the crisis of capitalism, but it is not its source. The final breakdown of the system, although it is not mechanical, does not have its ultimate source in the actions of the workers. However, it would be a mistake to think that, for him, historical necessity reduced freedom of action to a mere epiphenomenon. The question is rather that historical necessity and free revolutionary action coincide, in such a way that they become indistinguishable from each other. The Spinozist notion of freedom as being consciousness of necessity, which still had an essentially speculative dimension in Hegel, becomes in Marx an *active* principle identifying necessity and freedom. That is the reason why, for Marx, there is no possible distinction between the descriptive and the normative and why, as a result, Marxism cannot have an ethics independently grounded. And this is also why Žižek's distinction between proletariat and working class, subjective and objective, would have been anathema to Marx.

The difficulties started later on, with the increasing realization that there was an essential opaqueness that prevented the smooth transition from one economic category to the next and from one social antagonism to another. The Marxist view of the destiny of capitalist society was based on a postulate: the simplification of social structure under capitalism. The peasantry and the middle classes would disappear and, in the end, the bulk of the population would be a vast proletarian mass, so the last antagonistic confrontation of history would be a showdown between the bourgeoisie and the working class. Very quickly, however, it was seen that this strategic model showed all kinds of inconsistencies, both at the theoretical level and as a reading of what was going on in society. The labor theory of value was shown to be plagued by theoretical inconsistencies; the internal differentiations between sectors of the economy could not be intellectually grasped by any kind of unified law of tendency; social structure, far from being more homogeneous, became more complex and diversified; even within the working class, the splits between economic and political struggle became less and less politically manageable. In this situation, the initial reaction was to try to maintain the basic lines of classical theory, but to multiply the system of mediations that, while becoming the guarantors of its ultimate validity, would assume the heroic task of homogenizing the heterogeneous. Lukács's notion of false consciousness—whose correlatum was the location of the true consciousness of the proletariat in the Party—is a typical expression of this laborious but ultimately useless exercise. And, within structurally oriented Marxism, Nicos Poulantzas' distinction between "determination in the last instance" and "dominant role" did not fare any better. The only possible alternative was to accept heterogeneity at face value, without trying to reduce it to any kind of concealed or underlying homogeneity, and to address the question of how a certain totalization is possible, which is however compatible with an irreducible heterogeneity. To outline the contours of an answer to this issue is our next task.

Before embarking upon it, however, I would like to comment on pages 565–68 of Žižek's essay, for they present what most approaches a sustained and coherent argument in his piece. The main points are the following:

(1) There are two logics of universality that have to be strictly distinguished. The first would correspond to the state as conceived by Hegel, as the universal class, the direct agent of the social order. The second would be a supernumerary universality, internal to the existing order but without a proper place within it—"the part of no part" of Rancière. So we would not have a particular content that "will hegemonize the empty form of universality, but struggle between two exclusive *forms* of universality themselves" (p. 564).

(2) The proletariat would embody this second kind of universality. (This is the place where Žižek distinguishes between the proletariat and the working class in the way we have discussed.) Here Žižek criticizes my book's approach to the question of the *lumpenproletariat*, arguing that its difference from the proletariat *stricto sensu* is not "the one between an objective social group and a nongroup, a remainder-excess with no proper place within the social edifice, but a distinction between two modes of this remainder-excess that generates two different subjective positions" (p. 564). While the *lumpenproletariat*, as a nongroup, can be incorporated into the strategy of any social group—that is, it is infinitely manipulable—the working class *as a group* is in the contradictory position of having a precise location within capitalist accumulation and, yet, being unable to find a place within the capitalist order.

(3) The abstract logic of capital produces concrete effects. Here Žižek proposes his distinction between reality ("actual people involved in interaction and in the productive processes" [p. 566]) and the Real ("the inexorable abstract spectral logic of capital that determines what goes on in social reality"). I have already shown the inconsistencies of this distinction, and I will not go back to it. He adds, however, a further point: "the categories of political economy (say, the value of the commodity working force or the degree of profit) are not objective socioeconomic data but data that always signal the outcome of a political struggle" (p. 566). So the political cannot be an epiphenomenon.

(4) Žižek then adds a critique to the way I conceptualize, in an opposition A-B, the Bness of the B that resists symbolic transformation into a pure relation A-not A. As discussion of this point requires reference to some premises of my argument that I will present later on in this chapter, I postpone discussion of this criticism.

(5) Capitalism is thus not merely a category that delimits a positive social sphere but a formal-transcendental matrix that structures the entire social space—literally, a mode of production. (p. 567)

Which, among these various criticisms, has an at least tentative plausibility? The answer is simple: none. Let us consider them in turn.

(1) The two universalities described by Žižek cannot coexist in the same space of representation, not even under the form of an antagonistic presence. The mere presence of one of them makes the other impossible. The universality inherent in Hegel's universal class *totalizes* a social space, so nothing *ultimately* antagonistic could exist within it; otherwise, the state would not be the sphere of reconciliation of the particularities of civil society, and it would be unable to fulfill its universal role. What happens, however, if this role is threatened by a particularism that it cannot master? In that case there is, simply, no reconciliation; universality, *conceived as un-contaminated universality,* is a sham. Because the relation between the state's universality and what escapes its reconciling role is a relation of pure exteriority, it is essentially contingent, which is the same as saying that it should be conceived as a system of *power*. Universality is not an *underlying* datum, but a power that, as with all power, is exercised over something different from itself. Ergo, any kind of universality is nothing else than a particularity that has succeeded in contingently articulating around itself a large number of differences. But this is nothing other than the definition of a *hegemonic* relation. Let us now move to the second of Žižek's universalities—that of a sector that, although present within a social space, cannot be counted as a member of that space. The case of the *sans papiers* in France is frequently quoted as a relevant example. Let us say, to start with, that the mere fact of being outside the system of locations defining a social framework does not endow a group of people with any kind of universality. The *sans papiers* want to have *papiers,* and if the latter are conceded by the state, they could become one more difference within an expanded state. In order to become universal something else is needed—namely, that their situation of being outsiders becomes a symbol to

other outsiders or marginals within society—that is, that a contingent aggregation of heterogeneous elements takes place. This aggregation is what we have called "a people." This type of universalization, again, is what we understand by hegemony. We arrive at the same conclusion that we reached when we referred to the universality of the state. This is why Gramsci spoke of the "becoming State of the working class," which presupposes a reaggregation of elements at a certain nodal point at the expense of others. Gramsci called this movement "a war of position" between antagonistic universalities. The fact that Žižek hypostasizes his two universalities and cannot explain what the struggle between them could consist of and that, in addition, he conceives the hegemonic struggle as one particularity hegemonizing "the empty form of universality" shows that he has not understood even the ABCs of the theory of hegemony.

(2) Concerning the question of the *lumpenproletariat,* Žižek, again, clouds the issue. He says that, in the case of the proletariat, there is a contradiction between its precise location within capitalist accumulation and its lack of place within capitalist order; while in the case of the *lumpenproletariat* the first type of location would be absent, so its sociopolitical identity would be infinitely malleable. The real question, however, is whether the lack of place of the proletariat is so anchored in its precise location within capitalist accumulation that an equivalence could not be established with other out-of-place sectors, so a broader identity of the excluded could be formed that overflows *any* particular location. If so, the marginality of the *lumpenproletariat* would be the symptom of a much wider phenomenon. We will come back to this point.

(3) The economic field is, for Žižek, intrinsically political because it is the field where class struggle is structured. With an assertion of such a generality, I also, of course, agree. Gramsci wrote that the construction of hegemony starts at the factory level. The disagreement starts, however, when we try to define what we understand by the political. For me the political has a primary structuring role because social relations are ultimately contingent, and any prevailing articulation results from an antagonistic confrontation whose outcome is not decided beforehand. For Žižek, instead, socioeconomic data always signal the outcome of a political struggle—that is, if there is a logical transition from the economic data to the political outcome, the political is simply an internal category of the economy. It is not, perhaps, an epiphenomenon, in the sense that its ontological status is not merely reflective of a substantial reality but part of the latter, but precisely because of that it lacks any autonomy. While my analysis leads to a politicization of the economy, Žižek's ends in an "economization" of politics.

(5) As I said, we will discuss point 4 later on. As for point 5, Žižek does not simply sustain the idea that there is such a thing as a structured space called mode of production, but he also asserts that such a space (1) is a formal-transcendental matrix and (2) directly structures the entire social space—that is, that at no point social reality overflows what that matrix can determine and control (except, presumably, in the transition from one mode of production to another, but, as such a transition, if the model is coherent, would have to be governed by a logic internal

to the mode of production itself, this would not make any difference). Žižek's whole account stands or falls depending on the validity of these two assumptions. This is what we will discuss next.

Heterogeneity and dialectics

We will start our discussion by trying to determine the status of the heterogeneous. We understand by a heterogeneous relation one existing between elements that do not belong to the same space of representation.[11] This notion requires a set of specifications, for a space of representation can be multiply constituted. The unity of such a space can, first, be the result of dialectical mediations—that is, a type of connection between elements so that I have in each of them everything needed to move logically to all the others. In the duality A-not A the identity of each pole is exhausted in being the pure negation of the other. So dialectical transitions are not only compatible with contradiction but have to rely on contradiction as the condition of their unity within a homogeneous space. There is nothing heterogeneous in a dialectical contradiction. For that reason, dialectical transitions can only take place in a saturated space. Any remnant of a contingent empiricity that is not dialectically mastered by the whole would jeopardize the latter, for, in that case, the contingency of the unmastered element would make the whole equally contingent, and the very possibility of a dialectical mediation would be put into question (this is the Krug's pen objection to dialectics, which Hegel answered with a brisk dismissal that hardly concealed the fact that he had no answer). Žižek's assertion that socioeconomic data "signal the outcome of a political struggle" is a good example of a dialectical transition—that is, one taking place in a homogeneous space that thus entirely eliminates the possibility of radical negativity (p. 566). But homogeneity does not necessarily require dialectical transitions between the elements delimiting a space. A semiological relation between elements is also a possible alternative. Saussure's conception of language as a system of differences also presupposes homogeneity, as far as the identity of each element requires its difference from all the others. Heterogeneity only enters the game if it could be shown that the very logic of totality—being dialectical or semiological—fails at some point as a result of an aporia that cannot be solved within that totality's structuring principles.

Let us take as our starting point the Hegelian conception of history. The basic premise is that the movement of historical events is governed by an inner logic, conceptually apprehensible and conceived as a succession of dialectical reversals and retrievals. The arrival of various people on the historical arena is the phenomenic manifestation of such logic. There is, however, a blind spot in this picture: what Hegel calls the "peoples without history," who do not represent any differentiated moment in the dialectical series. I have compared them, in my book, with what Lacan calls the *caput mortuum*, the residue left in a tube after a chemical experiment. This non-historical presence is like the drop of petrol that spoils the bowl of honey, for the existence of a contingent excess overflowing the dialectics of history makes this dialectics equally contingent and, as a result, the whole vision of history as a coherent story is at the very least jeopardized. The same happens with Žižek's model of historicity. For capitalism to be "a formal-transcendental matrix that structures the entire social space" what is necessary is that such a matrix strictly functions as a ground, that is, that nothing in the social space exceeds the mastering abilities of the matrix (p. 567). Some sort of pragmatic version of the dialectical model is, however, possible; although this new version would considerably water down the dialectical ambitions, it could still be asserted that the "excess" is marginal *vis-à-vis* the main lines of historical development, so from the perspective of a universal history it can safely be ignored. If the whole issue comes to that, it is clear that it is just a matter of appreciation to decide whether the actual facts grant the assumptions of this pragmatic new version.

At this point we should move from Hegel to Marx, of whose work most of Žižek's analyses can be considered as derivative. Let us first, however, recapitulate our previous theoretical steps. First, as we have seen, any kind of dialectical transition is grounded in a saturated logical terrain where nothing can escape dialectical determination. Second, however, this logical closure is unachievable because something within that terrain escapes dialectical mastery; we have taken the example of peoples without history, but, obviously, many others could be brought forward. Third, referring now to the terrain of history, this excess *vis-à-vis* dialectical development can only be conceptualized through its contingent relation with the *main line* of historical development. Fourth, the fact that this main line has a contingent relation to something external to itself means that it, itself, becomes contingent. Fifth, the claims of that line to be the main one cease, as a result, to be grounded in a necessary dialectical development and can only be asserted as a historically *proved* contingent process. So the question is: Is there any entity in Marx's theory that, in its contingency, is homologous to Hegel's "peoples without history"? In my view there is, and it is the *lumpenproletariat*. And the result of its presence will be to destroy the claims of the proletariat to have an a priori central role as a necessary agent of historical development.

History for Marx, as far as it is a coherent story, is a history of production (the development of productive forces and its compatibility/incompatibility with the relations of production). So occupying a precise location within the relations of production is, for Marx, the only possible claim to be a *historical* actor. But this location is precisely what the *lumpenproletariat* does not have. Marx draws, without hesitation, what, starting from his premises, is the only possible conclusion: the *lumpenproletariat* should be denied any historicity; it is a parasitic sector inhabiting the interstices of all social formations. We see here the structural similitude with Hegel's "peoples without history"; *vis-à-vis* the main line of historical development its existence is marginal and contingent. If that were the whole matter, there would be no major problem; although the *lumpenproletariat* would have no place in a dialectically conceived historical narrative, its confinement as a category to the rabble of the city—which clearly is a marginal sector—would not put into question the pragmatic version of the dialectical story. The difficulties, however, persist. The *lumpenproletariat* has for Marx, no doubt, the rabble of the city as an intuitive referent, but he also gives a conceptual definition of that referent, to be found in the *lumpenproletariat's* distance from the productive process. Very soon, however, he realized that such a distance is not exclusive to the rabble of the city, but it is present in many other sectors; he speaks, for instance, of the financial aristocracy as the reemergence of the *lumpenproletariat* at the heights of society. And with the unfolding of the whole discussion concerning productive and unproductive labor—an issue that had already called the attention of classical political economists—the notion of history as history of production was increasingly under fire, and its defense required the most unlikely contortions. Clearly, the pragmatic test had not been passed. This is why the question of the *lumpenproletariat* is important for me. It is the royal road that makes visible a wider issue: the whole question of the logics structuring social totality. That is why I have said that the question of the *lumpenproletariat is* a symptom.

There is, however, something else that puts Žižek's approach even more radically into question. It is the whole issue concerning the theoretical status of social antagonisms. Let us go back to Žižek's assertion that the working class

> is a group that is in itself, as a group within the social edifice, a nongroup, in other words, one whose position is in itself contradictory; they are a productive force, society (and those in power) needs them in order to reproduce themselves and their rule, but, nonetheless, they cannot find a proper place for them.
>
> (p. 565)

This can only mean one of two things: *either* that the objective position of the worker within the relations of production is the *source* of his or her contradictory position within capitalist society as a whole *or* that the absence of that objective position within capitalist society as a whole derives from the idea that the worker is *beyond* his or her objective position within the relations of production. Given Žižek's general outlook, it is clear that he can only mean the first. But this is what is theoretically unsustainable. For the worker's position within the relations of production to be a purely objective one, the worker has to be reduced to the category of seller of labor power, and the capitalist to that of buyer of labor power as a commodity. In that case, however, we are not defining any antagonism because the fact that the capitalist extracts surplus labor from the worker does not involve antagonism unless the worker *resists* such an extraction, but that resistance cannot be logically derived from the mere analysis of the category of seller of labor power. That is why, in several places in my work, I have argued that social antagonisms are not objective relations but the limit of all objectivity, so society is never a purely objective order but is constructed around an ultimate impossibility.[12]

It is clear at this point that the only way out of this theoretical blind alley is to move to the second possible meaning of Žižek's assertion (which he systematically avoids), namely, that the capitalist does not negate in the worker something inherent in the category of seller of labor power, but that the worker is *beyond* that category (the fact that, below a certain wage level, he or she cannot have access to a minimal consumption, to a decent life, and so on). So antagonism is not internal to the relation of production but takes place *between* the relation of production and something external to it. In other words, the two poles of the antagonism are linked by a nonrelational relation; that is, they are essentially heterogeneous with each other. As society is crisscrossed by antagonisms, heterogeneity is to be found at the very heart of social relations.

The consequences of this displacement from the notion of a homogeneous, saturated space to one in which heterogeneity is constitutive rapidly follow. In the first place, asserting that a social antagonism emerges out of an insurmountable heterogeneity implies a necessary corollary that the antagonistic relation is conceptually ungraspable. There is no Absolute Spirit that can assign to it an objectively determinable content. This means that its two poles do not belong to the same space of representation. We are here in a strictly homologous situation to that described by Lacan through his famous dictum that there is no such thing as a sexual relation. By this he was obviously not asserting that people do not make love but that there is no single formula of sexuation that would absorb the masculine and feminine poles within a unified and complementary whole.[13] This is a radical outside that cannot be symbolically mastered. Heterogeneity is another name for the Real.[14] This fully explains why Žižek cannot understand the theoretical status of the Lacanian Real. If the mode of production was—as it is for him—a formal-transcendental matrix of the social, everything in society would have to be explained out of that matrix's own endogenous movements; ergo, there would be no place for heterogeneity (= the presence of a Real). Žižek's nonsensical attribution to the Real of a formal-transcendental content is at odds with the most elementary notions of Lacan's theory. It is interesting to observe that, within the Marxist tradition itself, the imperialistic epistemological ambitions of the category of mode of production have been downgraded a long time ago. To refer only to the Althusserian school, Étienne Balibar has demolished the essentialism of *Reading Capital* and shown that the unity of a social formation cannot be thought out of a mode-of-production matrix.[15]

There is, however, a still more important consequence of giving this constitutive role to heterogeneity, and it is that the category of class struggle is overflown in all directions. Let us just mention the most important.

(1) If antagonisms are not internal to the relations of production but take place *between* the relations of production and the way social agents are constituted *outside* them, it is impossible to determine the nature and pattern of an antagonism (at the limit: whether it is going to exist at all and its degree of intensity) from the mere analysis of the internal structure of the relations of production. We know that, empirically, groups of people can react to what, technically, are movements in the rate of exploitation in the most divergent ways. And we also know that, theoretically, it could not be otherwise, given

the heterogeneity inherent in antagonisms. So there is no longer any room for that childish talk about false consciousness, which presupposes an enlightened elite whose possession of the truth makes it possible to determine what the true interests of a class are.

(2) But heterogeneity destabilizes working-class centrality in still another sense. Once it is accepted that antagonisms presuppose a radical outside, there is no reason to think that locations within the relations of production are going to be privileged points of their emergence. Contemporary capitalism generates all kinds of imbalances and critical areas: ecological crises, marginalization and unemployment, unevenness in the development of different sectors of the economy, imperialist exploitation, and so on. This means that antagonistic points are going to be multiple and that any construction of a popular subjectivity will have to start from this heterogeneity. No narrow, class-based limitation will do the trick.

(3) This has a third capital consequence that I have discussed in detail in my book. The overflowing of any narrow class identity by equivalential logics has to take into account the fact that equivalences operate over a substratum of essentially heterogeneous demands. This means that the kind of unity that it is possible to constitute out of them is going to be nominal and not *conceptual*. As I have argued, the name is the ground of the thing. So popular identities are always historical *singularities*.

We now have all the elements to answer Žižek's objection concerning what he calls my reduction of the Real to the empirical determinations of the object. His target is a passage of my book where it is asserted that

> the opposition A-B will never fully become A-not A. The B-ness of the B will be ultimately nondialectizable. The people will always be something more than the pure opposite of power. There is a Real of the people which resists symbolic integration.
>
> (p. 566)

Against this passage Žižek raises the following objection: there is an ambiguity in my formulation, for it oscillates between accepting a formal notion of the Real as antagonism and reducing it to those empirical determinations of the object that cannot be subsumed under a formal opposition. The crucial question, for Žižek, is to find out what in the people exceeds being the pure opposite of power because if it were just a matter of a wealth of empirical determinations

> then we are not dealing with a Real that resists symbolic integration because the Real, in this case, is precisely the antagonism A-non-A, so that 'that which is in B more than non-A' is not the Real in B, but B's symbolic determinations.
>
> (p. 567)

This objection is highly symptomatic because it shows in the clearest possible way everything that Žižek does not understand concerning the Real, antagonisms, and popular identities. To start with, there are for him only two options: *either* we have a dialectical contradiction (A-not A), *or* we have the ontic empiricity of two objects (A-B) what Kant called *Real-repugnanz*. If that were an *exclusive* alternative it is clear that any B-ness in excess of not-A could only be of an empirical nature, and Žižek would obviously have an easy ride in showing that, in that case, we would not be dealing with the Real but with the symbolic determination of the object. But Žižek has missed the essential point. The real issue is whether I have in A everything that I need to move to its opposite (which, as a result, would be reduced to not-A). To go back to our previous discussion: whether I find in the *form* of capital everything I need to logically deduce the antagonism with the worker. If that were the case we would have a contradiction, but not an antagonistic one, because it would be fully representable within a unified symbolic space. And as it would be entirely symbolizable we would not be in the least dealing with the Real. A space constructed around the opposition A-not A is an entirely saturated space, which exhausts through that opposition all possible alternatives and does not tolerate any interruption. That is why the universe of Hegelian dialectics, with its ambition to obtain a complete overlapping between the ontic and the ontological orders, is incapable of dealing with the Real of antagonism that, precisely, requires the interruption of a saturated (symbolic) space. Our notion of antagonism as the limit of objectivity is another way of naming the Real, and its precondition is that we move away from any saturated A-not A space.

However, wouldn't we be in the same situation—that is, within a saturated space—if we move to the second Žižekian alternative, asserting a non-dialectizable B-ness of B? We would, indeed, if that excess were identified with the empiricity of the object. That fully symbolized space would no longer be dialectical but differential or semiotic; however, total objective representability would still be its defining dimension. But it is at this point that the full consequences of our analysis of heterogeneity can be drawn. We have asserted, in our previous discussion, that antagonism is not internal to the relations of production but that it is established between the relations of production and the way social agents are constituted outside them. This means that capitalist exploitation has an *interruptive* effect. This effect is, as we have seen, the Real of antagonism. So the presence of antagonism denies to social agents the fullness of an identity; there is, as a result, a process of identification by which certain objects, aims, and so on become the names of that absent fullness (they are "elevated to the dignity of the Thing"). This is exactly what the B-ness of B means. It is not simply an empirical object but one that has been invested, cathected, with the function of representing a fullness overflowing its ontic particularity. So, as we can see, Žižek's alternative is entirely misconceived. First, he conceives the Real of antagonism as a dialectical relation A-not A, in which the full representability of its two poles eliminates the interruptive nature of the Real. And, second, he reduces the B-ness of B to the empirical determinations of the object, thus ignoring the whole logic of the *objet a*. There is not the slightest substance in Žižek's objection.

On the genealogy of the people

Having reached this point in our argument, the next stage should be to say something about the way in which constitutive heterogeneity reflects itself in the structuration of social identities. Some dimensions of this reflection are already clear. In the first place, the dialectic homogenization/heterogenization should be conceived under the primacy of the latter. There is no ultimate substratum, no *natura naturans,* out of which existing social articulations could be explained. Articulations are not the superstructure of anything but the primary terrain of the constitution of social objectivity. This involves their essential contingency, for they consist of relational ensembles that do not obey any inner logic other than their factually being together. This does not mean that they can move in any direction any time. On the contrary, hegemonic formations can have a high degree of stability, but this stability is itself the result of a construction operating on a plurality of heterogeneous elements. Homogeneity is always achieved, never given. The work of Georges Bataille is highly relevant in this respect. A second dimension following from our previous analysis is that constitutive heterogeneity involves the primacy of the political in the establishment of the social link. It should be clear at this stage that by the political I do not understand any kind of regional area of action but the *contingent* construction of the social link. It is because of that that the category of hegemony acquires its centrality in social analysis. The consequence is that the category of hegemonic formation replaces the notion of mode of production as the actual self-embracing totality. The reasons are obvious. If the mode of production does not out of itself provide its own conditions of existence—that is, if the latter are *externally* provided and are not a superstructural effect of the economy—those conditions of existence are an internal determination of the primary social totality. This is even more clearly the case if we add that the links between different moments and components of the economic process are themselves the results of hegemonic articulations.

A third dimension to be taken into account is that, if heterogeneity is constitutive, the succession of hegemonic articulations will be structured as a narrative that is also constitutive and is not the factual reverse of a logically determinable process. This means that the reflection of heterogeneity in the constitution of social identities will itself adopt the form of a disruption (again, the irruption of the Real) of the homogeneous by the heterogeneous. As Marxism was, as we know, organized around the notion of necessary laws of history, it is worthwhile considering for a moment the way in which a heterogeneous other irrupted in the field of its discursivity and led to the reemergence of the people as a privileged historical actor.

The points in which classical Marxism as a homogeneous field of discursivity was interrupted by a heterogeneity unmasterable within its system of categories are legion. We will only refer, however, to the Leninist experience, both because of its centrality within the political imaginary of the Left and because it shows, with paradigmatic clarity, the type of politico-theoretical crisis to which we want to refer. There were a few principles that organized classical Marxism as a homogeneous space of discursive representation. One was the postulate of the class nature of historical agents. A second was the vision of capitalism as an orderly succession of stages dominated by a unified and endogenously determined economic logic. A third, and the most important for our argument, was an outlook according to which the strategic aims of the working class were entirely dependent on the stages of capitalist development. Russia being in a process of transition to a fully fledged capitalist society, the overthrowing of absolutism could only consist in a bourgeois-democratic revolution that, following the pattern of similar processes in the West, would open the way to a long period of capitalist expansion. All this was perfectly in tune with the political forecasts and the strategic vision of traditional Marxism. There was, however, a heterogeneous anomaly—an "exceptionality," to use the vocabulary of the time—that complicated the picture: the Russian bourgeoisie had arrived too late to the capitalist world market and, as a result, it was weak and incapable of carrying out its own democratic revolution. This had been recognized since the first manifesto of Russian social democracy, written by Peter Struve, and not even a diehard dogmatist like Plekhanov dared to attribute to the bourgeoisie a leading role in the revolution to come. In those circumstances, the democratic tasks had to be taken up by different classes (a workers'/peasants' alliance, according to Lenin; the working class, in Trotsky's vision). It is symptomatic that this taking up of a task by a class that is not its natural bearer was called by Russian social democrats hegemony, thus introducing the term into political language. Here we already find a heterogeneity disrupting the smooth sequence of Marxist categories. The discourses of Lenin and Trotsky were a sustained attempt to keep those disruptive effects under control. It was not a question that the class identity of the working class changed as a result of its taking up the democratic tasks or that the tasks themselves were transformed in nature when the workers were their bearers. The Leninist conception of class alliances is explicit in this respect: "to strike together and to march separately." And, for Trotsky, the whole logic of the permanent revolution is based on a succession of revolutionary stages that only makes sense if the class nature of both the agents and the tasks remains what it was from the very beginning. Moreover, the "exceptionality" of the situation was conceived as short-lived; the revolutionary power in Russia could survive only if a socialist victory in the advanced capitalist countries of the West took place. If that happened, the heterogeneous outside would be reabsorbed by an orthodox normal development.

The failure of the revolution in the West, important in its dislocating effecting as it was, was not, however, the only determining factor in the collapse of the classism of classical Marxism (its Russian variants included). In the Leninist vision of world politics there were already some seeds foretelling such a collapse. World capitalism was, for Lenin, a political and not only an economic reality; it was an imperialist chain. As a result, crises in one of its links created imbalances in the relations of forces in other links. The chain was destined to be broken by its weakest link, and nothing guaranteed that such a link was to be found in the most developed capitalist societies. The case was rather the opposite. The notion of uneven and combined development was the clearest expression of this dislocation in the orderly succession of stages that was supposed to govern the history of any society. When in the 1930s Trotsky asserted that uneven and combined development is the terrain of all social struggles in our age, he was extending (without realizing it) the death certificate to the narrow classism of the Second and Third Internationals.

Why so? Because the more profoundly uneven and combined development dislocates the relation between tasks and agents, the less possible it is to assign the tasks to an a priori determined natural agent and the less the agents can be considered as having an identity independent of the tasks that they take up. Thus we enter the terrain of what we have called contingent political articulations and in the transition from strict classism to broader popular identities. The aims of any group in a power struggle can only be achieved if this group operates hegemonically over forces broader than itself that, in turn, will change its own subjectivity. It is in that sense that Gramsci spoke of collective wills. This socialist populism is present in all successful communist mobilizations of that period. Žižek's assertion that populism—understood in this sense—is incompatible with communism is totally groundless. What was Mao doing in the Long March other than creating a wider popular identity, speaking even of "contradictions within the people," thus reintroducing a category, people, which was anathema to classical Marxism? And we can imagine the disastrous results that Tito, in Žižek's native Yugoslavia, would have obtained if he had made a narrow appeal to the workers instead of calling the vast popular masses to resist the foreign occupation. In a heterogeneous world, there is no possibility of meaningful political action except if sectorial identity is conceived as a nucleus and starting point in the constitution of a wider popular will.

On further criticisms

There are, finally, a few minor criticisms that Žižek makes of my work that I don't want to leave unanswered.

Concerning the distinction between my category of empty signifier and Claude Lefort's notion of the empty place of power, Žižek writes:

> The two emptinesses are simply not comparable. The emptiness of people is the emptiness of the hegemonic signifier that totalizes the chain of equivalences or whose particular content is "transubstantiated" into an embodiment of the social Whole, while the emptiness of the place of power is a distance that makes every empirical bearer of power deficient, contingent, and temporary.
> (p. 559)

I would be the last person to deny that the distinction made by Žižek is correct. In actual fact, I have myself made it in the very passage from my book that Žižek quotes: "'For me, emptiness is a type of identity, not a structural location'" (p. 559). Over several years I have resisted the tendency of people to assimilate my approach to that of Lefort, which largely results, I think, from the word *empty* being used in both analyses. But that the notion of emptiness is different in both approaches does not mean that no comparison between them is possible. What my book asserts is that if the notion of emptiness is restricted to a place of power that anybody can occupy, a vital aspect of the whole question is omitted, namely, that occupation of an empty place is not possible without the occupying force becoming itself, to some extent, the signifier of emptiness. What Žižek retains from the idea of "every empirical bearer of power (being) 'deficient,' contingent, and temporary" is only the possibility of being substituted by other bearers of power, but he totally disregards the question of the effects of that deficient, contingent, and temporary condition on the identity of those bearers. Given Žižek's total blindness to the hegemonic dimension of politics, this is hardly surprising.

Regarding the anti-segregationist movement in the U.S., epitomized by Martin Luther King, Jr., Žižek asserts that "although it endeavored to articulate a demand that was not properly met within the existing democratic institutions, it cannot be called populist in any meaningful sense of the term" (p. 560). Everything depends, of course, on the definition of *populism* that one gives. In the usual and narrow sense of the term, whose pejorative overtones associate it with sheer demagogy, there is no doubt that the civil rights movement could not be considered populist. But that is the sense of the term that my whole book puts into question. My argument is that the construction of the people as a collective actor requires extending the notion of populism to many movements and phenomena that traditionally have not been considered so.[16] And, from this viewpoint, there is no doubt that the American civil rights movement extended equivalential logics in a variety of new directions and made possible the incorporation of previously excluded underdogs into the public sphere.

I want, finally, to refer to an anecdotic point, just because Žižek has raised it. In an interview I gave in Buenos Aires I referred to another interview with Žižek, also in Buenos Aires, in a different newspaper, in which he asserted that the problem of the U.S. in world politics is that they act globally and think locally and in this way cannot properly act as universal policemen. From this call to the U.S. to both think and act globally I drew the conclusion that Žižek was asking the U.S. to become the universal class in the Hegelo-Marxist sense of the term. In his *Critical Inquiry* essay Žižek reacts furiously to what he calls my "ridiculously malicious" interpretation and asserts that what he meant was "that this gap between universality and particularity is structurally necessary, which is why the U.S. is in the long term digging its own grave" (p. 563). Let us see exactly what Žižek said in that interview. To the journalists question ("Do you think that invading Iraq was a correct decision from the United States?"), Žižek answers:

> I think that the point is different. Do you remember that ecologist slogan which said "think globally, act locally"? Well, the problem is that the United

States does the opposite: they think locally and act globally. Against the opinion of many left-wing intellectuals who are always complaining about American imperialism, I think that this country should intervene much more.

And, after giving examples of Rwanda and Iraq, he concludes:

This is the tragedy of the United States: in the short run they win wars, but in the long run they end up aggravating the conflicts that they should resolve. The problem is that they should represent more honestly their role of global policemen. They don't do it and they pay the price for not doing it.[17]

It is, of course, for the reader to decide if I have been particularly ridiculous and malicious in not realizing that when Žižek called the U.S. to "represent more honestly their role of global policemen" he meant to say that "the gap between universality and particularity is structurally necessary, which is why the U.S. is in the long term digging its own grave." If so, the world is full of ridiculous and malicious people. I remember that at the time of the publication of Žižek's interview I commented on it to several people in Argentina, and I did not find a single person who had interpreted Žižek's words the way he is now saying that they should be interpreted. Even the journalist interviewing him confesses to be puzzled by the fact that the one asking for the U.S. to act as an international policeman is a Marxist philosopher. And the title of the interview is "Žižek: The U.S. Should Intervene More and Better in the World." (What is the meaning of giving this advice if failure is considered "structurally necessary"?)

Why, however, is failure structurally necessary? Here Žižek asks Hegel's help: "*therein* resides my Hegelianism: the 'motor' of the historico-dialectical process is precisely the gap between acting and thinking" (p. 563). But Hegel's remark does not particularly refer to international politics because it applies to absolutely everything in the universe. So Žižek's answer to the question of whether the U.S. was right or wrong in invading Iraq is that this is not the important question, for the real issue is that there is, in the structure of the real, a necessary gap between thinking and acting. Anyway, with a lot of goodwill I am prepared to accept Žižek's interpretation of his own remarks. My friendly advice, however, is that, if he does not want to be utterly misunderstood, he should be more careful in choosing his words when making a public statement.

The ultraleftist liquidation of the political

We have put into close relationship a series of categories: the political, the people, empty signifiers, equivalence/difference, hegemony. Each of these terms requires the presence of the others. The dispersion of antagonisms and social demands, which are defining features of an era of globalized capitalism, needs the political construction of all social identity, something that is only possible if equivalential relations between heterogeneous elements are established and if the hegemonic dimension of naming is highlighted. That is the reason why *all* political identity is necessarily popular. But there is also another aspect that needs to be stressed. Antagonistic heterogeneity points, as we have shown, to the limits in the constitution of social objectivity, but, precisely because of that, it cannot be in a situation of *total* exteriority in relation to the system that it is opposing. Total exteriority would mean a topological position definable by a precise location *vis-à-vis* that system, and, in that case, it would be part of it. Total exteriority is just one of the forms of interiority. A true political intervention is never merely oppositional; it is rather one that displaces the terms of the debate, that rearticulates the situation in a new configuration. Chantal Mouffe in her work has spoken about the duality agonism/antagonism, pointing out that political action has the responsibility not only of taking a position within a certain context but also of structuring the very context in which a plurality of positions will express themselves.[18] This is the meaning of a war of position, a category that we have already discussed. This is what makes the ultraleftist appeal to total exteriority synonymous with the eradication of the political as such.

It is difficult to find a more extreme example of this ultraleftism than the work of Žižek. Let us see the following passage, which is worth quoting in full:

> There is a will to accomplish the "leap of faith" and *step outside* the global circuit at work here, a will which was expressed in an extreme and terrifying manner in a well-known incident from the Vietnam War: after the US army occupied a local village, their doctors vaccinated the children on the left arm in order to demonstrate their humanitarian care; when, the day after, the village was retaken by the Vietcong, they cut off the left arms of all the vaccinated children. ... Although it is difficult to sustain as a literal model to follow, this complete rejection of the enemy precisely in its caring "humanitarian" aspect, no matter what the cost, has to be endorsed in its basic intention. In a similar way, when Sendero Luminoso took over a village, they did not focus on killing the soldiers or policemen stationed there, but more on the UN or US agricultural consultants or health workers trying to help the local peasants—after lecturing them for hours, and then forcing them to confess their complicity with imperialism publicly, they shot them. Brutal as this procedure was, it was rooted in an acute insight: they, not the police or the army, were the true danger, the enemy at its most perfidious, since they were "lying in the guise of truth"—the more they were "innocent" (they "really" tried to help the peasants), the more they served as a tool of the USA. It is only such a blow against the enemy at his best, at the point where the enemy "indeed helps us," that displays true revolutionary autonomy and sovereignty.
>
> (I, pp. 83–84)

Let us ignore the truculence of this passage and concentrate instead on what matters: the vision of politics that underlies such a statement. One feature is immediately visible: the whole notion of rearticulating demands in a war of position is 100 percent absent. There is, on the contrary, a clear attempt to consolidate the unity of the existing power bloc. As usual, ultraleftism becomes the main source of support of the existing hegemonic formation. The idea of trying to hegemonize demands in a new popular bloc is rejected as a matter of principle. Only a violent, head-on confrontation with the enemy as it is is conceived as legitimate action. Only a position of total exteriority *vis-à-vis* the present situation can guarantee revolutionary purity. There is only one step from here to make exteriority qua exteriority the supreme political value and to advocate violence for violence's sake. That there is nothing "ridiculously malicious" in my suggestion that Žižek is not far from taking that step can be seen in the following passage:

> The only "realistic" prospect is to ground a new political universality by opting for the *impossible,* fully assuming the place of the exception, with no taboos, no a priori norms ("human rights," "democracy"), respect for which would prevent us also from "resignifying" terror, the ruthless exercise of power, the spirit of sacrifice ... if this radical choice is decried by some bleeding-heart liberals as *Linksfaschismus,* so be it![19]

We could, however, ask ourselves, What for Žižek are the political subjects of his *Linksfaschismus?* It is not easy to answer this question because he is quite elusive when it is a question of discussing left-wing strategies. So Žižek's book on Iraq is quite useful because there he devotes a few pages to the protagonists of what he sees as true revolutionary action. He refers mainly to three: the workers' councils of the Soviet tradition—which he himself recognizes have disappeared; Canudos—a millenarian movement in nineteenth-century Brazil; and the inhabitants of the Brazilian *favelas*. The connection between the last two is presented by Žižek in the following terms:

> The echoes of Canudos are clearly discernible in today's favelas in Latin American megalopolises: are they not, in some sense, the first "liberated territories," the cells of future self-organized societies? The liberated territory of Canudos in Bahia will remain forever the model of a space of emancipation, of an alternative community which completely negates the existing space of the state. Everything is to be endorsed here, up to and including religious "fanaticism."
>
> (I, p. 82)

This is pure delirium. The *favelas* are shanty towns of passive poverty submitted to the action of totally nonpolitical criminal gangs that keep the population terrified, to which one has to add the action of the police who carry out executions regularly denounced by the press. As for the assertion that the *favelas* keep alive the memory of Canudos, it involves being so grotesquely misinformed that the only possible answer is "Go and do your homework." There is not a single social movement in contemporary Brazil that establishes a link with the nineteenth-century millenarian tradition—let alone the inhabitants of the *favelas,* who have no idea what Canudos was. Žižek totally ignores what happened in Brazil today, yesterday, or ever—but that does not prevent him from making the most sweeping statements concerning Brazilian revolutionary strategies. This is the process of "Martianization" I referred to before: to attribute to existing subjects the most absurd features, while keeping their names so that the illusion of a contact with reality is maintained. The people of the *favelas* have enough pressing problems without paying any attention to Žižek's eschatological injunctions. So what he needs are *real* Martians. But they are too clever to come down to our planet just to satisfy Žižek's truculent dreams.

Notes

1 See Slavoj Žižek, "Against the Populist Temptation," *Critical Inquiry* 32 [Spring 2006]: 551–74; further page references in this chapter are to this article; see also Laclau 2005. I want to thank the editors of *Critical Inquiry* for inviting me to answer Slavoj Žižek's criticisms of my work.
2 Except, of course, when he identifies the particular feature of the No campaigns with defining characteristics of all possible populism.
3 A cheap trick to be found in several places in Žižek's work consists in identifying the assertion by some authors of a certain degree of comparability between features of the Nazi and the Stalinist regimes, with the impossibility of distinguishing between them postulated by conservative authors such as Nolte. The relationship between a political leader and his "ideology" is, actually, a very complicated business, involving multiple nuances. There is never a situation in which the leader would be *totally* exterior to his ideology and having a purely instrumental relation to the latter. Many strategic mistakes made by Hitler in the course of the war, especially during the Russian campaign, can only be explained by the fact that he actually identified with basic tenets of his own ideological discourse, that he was, in that sense, a "secondary" leader *vis-à-vis* the latter. But if it is wrong to make of the manipulative relation between leader and ideology the essence of some kind of undifferentiated "totalitarian" regime, it is equally wrong to assert, as Žižek does, a mechanical differentiation between a (communist) regime in which the leader would be purely secondary and a (fascist) regime in which he would have an unrestricted primacy.
4 In the passage quoted by Žižek I am just summarizing, approvingly, the analysis of Chartism by Gareth Stedman Jones, "Rethinking Chartism," *Languages of Class, Studies in Working Class History 1832–1902* (Cambridge, 1983).
5 See Laclau, "Why Do Empty Signifiers Matter to Politics?" *Emancipation(s)* (London, 1996), pp. 36–46; present volume, Chapter 3.
6 Here I am not using the term *symbolic in* the Lacanian sense but in the one frequently found in discussions concerning representation. See, for instance, Hanna Fenichel Pitkin, *The Concept of Representation* (Berkeley, 1967), ch. 5.
7 We now move to the strictly Lacanian notion of the Symbolic.
8 See the excellent book by Ian Steedman, *Marx after Sraffa* (London, 1977).
9 Karl Marx and Frederick Engels, *Manifesto of the Communist Party,* in *The Marx-Engels Reader,* trans and ed. Robert C. Tucker (New York, 1978), p. 478.
10 See Alain Badiou, *L'Être et l'événement* (Paris, 1988).
11 How a relation is possible between elements belonging to different spaces of representation is something we will discuss later on.
12 See Laclau and Chantal Mouffe, *Hegemony and Socialist Strategy: Towards a Radical Democratic Politics,* trans. Winston Moore and Paul Cammack (London, 1985), ch. 3; and Laclau,

New Reflections on the Revolution of Our Time (London, 1990), pp. 17–27; and Laclau 2005, pp. 139–56.
13 See on this subject the classic article by Joan Copjec, "Sex and the Euthanasia of Reason," *Read My Desire: Lacan against the Historicists* (Cambridge, MA, 1994), pp. 201–36.
14 Which involves the representation of the unrepresentable leading to what Hans Blumenberg called "the absolute metaphor."
15 See Balibar, "Sur la dialectique historique: Quelques remarques critiques à propos de *Lire le Capital*" *Cinq Etudes du materialisme historique* (Paris, 1974), pp. 205–45.
16 Whenever there is the definition of the ground organizing a certain area of subjectivity, the limits of the latter change, and, as a result, the referents addressed by that discourse are substantially modified. See, for instance, the following passage from Freud:

> By demonstrating the part played by perverse impulses in the formation of symptoms in the psychoneuroses, we have quite remarkably increased the number of people who might be regarded as perverts. Thus the extraordinarily wide dissemination of the perversions forces us to suppose that the disposition to perversions is itself of no great rarity but must form a part of what passes as the normal constitution.
> (Sigmund Freud, *Three Essays on the Theory of Sexuality*, in *The Standard Edition of the Complete Psychological Works of Sigmund Freud*, trans, and ed. James Strachey, 24 vols. [London, 1953–74], 7:171)

(The same can be said about populism).
17 See Laclau, "Las manos en la masa," *Radar*, 5 June 2005, p. 20, www.pagina12.com.ar/diaro/ suplementos/radar/9-2286-2005-06.09.html, and "Žižek: Estados Unidos debería intervenir más y mejor en el mundo: Pide que asuma su papel de policía global," *La nacion*, Mar.10, 2004, www. lanacion.com.ar/04/03/10dg_580163.asp.
18 It is some motive for celebration that Žižek, in his *Critical Inquiry* essay, has for the first time made an effort to discuss separately my work and that of Chantal Mouffe, instead of attributing to each of us the assertions of the other. To refer to a particularly outrageous example: after a long quotation from a work by Mouffe, he comments: "the problem here is that this translation of antagonism into agonism, into the regulated game of political competition, by definition involves a constitutive exclusion, and it is this exclusion that Laclau fails to thematize" (Žižek, *Iraq: The Borrowed Kettle* [London, 2004], p. 90; hereafter abbreviated *I*). The problem is not whether I agree or disagree with what Mouffe has said; the problem is that it is dishonest to criticize an author for what another author has said.
19 Žižek, "Holding the Place," in Judith Butler, Laclau, and Žižek, *Contingency, Hegemony, Universality: Contemporary Dialogues on the Left* (London, 2000), p. 326.

Bibliography

Laclau, Ernesto. 2005. *On Populist Reason*. London: Verso.

PART III
Critical engagements

9
'THE TIME IS OUT OF JOINT' (1995)

> Since this singular end of the political would correspond to the presentation of an absolutely living reality, this is one more reason to think that the essence of the political will always have the inessential figure, the very anessence of a ghost.
> (Jacques Derrida, *Specters of Marx*)

Halfway through *Specters of Marx*, Derrida links the concept of production to that of trauma and speaks of "the spectral spiritualization that is at work in any *tekhne*" (1994, p. 97). He immediately connects this assertion to Freud's remarks concerning the three traumas inflicted on the narcissism of the decentered man: the psychological trauma derived from the psychoanalytic discovery of the unconscious, the biological trauma resulting from the Darwinian findings about human descent, and the cosmological trauma proceeding from the Copernican revolution. To this Derrida adds the decentering effects coming from Marxism, which, according to him, accumulate and put together the other three:

> The century of "Marxism" will have been that of the techno-scientific and effective decentering of the earth, of geopolitics, of the *anthropos* in its onto-theological identity or its genetic properties, of the *ego cogito*—and of the very concept of narcissism whose aporias are, let us say in order to go too quickly and save ourselves a lot of references, the explicit theme of deconstruction.
> (1994, p. 98)

So deconstruction inscribes itself in a secular movement of decentering, to which Marxism itself belongs. In fact, at various points of *Specters of Marx*, Derrida insists that deconstruction would be either inconceivable or irrelevant if it were not related to the spirit or the tradition of a certain Marxism. And yet deconstruction is not *just* Marxism: it is a certain operation practiced in the body of Marxism, the locating in Marx's texts of an area of undecidability which, in Derrida's terms, is that circumscribed by the opposition between *spirit* and *specter,* between *ontology* and *hauntology.* The performing of this deconstructive operation—to which the last two chapters of the book are devoted—is far from a purely academic exercise: the very possibility of justice—but also of politics—is at stake. Without the constitutive dislocation that inhabits all hauntology—and that ontology tries to conceal—there would be no politics, just a programmed, predetermined reduction of the other to the same.

> It is easy to go from disadjusted to unjust. That is our problem: how to justify this passage from disadjustment (with its rather more technico-ontological value affecting a presence) to an injustice that would no longer be ontological? And what if disadjustment were on the contrary the condition of justice? And what if this double register condensed its enigma, precisely [*justement*], and potentialized its superpower in that which gives its unheard-of force to Hamlet's words: "The time is out of joint"? (Derrida 1994, pp. 19–20).

To find a double logic in Marx's work, to detect in the Marxian texts a double gesture that the theory makes possible but is unable to control conceptually in a credible synthesis: all this looks rather familiar. Since the end of the nineteenth century, this duality, deeply inscribed in Marx's work, has been the object of countless analyses. The duality of or the oppositions between economic determinism and the ethical orientation of socialism, between economism and the primacy of politics, even between the "scientific" and the "ideological" components of the theory, have been not only recurrent themes in Marxist discussions but the very issues that have made possible a history of Marxism. However, none of these apparent reformulations of the terms of a widely perceived dualism has been similar to the others. We are not dealing with a purely nominalistic operation of renaming: the displacement that these reformulations operate, the logics of the social they imply, and, above all, the political strategies they make possible are radically different.

Derrida does not trace the genealogy of his intervention in the Marxian text. This is regrettable, in part because the specificity, originality, and potentialities of his intervention do not come sufficiently to light. In what follows, I will try to stress some of these specific features, as well as their originality *vis-à-vis* other comparable attempts. To this end, I will refer to what I think are the two central theoretical points in Derrida's book: the logic of the specter (the hauntology) and the category of messianism.

The logic of the specter

> [T]he specter is a paradoxical incorporation, the becoming-body, a certain phenomenal and carnal form of the spirit. It becomes, rather, some "thing" that remains difficult to name: neither soul nor body, and both one and the

> other. For it is flesh and phenomenality that give to the spirit its spectral apparition, but which disappear right away in the apparition, in the very coming of the revenant or the return of the specter. There is something disappeared, departed in the apparition itself as reapparition of the departed.
> (Derrida 1994, p. 6)

Anachronism is essential to spectrality: the specter, interrupting all specularity, desynchronizes time. The very essence of spectrality is to be found in this undecidability between flesh and spirit: it is not purely body—for in that case there would be no spectrality at all; but it is not pure spirit either—for the passage through the flesh is crucial.

> For there is no ghost, there is never any becoming-specter of the spirit without at least an appearance of flesh, in a space of invisible visibility, like the disappearing of an apparition. For there to be ghost, there must be a return to the body, but to a body that is more abstract than ever. The spectrogenic process corresponds therefore to a paradoxical *incorporation*. Once ideas or thoughts (*Gedanke*) are detached from their substratum, one engenders some ghost by *giving them a body*.
> (Derrida 1994, p. 126)

From this point onward, Derrida makes a classic deconstructive move: the specter being undecidable between the two extremes of body and spirit, these extremes themselves become contaminated by that undecidability. Thus, having shown how, in Marx's analysis of commodity, exchange value depends for its constitution on a spectral logic, Derrida concludes that this logic is not absent from use-value either:

> The said use-value of the said ordinary sensuous thing, simple hulē, the wood of the wooden table concerning which Marx supposes that it has not yet begun to "dance," its very form, the form that informs its hulē, must indeed have at least promised it to iterability, to substitution, to exchange, to value; it must have made a start, however minimal it may have been, on an idealization that permits one to identify it as the same throughout possible repetitions, and so forth. Just as there is no pure use, there is no use-value which the possibility of exchange and commerce … has not in advance inscribed in an out-of-use—an excessive signification that cannot be reduced to the useless.
> (Derrida 1994, p. 160)

Similarly, if the spirit is something whose invisibility has to produce its own visibility, if the very constitution of spirit requires the visibility of the invisible, nothing is more difficult than to keep a strict separation between spirit and specter. Once this point has been reached, the conclusions follow quickly. We find in Marx a hauntology, an argument about spectrality at the very heart of the constitution of the social link. Time being "out of joint," dislocation corrupting the identity with itself of any present, we have a constitutive anachronism that is at the root of any identity. Any "life" emerges out of a more basic life/death dichotomy—it is not "life" as uncontaminated presence but *survie* that is the condition of any presence. Marx, however, attempted the critique of the hauntological from the perspective of an ontology. If the specter inhabits the root of the social link in bourgeois society, the transcendence of the latter, the arrival at a time that is no longer "out of joint," the realization of a society fully reconciled with itself will open the way to the "end of ideology"—that is, to a purely "ontological" society which, after the consummation of the proletarian millennium, will look to hauntology as its past. And since hauntology is inherent to politics, the transcendence of the split between being and appearance will mean the end of politics. (We could, in fact, put the argument in Saint-Simonian terms: the transition from the government of men to the administration of things.) If, however, as the deconstructive reading shows, "ontology"—full reconciliation—is not achievable, time is constitutively "out of joint," and the ghost is the condition of possibility of any present, politics too becomes constitutive of the social link. We could say of the specter what Groucho Marx said about sex: it is going to stay with us for a while.

This contamination of presence by the specter can be considered from the two perspectives involved in a double genitive. There are, in the first place, specters of Marx, insofar as Marx himself—an abbreviation for communism—is haunting us today as a horizon preventing the possibility of its final exorcism by the apparently triumphant capitalist "democracies" (here the main reference is to Fukuyama). But there are also the specters of Marx that visited Marx himself and prevented him from establishing a nonhaunted ontology. Thus, the ground we reach—that of a present never identical with itself—is the very terrain of this phantasmatic, an essential practice that we call politics.

What to say about this Derridean sequence? A first remark—first, both temporally and logically—is that I have nothing to object to. The deconstructive operation is impeccable, the horizons that it opens are far-reaching, and the intertextuality within which it takes place is highly illuminating. However, as with any deconstruction worthy of the name, there is a plurality of directions in which one can move, and it is to consider this plurality that I would like to pause for a moment. My own work has largely concentrated on the deconstruction of Marxist texts, and I could, *prima facie,* relate what I have called hegemonic logic[1]—which silently deconstructs Marxist categories—to the logic of the specter as described by Derrida. Others too have recently linked "deconstruction" and "hegemony." Simon Critchley, for instance, asserts:

> Against the troubling tendency to subordinate the political to the socioeconomic within Marx's "ontology" … Derrida's argument for a logic of spectrality within Marxism can be linked to the claim for the irreducibility of the political understood as that moment where the sedimented meanings of the socio-economic are contested. Following Ernesto Laclau's radicalization of Gramsci, one might link the logic of spectrality to the logic of hegemony;

that is, if one renounces—as one must—the communist eschatological "a-theodicy" of the economic contradictions of capitalism inevitably culminating in revolution, then politics and politico-cultural-ideological hegemonization is indispensable to the possibility of radical change.

(Critchley 1995, p. 5)

I hesitate, however, to entirely endorse such an apparently obvious assimilation. Although there is no incompatibility between hegemony and spectral logic as far as the latter goes, a hegemonic logic presupposes two further steps beyond spectrality that I am not sure Derrida is prepared to take:

1. Spectrality presupposes, as we have seen, an undecidable relation between spirit and flesh which contaminates, in turn, these two poles. It presupposes, in that sense, a weakened form of incarnation. Weakened because a full incarnation—an incarnation in the Christian sense—transforms the flesh into a purely transparent medium through which we can see an *entirely* spiritual reality with no connection to its incarnating body. God's mediation is what establishes the link between spirit and flesh insofar as He is at an infinite distance from both. So the lack of natural connection between both poles is what transforms the flesh into the medium through which the spirit shows itself. At the same time, however, it is this lack of connection that prevents the contamination of one by the other. No doubt this Christian polarity can be deconstructed in turn, but the point is that this deconstruction will not take place through the collapse of the frontier between spirit and specter. For in the specter the relation between spirit and flesh is much more intimate: there is no divine mediation that both sanctions and supersedes the essential heterogeneity of the two poles. Now, a hegemonic relation is one in which a certain body presents itself as the incarnation of a certain spirit. The hegemonic relation is certainly spectral: a certain body tries to present its particular features as the expression of something transcending its own particularity. The body is an undecidable point in which universality and particularity get confused, but the very fact that other bodies compete to be the incarnating ones, that they are alternative forms of materialization of the same "spirit," suggests a kind of autonomization of the latter which cannot be explained solely by the pure logic of spectrality.

2. Of what does this autonomization consist? This is our second step. Let us remember that any step that is taken out of the logic of spectrality cannot be in contradiction to the latter but must, on the contrary, presuppose it. If the autonomization of the "spirit" is to take place within spectrality, "autonomy" cannot mean identity with oneself, self-representation, because that would, precisely, restore a rigid frontier between "spirit" and "specter." But autonomy does not require full identity as its precondition: it can also emerge out of a constitutive impossibility, an absolute limit whose forms of representation will be necessarily inadequate. Let us suppose a situation of generalized social disorder: in such a situation "order" becomes the name of an absent fullness, and if

that fullness is constitutively unachievable it cannot have any content of its own, any form of self-representation. "Order" thus becomes autonomous *vis-à-vis* any particular order insofar as it is the name of an absent fullness that no concrete social order can achieve (the same can be said of similar terms such as "revolution," "unity of the people," etc.). That fullness is present, however, as that which is absent and needs as a result to be represented in some way. Now, its means of representation will be constitutively inadequate, for they can only be particular contents that assume, in certain circumstances, a function of representation of the impossible universality of the community. This relation, by which a certain particular content overflows its own particularity and becomes the incarnation of the absent fullness of society is exactly what I call a hegemonic relation. As we can see, it presupposes the logic of the specter: the fullness of the "spirit," as it has no content of its own, can exist only through its parasitic attachment to some particular body; but that body is subverted and deformed in its own particularity as it becomes the embodiment of fullness. This means, *inter alia,* that the anachronistic language of revolutions, which Marx refers to and Derrida analyzes, is inevitable: the old revolution is present in the new one, not in its particularity but in its universal function of being *a* revolution, as the incarnation of the revolutionary principle as such. And the Marxian aspiration of a revolutionary language that only expresses the present, in which the "content" overcomes "phraseology," is a pure impossibility. If the fullness of the revolution—as all fullness—is unachievable, we cannot but have a dissociation between the revolutionary content and the fullness of a pure revolutionary foundation, and this dissociation will reproduce *sine die* the logic of spectrality and the split between "phraseology" and "content."

What precedes is an attempt to show the type of move that I would make out of the logic of spectrality. But, as I said, it is not the only move that one can make. The steps that lead from the logic of spectrality to a hegemonic logic are steps that the former logic certainly makes possible, but are not necessarily corollaries derived from it.

But what political consequences does Derrida himself draw from his deconstruction of Marx's texts? Although these consequences are not entirely developed in his book, we can get a broad hint of the direction that Derrida is taking if we move to our second theme: the question of the messianic.

The question of the messianic

Let us quote Derrida again. After having indicated that both Marxism and religion share the formal structure of a messianic eschatology, he asserts:

> While it is common to both of them, with the exception of the content ... it is also the case that its formal structure of promise exceeds them or precedes them. Well, what remains irreducible to any deconstruction, what remains as undeconstructible as the possibility itself of deconstruction is, perhaps, a

certain experience of the emancipatory promise; it is perhaps even the formality of a structural messianism, a messianism without religion, even a messianic without messianism, an idea of justice—which we distinguish from law or right and even from human rights—and an idea of democracy—which we distinguish from its current concept and from its determined predicates today.
(Derrida 1994, p. 59)

Here Derrida summarizes themes that he developed in full in "Force of Law" (1992). However, these themes and concepts need to be reinserted in the various discursive contexts within which they were originally formulated, first because these contexts considerably diverge among themselves and, second, because the high metaphoricity of some of the categories employed—such as the messianic—can lead to an undue association of those categories with the concrete historical phenomena to which they are usually applied. I cannot do this properly in the limited space of this chapter, but let us, at least, lay down some guidelines. By the "messianic" we should not understand anything *directly* related to actual messianic movements—of the present or the past—but, instead, something belonging to the general structure of experience. It is linked to the idea of "promise." This does not mean this or that particular promise, but the promise implicit in an originary opening to the "other," to the unforeseeable, to the pure *event* which cannot be mastered by any aprioristic discourse. Such an event is an interruption in the normal course of things, a radical dislocation. This leads to the notion of "justice" as linked to an absolute singularity which cannot be absorbed by the generality of law. The chasm between law and justice is one which cannot be closed. The existence of this chasm is what makes deconstruction possible. Deconstruction and justice—or, rather, deconstruction *as* justice—is what cannot be deconstructed. Deconstructing law—which is finally what politics is about—is possible because of this structure of experience in which the messianic, the promise, and justice are categories in a relation of mutual implication.

On the basis of these premises, Derrida elaborates his concept of "democracy to come" *("démocratie à venir")*. This *"à venir"* does not involve any teleological assertion—not even the limited one of a regulative idea—but simply the continual commitment to keep open the relation to the other, an opening which is always *à venir*, for the other to which one opens oneself is never already given in any aprioristic calculation. To summarize: the messianism we are speaking about is one without eschatology, without pregiven promised land, without determinate content. It is simply the structure of promise which is inherent in all experience and whose lack of content—resulting from the radical opening to the event, to the other, is the very possibility of justice and gives its only meaning to the democracy to come. Singularity as the terrain of justice involves the radical undecidability which makes the decision possible.

> [I]t was then a matter of thinking another historicity ... another opening of event-ness as historicity that permitted one not to renounce, but on the

contrary to open up access to an affirmative thinking of the messianic and emancipatory promise as promise: as promise and not as onto-theological or teleo-eschatological program or design. ... But at a certain point promise and decision, which is to say responsibility, owe their possibility to the ordeal of undecidability which will always remain their condition.

(Derrida 1994, pp. 74–75)

What does one say about the various theoretical operations that Derrida performs starting from this conceptual construction? I think that we can distinguish three levels here. The first refers to the deconstruction of the concept of messianism that we have inherited from the religious but also from the Marxist tradition. This deconstruction proceeds by showing the contingent character of the articulations that have coalesced around the actual historical messianisms. We can do away with the teleological and eschatological dimensions, we can even do away with all the actual contents of the historical messianisms, but what we cannot do away with is the "promise," because the latter is inscribed in the structure of all experience. This, as we have seen, is not a promise of anything concrete; it is some sort of "existential," insofar as it is what prevents any presence from being closed around itself. If we link this to the relation law/justice, undecidability/decisions, we can see the general movement of Derrida's theoretico-political intervention, which is to direct the historico-political forms back to the primary terrain of their opening to the radically heterogenous. This is the terrain of a constitutive undecidability, of an experience of the impossible that, paradoxically, makes possible responsibility, the decision, law and—finally—the messianic itself in its actual historical forms. I find myself in full agreement with this movement.

However, Derrida's argument does not stop there. From this first movement (for reasons that will become clear presently, I keep this "from" deliberately vague, undecided between the derivative and the merely sequential) he passes to a sort of ethico-political injunction by which all the previously mentioned dimensions converge in the project of a democracy to come, which is linked to the classical notion of "emancipation." Derrida is very firm in his assertion that he is unprepared to put the latter into question in any way. But we have to be very careful about the meaning of such a stand, because the classical notion of emancipation is no more than another name for the eschatological messianism that he is trying to deconstruct.

Various aspects have to be differentiated here. If by reasserting the classical notion of emancipation Derrida does not mean anything beyond his particular way of reasserting messianism—that is, doing away with all the teleo-ontological paraphernalia of the latter and sticking to the moment of the "promise"—then I would certainly agree with him, but in that case the classic idea of emancipation, even if we retain from it an ultimately undeconstructible moment, is deeply transformed. I find it rather misleading to call this operation a defense of the classic notion of emancipation. But—a second aspect—the classic notion of emancipation was something more than the formal structure of the promise. It was also the crystallization and synthesis of a series of contents such as the elimination of economic exploitation and all forms of discrimination, the assertion of human rights, the consolidation of civil and political freedom, and so forth. Derrida, understandably, does not want to renounce this patrimony, and it would be difficult not to join him in its defense. The difficulty, however, is that in the classic notion of emancipation the defense and grounding of all those contents were intimately connected to the teleological eschatology that Derrida is deconstructing. So, if he wants to maintain the results of his deconstruction and at the same time to defend those contents, as the ground of the latter can no longer be an eschatological articulation, there are only two ways open to him: either to show that those contents can be derived from the "promise" as a general structure of experience, or to demonstrate that those contents are grounded in something less than such a general structure—in which case the "promise" as such is indifferent to the actual nature of those contents.

There is, finally, a third aspect to be distinguished. The previous distinctions have to be situated against the background of the real target of Derrida's discussion in *Specters of Marx:* the exposure of a prevalent common sense (that he exemplifies through his brilliant critique of Fukuyama) according to which the collapse of the communist regimes is supposed to mean humanity's arrival at a final stage where all human needs will be satisfied and where a messianic consummation of time is notto be expected any more. Derrida reacts against this new dominant consensus and its Hegelo-Kojèvian grounding by showing, at the empirical level, the gap between historical reality and the capitalist West's satisfied image of itself and, at the theoretical level, the inconsistencies of the notion of an end of History. It is against the background of this polemic that the whole discourse about the constantly returning specters of Marx has to be understood. What Derrida is finally saying is that isolated demands, grievances, injustices, and so forth are not empirical residues of a historical stage which has—in all essentials—been superseded, that they are, on the contrary, the symptoms of a fundamental deadlock of contemporary societies that pushes isolated demands to some kind of phantasmatic articulation which will result in new forms of political reaggregation. The latter are not specified beyond Derrida's quick allusions to the historical limits of the "party" form and to a "New International" in the making. It is, however, clear that any advance in formulating a theory of political reaggregation crucially depends on how the transition between the general structure of experience—the promise—and the contents of the classical emancipatory project is conceived.

This is the third level at which the argument of *Specters of Marx* can be considered: the type of link it establishes between the promise as a (post-)transcendental or (post-)ontological (non-)ground and the ethical and political contents of an emancipatory project. This is the level at which I find the argument of *Specters* less convincing. For here an illegitimate logical transition can easily be made. I am not necessarily asserting that Derrida is making that transition, but, nevertheless, it is one frequently made by many defenders of deconstruction and one to which the very ambiguity of the Derridean texts gives some credence. The illegitimate transition is to think that from the impossibility of a presence closed in itself, from an "ontological" condition in which the openness to the event, to the heterogeneous, to the radically other is constitutive, some kind of ethical injunction to be responsible and to keep oneself open to the heterogeneity of the other necessarily follows. This transition is illegitimate for two reasons. First, because if the promise is an "existential" constitutive of all experience, it is always already there, before any injunction. (It is like the voluntaristic argument criticized by Ortega y Gasset: on the one hand, it asserts that life is constitutive insecurity; on the other, it launches the imperative *Vivere pericolosamente,* as if to do it or not to do it were a matter of choice.) But, second and most important, from the fact that there is the impossibility of ultimate closure and presence, it does not follow that there is an ethical imperative to "cultivate" that openness or even less to be necessarily committed to a democratic society. I think that the latter can certainly be defended from a deconstructionist perspective, but that defense cannot be logically derived from constitutive openness—something more has to be added to the argument. Precisely because of the undecidability inherent in constitutive openness, ethico-political moves different from or even opposite to a democracy "to come" can be made—for instance, since there is ultimate undecidability and, as a result, no immanent tendency of the structure to closure and full presence, closure has to be *artificially* brought about from the outside. In that way a case for totalitarianism can be presented starting from deconstructionist premises. Of course, the totalitarian argument would be as much a non sequitur as the argument for democracy: either direction is equally possible given the situation of structural undecidability.

So far we have presented our argument concerning the nonconnection between structural undecidability and ethical injunction, starting from the "ontological" side. But if we move to the "normative" side, the conclusions are remarkably similar. Let us suppose, for the sake of the argument, that openness to the heterogeneity of the other is an *ethical* injunction. If one takes this proposition at face value, one is forced to conclude that we have to accept the other as different *because* she is different, whatever the content of that heterogeneity would be. This does not sound much like an ethical injunction but like ethical nihilism. And if the argument is reformulated by saying that openness to the other does not necessarily mean passive acceptance of her but rather active engagement which includes criticizing her, attacking her, even killing her, the whole argument starts to seem rather vacuous: what else do people do all the time without any need for an ethical injunction?

Yet I think that deconstruction *has* important consequences for both ethics and politics. These consequences, however, depend on deconstruction's ability to go down to the bottom of its own radicalism and avoid becoming entangled in all the problems of a Levinasian ethics (whose proclaimed aim, to present ethics as *first* philosophy, should from the start look suspicious to any deconstructionist). I see the matter this way. Undecidability should be literally taken as that condition from which no course of action necessarily follows. This means that we should not make it the necessary source of *any* concrete decision in the ethical or political sphere. In a first movement deconstruction extends undecidability—that is, that which makes the decision necessary—to deeper and larger areas of social relations. The role of deconstruction is, from this perspective, to *reactivate* the moment of decision that underlies any *sedimented* set of social relations. The political and ethical significance of this first movement is that by enlarging the area of structural undecidability it enlarges also the area of responsibility—that is, of the decision. (In Derridean terms: the requirements of justice become more complex and multifaceted *vis-à-vis* law.)

But this first movement is immediately balanced by another one of the opposite sign, which is also essential to deconstruction. To think of undecidability as a bottomless abyss that underlies any self-sufficient "presence" would still maintain too much of the imagery of the "ground." The duality undecidability/decision is something that belongs to the logic of any structural arrangement. Degrounding is, in this sense, also part of an operation of grounding, except that grounding is no longer to refer something back to a foundation which would act as a principle of derivation but, instead, to reinscribe that something within the terrain of the undecidables (iteration, re-mark, differance, etc.) that make its emergence possible. So, to go back to our problem, it is no longer a question of finding a ground from which an ethical injunction should be *derived* (even less to make of undecidability itself such a ground). We live as *bricoleurs* in a plural world, having to take decisions within incomplete systems of rules (incompletion here means undecidability), and some of these rules are ethical ones. It is because of this constitutive incompletion that decisions have to be taken, but because we are faced with incompletion and not with total dispossession, the problem of a *total* ethical grounding—either through the opening to the otherness of the other, or through any similar metaphysical principle—never arises. "The time is out of joint," but because of that there is never a beginning—or an end—of time. Democracy does not need to be—and cannot be—radically grounded. We can move to a more democratic society only through a plurality of acts of democratization. The consummation of time—as Derrida knows well—never arrives. Not even as a regulative idea.

> This leaves us, however, with a problem: how to conceive of emancipation within this framework. What kind of collective reaggregation is open to us once we have moved away from the eschatological dimension of the classical emancipatory model? This will be my last discussion, and I will broach it by locating Derrida's intervention within the tradition of critique and reformulation of Marxism.

The Question of the Tradition

Derrida very cogently maintains that one thinks only from within a tradition and shows that this thinking is possible only if one conceives one's relation with that past as a critical reception. Now, the reception of Marxism since the turn of the century has turned, in my view, around the discussion of two capital and interrelated issues: (1) how to make compatible—if it can be done at all—the various contradictory aspects of Marx's thought, as in Derrida's version, which relates the "ontological" and the "phantasmatic"; (2) how to think forms of reaggregation of political wills and social demands once the obviousness of the identification of the working class with the emancipatory agency started to dissolve. It is my contention that the deconstructionist intervention represents a crucial turn in connection with both issues. To show this, let us recapitulate the broad lines of the main classical attempts at recasting Marxism.

1. A first tendency represents the accentuation of the ontological dimension (in the Derridean sense) of Marx's thought. The absolute reconciliation of society with itself will arrive as a result of the elimination of all forms of distorted representation. The latter will be the consequence of the proletarian revolution. This tendency can be found in a vulgar materialist version (for example, Plekhanov) or in an apparently more "superstructuralist" one, centered in the notion of "false consciousness" (as in Lukács). There is here no reaggregation of collective wills (the revolutionary agent is the working class), and human emancipation is fixed in its contents by a full-fledged eschatology.
2. The various forms of "ethical" socialism, to be found in Bernstein and in some currents of Austro-Marxism. The common feature of all these tendencies is a return to a Kantian dualism. Here the ontological dimension becomes weaker: the "necessary laws of history" become more erratic, the agent of emancipation becomes more contingent and indeterminate, and the *Endziel* loses most of its eschatological precision. However, the determinacy which has been lost at the level of an objective history is retrieved at the level of an ethical regulative idea. The moment of the political decision is as absent as in Marxist orthodoxy.
3. The Sorelian-Gramscian tradition. It is here that the phantasmatic dimension finally takes the upper hand. The anchoring of social representations in the ontological bedrock of an objective history starts dissolving. The unity of the class is, for Sorel, a mythical unity. For Gramsci, the unity of a collective will results from the constitutive role of an organic ideology. History becomes an open and contingent process that does not reflect any deeper underlying reality. Two aspects are important for us: (a) the link between concrete material forces and the function that they fulfill in the classical Marxist scheme becomes loose and indeterminate. "Collective will," "organic ideology," "hegemonic group," and so forth become empty forms that can be filled by any imaginable political and social content. They are certainly anchored in a dialectics of emancipation, but as the latter is not necessarily linked to any particular content it becomes something like an "existential" of historical life and is no longer the announcement of a concrete event. Now, is this not something like a deconstruction of eschatological messianism: the autonomization of the messianic promise from the contents that it is attached to in "actually existing" messianisms? (b) The distinction between the ethical and the political is blurred. The moment of the ethico-political is presented as a unity. This can, of course, be given a Hegelian interpretation, but my argument is that what is really at stake in Gramsci's intervention is a politicization of ethics, insofar as the acts of

institution of the social link are contingent acts of decision that presuppose relations of power. This is what gives an "ontological" primacy to politics and to "hegemony" as the logic governing any political intervention.

I have said enough to make it clear that for me it is only as an extension and radicalization of this last tendency that deconstruction can present itself both as a moment of its inscription in the Marxist tradition as well as a point of turning/deepening/supersession of the latter. My optimistic reading of *Specters of Marx* is that it represents a step forward in the prosecution of this task. The main stumbling block that I still see for this to be accomplished—at least as far as Derrida is concerned—is that the ambiguity previously pointed out between undecidability as a terrain of radicalization of the decision and undecidability as the source of an ethical injunction is still hovering in Derrida's texts. Once this ambiguity is superseded, however, deconstruction can become one of the most powerful tools at hand for thinking strategically.

This rethinking of politics in a deconstructive fashion can (if we start from the Marxist tradition) produce three types of effect. In the first place, if we are thinking in the terms of the third tendency within Marxism, we can recast and extend its system of categories far beyond the intellectual tools to which Sorel or Gramsci had access. This recasting in terms of the logic of *différance* can open the way to much more refined forms of strategic thinking.

Second, the logics of hegemonic reaggregation face, in the contemporary world, much more serious challenges than those that a Gramsci was confronted with. Our societies are far less homogeneous than those in which the Marxian models were formulated, and the constitution of the collective wills takes place in terrains crossed by far more complex relations of power—as a result, *inter alia*, of the development of the mass media. The dissolution of the metaphysics of presence is not a purely intellectual operation. It is profoundly inscribed in the whole experience of recent decades. Deconstruction, as a result, faces the challenge of reinscribing the Marxian model in this complex experience of present-day society.

Finally, operating deconstructively within Marx's texts can help in a third vitally important task: reinscribing Marxism itself and each one of its discursive components as a partial moment in the wider history of emancipatory discourses. Derrida is quite right to combat the current amnesia of the Marxist tradition. But let us not make the opposite mistake and think that the history of Marxism overlaps with the history of emancipatory projects. Many more ghosts than those of Marx are actually visiting and revisiting us. Benjamin's angel should become a symbol constantly reminding us of our complex and multilayered tradition. I remember that during my childhood, in Argentina, in the cinemas of continuous performance there was an announcement saying, "The performance begins when you arrive." Well, I think that "emancipation" is the opposite: it is a performance at which we always arrive late and which forces us to guess, painfully, about its mythical or impossible origins. We have, however, to engage ourselves in this impossible task, which is, among other things, what gives deconstruction its meaning.

Note

1 The basic formulation concerning the concept of "hegemony" can be found in Laclau and Mouffe, *Hegemony and Socialist Strategy* (1985), chapters 3 and 4. I have reformulated the basic dimensions of this concept, linking it more closely to the category of "dislocation," in *New Reflections on the Revolution of Our Time* (1990).

Bibliography

Critchley, Simon. 1995. On Spectres de Marx. *Philosophy and Social Criticism* 21(3): 1–30.
Derrida, J. 1992. Force of Law: The "Mystical Foundation of Authority." In *Deconstruction and the Possibility of Justice,* ed. Drucilla Cornell *et al.* New York: Routledge.
——1994. *Specters of Marx: The State of the Debt, the Work of Mourning, and the New International.* Trans. Peggy Kamuf. New York: Routledge.
Laclau, E. 1990. *New Reflections on the Revolution of Our Time.* London: Verso.
Laclau, E. and Mouffe, C. 1985. *Hegemony and Socialist Strategy.* London: Verso.

10

CAN IMMANENCE EXPLAIN SOCIAL STRUGGLES? (2003)

In a recent interview, Jacques Rancière (2002) opposes his notion of "people" *(peuple)*[1] to the category of "multitude" as presented by the authors of *Empire* (Hardt and Negri 2000). As is well known, Rancière differentiates between *police* and *politics,* the first being the logic of counting and assigning the population to differential places, and the second, the subversion of that differentiating logic through the constitution of an egalitarian discourse which puts into question established identities. The "people" is the specific subject of politics and presupposes a sharp division in the social body that cannot be led back to any kind of immanent unity. *Empire,* on the contrary, makes immanence its central category and the ultimate ground of the multitude's unity.

It is worthwhile describing the main lines of Rancière's critique because they provide a good starting point for what we have to say about the book on which we are commenting. The immanentism of Hardt and Negri would be linked, according to Rancière, to their Nietzschean/Deleuzian ethics of affirmation, which does away with any reactive or negative dimension. *Empire* would belong, in that respect, to the whole tradition of modern political philosophy, which is profoundly metapolitical:

> the kernel of metapolitics is to lead back the precarious artifices of the political scene to the truth of an immanent power which organizes beings in a community and identifies the true community with the grasped and sensible operation of this truth.
>
> *(Rancière 2002, p. 96)*

From Hardt and Negri's rejection of any inherent negativity in political subjects it follows that the power inherent in the multitude has to be a disruptive power, "lodged in all states of domination as its ultimate content, a content destined to destroy all barriers. 'Multitudes' have to be a content whose continent is Empire" (Rancière 2002, p. 97). Disruptive forces operating through a purely immanent movement are what Marxist theory called "productive forces" and there would be, according to Rancière, a strict homology between the place of productive forces and that in which multitudes, as described in *Empire,* act. Rancière points out that productive forces should not necessarily be understood in any narrow productivist sense: there has been a constant widening of the concept from the strict economism of classical Marxism to the recent attempts to include within it the ensemble of scientific and intellectual abilities, passing through the Leninist attempt to supplement via political intervention a role that productive forces refused to fulfill.

I think that Rancière has rightly stressed what I see as the main source of several weaknesses of *Empire,* including a central one: that within its theoretical framework, politics becomes unthinkable. So I will start from a discussion of *Empire's* notion of immanence and move later to various other theoretical and political aspects of the book.

Let us start with the authors' discussion of the origins of European modernity. While the usual insistence is on the secularization process, that process would be:

> in our view ... only a symptom of the primary event of modernity: the affirmation of the powers of *this* world, the discovery of the plane of immanence. "Omne eus habet aliquod esse proprium"—every entity has a singular essence. Duns Scotus' affirmation subverts the medieval conception of being as an object of analogical and thus dualistic predication—a being with one foot in this world and one in a transcendental realm.
>
> (Hardt and Negri 2000, p. 71)

Duns Scotus's insistence on the singularity of being would have started an assertion of immanence that the authors describe as a process whose representative names would have been Nicholas of Cusa, Pico della Mirandola, and Bovillus—other names quoted are Bacon and Occam—and whose point of arrival is Spinoza:

> By the time we arrive at Spinoza, in fact, the horizon of immanence and the horizon of the democratic political order coincide completely. The plane of immanence is the one on which the powers of singularity are realized and the one on which the truth of the new humanity is determined historically, technically and politically. For this very fact, because there cannot be any external mediation, the singular is presented as the multitude.
>
> (Hardt and Negri 2000, p. 73)

The revolution, however, ran into trouble. It had its Thermidor. The Thirty Years War was the outcome, and the need for peace led to the defeat of the forces of progress and the instauration of absolutism.

The first striking thing that one finds in this analysis is that it gives us a truncated narrative. For the assertion of a radical immanentism does not start, as Hardt and

Negri seem to believe, at the time of Duns Scotus but much earlier, during the Carolingian Renaissance—more precisely, in Scotus Erigena's *De Divisione Naturae*. And in its initial formulations it had nothing to do with secularism, for it was an answer to strictly theological difficulties. The attempt to go back to those origins does not obey a purely erudite scruple; on the contrary, to clarify the context of theological alternatives of which immanentism was only one has direct relevance to the political issues that we are discussing today. The original theological question—which occupied the mind, among others, of no less a thinker than Saint Augustine—was how to make compatible the worldly existence of evil with divine omnipotence. If God is responsible for evil, he cannot be absolute Goodness; if he is not responsible for evil, he is not Almighty. Immanentism in its first formulations is an answer to this question. According to Erigena, evil does not really exist, for things we call evil are necessary stages that God has to pass through in order to reach His divine perfection. But this is obviously impossible without God being, somehow, internal to the world.

From that point onward, immanentism had a long career in Western thought. It is very much present in Northern mysticism and in some of the authors discussed in *Empire,* such as Nicholas of Cusa and Spinoza, and it is going to find its highest point in Hegel and Marx. Hegel's cunning of reason closely follows the argument that Erigena formulated one thousand years before. As the *Philosophy of History* asserts, universal history is not the terrain of happiness. And the Marxian version is scarcely different: society had to supersede primitive communism and pass through the whole hell of class division to develop the productive forces of humanity, and it is only at the end of the process, in a fully developed communism, that the rationality of all this suffering becomes visible.[2]

What are, however, really important in reference to these theological debates are the other existing alternatives in case the immanentist route *is not followed*. For in that case evil is not the appearance of a rationality underlying and explaining it, but a brute and irreducible fact. As the chasm separating good and evil is strictly constitutive and there is no ground reducing to its immanent development the totality of what exists, there is an element of negativity that cannot be eliminated either through dialectical mediation or through Nietzschean assertiveness. We are not very far here from the alternatives referred to by Rancière in his interview. (Let us observe that, strictly speaking, the category of *excess* is not incompatible with the notion of a nondialectical negativity that we are proposing. It is only if we try to combine excess with immanence that the nonpolitical turn that we will presently discuss is unavoidable.)

In the same way that, with modernity, immanence ceased to be a theological concept and became fully secularized, the religious notion of evil becomes, with the modern turn, the kernel of what we can call "social antagonism." What the latter retains from the former is the notion of a radical disjuncture—radical in the sense that it cannot be reabsorbed by any deeper objectivity that would reduce the terms of the antagonism to moments of its own internal movement, for example, the development of productive forces or any other form of immanence.

Now, I would contend that it is only by accepting such a notion of antagonism—and its corollary, which is radical social division—that we are confronted with forms of social action that can truly be called *political*. Why so? To show this I will consider an early text by Marx that I have discussed fully elsewhere.[3] In it, Marx opposes a purely human revolution to a merely political one. The differential feature is that in the former a *universal* subject emerges in and for itself. In the words of Marx: "By proclaiming the *dissolution of the hitherto world order* the proletariat merely states the *secret of its own existence,* for it *is in fact* the dissolution of that world order." To put it in terms close to Hardt and Negri: the universality of the proletariat fully depends on its *immanence* within an objective social order that is entirely the product of capitalism—which is, in turn, a moment in the universal development of the productive forces. But precisely because of that reason, the universality of the revolutionary subject entails the end of politics—that is, the beginning of the withering away of the State and the transition (according to the Saint-Simonian motto adopted by Marxism) from the government of men to the administration of things.

As for the second revolution—the political one—its distinctive feature is, for Marx, an essential asymmetry: that between the universality of the task and the particularism of the agent carrying it out. Marx describes this asymmetry in non-equivocal terms: a certain regime is felt as universal oppression, and that allows the particular social force able to lead the struggle against it to present itself as universal liberator—universalizing, thus, its particular objectives. Here we find the real theoretical watershed in contemporary discussions: *either* we assert the possibility of a universality that is not politically constructed and mediated *or* we assert that all universality is precarious and depends on a historical construction out of heterogeneous elements. Hardt and Negri accept the first alternative without hesitation. If, conversely, we accept the second, we are on the threshold of the Gramscian conception of hegemony. (Gramsci is another for whom—understandably given their premises—Hardt and Negri show little sympathy.)

It is interesting to see the consequences that *Empire* draws from its approach to immanence. There is an actual historical subject of what they conceive as the realization of a full immanence: it is what they call the "multitude." The full realization of the multitude's immanence would be the elimination of all transcendence. This can be accepted only, of course, if the postulate of the homogeneity and unity of the multitude as an historical agent is not put into question—a matter to which we will return shortly. But some of the results of this strict opposition between immanence and transcendence can be quickly detected. Let us take their way of dealing with the question of sovereignty. For them, modern political sovereignty—well anchored in the counterrevolutionary trend of the second modernity—is reduced to the attempt at constructing a transcendent political apparatus:

> Sovereignty is thus defined both by *transcendence* and by *representation*, two concepts that the humanist has posed as contradictory. On the one hand, the transcendence of the sovereign is founded not on an external theological

support but only on the immanent logic of human relations. On the other hand, the representation that functions to legitimate this sovereign power also alienates it completely from the multitude of subjects. ... Here [in Bodin and Hobbes] the concept of modern sovereignty is born in its state of transcendental purity. The contract of association is intrinsic to and inseparable from the contract of subjugation.

(Hardt and Negri 2000, p. 84; subsequent references below to this text are by page number).

So sovereignty was an essentially repressive device trying to prevent the democratic upsurge of an unspecified multitude. What a beautiful fabula! For as anybody acquainted with the modern theory of sovereignty knows, its practical implementation entailed a far more complicated process than the story proposed by Hardt and Negri. In the first place, the multitude they are speaking about is a purely fanciful construction. What we had in early modernity was an estamental society, profoundly fragmented, which did not move at all in the direction of constructing a unified political subject capable of establishing an alternative social order. Royal sovereignty was established fighting on a double front: against the universalistic powers—the Church and the Empire—and against local feudal powers. And many newly emerging social sectors—bourgeois, especially—were the social base that made possible the emergence of royal sovereignty. That the transference of control of many social spheres to the new social states is at the root of the new forms of biopower is incontestable, but the alternative to that process was not autonomous power of any hypothetical multitude but the continuation of feudal fragmentation. It is more: it was only when this process of centralization had advanced beyond a certain point that something resembling a unitary multitude could emerge through the transference of sovereignty from the king to the people.

This leads us to the second aspect of Hardt and Negri's dichotomy: the question of representation. What are the conditions for the elimination of any form of representation? Obviously, the elimination of any kind of asymmetry between actual political subjects and the community as a whole. If the *volonté générale* is the will of a subject whose limits coincide with those of the community, there is no need for any relation of representation but neither for the continuation of politics as a relevant activity. That is why, as we mentioned earlier, the emergence of a universal class heralded, for Marxism, the withering away of the State. But if we have an internally divided society, the will of the community as a whole has to be *politically* constructed out of a primary—constitutive—diversity. In that case, the *volonté générale* requires representation as its primary terrain of emergence. This means that any "multitude" is constructed through political action—which presupposes antagonism and hegemony.

The reason why Hardt and Negri do not even pose themselves this question is that for them the unity of the multitude results from the spontaneous aggregation of a plurality of actions that do not need to be articulated between themselves. In their words:

If these points were to constitute something like a new cycle of struggles, it would be a cycle defined not by the communicative extension of the struggles but rather by their singular emergence, by the intensity that characterizes them one by one. In short, this new phase is defined by the fact that these struggles do not link horizontally, but each one leaps vertically, directly to the virtual center of Empire.

(p. 58)

One cannot avoid finding it a little difficult to understand how an entity that has no boundaries—"[t]he concept of Empire is characterized fundamentally by a lack of boundaries: Empire's rule has no limits" (p. xix)—can still have a virtual center, but let it pass. Anyway, what we are told is: (1) that a set of unconnected struggles tend, by some kind of *coincidentia oppositorum,* to converge in their assault on a supposed center; (2) that in spite of their diversity, without any kind of political intervention, they will tend to aggregate with each other; and (3) that they could never have aims that are incompatible with each other. It does not take long to realize that these are highly unrealistic assumptions, to put it mildly. They clash with the most elementary evidence of the international scene, which shows us a proliferation of social actors fighting each other for a variety of religious, ethnic, or racial reasons. And the assumption that imperialism is over (*"The United States does not, and indeed no nation-state can today, form the center of an imperialist project.* No nation will be world leader in the way modern European nations were.") does not fare any better, as anybody looking at what is going on in the world after September 11 can easily realize (p. xiv; emphasis in original). What is totally lacking in *Empire* is a theory of *articulation,* without which politics is unthinkable.

This gap in the argument is particularly visible if we consider the way in which *Empire* deals with the distinction strategy/tactics. For Hardt and Negri the distinction collapses, but it is clear that the autonomous vertical struggles belong to the sphere of tactics rather than to strategic calculation. I want to be very precise on this point of my critique because I also think—although for reasons different from those of Hardt and Negri—that the distinction between strategy and tactics, as inherited from the socialist tradition, cannot be accepted any longer. For classical socialism there was a clear differentiation between both and a strict subordination of tactics to strategy. Now, a basic assumption in this vision was that the class identity of the strategic actors remained unchanged throughout the political process. For Kautsky, the strict working-class identity of the socialist actors was a basic dogma. For Lenin, class alliances did not transform the identities of the intervening forces ("to strike together and to march separated"). And for Trotsky, the whole strategy of the permanent revolution makes sense only if the taking up of democratic tasks by the working class does not contaminate the aims and nature of the latter.

It is precisely this assumption, in my view, that has to be put into question. For the present proliferation of a plurality of identities and points of rupture makes the subjects of political action essentially unstable and thus makes impossible a strategic calculation that covers long historical periods. This does not mean that the notion of strategy becomes entirely obsolete, but it does definitely mean that the strategies have to be short-term ones and that the various tactics become more autonomous. What is clear, however, is that this situation gives an increasing centrality to the moment of political articulation—the moment, precisely, which is entirely absent from Hardt and Negri's analysis as a result of their conception of struggles *spontaneously* converging in their assault on a systemic center.

There is another feature of Hardt and Negri's multitude that requires consideration: their inherent nomadism, which they explicitly link to the Deleuzian rhizomic movements. What is proper of the multitude is being-against:

> One element we can put our finger on at the most basic and elementary level is *the will to be against*. In general, the will to be against does not seem to require much explanation. Disobedience to authority is one of the most natural and healthy acts. To us, it seems completely obvious that those who are exploited will resist and—given the necessary conditions—rebel.
>
> (p. 210; emphasis in original)

Today, however, the very ubiquity of Empire—which is no longer an *external* enemy—would make it difficult to identify those to whom the multitude is against. The only solution would be to be against everything, in every place. The main pattern of this new kind of struggle is desertion:

> Whereas in the disciplinary era *sabotage* was the fundamental notion of resistance, in the era of imperial control it may be *desertion*. Whereas being-against in modernity often meant a direct and/or dialectical opposition of forces, in postmodernity being-against might well be most effective in an oblique or diagonal stance. Battles against the Empire might be won through subtraction and defection. This desertion does not have a place; it is the evacuation of the places of power.
>
> (p. 212; emphasis in original)

This desertion takes the form of nomadic migrations—economic, intellectual, and political exodus creates an essential mobility that is the new pattern of class struggle. Mobility would have been the privileged terrain of republicanism since early modern times (the examples quoted are the Socians of the Renaissance, the religious transatlantic migrations of the seventeenth century, the International Workers of the World agitation in the United States in the 1910s, and the European autonomists of the 1970s). These nomadic actors are the new barbarians. The concept of migration can, however, be expanded: it is a question not only of physical, literal migrations but also of figural ones—the transformation of bodies can also be considered as an *anthropological exodus*:

> We certainly do need to change our bodies and ourselves, and in perhaps a much more radical way than the cyberpunk authors imagine. In our

contemporary world, the now common aesthetic mutations of the body, such as piercing and tattoos, punk fashion and its various imitations, are all initial indications of this corporeal transformation, but in the end they do not hold a candle to the kind of radical mutation needed here. The will to be against really needs a body that is completely incapable of submitting to command. It needs a body that is incapable of adapting to family life, to factory discipline, to the regulations of traditional sex life, and so forth.

(p. 216)

From this perspective the proletarians of the nineteenth century could be seen as nomads, for although they did not displace themselves geographically, "their creativity and productivity define corporeal and ontological migrations" (p. 217).

What are the difficulties with this rather triumphalist vision? There are several. In the first place, the assertion that "the will to be against does not seem to require much explanation" is mere wishful thinking. Here the alternative is clear: either resistance to oppression is some kind of natural and automatic mechanism that will spontaneously operate whatever the circumstances, or it is a complex social construction that has conditions of possibility external to itself. For me the second is the correct answer. The ability and the will to resist are not a gift from heaven but require a set of subjective transformations that are only the product of the struggles themselves *and that can fail to take place*. What is missing in *Empire* is any coherent theory of political subjectivity—psychoanalysis, for instance, is entirely absent. Largely for that reason, the whole notion of being-against does not resist the slightest examination. It is easy to see the role that it plays in the economy of Hardt and Negri's argumentation: if one is "against" without defining an enemy, the idea that struggles against Empire should take place everywhere finds its justification (and, a fortiori, we have the guarantee that vertical struggles would coalesce around a single target without any need for their horizontal articulation). Unfortunately social struggles do not follow this simplistic pattern. All struggle is the struggle of concrete social actors for particular objectives, and nothing guarantees that these objectives will not clash with each other. Now, I would agree that no overall historical transformation is possible unless the particularism of the struggles is superseded and a wider "collective will" is constituted. But this requires the implementation of what in our work we have called the *logic of equivalence,* which involves acts of political articulation—precisely the horizontal linking that Hardt and Negri put aside. The "being-against" is, once more, a clear indicator of the antipolitical bias of *Empire*.

Finally, the notion of "anthropological exodus" is hardly more than an abusive metaphor. The role attributed to migration is already extremely problematic. It is true that the authors recognize that misery and exploitation could be determinant of the will of people to move across frontiers, but this element of negativity is immediately subordinated to an affirmative will to migrate that ultimately creates the possibility of an emancipatory subject. Needless to say, this martial conception of the migratory process does not correspond to any reality: reasons for various groups to migrate are very different and are not unified around any anti-Empire crusade. But when we are told that the rebellion against family life or the development of proletarian capacities in the nineteenth century has also to be conceived as a migratory act, the notion of migration loses all specificity: any kind of historical change—for better or worse—would be conceived as migration. A good metaphor is the one that, through analogy, reveals a hitherto concealed aspect of reality—but that hardly happens in the present case.

It is towards the end of their book that the authors address, to some extent, the question that we have been posing throughout this note: that of political articulation. Let us quote them:

> How can the actions of the multitude become political? How can the multitude organize and concentrate its energies against the repression and incessant territorial segmentations of Empire? The only response that we can give to these questions is that the action of the multitude becomes political primarily when it begins to confront directly and with an adequate consciousness the central repressive operations of Empire. It is a matter of recognizing and engaging the imperial initiatives and not allowing them continually to reestablish order; it is a matter of crossing and breaking down the limits and segmentations that are imposed on the new collective labor power; it is a matter of gathering together these experiences of resistance and wielding them in concert against the nerve centers of imperial command.
>
> (p. 399)

How, however, is this "gathering together [of] these experiences of resistance and wielding them in concert" going to operate? Hardt and Negri assert that about the specific and concrete forms of this political articulation they can say nothing. They, however, formulate a "political program for the global multitude" that is organized around three demands: the demand for global citizenship (so that the mobility of the working force under the present capitalist conditions is recognized and that groups of the population such as the *sans papiers* have access to full citizenship); the right to a social wage (so that an income is guaranteed to everybody); the right to reappropriation (so that the means of production are socially owned).

I can only say that I do not disagree with any of these demands—although it is clear that they do not amount to a full-fledged political program—but what sounds strange, after a whole analysis centered on the need to strike everywhere from a position of total confrontation with the present imperial system, is that these three political aims are formulated in a language of *demands* and *rights*. Because both demands and rights have to be *recognized,* and the instance from whom that recognition is requested *cannot be* in a relation of total exteriority vis-à-vis the social claims. Each of the three demands, in order to be implemented, requires strategic considerations concerning changes in the structure of the State, autonomization of certain spheres, political alliances and incorporation to the historical arena of previously excluded social sectors. That is, we are in the terrain of what Gramsci called "war of position." But this political game is strictly incompatible with the notion of a plurality of unconnected vertical struggles, all targeting—through some unspecified mechanism—an assumed virtual center of the Empire. Perhaps the ultimate incoherence of the book we are commenting on is that it proposes fragments of a perfectly acceptable political program, while its conditions of implementation are denied by the central theoretical and strategic categories on which its analysis is based. Multitudes are never spontaneously multitudinarious; they can become so only through political action.

Notes

1 For this concept, see Rancière 1995.
2 I have discussed these matters in more detail in my essay "Beyond Emancipation," in E. Laclau, *Emancipation(s)* (London: Verso, 1996), 1–19.
3 In my essay "Identity and Hegemony: The Role of Universality in the Constitution of Political Logics," in J. Butler, E. Laclau, and S. Žižek, *Contingency, Hegemony, Universality. Contemporary Dialogues on the Left* (London: Verso, 2000), 44–89. The text by Marx to which I am referring is "Contribution to the Critique of Hegel's Philosophy of Law, Introduction," in K. Marx and F. Engels, *Collected Works*, vol. 3 (London: Lawrence and Wishart, 1975), 186–87.

Bibliography

Hardt, M. and Negri, A. 2000. *Empire*. Cambridge, MA: Harvard University Press.
Rancière, J. 1995. *La Mésentente*. Paris: Galilée.
——2002. Peuple ou multitude: question d'Eric Alliez à Jacques Rancière. *Multitudes* 9 (May–June): 95–100.

11

ON 'REAL' AND 'ABSOLUTE' ENEMIES (2005)

I

The interest of Carl Schmitt's *Theory of the Partisan* (2007) is that it throws new light on central categories with which we have been familiar since the publication of his classical study, *The Concept of the Political* (2007) in 1928. What the work we are now considering adds to that book is a new emphasis on political subjectivity and new precisions on the links between war and politics, together with a differentiation between various kinds of hostility. It is to this differentiation that my commentaries will be mainly addressed, but before that I will briefly describe the logical sequence of the main categories of Schmitt's theory of the partisan.

Schmitt starts by pointing out a momentous event that took place in European military history: the emergence of an irregular kind of warfare whose first expression was the Spanish partisan resistance to the Napoleonic Armies between 1808 and 1813. At the epicenter of this new phenomenon we find the revolutionary restructuration of the art of war brought about by Napoleon, who broke with all the classical rules of the military art as they had been codified in the eighteenth century. Schmitt quotes a Prussian general as saying that the Napoleonic campaign against Prussia in 1806 had only been a partisan operation on a big scale. The Spanish example, however, was not widely followed in Northern Europe except for the brief guerrilla war in the Tyrol in 1809, and the long conflict was finally settled at the battle of Leipzig by a classical confrontation between regular armies. The restoration brought about by the Vienna Congress codified, *inter alia*, the rules of war between European states, rules that established neat distinctions between war and peace, between those engaged in the war and the civilian population, and between an enemy and a criminal. These rules dominated European history until the First World War, which started as a pure inter-state conflict in the most traditional sense, and whose nature was only modified by its revolutionary sequels.

It is this set of neat distinctions that the figure of the partisan starts blurring. Firstly, the popular resistance to an occupying power does not allow for a clear distinction between peace and war. Secondly, the partisans are an irregular force: they are part of the civilian population but participate in the armed struggle. Thirdly, the partisan, given his political motivation, cannot be assimilated to a criminal, yet he has no definable military status.

Schmitt gives several examples of appeals to the civilian population to resist foreign invaders. In German history he can only quote an edict from the Prussian king in 1813 that specifically refers to the Spanish precedent and calls on the population to be armed by any means and to disobey any orders coming from the invading power. This edict did not have any major effect or continuity, but in the case of Russia the partisan phenomenon—as described, for instance, in Tolstoy's *War and Peace*—went much deeper and was decisive in the defeat of the Napoleonic Armies. Stalin also called for partisan action against the German invasion, and in China and Indochina the partisan war was not, of course, a secondary phenomenon, but the main component of the military action.

There are four aspects of the partisan's identity that Schmitt especially underlines: its irregular character—the partisan has no uniform—its already mentioned political motivation, its high degree of mobility, and its telluric belonging, which anchors him to the land and governs the whole logic of his behavior. In some sense the partisan's presence is suspended between legality and illegality, and this is shown in the hesitations of the international legislation dealing with his status. The classical laws on war as stated by the *ius publicum europeum*—and restored by the Vienna Congress—did not leave any space for the recognition of the legality of the partisan, who either is considered some kind of light troop belonging to the regular army or is assimilated to a criminal *hors la loi*. The legal war took place between princes and regular armies. The historical evolution since the Franco-Prussian War, however, forced the international legislation to give some legal status to the partisan. Certain kinds of irregular combatants were assimilated into the regular armies. The decisive moments in this new recognition were the regulations of The Hague of 10 October 1907 and the four Conventions of Geneva of 12 August 1949. The Hague Regulations established four conditions for extending the rights enjoyed by the regular armed forces to the partisans: to be under the leadership of a person responsible for his subordinates; to have a distinguishable sign, visible at a distance; to carry arms openly; and to confirm themselves in their operations to the laws and customs of war. Failure to fulfill these conditions relegates the partisans to the status of illegal combatants and common criminals, unprotected by the laws of war. The Geneva Conventions extend the legal status of partisans to cases of civil war, insurrections, etc., specifying, however, that in inter-state wars an occupying power has the right to ask for the cooperation of the local police to ensure order and repress hostile acts from the local population.

It becomes immediately clear that these resolutions are highly contradictory. By its very nature, partisan resistance cannot operate within the requirement to show visible signs and openly carry arms. The impossibility of establishing a clear separation between combatants and the civilian population belongs to the essence of the partisan struggle. So what is involved in the latter? Simply, the extension and deepening of the antagonistic frontier separating friend from foe. "War" is some sort of mobile metaphor, whose limits of operation vary constantly and whose possibility of being contained within precise systems of rules such as those of the *ius publicum europeum* is, to say the least, precarious. It could only work if the social actors engaged in the confrontation see each other as belonging to a higher community of peers, as was the case with the eighteenth-century society of kings and princes. But the deeper the social chasm between the various forces in conflict, the more difficult it becomes to contain the conflict within legally defined limits. This is visible in the genealogy of the theory of the partisan war that Schmitt depicts in the next section of his essay. Between 1808 and 1813 Clausewitz had incorporated into this theory of war the possibility of a popular insurrection, and in September 1870 Gambetta had called the civilian population (the *franc-tireurs*) to arms to resist the advance of the Prussian Army. But it is Lenin who would extract all the consequences of the Clausewitz dictum that war is the continuation of politics by other means. Both inter-state wars and civil wars are now conceived as subordinated to class struggle—i.e., as grounded in an absolute hostility in which the adversary has become an enemy to be destroyed, and in which, as a result, there are no rules limiting what has become a total confrontation. The Russian and Eastern European movements of resistance to German occupation would continue and deepen this trend and would give an increasing centrality to the figure of the partisan; and with Mao Tse Tung the theory of the subversive war would reach its mature theorization as well as its most successful practical implementation. The war is now based on a total hostility towards a world enemy, and, as a result, it requires an equally total mobilization of the population: in that sense, nine-tenths of it is an irregular and not open war and only one-tenth consists of an openly military confrontation. The proportional importance of regular war and partisan war has been entirely inverted. The war in Indochina later followed the same pattern.

Later Schmitt discusses the defining aspects of the situation within which the modern partisan war takes place: the spatial aspect, the dismantling of social structures, the world political context, and the technical aspect. It is, however, in the last part of his essay that Schmitt presents his opposition between real and absolute enemy, on which we will center our discussion. His analysis starts from the distinction between legality and legitimacy. Here his position—which he illustrates with the example of General Salan and the clandestine actions of the Organisation de l'Armée Secrète (OAS) in Algeria and in the territory of metropolitan France— is unequivocal: in a republican regime there is no other source of legitimacy than legality itself. It is the break between these two principles that made Salan's position so hopeless. He had to fight a battle on two fronts: against the Algerian partisans and against his own government. But that not only weakened his position from a strategic point of view; it also weakened his own identity. As Schmitt reminds us, one's own identity is only defined in relation to an enemy; a duality of enemies can only result in a torn identity. He illustrates the case with the example of the Prussian general Yorck, whose conflict was between combating what he called the "real enemy"—the Napoleonic forces to which he was formally subordinated—or following loyally the directives of his king. He leaves the decision to the latter, but the very fact that he considered himself empowered to determine who the real enemy was meant that a breach in the link between legality and legitimacy had emerged that, if logically followed, would lead to partisan action. The dialectic between legality and legitimacy would lead to the one between the regular and the irregular. The option for the reality of the enemy led the Spanish anti-Napoleonic partisans to a serious war—a "real" war. And the transformation, by Lenin, of the partisan war to a revolutionary one, would dismantle all its limitations and lead to the emergence of an "absolute" enemy.

A central point of Schmitt's argument is that the hostility of the partisan war recognized a series of limitations. These came, on the one hand, from the presence of what he calls the "interested third," the friend that makes possible the connection between the regular and the irregular. This is a political limitation, e.g. the recognition, in the Spanish case, of the political character of the struggle of the "Empecinado" by the regular army and by England. In the same way, the telluric character of the partisans' war gives their struggle a mainly defensive character. But the absolutization of the political nature of the opposition friend/enemy leads to an equally necessary absolutization of the conflict. Clausewitz had already spoken of "absolute war" but had never put into question the regularity of an existing state. With Lenin, however, the civil war struggle of a party of professional revolutionaries turns the real enemy into an absolute one. The Party becomes the incarnation of an absolute hostility. In the same way, the development of nuclear arms in the present age opens the possibility of a type of conflict that declares the whole adversarial camp a criminal one, which has to be entirely eliminated. The limits to the criminalization of the adversary that had been achieved in the *ius publicum europeum* have been succeeded by a total war that transforms the real enemy into an absolute one.

II

Schmitt's argument is organized around three basic oppositions: politics/war; real/absolute enemy; legality/legitimacy. We will successively discuss each of them and their mutual relations.

Schmitt was clearly influenced by Clausewitz's dictum according to which war is the continuation of politics by other means. The dictum is, however, ambiguous. It can either assert the political character of war or the war-like nature of politics. But what is central in Schmitt's reception of Clausewitz is that there is an ultimate core of hostility that underlies both war and politics. Politics is structured around the friend/foe distinction that, obviously, belongs also to the substance of war. However, from the very beginning Schmitt introduces something different into the picture. The very progression from the *ius publicum europeum* to the real enemy and, finally, to the total enemy seems to suggest that the element of hostility—although having a central structuring role in the establishment of a political community—can be contained, under some circumstances, within certain limits. Before the partisans' war we have the inter-state war of the princes which, precisely because it was not a total war, could be submitted to rules. The situation could perhaps be compared to that of two chess players: the antagonistic moment is certainly present there—each wants the defeat of his adversary—but the rules of chess playing are accepted by both. The antagonistic situation only increases if one of them cheats or kicks the board.

So this suggests that politics cannot be simply reduced to the moment of hostility, that we have also a moment of structuring of the community through systems of rules that cannot be ignored and that, even in situations approaching what Schmitt calls total war, cannot be entirely eradicated. It is of the utmost importance to establish the kind of articulation existing between these two dimensions. We could call the moment of hostility the specifically "political" moment in the structuration of a community, while the system of rules limiting the field within which hostility can operate we could conceive as "administration." Classical political philosophy, starting with Plato, only recognized the latter as legitimate. The political task par excellence, as far as the community is concerned, consisted precisely in defining those conditions under which we could eliminate antagonism from the regulation of human affairs. The Saint-Simonian motto "from the government of men to the administration of things" expresses this trend of thought at its purest. And it is not for nothing that Marx adopted that motto to describe the situation that would exist in a classless society, i.e. a society from which politics would have been eliminated.

This duality has received, from different theoretical perspectives, a great deal of attention in recent years. Jacques Rancière, for instance, has referred to it in terms of his distinction between *police* and *le politique*. And in my work I have alluded to it through the distinction between *logic of difference* (which organizes the positivity of the social) and *logic of equivalence* (which introduces negativity and social division). The important point to stress is that although the relation between both always involves a tension, both are equally necessary for the constitution of a community. This means that a society will always have within itself antagonism and social division, and that the actors and the internal frontiers implementing "hostility" will experience constant processes of displacement.

There is, no doubt, something compelling in Schmitt's account of the emergence and development of the partisan war. It is undoubtedly true that after the French Revolution and Napoleon's transformation of the act of war, the nature of military confrontations drastically changed: they started embracing more social areas and wider sections of the population. What we should, however, ask ourselves is whether these changes did not lead to a metaphorization of the notion of "war" in a variety of directions that overflowed its purely military meaning. We can accept without difficulty that in a hierarchically organized society what we have called "administration" (logic of differences) tends to prevail in the internal affairs, while war is a purely military matter limited to inter-state confrontations (although, of course, such a picture involves a considerable degree of simplification). But when armed struggle by wider sections of the population takes the form described by Schmitt, the distinction between military and nonmilitary action becomes increasingly blurred. Disobedience to an occupying power, even when it does not involve physical confrontation, is an act of war as much as partisan action. "Class struggle," for instance, can be conceived as a permanent war taking place within society. With these changes, however, a new articulation between politics and administration emerges. Antagonistic forces have to organize themselves for a more permanent confrontation that covers most aspects of life. In this way, administration ceases to be neutral *vis-à-vis* the political. The question is to what extent Schmitt is really sensitive to these aspects of the problem. We should look for an answer by moving to the second of the oppositions structuring Schmitt's essay: the one between real and absolute enemy.

According to Schmitt, there is a real enemy whenever war, no longer conceived as a *Kriegespiel* against a conventional enemy, becomes a serious matter in which society as a whole is involved. We have seen, however, that a war against a real enemy finds a set of limitations: its political character (there are not only enemies but also friends) and the telluric nature of the partisan struggle which give the latter a purely defensive orientation. As Schmitt asserts, this establishes limits to hostility: the enemy is neither an absolute enemy nor is it declared to be the ultimate enemy of humanity. For Clausewitz, as we have seen, the theorization of war as being fought against a real enemy does not involve the dissolution of the apparatus of the state. For Lenin, however, as the Party becomes an absolute value, the partisan himself becomes absolute, and his struggle is inscribed in something like a world civil war. All restraints and limitations of hostility have been abandoned: the real enemy has become an absolute enemy.

What to think of this sequence? We see, in the first place, that the progression of conventional enemy/real enemy/absolute enemy consists in the constant expansion of the field of hostility. More and more elements that were at the beginning outside the field of war are now absorbed by the latter. We know what exactly that means: the increasing centrality of the equivalential logic at the expense of the purely differential one. Society is increasingly divided into two camps aiming at their mutual destruction. There is, undoubtedly, much that is true in this vision, but its very logic involves a set of possibilities that limit its apocalyptic consequences. Schmitt does not sufficiently take these possibilities into account. Let us enumerate them.

(1) To start with, the notion of an international civil war has effects that Schmitt's discourse cannot control within its own limits. As the very idea of an inter-state war has been superseded, the externality of the enemy *vis-à-vis* a given territory has to be superseded as well. The *civil war* nature of the confrontation requires now that such a *trench* war not respecting national boundaries take place. The national boundaries cease to define the identity of the enemy. This type of struggle is very different from the one involving a *given* external enemy. It approaches what Gramsci called a "war of position," whose basic requirement is

that the enemy has to be constantly constructed through the displacement and rearticulation of heterogeneous social elements. The universalization of war, and its concomitant effect, the establishment of the primacy of politics, has the paradoxical effect that there is no *given* absolute enemy, but a situation in which the two poles—real and absolute—are ideal extremes of a continuum that is constantly fluctuating.

(2) This very fluctuation means that the frontier separating the two camps is going to be essentially unstable. This is not a limitation of the role of the political conceived as hostility, but a consequence, on the contrary, of the fact that the political no longer recognizes any boundaries. This, however, means also that there can be a multiplicity of enemies—a situation Schmitt sees as anomalous—and that the formation of a more global social division into two camps can only be the precarious effect of a hegemonization of partial conflicts. The situation being so, the only possible conclusion is that the notion of an absolute enemy tends to disintegrate and must be replaced by that of a plurality of real enemies whose transition to absolutism will always be essentially incomplete.

(3) There is, finally, the question of the role of what we have called "administration," as distinguished from the political. The primacy of the political that we have asserted can only mean that the differential logic only takes place *within* a certain political camp. As a result, hegemonic victories in a trench war are going to involve not only the destruction of an enemy but also the construction of a new order on the basis of the rearticulation of the very elements that previously constituted the identity of the defeated power (this, obviously, cannot happen in the case of a totally external enemy). But this suggests yet another possibility: that the new differential order becomes more autonomous *vis-à-vis* the political forces that structured it in the first place. If this happens, the differential order starts operating as a framework within which political confrontation can take place. Ergo, we find here another limitation to the absolutism of hostility. Mao's long march—one of the cases Schmitt discusses would be a good example of what we have in mind.

There is, finally, the question of the opposition between legality and legitimacy. Here we have to invert, to some extent, the order of priorities that Schmitt establishes. In his discussion of Salan, Schmitt asserts that the French general found himself in an awkward position, because in a republican order only law can be a source of legitimacy. And he refers to De Gaulle's regime as having found its own legitimacy in the plebiscite that ratified the institutional changes that gave birth to the Fifth Republic. Schmitt's arguments are particularly unconvincing on this point. What about the De Gaulle of 1940? The legitimacy of his actions was certainly not grounded in any legality. He was actually acting as a partisan, in the sense Schmitt gives to the term. In more general terms we could say that if, as we have seen, the notion of war has to be generalized to the point of embracing any struggle against a real enemy, and if any kind of differential logic (legality included) has to be conceived as structured within an antagonistic camp, legality cannot be the source of legitimacy. Legitimacy can only proceed from the hegemonic practices of a group that organizes a certain social order in its opposition to a real enemy. Legality is part of that order and is, in that sense, an effect and not a cause. We have also seen, however, that such an order can acquire autonomy *vis-à-vis* the social forces that originally grounded it. This autonomy does not make it a "source" of legitimacy, but certainly a component of it. But no legal forms can survive when their breach with legitimacy goes beyond a certain point. When this happens, all social forces become partisans to a certain extent. It is what Schmitt calls the irregular that is at the source of the regular and not the other way round. If the matter is seen in this way, we can assert that the imbrication between administration and the political is indeed very intimate because of the reason we have given earlier; once the war is a civil one—even at the international level—there is no destruction of an enemy that is not, at the same time, construction of a new order. And this order is not instrumentally linked to the group that originally constructed it but becomes part of the identity of that group. We have to add to this that the multiplicity of struggles we have seen operating at the national level operate also in the international scene. We have seen, over the last few decades, a proliferation of international actors who are less and less reduced to the national states. War is a phenomenon larger than inter-state confrontations.

Let us summarize our argument. The merit of Schmitt's piece is to be found, in my view, in two points. The first concerns the grounding role he attributes to hostility in the structuration of political spaces. For him antagonism is at the very center of political analysis. The second merit is related to the way he conceives of the "real enemy": it involves the introduction of equivalential logics in the organization of an antagonistic camp. From this point of view the distinction between real and absolute enemy is secondary–only a matter of degree. But it is precisely the rigidity with which he presents this distinction that is at the root of the limitations of Schmitt's essay. As we have argued, it is the very generalization of the notion of war that the idea of a real enemy involves, what requires us to move in a variety of directions that Schmitt does not really explore. Even if we accepted his picture of Lenin as transforming the real enemy into an absolute one, the discussion of war in the Marxist tradition does not end there. In Gramsci, for instance, the notion of war is central, but it is displaced from its purely military connotations. The opposition war of maneuver/war of position is vital to properly develop the political implications of war. A consideration of these aspects involves rethinking the effects of a generalized notion of war: the possibility of a multiplicity of enemies—whose consequences, as we have pointed out, paradoxically lead to a limitation of hostility—and the possibility also of a more diversified vision of the forms of articulation between differential and equivalential logics.

Bibliography

Schmitt, C. 2007. *The Concept of the Political*. Chicago: University of Chicago Press.
——2007. *Theory of the Partisan*. Trans. G.L. Ulmen. New York: Telos Press.

12

BARE LIFE OR SOCIAL INDETERMINACY? (2005)

I have great admiration for the work of Giorgio Agamben. I particularly appreciate his dazzling classical erudition, his skill—both intuitive and analytical—in dealing with theoretical categories, and his ability to relate systems of thought whose connections are not immediately obvious. This appreciation does not go, however, without some deep reservations concerning his theoretical conclusions, and these reservations are what I want to elaborate upon here. If I had to put them in a nutshell, I would assert that Agamben has—inverting the usual saying—the vices of his virtues. Reading his texts, one often has the feeling that he jumps too quickly from having established the *genealogy* of a term, a concept, or an institution, to determine its actual working in a contemporary context, that in some sense the *origin* has a secret determining priority over what follows from it. I am not, of course, claiming that Agamben makes the naïve mistake of assuming that etymology provides the cipher or clue to what follows from it, but, I would argue, many times his discourse remains uneasily undecided between genealogical and structural explanation. Let us take an example from Saussurean linguistics: the Latin term *necare* (to kill) has become in modern French *noyer* (to drown), and we can examine as much as we want this diachronic change in the relation between signifier and signified and we will still not find in it any explanation of the meaning resulting from their last articulation—signification depends entirely on a *value* context which is strictly singular and which no diachronic genealogy is able to capture. This is the perspective from which we want to question Agamben's theoretical approach: his genealogy is not sensitive enough to structural diversity and, in the end, it risks ending in sheer teleology.

Let us start by considering the three theses in which Agamben summarizes his argument towards the end of *Homo Sacer*:

(1) The original political relation is the ban (the state of exception as zone of indistinction between outside and inside, exclusion and inclusion).

(2) The fundamental activity of sovereign power is the production of bare life as originary political element and as threshold of articulation between nature and culture, between *zoê* and *bios*.
(3) Today it is not the city but rather the camp that is the fundamental biopolitical paradigm of the West. (Agamben 1998, p. 181).

Let me start with the first thesis. According to Agamben—who is quoting Cavalca—"to ban someone is to say that anybody may harm him" (Agamben 1998, pp. 104–5). That is why the "sacred man" can be killed but not sacrificed—the sacrifice is still a figure representable within the legal order of the city. The life of the bandit clearly shows the kind of exteriority belonging to the sacred man:

> The life of the bandit, like that of the sacred man, is not a piece of animal nature without any relation to law and the city. It is, rather, a threshold of indistinction and of passage between animal and man, *physis* and *nomos*, exclusion and inclusion: the life of the bandit is the life of the *loup garou*, the werewolf, who is precisely *neither man nor beast*, and who dwells paradoxically within both while belonging to neither.
> (Agamben 1998, p. 105)

Sovereignty is at the source of the ban, but it requires an extension of the territory within which the ban applies, for if we were only to deal with the exteriority to law of the *loup garou* we would still be able to establish a clear line of partage between the "inside" and the "outside" of the community. Agamben is very much aware of the complexity of the relation between outside and inside. For that reason, speaking about Hobbes's "state of nature," he indicates that it is not a primitive condition which has been eradicated once the covenant has transferred sovereignty to the Leviathan, but a constant possibility within the communitarian order, which arises whenever the city is seen as *tamquam dissoluta*. In that sense, we are not dealing with a pure, pre-social nature, but with a "naturalization" which keeps its reference to the social order as far as the latter ceases to work. This explains how the state of exception emerges. Carl Schmitt had asserted that there is no rule applicable to chaos, and that the state of exception is required whenever the agreement between the legal order and the wider communitarian order has been broken.

Far from being a prejuridical condition that is indifferent to the law of the city, the Hobbesian state of nature is the exception and the threshold that constitutes and dwells within it. It is not so much a war of all against all as, more precisely, a condition in which everyone is thus *wargus, gerit caput lupinum*. And this lupization of man and humanization of the wolf is inaugurated by the state of exception at every possible moment in the *dissolutio civitatis*. This threshold alone, which is neither simple natural life nor social life but rather bare life or sacred life, is the always present and always operative presupposition of sovereignty (Agamben 1998, p. 106).

This explains why sovereign power cannot have a contractual origin:

> This is why in Hobbes, the foundation of sovereign power is to be thought not in the subjects' free renunciation of their natural right but in the sovereign's preservation of his natural right to do anything to any one, which now appears as the right to punish.
>
> (Agamben 1998, p. 106)

Thus, the ban holds together bare life and sovereignty. And it is important for Agamben to point out that the ban is not simply a sanction—which as such would still be representable within the order of the city—but that it involves *abandonment*, the *homo* sacer, and the other figures that Agamben associates with him are simply left outside any communitarian order. That is why he can be killed but not sacrificed. In that sense the ban is non-relational: the victims are left to their own separatedness. This is for Agamben the originary political relation, linked to sovereignty. It is a more originary extraneousness than that of the foreigner, who still has an assigned place within the legal order.

> We must learn to recognize this structure of the ban in the political relations and public spaces in which we will live. *In the city the banishment of sacred life is more internal than every interiority and more external than every extraneousness.*
>
> (Agamben 1998, p. 111)

The ban has, thus, been at the source of sovereign power. The state of exception, which reduces the citizens to bare life (he has in mind Foucault's biopolitics), has determined modernity from its very beginning.

Agamben has, no doubt, touched with the category of the ban something crucially important concerning the political. There is certainly, within the political, a moment of negativity that requires the construction of an inside/outside relation and requires that sovereignty is in an ambiguous position vis-à-vis the juridical order. The problem, however, is the following: does the articulation of dimensions through which Agamben thinks the structure of the ban exhaust the system of possibilities that such a structure opens? In other words: has not Agamben chosen just one of those possibilities and hypostatized it so that it assumes a unique character? Let us consider the matter carefully. The essence of a ban is given by its effects—that is, to put somebody outside the system of differences constituting the legal order. But in order to assimilate *all* situations of being outside the law to that of *homo sacer*, as described by Agamben, some extra presuppositions have to be added. In the first place, the sheer separatedness—absence of relation—of the outside involves the fact that he/she is a naked individuality, dispossessed of any kind of collective identity. But, secondly, it also involves the fact that the situation of the outsider is one of radical defencelessness, wholly exposed to the violence of those inside the city. Only at that price can sovereign power be absolute. Are, however, these two extra presuppositions justified? Do they logically emerge from the mere category of "being outside the law"? Obviously not. The outsider does not need to be outside *any* law. What is inherent to the category is only the fact of being outside the law *of the city*. Abandonment comes only from the latter. Let us consider the following passage from Frantz Fanon, which I have discussed in another context:

> The *Lumpenproletariat,* once it is constituted, brings all its forces to endanger the "security" of the town, and is the sign of the irrevocable decay, the gangrene ever present at the heart of colonial domination. So the pimps, the hooligans, the unemployed, and the petty criminals … throw themselves into the struggle like stout working men. These classless idlers will by militant and decisive action discover the path that leads to nationhood. … The prostitutes too, and the maids who are paid two pounds a month, all who turn in circles between suicide and madness, will recover their balance, once more go forward and march proudly in the great procession of the awakened nation.
> (Fanon 1968, p. 130)

Here we have actors who are entirely outside the law of the city, who cannot be inscribed in any of the categories of the latter, but such an exteriority is the starting point for a new collective identification *opposed* to the law of the city. We do not have lawlessness as against law, but two laws that do not recognize each other. In another work (2005), Agamben discusses the notion of "necessity" as elaborated by the Italian jurist Santi Romano and points out that, for Romano, revolutionary forces—strictly speaking, according to the state juridical order, outside the law—create their own new law. The passage from Romano quoted by Agamben is most revealing:

> After having recognised the antijuridical nature of the revolutionary forces, he adds that this is only the case with respect to the positive law of the state against which it is directed, but that does not mean that, from the very different point of view from which it defines itself, it is not a movement ordered and regulated by its own law. This also means that it is an order that must be classified in the category of originary juridical orders, in the now well-known sense given to this expression. In this sense, and within the limits of the sphere we have indicated, we can thus speak of a law of revolution.
> (Agamben 2005, pp. 28–29)

So we have two incompatible laws. What remains as valid from the notion of ban as defined by Agamben is the idea of an uninscribable exteriority, but the range of situations to which it applies is much wider than those subsumable under the category of *homo sacer*. I think that Agamben has not seen the problem of the inscribable/uninscribable, of inside/outside, in its true universality. In actual fact, what the mutual ban between opposed laws describes is the constitutive nature of any radical antagonism—radical in the sense that its two poles cannot be reduced to any super-game which would be recognized by them as an objective meaning to which both would be submitted.

Now, I would argue that only *when the ban is mutual do we have,* sensu stricto, *a political relation, for it is only in that case that we have a radical opposition between social forces and, as a result, a constant renegotiation and re-grounding of the social bond.* This can be seen most clearly if we go back for a moment to Agamben's analysis of Hobbes. As we have seen, he asserts that contrary to the contractarian view, the sovereign is the only one that preserves his natural right to do anything to anybody—that is, the subjects become bare life. The opposition between these two dimensions, however, does not stand; in order for the sovereign to preserve his natural right, he needs such a right to be recognized by the rest of the subjects, and such a recognition, as Agamben himself points out, finds some limits.

Corresponding to this particular state of the "right of punishing" which takes the form of a survival of the state of nature at the very heart of the state, is the subjects' capacity not to disobey but to resist violence exercised on their own person, "for … no man is supposed bound by Covenant, not to resist violence; and consequently it cannot be intended, that he gave any right to another to lay violent hands upon his person." Sovereign violence is in truth founded not on a pact but on the exclusive inclusion of bare life in the state (Agamben 1998, pp. 106–7).

Agamben draws from the minimal nature of the notion of a right to resist violence against one's person a further proof of his argument concerning the interconnections between bare life, sovereignty, and the modern state. It is true that the Hobbesian view invites such a reading, but only if a conclusion is derived from it: that it amounts to a radical elimination of the political. When a supreme will within the community is not confronted by anything, politics necessarily disappears. From this viewpoint the Hobbesian project can be compared with another which is its opposite but, at the same time, identical in its anti-political effects: the Marxian notion of the withering away of the state. For Hobbes, society is incapable of giving itself its own law and, as a result, the total concentration of power in the hands of the sovereign is the prerequisite of any communitarian order. For Marx, a classless society has realized full universality and that makes politics superfluous. But it is enough that we introduce some *souplesse* within the Hobbesian scheme, that we accept that society is capable of *some partial* self-regulation, to immediately see that its demands are going to be more than those deriving from bare life, that they are going to have a variety and specificity that no "sovereign" power can simply ignore. When we arrive at that point, however, the notion of "sovereignty" starts shading into that of "hegemony." This means that, in my view, Agamben has clouded the issue, for he has presented as a political moment what actually amounts to a radical elimination of the political: a sovereign power which reduces the social bond to bare life.

I have spoken of social self-regulation as being partial. By this I mean that social and political demands emerge from a variety of quarters, not all of which move in the same direction. This means that society requires constant efforts at re-grounding. Schmitt, as we have seen, asserted that the function of the sovereign—in the state of exception—is to establish the coherence between law and the wider communitarian order (one cannot apply law to chaos). If this is so, however, and if the plurality of demands requires a constant process of legal transformation and revision, the state of emergency ceases to be exceptional and becomes an integral part of the political construction of the social bond. According to Wittgenstein, to apply a rule requires a second rule specifying how the first one should be applied, a third one explaining how the second will be applied, and so on. From there he draws the conclusion that the instance of application is part of the rule itself. In Kantian terms—as Agamben points out—this means that in the construction of the social bond we are dealing with reflective rather than determinative judgments. Vico's remarks—also quoted by Agamben—about the superiority of the exception over the rule is also highly pertinent in this context. This explains why I see the history of the state of exception with different lenses than Agamben. While he draws a picture by which the becoming rule of the exception represents the unavoidable advance towards a totalitarian society, I also try to determine, with the generalization of the "exceptional," countertendencies that make it possible to think about the future in more optimistic terms. We discussed earlier what Santi Romano said concerning revolutionary laws. Now, that does not only apply to periods of radical revolutionary breaks—what Gramsci called "organic crises"—but also to a variety of situations in which social movements constitute particularistic political spaces and give themselves their own "law" (which is partially internal and partially external to the legal system of the state). There is a molecular process of partial transformations which is absolutely vital as an accumulation of forces whose potential becomes visible when a more radical transformation of a whole hegemonic formation becomes possible.

What we have so far already pre-announced is that in our view the second thesis of Agamben concerning bare life as resulting from the activity of sovereign power does not fare any better. To start with, the distinction between *zoê* and *bios* cannot play the central role in historical explanation to which Agamben assigns it. As he himself asserts at the beginning of *Homo Sacer,* the Greeks used two terms to refer to life: "*zoē*, which expressed the simple fact of living common to all living beings (animals, men or gods), and *bios*, which indicated the form or way of living proper to an individual or a group" (Agamben 1998, p. I). This means that living beings are not distributed between two categories—those who have exclusively *bios* and those who have exclusively *zoê*—for those who have *bios* obviously have *zoê* as well. So *zoê* is primarily an abstraction. Even the *oikos,* whose aim was merely concerned with reproductive life, has its own internal structure, based on a hierarchical distribution of functions, so that although its aims are not political, it is far from being bare life, for it has its own configuration and system of rules. Ergo, if Agamben's thesis is going to hold, he would have to prove that, in some circumstances, bare life ceases to be an abstraction and becomes a concrete referent.

It is at this point that Agamben brings into the picture Foucault's biopolitics. "According to Foucault, a society's 'threshold of biological modernity is situated at the point at which the species and the individual as a simple living body become what is at stake in a society's political strategies'" (Agamben 1998, p. 3). It is most revealing that Agamben links Foucault's biopolitical hypothesis to the earlier work of Hannah Arendt:

> Hannah Arendt had already analyzed the process that brings *homo laborans*—and, with it, biological life as such—gradually to occupy the very centre of the political scene of modernity. In *The Human Condition*, Arendt attributes the transformation and decadence of the political realm in modern societies to this primacy of natural life over political action.
>
> *(Agamgen 1998, p. 4)*

Of course, to present the argument in these terms is grotesquely biased. One could more plausibly make the opposite argument, namely that in modernity there is no primacy of natural life over political action, but rather a politicization of a terrain previously occupied by "natural" life (and it is already to concede too much to assume that that life was merely "natural"). Anyway, what is wrong in the argument about a rigid opposition between political sovereignty and bare life is the assumption that it necessarily involves an increasing control by an over-powerful state. All that is involved in the notion of a politicization of "natural" life is that increasing areas of social life are submitted to processes of human control and regulation, but it is a non sequitur to assume that such a control has to crystallize around a tendentially totalitarian instance.

Given Agamben's assertion of a strict correlation between ban and sovereignty, the postulation of an *ad quem* totalitarian trend was, of course, to be expected. The result is that he equates human situations whose nature is entirely dissimilar. In order to have a "bare life," as we have seen, the receiving end of the ban has to be entirely without defense and fully submitted to the "abandonment" dictated by the sovereign power. Some of the situations that Agamben describes actually approach the state of a bare life which is the mere object of a political intervention. Thus he refers to the figure of the *Muselmann*, an inhabitant of the concentration camps, "a being from whom humiliation, horror and fear had so taken away all consciousness and all personality as to make him absolutely apathetic" (Agamben 1998, p. 185). Or to a biochemist suffering leukemia who decides to transform his body in a laboratory:

> His body is no longer private, since it has been transformed into a laboratory; but neither is it public, since only insofar as it is his own body can he transgress the limits that morality and law put into experimentation. ... It is a *bios* that has, in every particular sense, so concentrated itself in its own *zoê* as to become indistinguishable from it.
>
> *(Agamben 1998, p. 186)*

Or to the body of Karen Quinlan, an over-comatose person whose organs are going to be transplanted:

> Here biological life—which the machines are keeping functional by artificial respiration, pumping blood into the arteries, and regulating the blood temperature—has been entirely separated from the form of life that bore the name Karen Quinlan: here life becomes (or at least seems to become) pure *zoê*.
>
> (Agamben 1998, p. 186)

Up to this point, Agamben's argument concerning "bare life" would be just plausible, although one could wonder about its political relevance. But later on he tries to extend it to entirely different situations. From the comatose we move to the bandit:

> His entire existence is reduced to a bare life stripped of every right by virtue of the fact that anyone can kill him without committing homicide; he can save himself only in perpetual flight or a foreign land. ... He is pure *zoê*, but his *zoê* is as such caught in the sovereign ban and must reckon with it at every moment, finding the best way to elude or deceive it. In this sense, no life, as exiles and bandits know well, is more "political" than his.
>
> (Agamben 1998, pp. 183–84)

The life of the bandit or the exile can be entirely political, but they are so in an entirely other sense than that of Karen Quinlan, because they, of the difference with Quinlan, are capable of engaging in antagonistic social practices. They have, in that sense, their own law, and their conflict with the law of the city is a conflict between laws, not between law and bare life. Agamben is aware of a potential criticism of the extreme and marginal character of his examples of bare life, and he tries to answer in anticipation with examples that he calls "no less extreme and still more familiar":

> the Bosnian woman at Omarska, a perfect threshold of indistinction between biology and politics, or—in an apparently opposite, yet analogous, sense—military interventions on humanitarian grounds, in which war efforts are carried out for the sake of biological ends such as nutrition or the care of epidemics.
>
> (Agamben 1998, p. 187)

At this point, however, we no longer know what is the issue under discussion: the care for the biological survival of populations or the reduction of people to *zoê*, entirely stripped of any *bios*? Agamben, in his argument, constantly mixes both levels.

If the example of the bandit already shows a displacement of the logic of exclusion to something which clearly exceeds the notion of "bare life," this excess is yet more visible when Agamben tries to expand the logic of sovereignty/bare life into a general theory of modernity. He starts by pointing out an undeniable fact: in most languages the notion of "the people" is ambiguous: on the one hand, it refers to the community as a whole (*populus*); on the other, to the underdog (*plebs*). His reading of this ambiguity, however, is that the community is sharply divided and that the totalitarian logic of modernity is an attempt to overcome that division.

> In this sense, our age is nothing but the implacable and methodical attempt to overcome the division dividing the people, to eliminate radically the excluded. This attempt brings together, according to different modalities and horizons, Right and Left, capitalist countries and socialist countries, which are united in the project—which is in the last analysis futile but which has been partially realized in all industrialized countries—of producing a single and undivided people (Agamben 1998, p. 179)

There is something basically wrong with this analysis. In the first place, division is perfectly compatible with the *status quo*, as far as the differences resulting from social diversity are not constructed in an antagonistic way. Hierarchy means, precisely, social differentiation, so that the elimination of division, conceived as multiplicity, is not something that the dominant groups are systematically aiming at. But, in the second place, if we are speaking about an antagonistic division, one which constructs "the people" as an underdog, the *plebs* that this division creates does not perpetuate but attempts to supersede the original division. We are dealing with a part that attempts to incarnate the whole, with a heterogeneity aspiring to be re-absorbed into a new homogeneity. So the dialectic between part and whole, between homogeneity and heterogeneity, is far more complex than Agamben's simplistic alternative of either "division" or "undivided people" allows us to think. The Gramscian distinction between "corporative" and "hegemonic" class allows for more complex strategic moves than Agamben's mechanical teleology. Differences can be partialities within a whole—as the *plebs* was for patrician eyes—or the names of alternative totalities (requiring the investment of the whole within the part, as in Lacan's *objet a*). Homogenizing logics can be, *reductio ad absurdum*, thoroughly totalitarian, but they can equally be emancipatory, as when they link, in an equivalential chain, a plurality of unsatisfied demands. Sovereignty, finally, can also be totalitarian in the extreme case in which it involves a *total* concentration of power; but it can also be profoundly democratic, if it involves an articulating rather than a determining power—that is, when it "empowers" the underdog. In that case, as we have already pointed out, sovereignty should be conceived as hegemony.

Needless to say, we fully reject Agamben's third thesis, according to which the concentration camp is the *nomos* or fundamental biopolitical paradigm of the West. He asserts:

> The birth of the camp in our time appears as an event that decisively signals the political space of modernity itself. It is produced at the point at which the political system of the modern nation-state, which was founded on the functional nexus between a determinate localization (land) and a determinate order (the state) and mediated by automatic rules for the inscription of life (birth or the nation), enters into a lasting crisis, and the state decides to assume directly the care of the nation's biological life as one of its proper tasks. ... Something can no longer function within the traditional

mechanisms that regulated this inscription, and the camp is the new, hidden regulator of the inscription of life in the order—or, rather, the sign of the system's inability to function without being transformed into a lethal machine.

(Agamben 1998, pp. 174–75)

This series of wild statements would only hold if the following set of rather dubious premises were accepted:

1. That the crisis of the functional nexus between land, state, and the automatic rules for the inscription of life has freed an entity called "biological—or bare—life".
2. That the regulation of that freed entity has been assumed by a single and unified entity called the state.
3. That the inner logic of that entity necessarily leads it to treat the freed entities as entirely malleable objects whose archetypical form would be the ban.

Needless to say, none of these presuppositions can be accepted as they stand. Agamben, who has presented a rather compelling analysis of the way in which an ontology of potentiality should be structured, closes his argument, however, with a naïve teleologism, in which potentiality appears as entirely subordinated to a pregiven actuality. This teleologism is, as a matter of fact, the symmetrical *pendant* of the "etymologism" we have referred to at the beginning of this chapter. Their combined effect is to divert Agamben's attention from the really relevant question, which is the system of structural possibilities that each *new* situation opens. The most summary examination of that system would have revealed that: (1) the crisis of the "automatic rules for the inscription of life" has freed many more entities than "bare life," and that the reduction of the latter to the former takes place only in some extreme circumstances that cannot in any way be considered as a hidden pattern of modernity; (2) that the process of social regulation, to which the dissolution of the "automatic rules of inscription" opens the way, involved a plurality of instances that were far from unified in a single unity called "the state"; (3) that the process of state building in modernity has involved a far more complex dialectic between homogeneity and heterogeneity than the one that Agamben's "camp-based" paradigm reflects. By unifying the whole process of modern political construction around the extreme and absurd paradigm of the concentration camp, Agamben does more than present a distorted history: he blocks any possible exploration of the emancipatory possibilities opened by our modern heritage.

Let me conclude with a reference to the question of the future as it can be thought of from Agamben's perspective. He asserts:

> Only if it is possible to think the Being of abandonment beyond every idea of law (even that of the empty form of laws being in force without significance) will we have moved out of the paradox of sovereignty towards a politics freed from every ban. A pure form of law is only the empty form of

relation. Yet the empty form of relation is no longer a law but a zone of indistinguishability between law and life, which is to say, a state of exception.

(Agamben 1998, p. 59)

We are not told anything about what a movement out of the paradox of sovereignty and "towards a politics freed from every ban" would imply. But we do not need to be told: the formulation of the problem already involves its own answer. To be beyond any ban and any sovereignty means, simply, to be beyond politics. The myth of a fully reconciled society is what governs the (non-)political discourse of Agamben. And it is also what allows him to dismiss all political options in our societies and to unify them in the concentration camp as their secret destiny. Instead of deconstructing the logic of political institutions, showing areas in which forms of struggle and resistance are possible, he closes them beforehand through an essentialist unification. Political nihilism is his ultimate message.

Bibliography

Agamben, G. 1998. *Homo Sacer: Sovereign Power and Bare Life*. Trans. Daniel Heller-Roazen. Stanford, CA: Stanford University Press.
——2005. *State of Exception*. Trans. Kevin Attell. Chicago: University of Chicago Press.
Fanon, F. 1968. *The Wretched of the Earth*. New York: Grove Press.

13

COMMUNITY AND ITS PARADOXES
Richard Rorty's "Liberal Utopia" (1991)

Anti-foundationalism has so far produced a variety of intellectual and cultural effects, but few of them have referred to the terrain of politics. It is one of the merits of Richard Rorty's work to have attempted, vigorously and persuasively, to establish such a connection. In his most recent book (1989), *Contingency, Irony, and Solidarity*, he has presented an excellent picture of the intellectual transformation of the West during the last two centuries and, on the basis of it, has drawn the main lines of a social and political arrangement that he has called a "liberal utopia." It is not that Rorty tries to present his (post-)philosophical approach as a theoretical grounding for his political proposal—an attempt (which Rorty rejects) that would simply "reoccupy" with an antifoundationalist discourse the terrain of the lost foundation. It is rather that antifoundationalism, together with a plurality of other narratives and cultural interventions, has created the intellectual climate in which certain social and political arrangements are thinkable.

In this chapter I will try to show that, although I certainly agree with most of Rorty's philosophical arguments and positions, his notion of "liberal utopia" presents a series of shortcomings that can be superseded only if the liberal features of Rorty's utopia are reinscribed in the wider framework of what Chantal Mouffe and I have called "radical democracy" (Laclau and Mouffe 1985).

I

Let me summarize, in the first place, the main points of Rorty's argument. At the beginning of the book he asserts his primary thesis in the following terms:

> This book tries to show how things look if we drop the demand for a theory which unifies the public and private, and are content to treat the demands of self-creation and of human solidarity as equally valid, yet forever

> incommensurable. It sketches a figure whom I call the "liberal ironist." I borrow my definition of "liberal" from Judith Shklar, who says that liberals are the people who think that cruelty is the worst thing we do. I use "ironist" to name the sort of person who faces up to the contingency of his or her own most central beliefs and desires – someone sufficiently historicist and nominalist to have abandoned the idea that those central beliefs and desires refer back to something beyond the reach of time and chance. Liberal ironists are people who include among these ungroundable desires their own hope that suffering will be diminished, that the humiliation of human beings by other human beings may cease.
>
> *(Rorty 1989, p. xv)*

The milieu in which these objectives are attainable is that of a postmetaphysical culture.

The specifically political argument about the contingency of the community is preceded by two chapters on "the contingency of language" and "the contingency of selfhood," which constitute its background. Rorty points out that two hundred years ago two main changes took place in the intellectual life of Europe: the increasing realization that truth is fabricated rather than found—which made possible the utopian politics of reshaping social relations—and the romantic revolution, which led to a vision of art as self-creation rather than as imitation of reality. These changes joined forces and progressively acquired cultural hegemony. German idealism was a first attempt at drawing the intellectual consequences of this transformation, but ultimately failed as a result of confusing the idea that nothing has an internal nature to be represented with the very different one that the spatiotemporal world is a product of the human mind. What actually lies behind these dim intuitions of the romantic period is the increasing realization that there is no intrinsic nature of the real, but that the real will look different depending on the languages with which it is described, and that there is not a metalanguage or neutral language which will allow us to decide between competing first-order languages. Philosophical argument does not proceed through an internal deconstruction of a thesis presented in a certain vocabulary but rather through the presentation of a competing vocabulary.

> Interesting philosophy is rarely an examination of the pros and cons of a thesis. Usually it is, implicitly or explicitly, a contest between an entrenched vocabulary which has become a nuisance and a half-formed new vocabulary which vaguely promises great things.
>
> *(Rorty 1989, p. 9)*

At this point, Rorty, faithful to his method, simply drops the old conception of language and embarks upon a new operation of redescription through Donald Davidson's philosophy of language, with its rejection of the idea that language constitutes a medium of either representation or expression, and its similarity with the Wittgensteinian conception of alternative vocabularies as alternative tools. Mary Hesse's "metaphoric redescriptions" and Harold Bloom's "strong poet" are also quoted in this connection.

After having shown the contingency of language, Rorty gives selfhood its turn. Here the main heroes are Nietzsche and (especially) Freud. For Nietzsche it is only the poet who fully perceives the contingency of the self.

> The Western tradition thinks of a human life as a triumph just insofar as it breaks out of the world of time, appearance and idiosyncratic opinion into another world – the world of enduring truth. Nietzsche, by contrast, thinks the important boundary to cross is not the one separating time from atemporal truth but rather the one which divides the old from the new. He thinks a human life triumphant just insofar as it escapes inherited descriptions of the contingencies of its existence and finds new descriptions. This is the difference between the will to truth and the will to self-overcoming. It is the difference between thinking of redemption as making contact with something larger and more enduring than oneself and redemption as Nietzsche describes it: 'recreating all it was' into a 'thus I willed it'.
>
> *(Rorty 1989, p. 29)*

But it is Freud who represents the most important step forward in the process of de-divinization of the self.

> He showed the way in which all the features of our consciousness can be traced back to the contingency of our upbringing. He de-universalizes the moral sense, making it as idiosyncratic as the poet's inventions. He thus let us see the moral consciousness as historically conditioned, a product as much of time and chance as of political or aesthetic consciousness.
>
> *(Rorty 1989, p. 30)*

In spite of their many points in common, Freud is more useful, according to Rorty, than Nietzsche, because the former shows that the conformist bourgeois is dull only on the surface, before the psychoanalytic exploration, while the latter relegates "the vast majority of humanity to the status of dying animals" (Rorty 1989, p. 35).

Finally we reach the contingency of the community, which should be dealt with in more detail because it concerns the main topic of this chapter. Rorty here finds an initial difficulty: he is attached to both liberal democracy and antifoundationalism, but the vocabulary in which the former was initially presented is that of Enlightenment rationalism. The thesis that he tries to defend in the following two chapters is that, although this vocabulary was essential to liberal democracy in its initial stages, today it has become an impediment to its further progress and consolidation. This involves him in an effort to reformulate the democratic ideal in a nonrationalist and nonuniversalist way.

Rorty starts by clearing out of his path the possible charges of relativism and irrationalism. He quotes Schumpeter as saying, "To realize the relative validity of one's convictions and yet stand for them unflinchingly is what distinguishes a civilized man from a barbarian"; and he includes Isaiah Berlin's comment on this passage: "To demand more than this is perhaps a deep and incurable metaphysical need; but to allow it to determine one's practice is a symptom of an equally deep, and more dangerous, moral and political immaturity" (Rorty 1989, p. 46). It is these assertions that Michael Sandel is brought into the picture to oppose: "If one's convictions are only relatively valid, why stand for them unflinchingly?" (Rorty 1989, p. 46). Thus the relativism debate is opened in its classical terms. Rorty steps into this debate by trying to make a nonissue of the problem of relativism. He starts by discarding two notions of absolute validity: that which identifies the absolutely valid with what is valid to everyone and anyone (because in this case there would be no interesting statement that would be absolutely valid); and that which identifies it with those statements that can be justified to all those who are not corrupted (because this presupposes a division of human nature [divine/animal] that is ultimately incompatible with liberalism). The only alternative is, as a consequence, to restrict the opposition between rational and irrational forms of persuasion to the confines of a language game, where it is possible to distinguish reasons for belief from causes for belief that are not rational. This, however, leaves open the question about the rationality of the shifts of vocabularies and, as there is no neutral ground upon which to decide between them, it looks as if all important shifts in paradigms, metaphorics, or vocabularies would have causes but not reasons. But this would imply that all great intellectual movements such as Christianity, Galilean science, or the Enlightenment should be considered to have irrational origins. This is the point at which Rorty concludes that the usefulness of a description in terms of the opposition rational/irrational vanishes. Davidson—whom Rorty quotes at this point—notes that once the notion of rationality has been restricted to internal coherence, if the use of the term is not also restricted we will find ourselves calling "irrational" many things we appreciate (the decision to repress a certain desire, for instance, will appear irrational from the point of view of the desire itself). If Davidson and Hesse are right, metaphors are causes and not reasons for changes in beliefs, but this does not make them "irrational"; it is the very notion of irrationality that has to be questioned. The consequence is that the question of validity is essentially open and conversational. Only a society in which a system of taboos and a rigid delimitation of the order of subjects have been imposed and accepted by everybody will escape the conversational nature of validity, but this is precisely the kind of society that is strictly incompatible with liberalism:

> It is central to the idea of a liberal society that, with respect to words as opposed to deeds, persuasion as opposed to force, anything goes. This open mindedness should not be fostered because, as Scripture teaches, Truth is great and will prevail, nor because, as Milton suggests, Truth will always win in a free and open encounter. It should be fostered for its own sake.

> *A liberal society is one which is content to call "true" whatever the upshot of such encounters turns out to be.* That is why a liberal society is badly served by an attempt to supply it with "philosophical foundations." For the attempt to supply such foundations presupposes a natural order of topics and arguments which is prior to, and overrides the results of, encounters between old and new vocabularies.
>
> (Rorty 1989, pp. 51–52; emphasis in original)

This question of the relationship between foundationalism (rationalism) and liberalism is treated by Rorty through a convincing critique of Horkheimer and Adorno's *Dialectic of Enlightenment*. He accepts their vision that the forces put into movement by the Enlightenment have undermined the Enlightenment's own convictions, but he does not accept their conclusion that, as a result of this, liberalism is at present intellectually and morally bankrupt. According to Rorty, the vocabularies that presided over the initiation of a historical process or intellectual movement are never adapted to them when they reach maturity, and in his view ironic thinking is far more appropriate to a fully-fledged liberal society than rationalism.

The poet and the utopian revolutionary, who are central historical actors in Rorty's account, play the role of "protesting in the name of the society itself against those aspects of the society which are unfaithful to its own self-image" (Rorty 1989, p. 60) And he adds in a crucial passage:

> This substitution (of the protest of alienated people by the revolutionary and the poet) seems to cancel out the difference between the revolutionary and the reformer. But one can define the *ideally* liberal society as one in which the difference is canceled out. A liberal society is one whose ideals can be fulfilled by persuasion rather than force, by reform rather than revolution, by the free and open encounters of present linguistic and other practices with suggestions for new practices. But this is to say that an ideal liberal society is one which has no purpose except freedom, no goal except a willingness to see how such encounters go and to abide by the outcome. It has no purpose except to make life easier for poets and revolutionaries while seeing to it that they make life harder for others only by words, and not deeds. It is a society whose hero is the strong poet and the revolutionary because it recognizes that it is what it is, has the morality it has, speaks the language it does, not because it approximates the will of God or the nature of man but because certain poets and revolutionaries of the past spoke as they did.
>
> (Rorty 1989, pp. 60–61)

Rorty brings into focus the figure of the liberal ironist by comparing it with Foucault (an ironist who is not a liberal) and with Habermas (a liberal who is not an ironist). In the case of Foucault there is an exclusive emphasis on self-realization, self-enjoyment. Foucault is unwilling to consider the advantages and improvements of liberal societies because he is much more concerned with the ways in which these societies still prevent this process of self-creation. In many cases they have even imposed upon their members increased controls, which were unknown in premodern societies. Rorty's main disagreement with Foucault is that, in his view, it is not necessary to create a new "we"; "we liberals" is enough. With Habermas the situation is the opposite. For him it is essential that a democratic society's self-image has an element of universalism, which is to be obtained through what he calls a process of domination-free communication. He tries to maintain—even if through a radical recasting—a bridge with the rationalistic foundation of the Enlightenment. So, Rorty's disagreement with Foucault is essentially political, whereas with Habermas it is purely philosophical.

Finally, we should consider for our purposes two possible objections to Rorty's liberal utopia, which he tries to answer. The first is that the abandonment of the metaphysical grounding of liberal societies will deprive them of a social glue that is indispensable for the continuation of free institutions. The second is that it is not possible—from a psychological point of view—to be a liberal ironist and, at the same time, not to have some metaphysical beliefs about the nature of human beings. Rorty's answer to the first objection is that society is pulled together not by any philosophical grounding but by common vocabularies and common hopes. The same objection was made in the past about the disastrous social effects that would derive from the masses' loss of religious beliefs, and the prophecy proved to be wrong. The answer to the second objection is that there is something to it. Ironists have been essentially elitist and have not contributed excessively to the improvement of the community. The redescription in which they engage frequently leads to an attack on the most cherished values of people and to their humiliation. On top of that, though the metaphysicians also engage in re-descriptions, they have the advantage over ironists in that they at least give people something they claim to be true in nature, a new faith to which they can adhere. But here Rorty says that the primary difficulty is that people are demanding from ironist philosophers something that philosophy cannot give: answers to questions such as "Why not be cruel?" or "Why be kind?" The expectation that a *theoretical* answer can be given is simply the result of a metaphysical lag. In a postphilosophical era it is the narratives that perform the function of creating those values:

> Within an ironist culture ... it is the disciplines which specialize in thick description of the private and idiosyncratic which are assigned this job. In particular, novels and ethnographies which sensitize one to the pain of those who do not speak our language must do the job which demonstrations of a common human nature were supposed to do.
>
> (Rorty 1989, p. 97)

II

I am in agreement with a great deal of Rorty's analysis, especially with his pragmatism and with the account that he gives of what is happening in contemporary theory. I certainly subscribe to his rejection of any metaphysical grounding of the social order and with his critique of Habermas. Finally, I also endorse his defense of the liberal democratic framework. However, I think that there is in his "liberal utopia" something that simply does not work. And I do not think that it is a matter of detail or incompletion but rather that it is an internal inconsistency of his "ideal society."

Let us start with his characterization of liberal society as a type of social arrangement in which persuasion substitutes for force. My main difficulty is that I cannot establish between the two as sharp a distinction as Rorty does. Of course in one sense the distinction *is* clear, in persuasion there is an element of consensus, whereas in force there is not. But the question that remains is to what extent in persuasion/consensus there is not an ingredient of force. What is it to persuade? Except in the extreme case of proving something to somebody in an algorithmic way, we are engaged in an operation that involves making somebody change her opinion without any ultimate rational foundation. Rorty quite correctly limits the domain of reason to the interior of any particular language game, but the difficulty subsists, because language games are not absolutely closed universes and, as a consequence, decisions within them have to be made that are undecidable by the system of rules that define the structure of the game. I agree with Rorty/Davidson that recognition of this fact does not justify describing the decision as irrational, and that the whole distinction between rational and irrational is of little use. But what I want to point out is something different: it is that a decision to be made under those conditions is inevitably going to include an element of force. Let us take Davidson's example of somebody who wants to reform herself and decides to suppress a desire—e.g., an alcoholic who decides to stop drinking. From the point of view of the desire there is only repression—that is, force. And this argument can be generalized. Let us consider various possible situations:

Situation A. I am confronted with the need to choose between several possible courses of action, and the structure of the language game that I am playing is indifferent to them. After having evaluated the situation, I conclude that there is no obvious candidate for my decision but I nevertheless make *one* choice. It is clear that in this case I have repressed the alternative courses of action.

Situation B. I want to persuade somebody to change his opinion. Since the belief I want to inculcate in him is not the Hegelian truth of the opposed belief that he actually has, I do not want to develop his belief but to *cancel it out of existence*. Again, force. Let us suppose that I succeed in my efforts. In that case he has been *converted* to my belief. But the element of force is always there. All I have done is convince my friend that by killing his belief he will become my ally. Persuasion, consequently, structurally involves force.

Situation C. There are two possible courses of action and two groups of people are split about which to follow as the two courses of action are equally possible within the structure of the situation, the difference can only be solved by force. Of course this element of force will be actualized in many different ways: either by one group persuading the other (and we are back to situation B); or through a system of rules accepted by both parties to settle the difference (a vote, for instance); or by the *ultima ratio*. But the important point to see is that the element of force is going to be present in all cases.

Clearly the kind of society that Rorty prefers is one in which the third solution to situation C is excluded, but this still presents various difficulties. The first is that it is simply not possible to oppose force and persuasion since persuasion is one form of force. The discussion is thus displaced to an analysis of the way in which force is organized in society and of the types of force that are acceptable in a liberal society. The second problem is that the element of physical force cannot be eliminated even in the most free society. I doubt that Rorty would advocate persuasion as an adequate method for dealing with a rapist. And strikes, or student sit-ins—which are perfectly legitimate actions in a free society—try to achieve their goals not only through persuasion but also by forcing their antagonists to surrender to violence. There are, of course, many intermediate cases.

For the same reasons I tend to deal in a way different from Rorty with the distinction between reform and revolution. In my view, the problem is to displace the terrain that made the distinction possible. For the classical idea of revolution involves not only the dimension of violence that Rorty underscores but also the idea that this violence has to be directed toward a very specific end, which was to give a *new foundation* to the social order. Now, from this point of view I am a reformist, not because my social aims are limited but simply because I do not believe that society has such a thing as a foundation. No doubt Rorty would agree with me on this point. Even the events that in the past *have been called* revolutions were only the overdetermination of a multiplicity of reforms that cover vast aspects of society but by no means the totality of them. The idea of turning the whole society upside down does not make any sense. (Which does not mean that many ugly things were not committed in the attempt to perform this impossible operation.) But if, on the one hand, I am trying to relocate revolution within reform, on the other hand, I am very much in favor of reintroducing the dimension of violence within reform. A world in which reform takes place without violence is not a world in which I would like to live. It could be either an absolutely uni-dimensional society, in which 100 percent of the population would agree with any single reform, or a society in which the decisions would be made by an army of social engineers with the backing of the rest of the population. Any reform involves changing the *status quo*, and in most cases this will hurt existing interests. The process of reform is a process of struggles, not a process of quiet piecemeal engineering. And there is nothing here to regret, it is in this active process of struggle that human abilities—new language games—are created. Could we, for instance, think what the workers' identity would have been without the active struggles with which they were involved during the first stages of industrial societies? Certainly many of the workers' abilities that will be essential to the process of democratization of Western societies would not have developed. And the same, of course, can be said of any other social force. Thus, the radical democratic "utopia" that I would like to counterpose to Rorty's liberal one does not preclude antagonisms and social division but, on the contrary, considers them as constitutive of the social.

So, in my view Rorty has based his argument on certain types of polarizations—persuasion/force, reform/violence-revolution—that are not only simplistic but also inconsistent because the role of the goodies presupposes the presence, inside it, of baddies. Any theory about power in a democratic society has to be a theory about the forms of power that are compatible with democracy, not about the elimination of power. And this is the result not of any particular persistence of a form of domination but of the very fact that society, as Rorty knows well, is not structured as a jigsaw puzzle and that consequently it is impossible to avoid the collision of different demands and language games with each other. Let us take the case of recent debates in America concerning pornography. Various feminist groups have argued that pornography offends women—something with which I could not agree more. But some of these groups have gone so far as to ask for legislation permitting any woman to take the publishers of pornographic material and advertisements to court. This has raised the objection—which I also share—that such actions would create a climate of intimidation that could affect freedom of expression. Where should the line be drawn between what is pornographic and what is artistic expression, for instance? Obviously a balance has to be established between antagonistic demands. But it is important to stress that the balance is not going to be the result of having found a point at which both demands harmonize with each other, in which case we would be back to the jigsaw puzzle theory. No, the antagonism of the two demands is, in that context, ineradicable, and the balance consists of limiting the effects of both so that a sort of social equilibrium—something very different from a rational harmonization—can be reached. But in that case the antagonism, though socially regulated and controlled, will subsist under the form of what could be called a "war of position." Each pole of the conflict will have a certain power and will exercise a certain violence over the other pole. The paradoxical corollary of this conclusion is that the existence of violence and antagonism is the very condition of a free society. Antagonism exists because the social is not a plurality of effects radiating from a pregiven center, but is pragmatically constructed from many starting points. But it is precisely because of this, because there is an ontological possibility of clashes and unevenness, that we can speak of freedom. Let us suppose that we move to the opposite hypothesis, the one contained in the classical notion of emancipation, i.e. a society from which violence and antagonisms have been *entirely* eliminated. In this society we only enjoy the Spinozan freedom of being conscious of necessity. This is a first paradox of a free community: that which constitutes its condition of impossibility (violence) constitutes at the same time its condition of possibility. Particular forms of oppression can be eliminated, but freedom exists only insofar as the achievement of a total freedom is an ever-receding horizon. A totally free society and a totally determined society would be, as I have argued elsewhere, exactly the same. I think that the reason

Rorty is not entirely aware of these antinomies is the result of his insufficient theorization of what is involved in the notion of "persuasion" and of the total opposition that he has established between "persuasion" and "force."

III

Persuasion is an essentially impure notion. One cannot persuade without the other of persuasion—that is, force. One can speak of the force of persuasion, but one would never say that one has been persuaded of the correctness of the Pythagorean theorem. The latter is simply *shown,* without any need for persuasion. But one cannot say either that persuasion is simply *reducible* to force. Persuasion is the terrain of what Derrida would call a "hymen." It is the point at which the "reasons" for a belief and the "causes" of the belief constitute an inseparable whole. The adoption of a new paradigm in Kuhnian terms is a good example of what I mean. A multitude of small reasons/causes ranging from theoretical difficulties to technical advances in the tools of scientific research overdetermine each other in determining the transition from normal to revolutionary science. And for reasons that I have explained earlier—and which are also clearly present in some way in Kuhn's account—this transition is not an indifferent and painless abandonment but involves repression of other possibilities: it is the result of a struggle. This is obviously more clearly visible when we refer to the politico-ideological field. Now, as Chantal Mouffe and I (1985) have argued in *Hegemony and Socialist Strategy,* there is a word in our political tradition that refers to this peculiar operation called persuasion, which is only constituted through the inclusion, within itself, of its violent opposite: this word is "hegemony."

I refer to our book for all aspects concerning the genealogy of the concept of hegemony from the Russian Social Democrats to Gramsci, for its structural characteristics, and for its forms of theoretical articulation with the project of a radical democracy. Here I want only to underscore some aspects that are relevant to the present discussion. The most important one is that "hegemony" is the discursive terrain in which foundationalism began disintegrating in the history of Marxism. What had been presented until then as a necessary consequence of an endogenous development determined by the contradiction between development of the productive forces and existing relations of production, became, escalating from Lenin to Gramsci, the result of a contingent process of political articulation in an open ensemble whose elements had purely relational identities. That is, History (with a capital *H*) was not a valid object of discourse because it did not correspond to any *a priori* unified object. The only thing we had was the discontinuous succession of hegemonic blocs, which was not governed by any rationally graspable logic—neither teleological, nor dialectical, nor causal. As in the relation between the desire that I want to suppress—in Davidson's example—and the decision to suppress it, there is no internal connection at all. On the other hand, there is here an important dialectic to detect between necessity and contingency. If each of the elements intervening in a hegemonic bloc had an identity of its own, its relations with all the others would be merely contingent; but if, on the contrary, the identity of each element is contingent upon its relations with the others, those relations are absolutely necessary if the identity is going to be maintained.

Now the problem to be discussed is the internal logic of this hegemonic operation that underlies the process of persuasion. We will approach it by bringing into the analysis various devices that are thinkable as a result of the transformations that have taken place in contemporary theory. Let us start with the Wittgensteinian example of the rule governing the sequence of a numerical series. I say 1, 2, 3, 4 and ask a friend to continue the series: the spontaneous answer would be to say 5, 6, 7, and so on. But I can say that the series I have in mind is not that but 1, 2, 3, 4, 9, 10, 11, 12, *et cetera*. My friend thinks that he has now understood and proceeds accordingly, but I then say that the series is still not what I had in mind, and so on. The rule governing the series can be indefinitely changed. Everything depends, as Lewis Carroll would put it, on who is in command. Now let us change the example slightly. Let us suppose that we are speaking of a game in which player A starts a series and player B has to continue it the way he wants, providing that there is some visible regularity. Now, when it is A's turn again, he has to invent a new rule that takes as its starting point the series as it has been left by B, and so on. In the end the loser is the one who finds the whole business so complicated that he is unable to imagine a new rule. The corollaries that follow from this example are the following: (a) that there is no ultimate rule: it can always be subverted; (b) that since an indefinite number of players can come to participate in the game, the rule governing the series is essentially threatened—it is, to use Rorty's expression, *radically contingent*; (c) that the identity of each of the individual figures within the series is entirely relational; it is only given by its structural position within the rule that is at that moment hegemonizing the series, and it will change with the formulation of a new rule. I think this is important because the process of persuasion is frequently presented as if somebody who has a belief A is presented with a belief B and the suggestion of moving from one to the other. Things never happen this way. What happens is that new elements enter into the picture and that the old rule is unable to hegemonize them—for instance, if an apparently chaotic series of numbers is introduced in our series and the challenge is to find a coherent rule that will be compatible with the new state of affairs. Very frequently the new rule is accepted, not because it is liked in itself, but just because it is *a* rule, because it introduces a principle of coherence and intelligibility in an apparent chaos. In the confused Italian situation of the early 1920s many liberals accepted fascism, not because they particularly liked it, but because an explosive social situation existed that was both unthinkable and unmanageable within the framework of the traditional political system, and fascism appeared as the *only* coherent discourse that could deal with the new chaotic events. And if liberalism had wanted—which it did not—to present itself as an alternative hegemonic discourse articulating the new elements, it could only have done so by transforming itself. Between the liberalism of 1905 and the liberalism of 1922 there are only "family resemblances." This is because, among other reasons, the latter had to be antifascist and this involved dealing with a new series of problems that radically transformed the discursive field. This is the reason I do not agree with Rorty's assertion that we can *be just* liberals; that our "we" has reached a point that does not require any further transformation. Even if we want to continue being liberals we will *always* have to be something more. Liberalism can only exist as a hegemonic attempt in this process of articulation—as a result of the radically relational character of all identity. Here I think that Rorty has not been historicist enough.

This is also the point—moving now from Wittgenstein to Derrida—at which deconstruction becomes central for a theory of politics. Derrida has shown the essential vulnerability of every context:

> Every sign, linguistic or not linguistic, spoken or written (in the current sense of this opposition), in a small or large unit, can be *cited,* put between quotation marks; in so doing it can break with every given context, engendering an infinitude of new contexts in a manner which is absolutely illimitable. This does not imply that the mark is valid outside of a context, but on the contrary that there are only contexts without any center of absolute anchorage (*ancrage*). This citationality, this duplication or duplicity, this iterability of the mark is neither an accident nor an anomaly, it is that (normal/abnormal) without which a mark could not even have a function called "normal." What would a mark be that could not be cited? Or one whose origins would not get lost along the way?
>
> (Derrida 1988, "Signature," p. 12)

Now, what is this saying if not that all context is essentially vulnerable and open, that the fact that one of the possibilities rather than the others has been chosen is a purely *contingent* fact? If the choice is not *determined* by the structure, it is down to the bottom a hegemonic operation, an essentially *political* decision.

Let us go back, with these distinctions in mind, to Rorty's text. The first aspect of his liberal utopia I would take issue with is his sharp division between the public and the private, it is not, of course, that I want to return to some "grand theory" that would embrace both. The reason for my disagreement is exactly the opposite: Rorty sees as necessarily united many things that for me are radically discontinuous and only held together by contingent articulations. Is the realm of personal self-realization really a *private* realm? It would be so if that self-realization took place in a neutral medium in which individuals could seek unimpeded the fulfillment of their own aims. But this medium is, of course, a myth. A woman searching for her self-realization will find obstacles in the form of male-oriented rules that will limit her *personal* aspirations and possibilities. The feminist struggles attempting to change those rules will constitute a collective "we" *different* from the "we" of the abstract public citizenship, but the space that these struggles create—remember the motto "the personal is political"—will be a no less communitarian and public space than the one in which political parties intervene and in which elections are fought. And the same can be said, of course, of any struggle that begins as a result of the existence of social norms, prejudices, regulations, and so forth that frustrate the self-realization of an individual. I see the *strength* of a democratic society in the multiplication of these public spaces and its *condition* in the recognition of their plurality and autonomy. This recognition is based on the essential *discontinuity* existing between those social spaces, and the essential character of these discontinuities makes possible its exact opposite: the contingent-hegemonic articulation among them in what could be called a global sense of community, a certain democratic common sense. We see here a second paradox of community: it has to be *essentially* unachievable to become pragmatically possible. So, what about the private? It is a residual category, limited to those aspects of our activity in which our objectives are not interfered with by any structural social barrier, in which their achievement does not require the constitution of any struggling community, of any "we." So, as we see, the classical terms of the problem are displaced: it is no longer a question of preventing a public space from encroaching upon that of private individuals, given that the public spaces have to be constituted in order to achieve individual aims. But the condition for a democratic society is that these public spaces have to be plural: a democratic society is, of course, incompatible with the existence of only *one* public space. What we should have is a multiple "civic republicanism."

As is clear, my idea of a democratic society is different in central respects from Rorty's liberal utopia. Rorty's utopia consists of a public space limited—as for all good liberals—to minimal functions and a private sphere in which individual agents seek their own ends. This system can certainly be reformed and improved, but one has the impression that such improvements are like improving a machine by designing a better model, not the result of struggles. Antagonism and violence do not play either a positive or a negative role, simply because they are entirely absent from the picture. For me, a radically democratic society is one in which a plurality of public spaces, constituted around specific issues and demands, and strictly autonomous of each other, instills in its members a civic sense that is a central ingredient of their identity *as* individuals. Despite the plurality of these spaces, or, rather, as a consequence of it, a diffuse democratic culture is created, which gives the community its specific identity. Within this community, the liberal institutions—parliament, elections, division of powers—are maintained, but these are *one* public space, not *the* public space. Not only is antagonism not excluded from a democratic society, it is the very condition of its institution.

For Rorty the three words "bourgeois, liberal democracy" constitute an indivisible whole; for me there is between them only a contingent articulation. As a socialist I am prepared to fight against capitalism for the hegemony of liberal institutions; and as a believer in the latter, I am prepared to do my best to make them compatible with the whole field of democratic public spaces. I see this compatibility, however, as a hegemonic construction, not as something granted from the beginning. I think that a great deal of twentieth-century history can be explained by the dislocations in the articulation of the three components just mentioned. Liberal institutions (let alone capitalism) have fared badly in Third World countries, and the record of the attempt to articulate socialism and democracy (if attempt it can be called) in the countries of the Eastern bloc is simply appalling. Though my preference is for a liberal-democratic-socialist society, it is clear to me that if I were forced in given circumstances to choose one of the three, my preference would always be for democracy. (For instance, if in a Third World country I had to choose between, on the one hand, a corrupt and repressive liberal regime, in which elections are a farce manipulated by clientelistic gangs, with no participation of the masses; and, on the other, a nationalistic military regime that tends toward social reform and the self-organization of the masses, my preference would be for the latter. All my experience shows that, while in some cases the second type of regime can lead—with many difficulties—to an increasing liberalization of its institutions, the same process does not take place in the first case: it is just a blind alley.)

IV

Finally, I want to address the two possible objections to his argument that Rorty raises (see *supra*), and his answers to them. Regarding the first objection, I think that Rorty is entirely correct and I have nothing to add. But in the case of the second objection, I feel that Rorty's answer is unnecessarily defensive and that a much better argument can be made. I would formulate it in the following way. The question is whether the abandonment of universalism undermines the foundation of a democratic society. My answer is yes, I grant the whole argument. Without a universalism of sorts—the idea of *human* rights, for instance—a truly democratic society is impossible. But in order to assert this it is not at all necessary to muddle through the Enlightenment's rationalism or Habermas's "domination-free communication." It is enough to recognize that democracy needs universalism while asserting, at the same time, that universalism is one of the vocabularies, one of the language games, which was constructed at some point by social agents and which has become an increasingly central part of our values and our culture. It is a *contingent* historical product. It originated in religious discourse (all men are equal before God), was brought down to this world by the Enlightenment, and has been generalized to wider and wider social relations by the democratic revolution of the last two centuries.

A historicist recasting of universalism has, I would think, two main political advantages over its metaphysical version, and these, far from weakening it, help to reinforce and to radicalize it. The first is that it has a liberating effect: human beings will begin seeing themselves more and more as the exclusive authors of their world. The historicity of Being will become more apparent. If people think that God or Nature has made the world as it is, they will tend to consider their fate inevitable. But if the Being of the world that they inhabit is only the result of the contingent discourses and vocabularies that constitute it, they will tolerate their fate with less patience and will stand a better chance of becoming *political* "strong poets." The second advantage is that the perception of the contingent character of universalist values will make us all more conscious of the dangers that threaten them and of their possible extinction. If we happen to believe in those values, the consciousness of their historicity will not make us more indifferent to them, but, on the contrary, will make us more responsible citizens, more ready to engage in their defense. Historicism, in this way, helps those who believe in those values. As for those who do *not* believe in them, no rationalist argument will ever have the slightest effect.

This leads me to a last point. This double effect—increasing the freeing of human beings through a more assertive image of their capacities, increasing social responsibility through the consciousness of the historicity of Being—is the most important possibility, a radically *political* possibility, which contemporary thought is opening to us. The metaphysical discourse of the West is coming to an end, and philosophy in its dusk has performed, through the great names of the century, a last service for us: the deconstruction of its own terrain and the creation of the conditions for its own impossibility. Let us think, for instance, of Derrida's undecidables. Once undecidability has reached the ground itself, once the organization of a certain camp is governed by a hegemonic decision—hegemonic because it is not objectively determined, because different decisions were also possible—the realm of philosophy comes to an end and the realm of politics begins. This realm will be inhabited by a different type of discourse, by discourses such as Rorty's "narratives," which tend to *construct* the world on the grounds of a radical undecidability. But I do not like the name "ironist"—which evokes all kinds of playful images—for this political strong poet. On the contrary, someone who is confronted with Auschwitz and has the moral strength to admit the contingency of her own beliefs instead of seeking refuge in religious or rationalistic myths is, I think, a profoundly heroic and tragic figure. This will be a hero of a new type who has still not been entirely created by our culture, but one whose creation is absolutely necessary if our time is going to live up to its most radical and exhilarating possibilities.

Bibliography

Derrida, J. 1988. *Limited Inc*. Evanston, IL: Northwestern University Press.
Horkheimer, M, and Adorno, T.W. 1997. *Dialectic of Enlightenment*, new edn. London: Verso.
Laclau, E. and Mouffe, C. 1985. *Hegemony and Socialist Strategy*. London: Verso.
Rorty, R. 1989. *Contingency, Irony, and Solidarity*. Cambridge: Cambridge University Press.

AN INTERVIEW WITH ERNESTO LACLAU

Questions from David Howarth

The re-presentation of the chapters in this book exemplifies the major innovations your work has brought about over the last thirty-five years or so. Put very simply, in my view, your various contributions can be divided into three basic phases. First, in texts like Politics and Ideology in Marxist Theory, *you endeavour to elaborate a non-reductionist theory of ideology and politics in the Marxist tradition by engaging with the work of Antonio Gramsci, Louis Althusser, Nicos Poulantzas and others. Then in* Hegemony and Socialist Strategy *and* New Reflections on the Revolution of Our Time *you elaborate a distinctively post-Marxist theory of hegemony that incorporates different aspects of poststructuralist philosophy (e.g. the writings of Derrida, Foucault and Lacan), and that breaks decisively with the residual determinism and essentialism of the Marxist paradigm. And, finally, in texts like* Emancipation(s) *and* On Populist Reason, *you further refine this post-Marxist approach to political analysis through a deeper engagement with deconstructionist philosophy and Lacan's interpretation of Freudian psychoanalysis.*

Each of these theoretical developments connects in a rough fashion with a series of pressing issues in contemporary politics: the construction and representation of working-class and popular demands in an expanded project for socialist transformation; the development of a project for radical democracy as a way of articulating the demands and identities associated with the new social movements; and finally a stress on the creation of new forms of 'contingent universalism' in the face of a worrying fragmentation of radical politics caused by the rise of new forms of particularism and identity/difference. But though it is possible to delineate and chart these shifts in your approach to the study of ideology and politics, there are also significant continuities. Each of the different phases of your writings is informed by the search for an anti-essentialist and non-reductionist account of social relations and practices. All your interventions seek to make greater room for the relatively autonomous role of politics and ideology in explaining social processes. And at each stage of your writings, you explore and sometimes integrate non-Marxist currents of thinking into your approach.

In asking you to reflect on the overall development of your work, do you recognize these broad descriptions? Do you see important continuities and discontinuities in your writings? Are these theoretical and philosophical influences decisive, or are there are others that are not mentioned? Are you still happy to describe your work as post-Marxist? And, if so, what content do you now give to that term?

I think that you have quite accurately described the main stages of my thought. Let me add, however, that as far as the continuities is concerned, in moving from one phase to another I have not conceived that movement as a simple 'leaving behind' what had preceded it, but as a recovery, at a higher level of reflection, of something which was there *in nuce* from the very beginning. And I would add something more: some of the intuitions which later took theoretical shape were already present in my mind in the 1960s, at a time at which I had written nothing. But coming to your point, I see the question of the continuities and discontinuities in the following way. I have never abandoned my post-Marxist perspective. By the 'post' we should not understand a 'leaving behind', but rather a dealing with actual *aporias* deeply ingrained in the heart of Marxism, which forced political thought to go beyond the straightjacket constituted by classical Marxist categories and which, however, could only be posed within the horizon opened by Marxist theorization. As you have rightly pointed out, at the beginning it was a question of confronting that theorization with the arsenal of categories coming not only from the post-structuralist tradition, but also those connected with the avenues opened by the Wittgensteinian breakthrough. The result of this theoretical exercise was peculiar: it did not replace Marxist categories with totally new ones, but uncovered logics secretly operating within those categories and subverting them. This gave them a new inflection. Such was the task carried out in *Hegemony and Socialist Strategy*, written together with Chantal Mouffe, where the central category that was deconstructed was that of 'hegemony'.

As for the third stage to which you refer, it came quite logically, as a deepening of what was already present, in an inchoate form, since *Hegemony and Socialist Strategy*. The way I see the matter today, there were three main developments in this third stage. In the first place, while in *Hegemony* we had presented 'antagonism' as the limit of all objectivity – something that I still maintain – there was still a certain ambiguity in the argument, for in one of its dimensions an antagonism is already a form of discursive inscription. It is internally divided between its ontic content and the ontological function of representing the very limits of representation – the *Abgrund* – in the Heideggerian sense of the term. That is why I gave an increasing role to the notion of 'dislocation'. A pure dislocation is, of course, impossible, and it can only show itself through the distortions that it introduces into what would have otherwise been fully objective ontic contents. This duality antagonism/dislocation allows us, I think, to reach a richer and more complex notion of hegemony.

The other two departures from the original formulation are related to the first. One is the increasing centrality that I have given, in my recent work, to the logic of representation. As I said before, a dislocation can only be shown through the distortion of particular ontic contents. This means that such contents will represent something different from themselves; so that 'representation' is a primary and constitutive ontological terrain, because there is no full 'presentation' *vis-à-vis* which that representation would be a simple copy (in the Platonic sense). I think that, in different ways, the writings of Derrida and Deleuze have moved in a comparable direction. Finally, in my recent work there is a far more serious engagement with Lacanian psychoanalysis than in the past. In *On Populist Reason*, I have argued that, on the one hand, the hegemonic logic, and, on the other hand, Lacan's concept of the *object petit a* are, from a certain theoretical point of view, indistinguishable from each other. I have explored this question in a graduate seminar that I organized, together with my colleague Joan Copjec, at SUNY, Buffalo for a number of years.

One important contribution of your approach is the development of a range of categories and concepts with which to critically explain social phenomena. Actually, four basic categories run through your work, though with different emphases and inflections: discourse, antagonism, hegemony and the primacy of politics or 'the political'. I would like to discuss each in turn. Let's begin with the category of discourse. This category has enabled you to deconstruct and rework problematic oppositions, which continue to haunt modern social and political theory in the Marxist and non-Marxist traditions. These include sharp separations between linguistic and non-linguistic practices, as well as the opposition between thought/consciousness and so-called material conditions. The category has also enabled you to draw on the rich resources of linguistic and rhetorical theory to develop new concepts and logics of political analysis.

Yet there are still persistent questions about the extension of the category of discourse to embrace a wide range of social practices, institutions and objects. Indeed, even those who are very sympathetic to your poststructuralist theory of politics have sought to supplement the discursive with other dimensions. For example, in his excellent book The Lacanian Left, *Yannis Stavrakakis seeks to explore 'the interface between the symbolic and the real of jouissance as two distinct but inter-implicated dimensions', and he emphasizes the affective, libidinal dimension as an important supplement to the discursive. In a related fashion, William Connolly draws on neuroscience, biology and evolutionary theory, as well as Deleuze and complexity theory, to rework cultural theory by incorporating the 'visceral register' of the self.*

Such developments raise a number of questions, especially in light of your suggestions that the concept of discourse could be replaced by notions like 'practice' or 'relationalism'. Does the category of discourse run the risk of obscuring a set of more regional distinctions between institutions, practices, organizations, talk, nature, the body and so forth, even though these entities are still discursively constructed? Do you see notions like affect, jouissance and libidinal investment as inhabiting a kind of pre- or extra-discursive realm, or can they only be understood discursively? If so, how is this possible? Does your idea of 'radical materialism', which stresses 'the relational, historical, and precarious character of the world of forms', make possible a rethinking of the concepts like nature, the body and materiality?

Let us be clear about the status of the category of discourse in my theoretical approach. It corresponds to what would be the equivalent of a *general ontology*. In the same way that Alain Badiou attempts to conceptualize this primary level in terms of a mathematical ontology, which is grounded in set theory, I have tried to do something comparable, although my theoretical approach is not grounded in mathematics but in linguistics. The reasons for this choice would require a long explanation, but, in any case, I think it makes possible an understanding of social and political relations that I don't think can be represented in terms of the categories which govern set theory.

Having said this, some precisions are required to make sense of this primary choice. The first is that to speak of 'discourse' is not to refer to any priority of speech or writing conceived in a narrow sense, but to a relation of signification which is inherent in any social practice. What is asserted is that a social practice constitutes itself around the logic of the signifier – i.e. around the complex movements dominating the relationship signifier/signified. And this includes not only words but also actions, as in Wittgenstein's notion of a 'language game'. All the differentiations that you refer to in your question can and should be represented in discourse theory in terms of alterations in the relation signifier/signified. Marx starts *Das Kapital* by asserting that the wealth of modern societies presents itself as an immense arsenal of commodities, and commodity as its elementary form. Evidently, in making this claim he is not saying that we have only commodities and not banks, financial systems and international trade; what he is saying is that he will attempt to produce in a conceptual form this differentiation through an analysis which starts from the internal logic of the commodity. In the same way, when we are asserting the ontological centrality of the sign, our commitment is to construct the differentiations to which you refer, out of the logic of the signifier.

Let me give you some examples. Rhetoric was traditionally conceived as an adornment of language and, as such, external to linguistic rules. So we have in classical rhetoric all those long and totally unstructured lists of figures, without any clear principle of classification. Since at least Jakobson we know better: we know that all rhetorical figures are organized around the two poles constituted by metaphor and metonymy, which strictly correspond to the two axes of language discerned by structural linguistics, that is, the syntagmatic and the paradigmatic poles. Even more: as Saussure himself had found out, while the syntagmatic pole was subjected to strict syntactic rules, the paradigmatic pole – which he called the 'associative' – was submitted to no rules and could advance in the most diverse directions. In other words, its functioning was strictly tropological. But this means that rhetoric is not a province separated from linguistics, but that it is an essential dimension of linguistic structuration.

To give you a second example: psychoanalysis. Here you have the distinction – homologous to those you find in linguistics and rhetoric – between condensation and displacement, studied by Freud since *The Interpretation of Dreams*. And this, again, poses the same questions. Any psychic element is overdetermined, that is, differentially cathected. This leads us to the problem of the relation between discourse and *jouissance* that you mentioned. You quoted Stavrakakis – whose book, I agree, is extremely valuable – as speaking about 'the interface between the symbolic and the real of *jouissance* as two distinct but inter-implicated dimensions'. The difficulty with this formulation is that it is ambiguous. Everything depends on the way in which both the distinction and the inter-implication are going to be conceived. If it is a question of asserting the presence of two entities, which are independently constituted, and that only later react with one other, then I do not believe at all that this is the case. The paradigmatic pole of language is essential to linguistic functioning as such, and it is dominated by unconscious associations, not submitted to syntactically *a priori* rules. So affect is internal to language. But the reverse is also true: affect is not a mysterious force operating outside language, but only constitutes itself through the differential cathexis of the components of a signifying chain. There is no 'real of *jouissance*' constituted outside the symbolic, because 'the Real' only emerges as a result of the failure of the symbolic in reaching a full constitution. Discourse is the underlying unity of the two dimensions.

With these clarifications you can glimpse the ontological task as I conceive it. On the one hand, we have the reproduction of a basic homology at all levels of analysis of human reality: in linguistics it is the duality paradigm/syntagm; in rhetoric, metaphor/metonymy; in psychoanalysis, condensation/displacement; and in politics, equivalence/difference. On the other hand, each field has its own specificity. It is on the basis of comparing such specificities, of making them interact with each other, that we can advance towards a more formal general ontology. In my own terms, the latter would exhibit a linguistic character, though only once the linguistic categories have superseded their regional anchoring. This double dimension is essential to my intellectual project. Many of the distinctions developed by other theoreticians, such as those formulated by Connolly, for example, which you have just mentioned, and which are very valid, can quite justifiably be adopted and reproduced in my approach, but I have to construct them starting from different points of departure.

I would like now to turn to the category of antagonism. One of the key moves in your approach is to connect the construction and experience of antagonism to the question of identity. Antagonisms are constitutive and liminal phenomena in your approach because they prevent the full constitution of the self, and indeed society itself. But in teaching and discussing your work I am often asked about the role of interests in accounting for the construction of antagonistic relations. (On another register, this issue surfaces in the recent debates about the relation between a 'politics of recognition' and a 'politics of redistribution'.) What, if anything, does your approach say to those struggles and conflicts that are organized around specific demands and grievances that are best described in terms of interests? I am thinking here of those situations where workers demand better wages or conditions, or environmental protesters campaign to prevent the building of a road or airport. At times, it is clear that these demands are structured around the dynamics of identity/difference, but in other cases they are often struggles to achieve particular outcomes, and the question of identity is not so evident. Are these instances of conflict and struggle not to be viewed as antagonisms, so that the use of the term antagonism is restricted to those instances where the challenge to the subject's identity is prominent? Do you see a conceptual or even ontological connection between interests and the construction of political identities, or do you see the notion of interests as belonging to a different and opposed paradigm? If the former, how do you conceive of the conceptual relationship between identity and interests?

I think that the whole distinction between recognition and redistribution is based on a misunderstanding. I do not accept it in the least. Behind it there is a very traditional paradigm, which relegates recognition to the cultural sphere and redistribution to the economic field. This is a simple reproduction of the old base/superstructure model. In order to advocate a politics of redistribution one has to assert that some economic demands are just, and that requires the recognition of certain identities that presently are denied. For the same reason, even the most cultural of the demands for recognition involves the redistribution and reconfiguration of symbolic values in a certain society. As for the notion of 'interests' something similar could be said. What is an interest? The demand for the recognition of a right that social agents think is actually negated. It is simply impossible to defend an interest without, at the same time, asserting an identity which is felt to be either negated or, at the very least, jeopardized by the existing *status quo*. And this vulnerability of certain demands both creates interests to be defended and requires the recognition of the identities constituted around them. Even in classical socialist discourses, the process of the so-called 'conscientization' of certain social actors, involved both the perception of an interest and the construction of an identity sustaining it. With this I am not saying that the construction of interests has no differential features in the various social spheres. But these differences do not affect the basic components of the interests/identities complex, and do not have anything whatsoever to do with the constitutive role of antagonism in the structuration of the social field.

The category of hegemony has been a central device for linking together the different elements and concepts of your approach. Yet there are different formulations and emphases in your writings in this regard. In Hegemony and Socialist Strategy, *hegemony is a type of practice that links together different demands and identities in the construction of hegemonic projects. This articulatory practice in turn presupposes the incomplete and open character of the social, coupled with the presence of antagonistic forces and the instability of the frontiers which separate them. In this view, it is only the presence of a vast area of floating elements and the possibility of their articulation into opposed formations that makes a hegemonic practice possible. Without equivalence and without frontiers, it is impossible to speak strictly of hegemony. In your more recent writings, the notion of hegemony is closely connected to the functioning of empty signifiers. In* On Populist Reason, *for instance, hegemony is described as an operation in which 'one difference ... assumes the representation of an incommensurable totality', so that in the consequent interplay between universality and particularity, where the embodied totality is an impossible object, the hegemonic identity assumes the form of an empty signifier.*

A series of questions thus arise. Have you modified your thoughts about the concept of hegemony over the years? Is there a basic concept with different variations, or are there different concepts of hegemony at play? Another set of questions emerges from a certain degree of scepticism amongst some political theorists about the very category of hegemony itself. Some poststructuralists equate the term with simple domination and the erasure of pluralism, whilst others have begun to speak about the notion of 'post-hegemony'. Do you think that the category of hegemony is still crucial for interpreting, explaining and transforming our increasingly heterogeneous and globalized world? Are hegemonic struggles restricted to the terrain of the 'nation-state', which is no longer as central as it once was? Do arguments for the importance of radical pluralism and the respect for difference problematize the very idea of hegemony? Does the category of hegemony have a critical import in your work?

Let us carefully consider your various questions. Concerning the one referring to the possible continuities or discontinuities in my treatment of 'hegemony', my answer is that I do not see any major discontinuity – at most there is only an emphasis of different dimensions of the same category. In *Hegemony and Socialist Strategy* we wanted to stress the essentially articulatory nature of the unity existing between elements composing a social formation. Thus hegemony had to be presented as a contingent bringing together of those elements, as against various essentialist readings of their type of unification. That left open, however, the question of the forms of crystallization of such a unity, and it is there where the notion of an 'empty signifier', which I have explored in my later work, emerges. But both are just phases of a single research.

As for the scepticism of some readers, I think it is grounded in some basic misunderstandings. Anybody who has read my work carefully – and, indeed, that of Gramsci – knows that hegemony cannot be equated with domination, for the simple reason that the consensual dimension (which is presupposed by the notion of a democratic equivalence) is an essential component of the hegemonic operation. What, actually, is pluralism? If the term refers to struggles that are unconnected with each other, and thus reduced to some kind of monadic existence, my answer is that such a conception of pluralism leads to a sterile isolationism which condemns social struggles to impotence. There would be nothing democratic in such a corporative closure. If, on the contrary, pluralism means the attempt to avoid the subordination of concrete social agents to the *diktats* of a rigid centre, my answer is that because such a centre is an empty signifier its only identity is the one given to it by the interaction of a plurality of demands within a signifying chain – an interaction which is in a constant process of flux. Any hegemonic stabilization is thus the achievement of a plural interaction, and not something that irradiates from an *a priori* and given centre of power. This confronts us with two dangers which could lead to the death of politics: one is the transformation of equivalence into identity, which would do away with the concrete plurality of social struggles; the other is to transform such a plurality into a corporative isolation, which is incapable of agglutinating social struggles around the prosecution of broader popular aims. It is for this reason that the notion of 'post-hegemony', from a democratic viewpoint, does not cut any ice for me.

Coming to the question of heterogeneity, I think that it is precisely the increasing heterogeneous character of our globalized world that gives greater centrality to hegemonic practices. You must have in mind that 'hegemony' is not a regional category, but one referring to what we could call the general field of a social ontology. Hegemony means the practice of contingent articulation, in which neither the articulated elements, nor the articulating force, have necessary links, which would precede their relations within a hegemonic configuration. In other words, there is no aprioristic foundation operating as a *fundamentum inconcussum*, as a *natura naturans* against which the surface of the social world would be reduced to a *natura naturata*. So once we reach full visibility of this radical contingency, essentialist social ontologies collapse, and the cluster of concepts linked to the hegemonic paradigm extend their area of validity. That applies, of course to the international arena to which you referred. I am not among those who sustain that the national state is totally obsolete as a framework of political action. It retains a partial validity, but it is also true that its past centrality has been eroded in many respects. Relations of equivalence, relations of difference and the constitution of hegemonic centres increasingly take place across national frontiers. The development of new technologies and the new forms of communication associated with them are creating networks which go far beyond the traditional frontiers of politics.

One powerful feature of your approach is the emphasis you place on the primacy of politics, or what some refer to as 'the political'. This follows from the centrality you attribute to radical contingency and the role of antagonisms, which disclose the undecidable character of any identity or social relation. Because of this, as you put it in New Reflections, *any social relation 'can be radically transformed through struggle', and you draw on Edmund Husserl to capture the way in which politics involves reactivating the contingent foundations of a sedimented practice or relation, thus enabling political subjects to decide and act anew. But how precisely should we understand this primacy? If the Marxist tradition has stressed the determining role of the economy and the relations of production, does your approach attribute a determining role to political practices? Is this determining role to be understood in causal terms? And if it is, how do you factor in the role of economic logics and practices in the articulation of critical explanations?*

I think we have to distinguish between a conception of social totality grounded in discriminating levels of social totality – e.g. the political, the economic and the ideological, as in Althusserian Marxism – and one which privileges, as mine does, the political logic as constitutive of the social. Here there is no question of a regional level having priority over the others, and, as a result, the question of causality does not even arise. The economic 'level' – as envisaged in classical Marxism – is a terrain as structured by political logics as any other level of society,

A further set of issues in this regard concerns the scope and specificity of the political in your work. It is clear that your approach expands the political beyond the state, as well as the usual liberal divisions between the public or political and the private spheres; it also questions the idea of prioritizing notions like justice or rights as the ground of politics. But where and how does your approach draw the line between the political and the social or the cultural? Do all struggles and contestations qualify as political? Is the political exhausted by the friend/enemy opposition, or are there other criteria that supplement your stress on the construction and mediation of social antagonisms? Finding inspiration in Arendt, for instance, does politics involve a peculiarly public dimension? Should it not involve the activity of publicly contesting the norms of a practice or regime in the name of alternative principles or ideals?

Let us not mix different issues in this regard. Because the notion of antagonism is ontologically primary for me, it is previous to distinctions between the public and the private, as you find for example in Arendt's work. The social – which for me is a partial crystallization of the political – emerges when a hegemonic configuration achieves a certain stability. For that reason, it is not a question of differentiating the political from the social – even less from the cultural, which is a merely regional category – except in terms of discriminating between degrees of sedimentation, which do not put into question the ontological priority of the political.

A significant continuity in your writings is the topic of populism. One reason for this (I presume) is your long-standing experience and engagement with Latin American politics. But the theme of populism assumes a much more ontological, rather than merely ontical, focus in your approach. Indeed, in On Populist Reason, *you elaborate a theory of populism that shares important features with your overall theory of politics. This account has attracted some criticisms, though in my view they are mostly wide of the mark because they fail to note the ontological character of your intervention.*

Yet there are some questions that I would like to ask. First, as you have noted, the act of naming is important in constituting an object, even if in this case it is a theoretical object of inquiry, with a reasonably clear conceptual form that can encompass various instances. But is there a difficulty that the connotative articulations evoked by this name are likely to cause consternation amongst theorists and citizens who associate populism with a particular set of practices and forces: ideological simplification, anti-liberalism, authoritarianism, emotivism, leadership cults and so forth? The tactical question in this regard is whether or not an alternative name – 'popular democratic politics' or 'equivalential politics' or just political practices as such – would better capture the logics and processes to which your approach refers, without evoking or implying the negative associations that commonsensical usages of the terms 'populism' and 'populist' suggest? Secondly, your approach to populism stresses the importance of linking together a number of demands in a range of sites to constitute an equivalential chain against a common enemy. Yet there is no mention of the salience or intensity of each demand, and how this dimension must be factored in. Are each of the demands formally and substantially equivalent to one another, or are some more important than others?

A third issue that arises from your theory of populism concerns the relationship between the horizontal and vertical axes of your model. A virtue of your account is that the vertical relationship that connects heterogeneous social demands to a singular signifier and leader in a populist movement or force is always supplemented by a series of horizontal linkages between demands. Both elements must be in some sort of equilibrium. However, the danger of populism for some commentators is the overshadowing of the horizontal by the vertical: populism always runs the risk of a purely vertical connection between the leader and the people at the expense of the overdetermined relations between demands that have been constituted in the various spaces of the state and civil society. A democratic populism, therefore, cannot sacrifice the carefully constructed equivalences between identities and subjectivities on the altar of a leadership cult or a transcendental signifier that promises the end of history. If it does so, then it risks the strong possibility of an 'authoritarian populism'. How would you respond to such views? Does a democratic populism require certain institutional forms and constraints?

Yes, as far as your first point is concerned, I also feel that a few of the criticisms that my views on populism have received are to do with the fact that those critics had a particular referent in mind when thinking about populism and have not paid enough attention to the enlargement of the category that I was proposing. It is clear that if you identify populism with demagogy, manipulation of the popular will by a cynical leadership, irresponsible political practices and so forth, any defence of populism would look scandalous. I would respond by saying two things. First, that by populism I do not understand those referential contents but, rather, a way of constructing the political on the basis of interpellating the underdog to mobilize against the existing *status quo*. This can be done from the most diverse ideologies and involves, as a result, a far wider ensemble of differences. Secondly, that behind the discourse of my critics there is also, very often, a discursive strategy of enlargement of the notion, but of an opposite sign. It consists in firmly sticking to the primary negative reference – demagogy, manipulations and so on – but then extending it non-critically to completely different sorts of political movements and practices as a way of disqualifying them. This has, for instance, been a frequent strategy to disqualify the national-popular regimes which have emerged in Latin America over the last decade and a half. So for me it was a matter of fighting the anti-populist crusade on its own terrain. To do this, one had to do what the Christians did with the Cross: to transform a symbol of ignominy into a positive value. We have won some important victories in this confrontation.

As for your second point, it is clear that if all the demands were at the same level, without differences of saliency or intensity between them, it would also be impossible to have any overdetermination between them. As a result there would be no generation of empty signifiers and, *ergo*, no populism. The unevenness between what you call the saliency or intensity between demands is the very condition of the structuration of a politico-hegemonic field. A different question is the one concerning what determines this difference in centrality, that is, its overdetermined centrality. It is obvious that it is not the case that some demands, considered in isolation, have inscribed in their internal structure, a hegemonic centrality given to them by some sort of manifest destiny. It is only the interaction between those demands in a politico-discursive field that will be the source of those overdetermining effects. And here there are no *a priori* rules establishing a differential saliency. Only a contextual analysis can determine that.

Concerning the horizontal and vertical axes I would invert the roles attributed to them by you in your initial formulation. It is not that the vertical axis has to be supplemented by the horizontal one. What happens is that without the horizontal axis there would be no vertical axis either. It is because the equivalential/horizontal axis is already there that the need emerges of signifying it as a totality. The answer to that need is the production of empty signifiers, that is, the constitution of the vertical axis. But this second axis is strictly functional to the presence of the first: without equivalential chains needing some global representation there would be no social logic giving the rationale for the emergence of a leadership. Let us think, *reductio ad absurdum*: What kind of society would exist in which there was only a vertical axis? It would be an entirely authoritarian one in which, given the absence of any equivalence between democratic demands, there could not be any 'emptying' practices leading to the constitution of hegemonic signifiers. No centre would be overdetermined; instead we would be faced with a situation in which the ontic, concrete content of the central element would establish pure relations of domination with atomized, monadic subjects. Even Hobbes' Leviathan has to accept an equivalential/horizontal moment in the contract between wills from which the Commonwealth emerges. This consensual element, although minimal, is present there and is what makes it possible to distinguish the Hobbesian Leviathan from what would otherwise be naked despotism. A hegemonic practice extends the field of operation of this equivalential/consensual axis, which Hobbes reduced to a single, originary act.

That the relation between the two axes is one of tension is something that I fully accept. But that tension belongs to the way society is structured and is not the result of any logical difficulties inherent in my theory. It is true that the privileging of the vertical axis beyond a certain point leads to authoritarian politics – let us just think of Mugabe's Zimbabwe – but when this happens we can no longer speak of populism. The horizontal axis has been destroyed and it can no longer operate as the source of political legitimacy of a political regime – which, consequently, ceases to be democratic at all. But it is important to stress that a total elimination of the vertical axis, as postulated by some ultra-libertarian currents, is not a democratic alternative either. Isolated demands, left to themselves, do not tend to coalesce by themselves in some kind of spontaneous miracle or *coincidentia oppositorum* but, most likely, would disperse themselves in a variety of directions – not necessarily all of them of a progressive nature. And this could easily lead to the implosion of the equivalential chain and the disintegration of the democratic camp. So democracy can only be constructed within the balance/tension constituted by the joint operation of the two axes. The different language games that this tension inaugurates and makes possible is exactly what we call politics. The institutional forms that will make possible the agonistic exchanges within that tension will vary from society to society and no blueprint of an ideal democratic society can be given. To give you just another example from the African context: while the Mugabe experience led to the collapse of populism into authoritarianism, the regime of Nyerere in Tanzania led to a democratic balance between the two axes we were speaking about.

My last question touched upon the relationship between populism and radical democracy, as well as the relationship between universality and particularity. Perhaps you can say a little more about this important topic. In Hegemony and Socialist Strategy, *you and Chantal Mouffe problematize discourses of universalism because they are incompatible with radical and plural democracy. But in your later writings, the notion of universality is not rejected in the name of democratic pluralism and diversity. Instead, we see a dialectical play between universality and particularity, as every hegemonic project – every set of equivalences – necessarily seeks to universalize its discourse by constructing an empty signifier in the struggle to 'occupy the empty place of power', if not necessarily to 'identify with it'.*

In On Populist Reason *you go further to flesh out the relationship between democracy and populism by drawing a strong link between the two, in which 'democracy is grounded only on the existence of a democratic subject, whose emergence depends on the horizontal articulation between equivalential demands' (p. 171). One implication of this view is that the articulation between democracy and liberalism is contingent; another stresses an inner connection between democracy and popular subjectivity. An important consequence of this reformulation is the distancing of democracy from any one set of institutional forms or practices, as the populist logic transcends and then underpins any particular organizational configuration. Do you need to say more about the composition of these other institutional forms? If not, does your approach run the risk of an institutional deficit?*

On the question of the relationship between liberalism and democracy, I have to go back to something that I have said several times: that relation is merely contingent and it is a vain attempt to try to universalize the kind of link between liberalism and democracy based on the experience of Europe and the Anglo-Saxon world. C.B. Macpherson, in one of his essays, pointed to the existence of many kinds of democratic arrangements, the liberal-democratic one of the West being only one of them. At the beginning of the nineteenth century, in Western Europe, liberalism was a highly respected form of political organization, while democracy had a pejorative connotation – as populism does today – because it was associated with mob rule. It took a long time to reach some kind of integration between the two in Europe, an integration that has always been precarious anyway. But in other latitudes that integration has been even less solid. In Latin America, for instance, liberal states became dominant from the second half of the nineteenth century, but they were never really democratic, for they were the typical political expressions of local landowning oligarchies based on clientelistic mechanisms. So the democratic aspirations of the masses, when they emerged in the twentieth century, tended to express themselves through non-liberal forms: the support of popular leaders who represented a counterbalance to a parliamentary power that was the stronghold of conservative oligarchies. These new popular expressions required the reinforcement of the executive at the expenses of the legislative power, that is to say, the agglutination of democratic demands around a populist pole. Today, in Latin America, national-popular regimes do not put into question liberal form as such – elections, division of powers, etc. – but they are strongly presidentially oriented regimes, in which mass mobilization is a constant condition of democratic advances. In the Middle East, whatever the democratic institutional settlements that emerge from the Arab Spring, we already know that they are going to be rather different from the liberal democracies of the West. Democratic institutional settlements do not follow a unique pattern, so that if somebody says that this shows that there is an institutional deficit in my theory, my answer is: I am very proud of it.

This leads me to the question of universality. My approach should be distinguished, in this respect, from two opposing views. One is the strong universalism of, for instance, the Habermasians, for whom the universal has a content of its own, determinable in a direct act of conceptual apprehension. The other is the extreme particularism to be found, among others, in some forms of multiculturalism. For me, the dimension of universality cannot be eradicated, but it will be the universality corresponding to the logic of tendentially empty signifiers. As against a strictly universalistic approach, we sustain that the universal has no content of its own, but that it always emerges from a certain particularity which transforms its own body into a medium capable of expressing something transcending it. And against a strict particularism, we sustain that there is no particularity which is not overdetermined – i.e. that there is not something such as a pure particularity – for the relational context of that particularity enters into the constitution of its own identity. This convergent movement from universality to particularity and from particularity to universality means that the universal dimension cannot be eliminated, but that its status will always be that of a hegemonic universality, never one of a fully fledged identity.

There have been two striking developments in political theory since you began your work. First, there was the publication of A Theory of Justice *in 1971, which in some quarters signalled the rebirth of normative political philosophy, and provoked a host of critical responses, such as communitarianism, libertarianism, republicanism and so forth. Secondly, there arose a range of voices that challenged behaviouralist and positivist models of (mainly American) political science, whether in the name of interpretivism, hermeneutics, social constructivism, feminism, postmodernism or critical theory. Of course, this characterization is rather parochial, because it largely reflects developments in the Anglo-American traditions. In the European context, by contrast, there were other developments – different varieties of Marxism, phenomenology, structuralism, Critical Theory, deconstruction, poststructuralism and other tendencies – which tended to problematize and transcend traditional Anglo-American disciplinary boundaries.*

Nonetheless, it is striking that your work does not overtly engage with these trends in Anglo-American political theory. It is not much concerned with strictly normative issues and theory, nor is it obsessed with questions of method and epistemology, which is characteristic of much debate in contemporary political science. How do you react to these observations? Would you agree that your work is much more concerned with ontological questions, rather than epistemological and methodological matters? How would you respond to the claim that your work suffers from what some have labelled normative and methodological deficits, and that more attention ought to have been directed at the justification of your putative explanations and normative alternatives? Would you say that there is a model – or different models – of critical explanation at play in your work? Do you feel at all inclined to engage with the debates and discussions surrounding the so-called perestroika movement in political science, which has advocated more qualitative and interpretive styles of thinking and research?

It is true that I have worked far more within the Continental tradition of political reflection than in connection with the Anglo-Saxon one. The issues raised by an author like John Rawls are quite alien to my way of addressing the political. I have drawn a great deal on Wittgenstein and I have been very interested in the debate between descriptivists and anti-descriptivists concerning naming, but these are issues concerning general philosophy which led me to explore their possible projections for political analysis, rather than influences coming from the specific terrain of political philosophy.

As for the question concerning epistemology and methodology, I can tell you the following. Before Kant, ontological and epistemological questions belonged to two entirely different disciplines. Ontology studied the structure of reality; epistemology, the ways of knowing it. But Kant's transcendental turn blurred the separation between them, for the subjective ingredient of knowledge was no longer external to the object to be known but plays an essential and active role in its constitution. Everything that has happened in philosophy after Kant has reinforced this tendency. The social construction of reality is incompatible with a strict separation between ontology and epistemology. I think that the era of normative epistemology is definitely over. Something similar can be said about methodology. I am as much allergic to general methodologies as is Feyerabend. Of course there are rules that you have to follow when engaging in particular fields of research. If you are making a statistical study, for instance, you have to accept particular rules dictated by the structural properties of numerical series. But I think it is a dangerous illusion to think that the ensemble of these rules converges in constituting a unified whole called 'methodology'. The social scientist is an underworker who should not expect that an infallible method should orient decisions which should be actually dictated by his intuition or his common sense.

One important characteristic of your work is your willingness to engage publicly with a wide range of different thinkers and theorists. Some of these dialogues are reproduced in this volume. Yet it is striking how some of your interlocutors have lacked a sense of agonistic respect in these exchanges. I am thinking here of Norman Geras's various rants about Hegemony and Socialist Strategy, *or Slavoj Žižek's increasingly hostile reactions to some aspects of your work. This is not to mention the more generalized hostility one encounters from many positivist or behavioural political scientists about any research that dares to be theoretical and critical. Why do you think this is? Do you think this says anything more general about the culture of academic debate today, especially amongst the Left? Do you think it is worthwhile to continue to try and engage with currents that appear increasingly closed and dismissive?*

One always has to select not only one's own friends but also one's own adversaries. In each historical period there is a plurality of intellectual paradigms and it would be a mistake to enclose oneself in one's own approach without confronting it with what is taking place in alternative currents of thought. One can only enrich one's own approach through an agonistic confrontation. Of course, such an openness has its limits. There are some approaches which are so alien that one knows beforehand that nothing profitable would come from a dialogue with them. For instance, I would never dream of intellectually interacting with the behaviouralist tradition, and I don't think they would be interested in interacting with me in a scholarly way either. As Lacan said on a famous occasion, 'I do not need too many people and there are some people that I do not need at all'. But apart from these extreme cases, there are many currents in contemporary thought with whom interaction is for me not only profitable but also necessary. As for the case of Žižek, which you mention, it is a rather special one. He was my friend for many years and we had many interests in common. We had, however, also intellectual disagreements right from the beginning. His discourse was based in an assimilation of Hegel to Lacan that I always thought was utterly mistaken. Hegel and Lacan are not only not saying the same thing, but they are saying exactly the opposite. For Hegel, there is, through dialectical mediation, a universal medium of representation; while what is central in Lacan's approach is the notion of the 'Real', that is, something that radically interrupts any process of representation. Those disagreements, however, would have been no reason to put an end to our friendship, if they had not been accompanied by an increasing political chasm between us. Žižek went through a process of political involution, as his discourse was progressively dominated by a frantic ultra-Leftist stance, wrapped in a Leninism of kindergarten, so that in the end any communication with him was impossible. To summarize, David, I want to say that I do not feel isolated in the least. I have received many expressions of intellectual appreciation from colleagues from many different quarters, and I feel myself as part of a huge political and academic community which, with many nuances and differences, is working together in the struggle for social progress and political emancipation.

INDEX

abandonment of ideology 76, 233–4
Abgrund 258
abolition of duality 51–2
absent fullness 12, 14, 48, 71, 80–82, 84–6
absent rationality 92
absent totality 71
"absolute" enemies 223–30
absolute metaphors 107
absolute power 44
Absolute Spirit 184
absolute value 228
the Absolute 89
absolutism of hostility 229
absolutization 226
abstract universality 59
abstraction 113
acoustic images 24
act of opposition 69
actuality 31, 240
actualization 67
administration 227–9
Adorno, Theodor W. 38, 246
adventurism 38
affective nature 103
affectivity of forces 71
affirmation of values 82
Agamben, Giorgio 231–41
agent/structure alternative 45–65; constitution of social imaginaries 48; constitutive metaphor 46–8; subject as myth 46; surfaces of inscription 48

agonism 192
agrarian underdevelopment 119
Alessandri, Arturo 139
Alfonzo Lopez 139
alienation 40, 51–2, 77, 79, 126, 176
allegory 86
alternative vocabularies 244
Althusser, Louis 1, 3, 6–9, 77–9, 153, 184, 257, 264
Alvear, Carlos de 142
Amaru, Tupac 128
ambiguity 49, 66, 70–72, 90, 93, 126, 154, 207, 233, 239
anachronism 201
analogical ambiguity 126–7
analysing populism 109–196; constructing a people 165–95; definition of populism 152–64; towards theory of populism 111–51
analytical philosophy 2
ancien régime 40, 157
A–not A 98, 104, 179, 181, 185–6, 252
anomaly 229
antagonisms 52–4, 61–3, 67, 97–9, 101, 103–5, 122–6, 133–4, 141, 144–9, 159–62, 166–8, 177–9, 184–6, 192, 228, 250
antagonistic confrontation 180, 238
anthropological exodus 219–21
anti-community 101
anti-descriptivism 102
anti-establishment protest 61, 73
anti-fascism 82

anti-foundationalism 242–4
anti-hegemonic orientation 106
anti-imperialism 142–3
anti-institutionalism 116, 156, 162
anti-intellectualism 114
anti-liberal ideology 139–40, 144, 149
anti-political effect 235
anti-space 52
anti-state ideology 130
anti-system mobilization 106
apocalypse 55–7, 59–60, 62, 64
aporia 98
appropriation 34
Apter, David 111
Arab Spring 269
arbitrary arrest 3, 85, 88, 94
archaeology 27, 29
Arendt, Hannah 237, 265
argumentative discourse analysis 4
Aristotle 31, 53, 81, 91, 126
articulation 6, 16–17, 34–7, 63, 85, 96, 105, 124–5, 147–50, 155, 161, 190, 218, 233
articulatory practice 5
associative language 103
asymmetry 62, 164, 216
asynchronism 114–15, 117–21
Auschwitz 256
Austro-Marxism 210
autarchy 45
authoritarianism 8, 116, 139–40, 142, 266
automatic rules of inscription 240
autonomization 203
autonomous organization 118
autonomy 7, 38, 42, 153, 159–60, 180, 203–4, 218–19
availability 50

backwardness 137
Bacon, Francis 214
Badiou, Alain 6, 128–30, 148, 177, 260
Balibar, Étienne 3, 184
Balmès, François 128–30, 148
barbarianism 219, 245
Barbosa, Ruy 139, 145
bare life 231–41
Barthes, Roland 3, 25–6, 75–6
base–superstructure of social relations 7, 63
Bataille, Georges 187
Batlle y Odorñez 139
Bauer, Bruno 176
bearer of negation 158
beautiful fabula 217
being-against 219–20

belief 75
Benjamin, Walter 211
Benjamin's angel 211
Benveniste, Jacques 5
Bernstein, Eduard 210
between requests and claims 171–4
beyond all differences 71
bios 232, 236, 238
Bismarck, Prince Otto von 33, 123
Bloom, Harold 244
Blumenberg, Hans 57, 107
B-ness of B 179, 185–6; *see also* A–not A
Böhm-Bawerk, Eugen von 175
bolshevism 90
bolshevization 106
Bonapartism 149
Bortkiewicz, Ladislaus 175
bourgeois revolution 33
bourgeoisie 33–5, 112, 125, 188, 254
bricoleurs 209
Bryan, William Jennings 112
bureaucratization 40, 42
buyer of labour power 104–5

cancellation of determinations 60
Canovan, Margaret 15
Canudos 193–4
Capital 168, 260
capitalism 8, 30–65, 116, 172, 174–9, 188–9, 239, 254; opposition to 174–6
capitalist accumulation 42–3
capitalist asceticism 115–16
capitalist expansion 137
caput mortuum 181–2
Carolingian Renaissance 215
Carolus Bovillus 214
Carroll, Lewis 252
Cartesian assertion 24, 64
catachresis 100, 169–70, 186
category of articulation 153
caudillo 132, 139
Cavalca, Ernesto 232
Ceaușescu, Nicolae 58
change 31
chaos 54, 144
chaotic enumeration 116
Chartism 167
Chiang Kai-Shek 128
chiliastic world 57
Chouliaraki, Lillie 4
Christian polarity 203
Cicero 99–100
circulation of signifiers 161
civic republicanism 254

civil war 228
civilization 137
class alliances 188, 218
class analysis 113
class consciousness 122–3, 126
class essentialism 38
class ideology 118
class reductionism 8, 139–40, 150
class struggle 9, 38, 97, 104, 107, 125–7, 147, 165–71, 228
Class Struggles in France 33
Classical Age 27
classical antiquity 55
classical structuralism 25
classism 106
classless society 163
Clausewitz, Karl Marie von 225–6, 228
clientelism 132
closure 78–80, 86, 93–4, 100, 107
coercion 6
coherence 160
coincidentia oppositorum 218, 267
collapse of objectivity 46
collective bargaining 44
collective identification 234
collective will 38, 62, 107, 154, 164, 189, 210, 220
collision 37
Comintern 106, 119
commodification 38–9, 42, 51, 201
communism 106, 129–30, 152, 159, 161, 202
communist constants 130
Communist Manifesto 34, 96, 176
communitarian fullness 71–2, 154, 163
communitarian order 54
community paradoxes 242–56
concealment 79
concentration camps 237, 239–41, 256
Concept of the Political 223
conception of history 96, 181
conception of progress 48
conception of the world 136
conceptual mediation 101–2
conceptual substance 24
conceptual subsumption 101–2
concretization 167
condemnation to be free 32
conditions of possibility 23
conscientization 262
constitution of social imaginaries 48–9, 64
constitutive antagonism 97–100
constitutive asymmetry 16
constitutive dislocation 31, 78

constitutive distortion 93
constitutive exclusion 169
constitutive lack 69
constitutive metaphor 46–8, 51
constitutive openness 208
constructing a people 165–95; class struggle 165–71; criticisms 189–91; demands 171–4; dialectics 181–7; genealogy 187–9; heterogeneity 174–87; social practices 174–81; ultraleftist liquidation of political 191–4
consummation 52
consumption 120
contamination of closure 78
contemporary theorization 107
contextualization 85
contingency 2, 5–6, 16, 28, 45, 53, 59–60, 90, 190, 243–4, 255–6
Contingency, Hegemony, Universality 11
Contingency, Irony, and Solidarity 242
contingency of language 243
contingent articulation 34, 105
contingent construction 187
continuum of features 120
contradictio in adjecto 78
contradiction 34, 42, 97, 122–7, 131, 145, 177, 189
control of monopoly capital 146
Copernicus, Nicolas 199
Copjec, Joan 14, 103, 169, 259
corporatist classes 49, 106, 239
corrosion 137
corruption 55, 57–8, 62, 90
coterminousness 169
counter-society 62
crass opportunism 128
creation ex nihilio 170
crisis of Marxism 89, 96
crisis of transformism 134–5, 146
Critchley, Simon 202–3
critical engagements 197–272; bare life/social indeterminacy 231–41; immanence and social struggle 213–22; interview with Laclau 257–71; paradox of community 242–56; "real" and "absolute" enemies 223–30; "time out of joint" 199–212
Critical Inquiry 190
criticisms of ideology 189–91
critique of ideology 77
Critique of Political Economy 96, 176–7
Croce, Benedetto 89, 92
crystallization of Jacobin inflexion 134
Cultural Revolution 162

cunning of Reason 97, 215
cyberpunk 219–20

Darwin, Charles 199
Davidson, Donald 3, 243–5, 248, 251
De Divisione Naturae 215
De Gaulle, Charles 229
de Man, Paul 75–6
de Tocqueville, Alexis Charles 40
de-divinization of self 244
death of the subject 25
death of theory of ideology 75–95
debate on poststructuralism 2–3
decadence 90
deceit 84, 119
deconstruction 26, 199–212; logic of the specter 200–204; question of the messianic 204–9; question of tradition 209–211
decontextualization 85
definition of populism 152–65; empty/floating signifiers 156–60; representation 160–64; social demands/social totality 153–6
deformation 80–81, 89, 94
degrounding 208–9
dehumanization 176
Deleuze, Gilles 213, 219, 259
Delia Volpian School 97
deliberative behaviour 115
delimited positivity 6
delirium 193
della Mirandola, Pico 214
demagogy 119, 190
demands 154, 171–4, 221
democracy 73–4, 136, 143, 202, 209; and hegemony 73–4
democratic interaction 17
democratic revolution 30–65; agent/structure alternative 45–64
democratic subject 156
démocratie à venir 205–6
demonstration effect 115, 119–20
demos 163
derivative analysis 114, 209
derivative antagonism 97–8
Derrida, Jacques 1, 3, 5, 8, 26, 199–212, 251, 253, 256–7, 259
descriptivism 102
destructuration 47
determinate social formation 125–6, 135
determination in the last instance 103, 178, 185–6
determinative judgement 101–3

deus absconditus 86
Deus sine Natura 31–2
deviance 10–11
Di Tella, Torcuato 114, 117–18
diachrony 30, 37, 55–6, 59, 64, 231
Dialectic of Enlightenment 246
dialectics 80, 98, 167, 181–7
dichotomic construction 156
dichotomies 76
dictatorship 8, 59, 63
différance 211
differential limits 158
differential logic 229–30
differential universe 24, 170
differentiated particularity 91, 218
diktats 42, 263
disarticulation 9, 122, 142, 1443
discourse 1–20, 23–9; theories of 24–7; theory and politics 27–9
discourse analysis 1, 4
discursive chains 82
discursive formations 10, 26–7, 49, 55, 59–61, 187–8
disintegration 251
dislocation 30–65, 79, 201–2, 258
dislocatory junctures 34
disobedience 228
disorganized capitalism 43, 51, 62
displacement of political frontiers 14–15
Disraeli, Benjamin 155, 159
disruption 213–14
dissolutio civitatis 232–3
dissolution of imaginary 49, 76, 216
distance 70
distortion 77–9, 117, 168
divine omnipotence 215
division of labour 42
doctrine 75
domination-free communication 247, 255
double articulation 128
duality of space 49, 60–62, 92
Ducrot, Oswald 76

eclipse of God 60
economic determinism 8
economization of politics 180
effectiveness of myth 46
egalitarianism 130
eidetic purity 55
eidos 58, 62
elimination of frontiers 159
elitism 139–40
emancipation 60, 63–4, 80, 206–7, 211–12, 271

Emancipation(s) 11, 257
embodiment 61–2, 64
emergence of populism 134
Empecinado 226
Empire 213–22
empirical circumstantial fault 53
empirical determinations 185–6
empiricity 59
empowerment 239
emptiness 190
empty form of universality 180
empty place of power 16
empty signifiers 11–13, 66–74, 82, 84–5, 87–8, 93, 99–103, 156–61, 263; democracy 73–4; and floating 156–60; hegemony 69–73
end of history 64, 105, 207
end of politics 163, 216
Endziel 210
"enemy within" 10
Engels, Friedrich 33–4, 128–9, 176
enigma of populism 126
Enlightenment 48, 58, 64, 244–5, 247, 255
énoncé 27
ens creatum 45–6, 57, 86
enumeration 81, 86–8, 116
episteme 27
equivalence 71, 80–82, 156, 158, 172, 220, 227, 264
equivalential aggregation 156
equivalential chain 155–62
equivalential enumeration 81, 93–4, 100, 156, 162
equivalential logic 161–2, 265
equivocal ambiguity 126–7
equivocation 66
Erigena, Scotus 215
eschatological identity 56–7, 60, 203, 210
essence 2
essential distortion 100
essential symmetry of development 75
essentialism 3–4, 38
eternal ideology 77, 103
ethical injunction 208
ethical socialism 210
European Union 45
Europeanization 140–41
exceptionality 188, 236
excess 215
exclusion 67–8
exclusionary limits 67
existence of class 123–4
existential phenomenology 3, 32, 210
exodus 219–21

exploitation 89–90, 121–2, 176–7, 186, 220–21
expressing the inexpressible 87–8
extension 158
exteriority 192, 221, 234
external necessity 37
extra-discursive reality 76
extroversion 88
extrovertive mysticism 88

facile teleology 58
facticity of strata 64
failed objects 48
Fairclough, Norman 4
false consciousness 107, 126, 169, 210
false representation 76–7
family resemblances 252–3
Fanon, Frantz 234
fascism 8, 82, 90, 118–19, 134, 139, 149, 152, 159, 161, 166–7, 170
Fatherland 167
favelas 193–4
federalism 138
feminism 250
feudal particularism 123
Feyerabend, Paul 270
fiat of power 45
field of discursivity 5
field of objectivity 46
Fifth Republic 229
figural language 99–100
final showdown of history 105
First World 44
First World War 134, 223–4
flexible organizations 44
floating signifiers 10, 13–14, 28, 82, 156–60; *see also* empty signifiers
folklore 132
force of law 205
form of freedom 31
Form of the Good 53
formal populism 16
formalism 25
forms of existence 122–3
Fort/Da game 30
Foucault, Michel 1, 3–4, 23–4, 26–9, 76, 236–7, 246–7, 257
Frankfurt School 3, 39
fraud 142
free world 82
freedom 31–2, 82
French Revolution 33, 40, 227
Freud, Sigmund 1, 26, 30, 103, 167, 169, 199, 244, 257, 261

Fukuyama, Francis 207
fullness 49–51, 55, 59–60, 71–2, 80, 101
fundamental deadlock 207
fundamentum inconcussum 103, 175, 264
fusion effect 115, 119–21
"The Future of Radical Democracy" 17

Gambetta, Léon Michel 225
Gandhi, M.K. 171
Garibaldianism 161
genealogy 28–9, 187–9, 200, 231
generalization 113
Geneva Conventions 224
geographical asynchronism 114–15
Geras, Norman 271
German economic crisis 50, 134
Germani, Gino 114–21
The German Ideology 176
givenness 23
global policemen 191
global totality 35
globalization 85, 172
glossematic school of Copenhagen 24
Gödel's theorem 26
Goulart, João 146
governing change 31
Gramsci, Antonio 1, 3, 6–8, 28, 38, 49, 72, 106–7, 159, 162, 180, 189, 210–211, 216, 221–2, 228–30, 236, 239, 250–51, 257, 263
Great Depression 51
great narratives 58
Greater Hekhaloth 87
ground of things 99, 102
Grundrisse 176

Habermas, Jürgen 2, 77, 83, 246–8, 255, 269
Hague Resolutions 224
Hajer, Maarten 4
Hardt, Michael 213–21
hauntology 200–202
Hegel, Georg Wilhelm Friedrich 28, 34, 40, 51–2, 67, 75, 97–8, 153–4, 169, 174, 177–9, 181–2, 191, 207, 210, 215, 271
Hegelian–Marxist moment 34, 57
hegemonic classes 106, 239
hegemonic force 28
hegemonic logic 202
hegemonic relationships 72
hegemonization 30, 103, 193
hegemony 27–8, 69–73, 191
Hegemony and Socialist Strategy 9, 12, 16, 69, 97, 251, 257–8, 262, 268, 271

Heidegger, Martin 3, 5, 258
Hesse, Mary 244–5
heterogeneity 15, 98, 174–87, 192, 239
heterogeneous anomaly 188–9
heterosexuality 10–11
hierarchy 239
Hilferding, Rudolf 43
historical discourse analysis 4
historical limitation of social agents 62
historical messianisms 206
historical necessity 104
historical positivism 89
historicism 64, 182, 255–6
historicity of being 255–6
Hitler, Adolf 128, 133, 167
Hjelmslev, Louis 5, 24–5
Hobbes, Thomas 54–5, 71–3, 163, 232–3, 235, 267
Hobbesian monarch 54
Holocaust 171
The Holy Family 176
Homo Sacer 231–41
homogenization 170, 181, 187–8, 239
homology 214
homosexuality 10–11
Horkheimer, Max 246
hostility 226–9, 271
Howarth, David 76
humanity 64, 107, 192
Husserl, Edmund 23, 264
hymen terrain 251

Ianni, Octavio 135
ideal of undistorted communication 77
identification 28, 32, 45
identifying the Real 174–5
identity 37–8, 45–7, 67
ideological crisis 142–3
ideological discourse 8–9
ideological misconception 76
ideological state apparatuses 76
ideology of oligarchy 138–9
illusion of closure 86
illusion of immediacy 3, 113
imaginaries' pattern 49
imaginary aggregation 63
immanence 44, 47, 62, 155, 168, 173, 213–22
immanent unity 213
immanentism 214–15
impartial law enforcement 85
imperialist penetration 136, 142, 218
importance of empty signifiers 66–74
imposition 72

impossibility of signification 67, 92
impossible autarchy 45
impossible fullness 80, 101, 172
inanity of unification of historical process 89
incarnation 56–8, 80–81, 86, 89, 167; of omnipotence 56–8
incommensurable totality 100, 263
indeterminacy 60, 62
indetermination 38
indetermination of myth 48
indigenism 132
individualization 161
industrial society 119–20
industrialism 143
inherent negativity 213–14
inscrutability of divine plans 57
institutional asynchronism 114–15
Institutional Revolutionary Party 106
integration 115–16
intelligibility 50, 252
intension 158
inter-regional conflict 145
interested third 226
internal migration 62
International Workers of the World 219
internationalization of capital 44
Interpretation of Dreams 261
interruption 67, 186
intervention 56
interview with Laclau 257–71
intimidation 250
introversion 88
introvertive mysticism 88–9
intuition 160
inversion 172
Irigoyen, Hípolito 139, 142, 145
irradiation effect 102
irrationalism 51, 245
irruption of Real 187
ius publicum europeum 224–7

Jacobinism 124, 130, 134, 137–9, 145, 162
Jakobson, Roman 5, 99, 260
job satisfaction 118
jouissance 259–61

Kant, Immanuel 23, 69, 97–8, 101–2, 175, 185, 210, 236, 270
Kautsky, Karl Johann 218
King, Martin Luther 190
Kingdom of God 62
know-how 53
knowing/being duality 51–2

knowledge 54, 59, 87–8
Kojève, Alexandre 207
Kriegespiel 228
Kripke, Saul 28, 102
Kristeva, Julia 3
Krug's pen 181
Kuhn, Thomas Samuel 251

Lacan, Jacques 1, 5, 8, 14, 26, 28, 68, 99–103, 169, 171, 174–5, 181, 184, 239, 257, 271
The Lacanian Left 259
language games 3, 25, 83, 99
langue de bois 162
large-scale industry 41–3
Lash, Scott 43–4
"leap of faith" 19
Lefort, Claude 16, 41, 189–90
legitimacy 73, 226–30
The Legitimacy of the Modern Age 57
Lenin, Vladimir 38, 125, 188–9, 218, 225–6, 228, 230
Leninism 38, 187–8, 214, 271
levels of development 119, 125–6
Leviathan 163, 232, 267
Levinasian ethics 208
liberal capitalism 44
liberal utopia 242–56
liberalism 75, 131, 136, 138–40, 152, 245–6, 252
liberal–democratic regimes 16, 125, 130–31, 143, 255
liberation 72–3, 85, 161
libidinal investment 259–60
limited transformism 146
limitless representability 58
limits of what is "sayable" 107
lines of flight 14
linguistic identities 67, 231
linguistic turn 2
linguistics of discourse 24
Linksfaschismus 193
liquidation of political 191–4
literality 47
Local Government Act 1988 10–11
logic of articulation 153
logic of populism 12–15
logic of the signifier 26
logic of the specter 200–204
logical resolution 130
logics of difference 155
logics of equivalence 71, 155
Long March 107, 189, 229
Lopez Jordan 136

loup garou 232
Löwy, Michel 36
Lukács, György 52, 168, 210
Lumpenproletariat 178–83, 234; *see also* proletariat
Luxemburg, Rosa 6, 69–70

Macpherson, C.B. 125, 130–31, 137, 268
Madero, Francisco 139
maladjustment 53
malign power 56
manifest destiny 159
manifestation 70
manipulation 119
Mao Tse Tung 25, 107, 111, 124, 128, 133, 148, 189, 225, 229
Maoism 111, 130
March Revolution 129
martial conception 220–21
Marx, Groucho 202
Marx, Karl 33–4, 41, 154, 163, 168, 175–7, 182–3, 200–201, 204, 207, 209–210, 215–16, 227, 235, 260
Marxism 1–3, 6, 8, 28, 33, 37–9, 42, 77, 89–90, 93, 96–107, 148, 177–8, 187–9, 199–200, 202, 209–211, 213–17, 258; crisis of 89, 97
mass communism 129, 131
mass integration 116
mass mobilization 135
mass psychology 161
materialism 97, 260
materiality 158
Maurras, Charles 140
maximalism 83
Mazzinism 161
mechanical teleology 239
mediation 168, 216
Meister Eckhart 88–9
the messianic 204–9
metamorphoses of the people 147
metaphoric redescriptions 244, 247
metaphorization 49
metaphysics 4
Metaphysics 31
metonymical transference 58–9
migrations 219–21
militancy 63, 140
Mill, John Stuart 102
minimalism 83
misrecognition 77–8
misrepresentation 79
Mitrism 138

mobilization 33, 69–70, 72–3, 106, 115–16, 121, 135, 173, 219
mode of articulation 153
models of hegemony 7–12
modern rationalism 57
modernity 17, 27, 214–15, 236–7, 239–40
modernization 120–21
modes of production 125–6
monopoly capital 125, 146
Montonero Rebellion 136–8, 141
moral majority 159
motivational asynchronism 114–15
Mouffe, Chantal 1, 5–10, 16, 25, 27–8, 97, 192, 242, 251, 258, 268
multiplication of dislocation 62
multiplication of regionalisms 134
multiplicity of enemies 229, 239
multitude's immanence 216
Münzer, Thomas 129
Muselmann 237
mutual dependency 93
mutual implication 205
mystical Nothing 86
mysticism 86–9, 92, 215
myth of liberal capitalism 44
myth of origins 52
mythical unity 210

Napoleon III 33, 149, 223
narodnichestvo 111–12
national capitalism 144
National Front 159
National Socialism 50, 144
nationalism 8, 106, 116, 123–4, 128, 142–3, 166–7
nationalization 80
national–popular movement 116
natura naturans 123, 187, 264
natura naturata 123, 264
naturalism 93
Nazism 50, 111, 128, 133–4, 149, 170–71
necessary embodiment 63
necessary laws of history 106, 122–3, 210
necessary misrecognition 78
negativity 68, 170, 183–4, 213–14
Negri, Antonio 213–21
neo-Gramscian theory 3, 14
neutralization 133, 149
New Deal 159
New International 207
new order discourse 50
New Reflections on the Revolution of Our Time 11, 264
Nicholas of Cusa 214–15

Nietzsche, Friedrich Wilhelm 4, 213, 215, 244
nihilism 113–14, 170, 208, 241
nomadism 219–20
nomos 239–40
non-being 57, 90
non-class contents 124–5, 127
non-dislocation 57
non-equalitarianism 71
non-liberal oligarchic ideologies 139–40
non-place of dislocation 47
nonissue of relativism 245
nostalgia 63
notion of discourse 23–9; *see also* discourse
noumenon 98
Novo, Estado 145

objective society 51
objectivity 45–8, 51–2, 54, 93, 106
objet a 169, 187, 239, 259
object petit a 14, 259
obliqueness 100
obscurantism 137
obvious assimilation 203
Occam *see* William of Ockham
oikos 236
oligarchic hegemony 138, 140–43, 146
oligarchy 120, 136, 138–9, 269
omnipotence 56–8, 215
On Populist Reason 11–12, 16, 102, 165, 169–70, 172, 176, 257, 259, 263, 265, 268
"one nation" 155, 159
ontology 200–203, 207–211, 220, 259–60
opportunist accommodation 106
opposition against the system 69
opposition of spirit and specter 200, 203–4
oppression 70, 84, 216, 250–51
optimism 63
Order 62, 72–3
orderly overflow 104
The Order of Things 3–4
organic constitution of worker 41–2
organic crises 162, 236
organic ideology 210
Organisation de l'Armée Secrète 225
organized capitalism 40, 43–4
origin of dislocation 47
original position 85
originary meaning 79
Ortega y Gasset, José 64, 208
the Other 10–11
outsiders 15; *see also* underdogs
overdetermination 26, 50, 69–70
own law 234–36

paradigm/syntagm 99, 261
paradigmatic pole of language 103
paradoxes of community 242–56
parasitic attachment 204
"part of no part" 178
partial autonomy 159–60
partial struggle 69
particular conjuncture 71–2
particularity 60–62, 91, 93, 100, 156, 163–4, 186
partisanship 107, 223–30
Parvus, Alexander 35
passionate attachment 14
Pax Romana 62
peaceful liberation 85
peasant ideology 112
Peasant Wars in Germany 128–9
Pêcheux, Michel 76
people's genealogy 187–9
peoples without history 181–2
permanent revolution 33, 188–9
permanentist approach 38
Peron, Isabel 144
Peron, Juan 111, 143, 145
Peronism 111, 118, 132, 135, 141, 143–5, 149, 162, 171
personification of evil 56
persuasion 248–9, 251
pessimism 38–9
petitio principii 76
petty-bourgeoisie 112
phantasmagoria 209–210
phenomenology 2, 23, 26–7
phenomenon of bureaucratization 40
Philosophy of History 215
philosophy of praxis 3
phonic substance 24
phronimos 53
planism 43
Plato 52–5, 227, 259
Platonic philosopher–king 54, 59
plebeians 129, 238–9
Plekhanov, Georgi 188, 210
pluralism 17, 63
plurality of antagonistic projects 159
plurality of democratic demands 156
polarization 250
political agency 7, 33
political articulation 17, 155, 161, 220–21
political fruitfulness 33
political optimism 63
political philosophy 53
political rearticulation 37
political representation 16, 160–64

political sovereignty 216
political theory 1–20; conclusion 17–18; logic of populism 12–15; Marxism and the post-Marxist turn 3–7; models of hegemony 7–12; philosophical background 2–3; radical democracy 15–17
political transformation 58
political will 154
politicization of economy 180–81
politico-theoretical crisis 188, 206
Politics and Ideology in Marxist Theory 8, 12, 257
Polybius 54–5
popular fronts 141
popular parties 138
popular subjectivity 156
popular traditions 128, 137, 139
popular–democratic interpellation 112, 130–35, 139–40, 147
populism theory 8, 106, 111–51, 160–63, 168, 190; part I 112–22; part II 122–34; part III 134–47; part IV 147–50
populist credentials 162–3
pornography 250
positive identity 45, 69, 170
positivism 48, 68, 137, 227
possibility 31
post-analytical philosophy 1
post-Marxism 96–107, 258; and ideology 96–107
post-Marxist turn 3–7
post-modernism 83
post-Saussurean linguistics 23
poststructuralism 1–3, 5, 23–8, 82
potentiality 31, 59, 131, 240
Poujadisme 118
Poulantzas, Nicos 3, 6, 8, 178, 257
poverty 157
power 13, 17, 29, 38–40, 44–5, 53, 55–6, 59, 70, 73, 125, 137–8, 189, 217, 232–3, 235
powerful elite 13
pragmatic politics 15
pragmatism 64, 247–8
pre-given organizational principles 72
presence of something 61
press freedom 82
primacy of politics 7, 98, 211
primitive communism 215
private property 82
privilege of backwardness 34, 36
problem of politics 53; *see also* dislocation
process of reduction 123–4

productive forces 214
projection 79
proletariat 35, 90–92, 129, 142, 176–8, 219–20
promise 204–6
pseudo-answers 66
pseudoconcreteness 166
psychoanalysis 1–2, 26, 169–70, 220, 244, 247, 257, 261
psychotic universe 31
pure Being 68
pure moralism 119
purpose of radical politics 165–95

Qualunquismo 118
quasi-objects 48
quasi-transcendental movement 26–7, 64
question of the messianic 204–9
question of tradition 209–211
Quinlan, Karen 237–8

racism 133
radical centre 159
radical contingency 5, 46, 53, 57, 252
radical democracy 15–17, 242
radical disjuncture 215–16
radical disorder 73
radical exclusion 68, 73
radical indeterminacy 60
radical investment 99, 103, 169
Radical Party 139, 141–2
radical politics 165–95
radicalization 49, 63, 138–9, 142, 145, 208, 211
Rancière, Jacques 178, 213–15, 227
rape 249
rational essentialism 3, 39–40, 57, 59
rationalization 39–40
Rawls, John 85, 270
re-distributive capacity of oligarchy 138
re-grounding 235–6
Reading Capital 184
reaggregation of elements 180
"real" enemies 223–30
realization of society 90
Realrepugnanz 97, 186
rearticulation 37, 63, 159
recasting Marxism 210
reconciled society 59
reconciliation 62, 202, 210
reconstruction 63
redemptive politics 15
reductio ad absurdum 239, 267
reduction of time to space 55

reductionism 123–6, 148, 150
reformism 124–5, 141
regeneration 91
regionalism 134
regularity 56
reification 167–72
Reisigl, Martin 4
relational systems 5
relationalism 259
relations of combination 159
relations of production 105
relative autonomy 153
relative continuity 128
relative universalities 62
relativism 244–5
Renaissance 27, 219
renaming 200
renegotiation 85
reoccupations 57–9, 242
representation 16, 34, 49, 51, 61, 79, 98, 105, 160–64, 181, 216–17, 259
repression 45, 70, 138–9, 144, 217
reproach 175
resistance 104–5, 137
resonances of communism 129–30
resurrection of theory of ideology 75–95
revolution of rising expectations 117–18
revolutionary agency 92, 173–4
revolutionary mass identity 69–70, 133
revolutionary perspective 106
rhetorico-discursive text devices 77
rhetorics 99–100, 169–70, 260
rhizomic movements 219
right of punishing 235
right-wing nationalism 142, 159
right–left dichotomy 116
rigid geometry of social effects 173–4
rising expectations 117
Risorgimento 161
ritual 75
Robinson, Joan 175
Roca, Julio Argentino 138
Roman Constitution 54
Roquism 139
Rorty, Richard 1, 3, 242–56
Rousseau, Jean-Jacques 153, 163
royal sovereignty 217
rules of engagement 83
rules of formation 4–5
Russell, Bertrand 102
Russian Revolution 35, 58, 172

sabotage 219
sacred life *see* bare life

Saint Augustine 215
Saint-Just, Louis Antoine 166
Saint-Simon, Claude 106, 155, 202, 227
Salan, Raoul 225, 229
Sandel, Michael 245
sans papiers 179–80, 221
Santi Romano 234, 236
Saussure, Ferdinand de 5, 23–7, 67, 99, 103, 231
Scargill, Arthur 11
Schmitt, Carl 223–30, 232, 235–6
Scholem, Gershom 86–7
Schumpeter, Joseph 245
scientific certitude 89–90
scientific gaze 4
Scotus, Duns 214–15
Second International 28, 33, 38, 104, 123, 189
secondary leadership 167
Section 28 10–11
sectorialization 105
secular struggle 128
secularization 215
security levels 155
sedimented forms of status quo 63
sedimented set of social relations 209
self-awareness 60
self-creation 247
self-defeating relativism 2, 152
self-defined totality 6
self-determination 31–2, 154, 175
self-identity 50
self-realization 253
self-recognition 4
self-regulating totality 39, 42, 44, 235
self-representation 203–4
self-sufficient "presence" 209
self-transformation 34
self-transparency 78–9
self-transparent discourse 49
self-unfolding 123
selfhood 243
seller of labour power 183–4
semi-colonial social formation 131
September 11 218
serious speech-acts 27
sermo humilis 139
Shklar, Judith 243
signification 21–108, 157, 169–70; discourse 23–9; dislocation 30–65; empty signifiers 66–74; ideology and post-Marxism 96–107; theory of ideology 75–95
the signified 24–7

signifiers 24–7, 66; *see also* empty signifiers; floating signifiers
signifying systems 67
simultaneity 53
singularities 185, 205–6, 214
Skinner, Quentin 2
slippage 13
so-called poverty 157
social action 32
social change 7
social control 63
social crisis 134
social demands 13–15, 59, 105, 153–6, 161
social diversity 85–6, 163
social functioning 43
social "grandeur" 90
social imaginary revolution 12, 30–65
social indeterminacy 231–41
social logics 155
social management 58–9
social objectivism 93
social order 62
social practices 174–81, 238
social production of empty signifiers 66–74; *see also* empty signifiers
social regulation 38–9, 240
social relations 7, 90, 97
social reproduction 51, 58, 77
social spaces 15, 182
social struggles 213–22
social totality 153–6
social whole 154
socialism 35, 116, 141, 176
socialist hegemony 148–9
Socians of the Renaissance 219
socio-political objectivity 54
sociological asynchronism 114–15
sociologism 160
solidarity 106
Solidarnoś 157, 170
Sorel, Georges 89–92, 210–211
sound-images 5
souplesse 235
source of dislocation 47
sovereignty 216–17, 232–3, 235–7, 241
spaces of representation 105
spatial society 51
spatiality 30, 52–4, 64
spatialization 30–31, 37, 50, 55
specific articulating principle 123, 125, 136
specificity 112
Specters of Marx 199, 207, 211
spectral logic of capital 179

spectrality 201–4
speech–act theory 26
Spinoza, Baruch 31, 103, 177, 215
split identity 47
spontaneous democracy 131, 219, 222
Sraffa, Piero 175
Stace, W.T. 88
stagism 35, 38
stagnation 137
Stalin, Josef 106–7, 167
state building 240
state of nature 72, 232
status incongruence 118–19
Stavrakakis, Yannis 259
strategic calculation 218
strict classism 189
structural dislocation 33–4, 47
structural linguistics 5
structural objectivity 46, 158
structural stage 37
structural undecidability 11
structurality 47
structure of the sign 66
struggle against evil 58
Struve, Peter 188
subject as myth 46
subject position 46
subjective alienation 77
subjectivity 37–8, 156, 220
sublimation 103, 169
subordination to the Idea 167
substantial difference 25
substitution 84
subsumption 101, 113–14
subversion 61, 68–9, 99, 101–2, 204
superstructure of ideology 122–3, 210
supranational communities 45
surfaces of inscription 48, 56, 59–61
surrealism 116–17
sutured totality 6
symbolic fabric 102
symbolization 30, 86, 170, 175
symmetry 75, 166
synchrony 30, 37, 55
synthetic–antagonistic complex 132
Syracuse 53
system of differences 67, 99
system of ideas 75
system of locations 179–80
system of needs 154
system as pure presence 67
systematicity 67–9
systematicity of system 69
systemic violence 174

tamquam dissoluta 232
Taylor, Charles 2
Taylorism 44
technical transformation 41
technological progress 177
tekhne 199
teleology 58, 239–40
telos 31
temporality 30–31, 49, 55, 57
tendentially empty signifiers 157, 170
tenentes 145
tension 162, 171–2
terrain of emergence 217–18
Thälmann, Ernst 128
Thatcher, Margaret 10–11
theoretical inconsistency 178
theoretical nihilism 113
theoretical watershed 216
theory of ideology 75–95; part I 75–8; part II 78–82; part III 82–6; part IV 86–9; part V 89–92; part VI 92–4
theory of organized capitalism 48
Theory of the Partisan 223
A Theory of Justice 269–70
Thermidor 214
thick morality 83–5
Thick and Thin 82–3
thin morality 83–5
a Thing 14, 103
think locally, act globally 191; *see also* Žižek, Slavoj
Third International 90, 123, 189
Third Way 159
Third World 44, 61–2, 80, 111, 171, 254
Thirty Years War 214–15
Tiananmen Square 58
"time is out of joint" 199–212; *see also* deconstruction
Tito, Josip 107, 133, 189
Togliatti, Palmiro 148
Tolstoy, Lev 224
torture 84
totalitarianism 50, 58, 64, 149, 208, 236–7
totality 6, 31, 35, 39, 71, 100, 103, 153, 157, 169, 179, 183–4
totality of language 67
towards theory of populism 111–51
Tractatus 47
trade unionism 124–5
tradition 209–211
traditions of struggle 128
transcendental turn 23, 47, 51, 64, 207, 216–17

transcultural core 83
transformation 58, 121–2, 134–5, 138–9, 141, 146, 159, 175, 236
transitory autonomy 159–60, 216
transparency 51, 78, 80; *see also* self-transparency
trauma 199
tribunicial function 159
Trotsky, Leon 34–8, 188–9, 218
true consciousness 107
tsarism 35, 70
tyranny 84

ubiquity of power 29, 219
ultimate universality 164
ultraleftist adventurism 106, 192
ultraleftist liquidation of political 191–4
unchallengeable state 163
uncontaminated universality 179
undecidability 208–9, 211, 256
underdogs 15, 106, 156, 161–3, 190, 238–9, 266
undifferentiated One 94
undistorted communication 77
unevenness 99
unevenness and combination 36, 73
ungroundedness 92
uninscribable exteriority 234–5
unintelligibility of evil 56
unity 142, 204
universal class 40, 63, 190, 217
universalism 16–17, 51, 58–61, 64, 178–9, 247, 255
universalistic power 217
universalization 49, 59, 172–3, 229
univocal ambiguity 126–7
urban reformulation 132
Urry, John 43–4
utopia 91–2, 154, 246, 250, 253–4

Vargas, Gertulio 145–6
Varguismo 112, 135, 145–6
vertical struggles 222
Vico, Giambattista 236
Vienna Congress 223–4
violence 6, 91–2, 193, 250
vivere pericolosamente 208
volonté générale 217
voluntarism 38, 208
vulgar materialism 210
vulnerability 253

"Waiting for the Martians" 173–4, 194; *see also* Žižek, Slavoj

Wall Street 171
Wallace, George 159
Walzer, Michael 82–5, 93
war of liberation 161
War and Peace 224
war of position 180, 221–2, 228–9, 250
wargus, gerit caput lupinum 232–3
Weber, Max 39–40
Weberian theory of bureaucracy 40
Weffort, Francisco 135
welfare of the people 81, 155
welfare scroungers 10, 12
Weltanschuung 124
Western philosophy 2–3
whip of external necessity 37
why empty signifiers matter to politics 66–74

wider masses 72
William of Ockham 214
Winter of Discontent 10
withering away of State 217–18
Wittgenstein, Ludwig 1, 3, 25, 47, 99, 236, 244, 252–3, 260
Wodak, Ruth 4
working classes 38, 177, 180, 183–5
working-class ideologies 140–41
world history 35–6
Worsley, Peter 113

Zasulich, Vera 34
zero level 76
zigzag oscillation 106
Žižek, Slavoj 11, 14, 28, 75–6, 165–95, 271
zoê 232, 236

eBooks
from Taylor & Francis

Helping you to choose the right eBooks for your Library

Add to your library's digital collection today with Taylor & Francis eBooks. We have over 45,000 eBooks in the Humanities, Social Sciences, Behavioural Sciences, Built Environment and Law, from leading imprints, including Routledge, Focal Press and Psychology Press.

Choose from a range of subject packages or create your own!

Benefits for you
- Free MARC records
- COUNTER-compliant usage statistics
- Flexible purchase and pricing options
- 70% approx of our eBooks are now DRM-free.

Benefits for your user
- Off-site, anytime access via Athens or referring URL
- Print or copy pages or chapters
- Full content search
- Bookmark, highlight and annotate text
- Access to thousands of pages of quality research at the click of a button.

ORDER YOUR FREE INSTITUTIONAL TRIAL TODAY

Free Trials Available

We offer free trials to qualifying academic, corporate and government customers.

eCollections

Choose from 20 different subject eCollections, including:

- Asian Studies
- Economics
- Health Studies
- Law
- Middle East Studies

eFocus

We have 16 cutting-edge interdisciplinary collections, including:

- Development Studies
- The Environment
- Islam
- Korea
- Urban Studies

For more information, pricing enquiries or to order a free trial, please contact your local sales team:

UK/Rest of World: online.sales@tandf.co.uk
USA/Canada/Latin America: e-reference@taylorandfrancis.com
East/Southeast Asia: martin.jack@tandf.com.sg
India: journalsales@tandfindia.com

www.tandfebooks.com